READING BY DESIGN

The Visual Interfaces of the
English Renaissance Book

PAULINE REID

Reading by Design

The Visual Interfaces of the English Renaissance Book

UNIVERSITY OF TORONTO PRESS
Toronto Buffalo London

ISBN 978-1-4875-0069-6

 Printed on acid-free paper with vegetable-based inks.

Library and Archives Canada Cataloguing in Publication

Title: Reading by design : the visual interfaces of the English Renaissance
    book / Pauline Reid.
Names: Reid, Pauline, 1985– author.
Description: Includes bibliographical references and index.
Identifiers: Canadiana 20189066458 | ISBN 9781487500696 (hardcover)
Subjects: LCSH: Books and reading – England – History – 16th century. |
    LCSH: Books and reading – England – History – 17th century. | LCSH:
    Early printed books – England – 16th century. | LCSH: Early printed
    books – England – 17th century. | LCSH: Literature publishing –
    England – 16th century. | LCSH: Literature publishing – England –
    17th century. | LCSH: Visual perception – History – 16th century. |
    LCSH: Visual perception – History – 17th century. | LCSH: English
    literature – Early modern, 1500–1700 – History and criticism.
Classification: LCC Z1003.5.G7 R45 2019 | DDC 002.094209/031—dc23

University of Toronto Press acknowledges the financial assistance to its
publishing program of the Canada Council for the Arts and the Ontario
Arts Council, an agency of the Government of Ontario.

For my husband

Contents

Illustrations

Acknowledgments

One of the primary tenets of this work, and indeed of book history as a whole, is that book production and reception is a collective enterprise: no single author could solely and successfully get out her ideas to the larger world without continuing support from colleagues and collaborators, editors, publishers, readers, friends, and family. This tenet is of course true of this book as well, and I would like to express gratitude to all who have contributed to this scholarship's development. As a mentor, Sujata Iyengar first saw the early potential in my ideas and became a supportive, rigorous audience for their growth throughout this project's writing process, as my ideas progressed from a rough-edged research proposal to a polished, even publishable, book manuscript. She, and Michelle Ballif, who also gave insightful, substantial feedback on my work throughout its many different iterations, helped me not only to delve into the interesting details and potential contributions of my research, but also to organize and explain what I discovered to a larger readership. Frances Teague was another important influence and astute reader for this work, as she helped me fill the gaps in my knowledge base on book history and Renaissance historiography. Kathryn Murphy at the University of Oxford read early versions of chapters 3 and 4 and fostered thoughtful, enjoyable discussions of how to choose a theoretical lens and build further methodological substance into my research. I am grateful to the University of Georgia's UGA-Oxford Study Abroad Program and the UGA-Liverpool graduate research exchange for their financial support that enabled me to have crucial access to rare, early print books overseas. I would also not have gotten through the writing and revision process for this project without the continued support of my friends and colleagues at the University of Georgia and the University of Denver, including our director, Doug Hesse.

I am grateful for the opportunity to present portions of my research for this project at the Shakespeare Association of America (SAA) conferences of 2013 and 2014 and the Renaissance Society of America (RSA) conferences of 2015 and 2016. I appreciate the attention given by my co-presenters, chairs, and audience members to my work. Specifically, Jeffrey Cohen and Julian Yates, as editors, included one of these SAA papers in their collection *Object-Oriented Environs*. My development of that work for their collection, in addition to our panel conversation, helped me to develop my understanding of phenomenology as it applies to material history. Earlier versions of chapter 1 and chapter 4 have been published as articles in *Rhetorica* and *Word and Image*, respectively. I am grateful to their editors and anonymous readers for their feedback on my work and their permission to reprint the later versions of these chapters in this book.

Several libraries have also been crucial to the production of this book. I am grateful especially to the librarians and staff of the Bodleian Library, in addition to Cambridge University Library, the John Rylands Library at the University of Manchester, and the Sydney Jones Library at the University of Liverpool for allowing me full access to rare and early books during my research process, without which this project's potential would not have been fulfilled. Additionally, I am grateful to these libraries, as well as the British Library, the Huntington Library, the Folger Shakespeare Library, the University of Glasgow Library, the National Portrait Gallery, the University of Ghent Library, the University of Utrecht Library, and the Pepys Library at Cambridge University for their kind permission to reproduce the images included in their holdings in this book.

I am also grateful to the University of Toronto Press for its support of my scholarship. Suzanne Rancourt has been an unflaggingly helpful and informative editor, particularly as this is my first published academic book: I am grateful to Suzanne for both recognizing my work's potential as a publishable manuscript and assisting me through the publication process. My anonymous readers also gave both generous and helpfully critical feedback that aided me in further defining my approach and connecting my individual ideas and chapters to build a more cogent, readable whole. I also appreciate the work of this press's board, staff, and production team, without whose work our scholarship would stay in the ether.

My family has also been a continued support through this process, particularly my husband, without whose emotional encouragement and practical aid this book would not have been written. I especially appreciate that, in this very moment, he is comforting our crying infant son so that I can write these acknowledgments.

Finally, I appreciate you, dear reader, in your willingness to pick up this book and give it a read or a glance. I will leave you with not an imprecation, as is the Renaissance tradition, but rather a benediction: may you find something here of value, of interest, of use, and of enjoyment.

READING BY DESIGN

The Visual Interfaces of the
English Renaissance Book

Introduction

For now we see through a glass, darkly; but then face to face: now I know in part; but then I shall know even as also I am known

KJV, Corinthians 13:12

And in her other hand she fast did hold
A booke, that was both signd and seald with blood,
Wherein darke things were writ, hard to be understood

Edmund Spenser, *The Faerie Queene*,
Book 1, Canto 10, sig. I4v

This book envisions early modern English print as a fragile, fragmented material object. In this study, I will explore how the English Renaissance book was culturally coded as both a thing and a medium. Renaissance readers perceived the print book as a thing that could be broken or reassembled, as well as a visual apparatus that had the power to reflect, transform, or deceive. My approach to the hand-press–era book as a phenomenally troubling medium in its own right counters the long-standing binary of print as linear and monologic, as opposed to oral or digital media, often viewed as more hypertextual and dialogic. Early print texts often seem to be caught between sweeping narratives of declension or progression, such as Walter Ong's claim that the visual nature of print led to the death of scholastic rhetoric, or Elizabeth Eisenstein's much-cited characterization of print as an "agent of change," a harbinger of modernity.[1] These binaries, prominent in the works of media theorists and rhetoricians such as Ong, Eisenstein, Marshall McLuhan, and Jay Bolter, still structure – and limit – how we use and discuss books in composition and literature classrooms, in popular conversations about visual media, and in our scholarship. In this study, I instead approach the early modern book as a complex visual, rhetorical, and political spectacle. I situate the culturally and intellectually problematic relationship between visual perception and knowledge in the English Renaissance as fundamental to how early print books' visual interfaces were constructed, displayed, read, perceived, and dismantled. I argue that the physical, and specifically visual, features of early modern print books expressed conflicting theories of perception and knowing.

New bibliographic studies of early modern print, such as those of Ann Moss, Peter Stallybrass, Jeffrey Todd Knight, Jennifer Summit, and Adam Smyth, have recently led to a greater recognition of the Renaissance book's cultural and material complexity as a product of its own historical crises. My approach to the early modern English book's unique visual, phenomenological, and rhetorical properties draws inspiration from such recent cross-disciplinary readings of the print book. Peter Stallybrass's research on visual materials in early modern literature has brought a renewed energy to textual and bibliographical studies.[2] Several innovative studies within this field investigate textual compilation and decomposition in early modern culture. For instance, Jennifer Summit's *Memory's Library: Medieval Books in Early Modern England* (2008) analyses the collection and, at times, erasure of medieval books within the early modern English library's post-Reformation context, and Jeffrey Todd Knight's *Bound to Read: Compilations, Collections, and the Making of Renaissance Literature* (2013) champions the material diversity of early modern texts and the agency of their readers as he tracks the unique ways readers compiled, bound, and recycled assemblies of texts.

Early modern books' material fungibility and the agency of their readers stands against any interpretation of them as monologic or logocentric. The collective discoveries of recent book-history scholarship demonstrate that early modern print encouraged active and interactive reading practices. Christopher D'Addario asserts that "readers viewed books as malleable collections rather than unified totalities" (73); readers compiled their book collections according to individual interest and intellectual pursuit. In *Used Books: Marking Readers in Renaissance England*, William H. Sherman discusses the extent to which readers altered and "customized" their books, particularly in their use of written marginalia alongside the printed text (9).

Reading was not a passive activity in the Renaissance, as Sherman charts: instead, readers cross-referenced quotations between texts (127), "regularly turned one print book into another," and left their books "startlingly full of marks" (119). Steven N. Zwicker also tells us that "to read with pen in hand underscoring or otherwise marking memorable passages; to correct errors," "to gloss," "to outline," "to ... provide interpretations" "were the commonplaces of Renaissance reading" (176). Renaissance readers would also mark texts they disagreed with, through cross-hatching, as a form of contestation and "repudiation" (192), particularly in the Civil War era. Stephen B. Dobranski focuses on ways that texts were left incomplete, to be fulfilled and corrected by readers: "readers in the early modern period could help to make the books they read – by cutting the outer sheets, correcting the errata, writing in notes, transcribing commonplaces, and borrowing select words and ideas" (62). Craig Kallendorf claims that such forms of reading were a type of "self-fashioning" in the Renaissance, as annotations would define the reader as individual subject (114). We may not be able to fully recover the practicable habits of each early modern reader, but these acts of annotation and commonplacing suggest that early modern readers viewed their books intertextually and with active engagement through both body and mind. This potential for readers' interaction and active gaze would certainly have shaped books' visual composition. While my study does not primarily focus on readers' material engagement with books, *Reading by Design* broadly considers the rhetorical and phenomenal situation in which readers would have been placed by books' interfaces, and the ways in which books themselves were shaped by a visual culture where the interactivity between material and gaze would have been rife with ambivalence and anxiety. Book history's recent focus on the collection, construction, and (re)compilation of books by readers may also in fact lead to more explorations of books' destruction and disintegration, an approach to which my own study turns. Indeed, in the recent collection *Book Destruction from the Medieval to the Contemporary* (2014), Adam Smyth uses early modern books' material fungibility to argue that a "culture" where "books were often simply read to pieces" disrupts the commonplace "coupling of print with permanence": "early modern writers wrote, and early modern readers read, with a comparable expectation of quotidian loss" (35).[3] This cultural sense of books' fragmentation, destruction, and recyclability was not only material, as I will argue, but also perceptual.

Further, several recent textual studies have used the concept of spatial ecologies, both internal and external to the page, as a framework for reconceptualizing reading practices. Andrew Gordon's *Writing Early Modern London* (2013) situates text as a negotiation of spatial memory and community building in Renaissance London's urban landscape. Leah Knight also reads early modern print as a negotiation of space: her *Reading Green in Early Modern England* (2014) combines environmental ecologies with textual ecologies as she historicizes reading practices through early modern optics and horticulture. Bonnie Mak's *How the Page Matters* (2012) charts the material transformation of the text *Controversia de nobilitate* to make a larger argument for the page's status as an interface between designer and reader (9). Further, the collection *Printed Images in Early Modern England* (2010) and Katherine Acheson's *Visual Rhetoric and Early Modern English Literature* (2013) begin to remedy the neglect of print's visual imagery in studies of the early modern book, fusing neo-bibliographical, new historical, rhetorical, and cognitive methodologies. Yet the growing focus on books as "things" or material artefacts in early modern studies often centres on books' physical, graphical construction and deconstruction alone, rather than crucial moments of their epistemic fragmentation and disunity. This approach potentially risks relegating the book to the status of fetishized object. Because of its dual role as object and medium, the materiality of the book does not allow us to evade its philosophical and epistemic concerns.

As Bill Brown contends, the history of the book as a field represents a complication and deepening of textual criticism rather than a purely material "relief from theory" ("Textual Materialism," 24). In a similar merging of theory with thing, Graham Harman, drawing from Husserl, argues that what we encounter when we interact with a thing is not its totalizing, ontic presence but its intersection with human perception. From this understanding, Harman hypothesizes a "global ether" or "network" that connects objects, a "stuff of perception" that is "neither form nor matter, neither object nor quality" (3). This perceptual "stuff" recalls classical and early modern concepts of *species*, or the image-replicas that visible things were thought to give off. This "stuff" or *species* of perception was believed to mediate the relationship between viewer and the object viewed. Both Harman's concept of the global network and the classical idea of visual *species*, still in place during much of the Renaissance, mediate between a thing-in-itself and a subjective experience of perception.

We may, however, hesitate to uphold Harman's ahistorical network-in-itself as an ontological solution to phenomenal problems. Harman himself employs the culturally specific, media-centric terminology of a *network* to describe our encounter with things. Our cultural and material experiences (in this case, digital media) constantly shape our phenomenological assumptions. In other words, material things shape how we *perceive* perception, even as our cultural and historical models of perception necessarily shape and colour how we approach these things: material things and our experience of them exist in a state of recursion. Like Harman's "network" of perceptual stuff, early modern texts often described the process of perception in material terms specific to print: impressions, engravings, illustrations, and types. This book explores how such metaphors, used to describe visual and cognitive perception, in turn structured early modern readers' experiences of books and their visual features. The intellectually complex ways that print books patterned visual materials alongside textual matter could even be deemed a political act, one that transformed how people saw and perceived their world: as Jane Bennett describes in *Vibrant Matter*, "a political act not only disrupts, it disrupts in such a way as to change radically what people can 'see': it repartitions the sensible; it overthrows the regime of the perceptible" (106).

Hence, I build upon the concept of rhetorical vision to investigate the ways that early modern books responded to – and constructed – the phenomenological crisis of visual perception. Debra Hawhee distinguishes "rhetorical vision" from the more commonly studied "visual rhetoric" (140).[4] Rhetorical vision, she proposes, indicates a concern for how rhetoric creates and responds to perception, whereas the term "visual rhetoric" conventionally ties rhetoric to a specific material index. Visual rhetoric has a more material basis, while rhetorical vision, as Hawhee defines it, is a way of perceiving the world through a rhetorical lens. Rhetorical vision "attends" to the "conjuring" of visual images and how they are brought to mind, and hence treats with how rhetoric affects cognition and perception (139), while visual rhetoric treats with the force of visual media: "put most simply, through rhetorical vision, words come to life" (140). More broadly, as Thomas Rickert advocates, a rhetorical situation or experience may be brought into the realm of the experiential and ambient, as a rhetorical situation is defined by its location, inhabitation, and environing (12–16). Rickert shifts rhetoric from ontology (being) to ambience, or a "dwelling" that includes our own "affective" situation in our environs, in an agency that is diffuse

(16). In my analysis, rhetorical vision and visual rhetoric work dialectically, within the book's status as both an object (techne) and an interface (episteme), while being surrounded by a cultural and phenomenal environ that modifies and mediates the reading experience. In other words, I attempt to draw from discussions of the book as a visual media to interrogate how book visuals constructed and called to mind different forms and ideologies of perception and cognition. *Reading by Design* investigates the following question: how do the visual media of early modern books transform, produce, or uproot structures of knowledge and perception?

Partial Visions and Visual Rhetorics

The relationship between sight and perception was fundamentally called into question at the same historical moment that print books remediated the visual and material structures of manuscript, iconic, and oral rhetoric.[5] As Stuart Clark has recently explored in *Vanities of the Eye*, Platonic, Aristotelian, and empirical models of sight vied with one another in a culture in which "vision was anything but objectively established or secure in its supposed relationship to 'external fact'" (1). Physiological, diabolical, or psychological forces could undermine visual perception. Further, as Sergei Lobanov-Rostovsky claims, the Platonic "projective" model of sight was not yet passed over in favour of the Aristotelian "receptive" model. Lobanov-Rostovsky describes how, in Platonic thought, the eye projected an "inner fire, which coalesced with daylight to extend from the eye to an object of vision" (198). Alternatively, the Aristotelian eye, made of water, receives images (199).[6] In the context of readers' sensory interaction with the book as a medium, the question of whether their eyes received book images or projected their own visual perceptions onto them is important to how we explore early modern books' intersection with readers' perceptive gazes. The epistemic problem of vision is discussed at length in classical works that influenced early modern thought and culture, such as Aristotle's *De Anima* and Plato's dialogues. In a notoriously thorny passage of *De Anima*, Aristotle claims that the eye receives form (sensory objects) without matter (meaning). The process of *phantasia*, loosely translated as imagination or fantasy, allows perception to take place without the material presence of the object. The retained image becomes hazy, shadowy, or partial.[7] In an Aristotelian reading process, then, the form of an object, like a book, can be grasped immediately by sight; however, the process of interpretation requires its images to become partial, fragmented, and transformed by cognitive perception.

Neo-Platonic and neo-Aristotelian phenomenologies in vogue in the early modern era had more in common with one another intellectually than the projective-versus-receptive controversy may indicate. Both exhibit a high degree of scepticism regarding the ability of the visual senses to represent truth or lead to understanding. In *Theaetetus*, Plato's Socrates demands,

> What we say a given colour is will be neither the thing which collides, nor the thing it collides with, but something which has come into being between them; something peculiar to each one. Or would you be prepared to insist that every colour appears to a dog, or any other living thing, just the way it appears to you? (19)

While Aristotle describes the movement from sight to perception as partial and imaginative, Plato casts doubt on the capability for sight to operate as a mode of perception at all. Plato compares the perceiving mind in *Theaetetus* to an aviary full of flying birds. These birds of knowledge swarm about at their own whim, unreliably. Socrates claims that it is

> possible not to have one's knowledge of that thing, but to have some other piece of knowledge instead of it. That happens when, in trying to catch some piece of knowledge or other, among those that are flying about, one misses, and gets hold of the one instead of the other ... as one might get hold of a dove instead of a pigeon. (199)

As I will discuss at greater length in this project, early modern books often resemble this aviary. They are assembled among fragmented material pieces that surprise and confound the reader's perception. This historical attitude towards the materials of sensory perception is illustrated by Herbert's description of a "broken altar" "cemented with tears" in his iconic shape poem, "The Altar"; by Francis Quarles's description of his *Emblemes* as reflective of the patterned, mysterious hieroglyphics of creation; and by Henry Vaughan's description of "Hyerogliphicks quite dismembred, / And broken letters scarce remembred" in *Silex Scintillans*. The partial images and fragmented materials of this book's primary texts recall Plato's description of representation in *The Republic* as the shadowy, unknowable projections of real forms to cave-dwelling prisoners.[8] The partial and subjective sight of Aristotle's *De Anima*, in other words, is not only partial or foggy but also deceptive in Plato's metaphors of visual perception. Early print-book visuals meditate on this sense of partial, fractured, and potentially deceptive sight. But they are not, as is the strain in Platonic and dissenting Puritan thought, necessarily anti-representational. They are instead representations that often point towards the visual construction of their own representational problems. The importance of readerly watchfulness – and a sense of formal playfulness – is a dominant ethos of early modern book visuals. Of course, each text in this study responds uniquely to a culture where iconicity and visual spectacle is both ubiquitous and ubiquitously interrogated.

Conditions of forgery and piracy rendered the book epistemically unstable as a material: as Adrian Johns asserts, book culture was "characterized by nothing so much as indeterminacy" in its variances of physical form and reader reception (36). Johns describes the early modern understanding of the reading process as filtered through the untrustworthy avenues of the passions and senses, such that those "who failed to control their passionate reading practices, and thereby fell prey to them, could then be diagnosed by a series of symptoms that were likewise understood in terms of the passions" (387). One victim of this circumstance was "Laudian scholar Peter Heylyn," whose "excessive reading engendering blindness as the *"Laboratory"* of his brain overheated and destroyed the crystalline humour of his eyes" (383). Print visuals, as Johns and I examine, were important to the imaginative and perceptual faculties, yet this imaginative function caused anxiety that vision would overwhelm reason (443). This tension between the productive, generative features of visual reading and its potential to erase and even blind readers to truth and reason will be an ongoing thread in my investigation. Vision's changing nature in its cultural context was shaped by both the Reformation and by the inheritance of Aristotelian notions of sight that competed with more empirical understandings. Matthew Milner argues that the senses and their "misuse" were certainly feared in a Reformation context, but that Reformers were as much "shaped" by "sensory culture" at large as iconoclasm (2–3). The Reformation drew from "traditional Aristotelian theories of perception," but also reshaped and at times undermined them, further destabilizing the role of visual perception (349–50).

Early modern philosophical and cognitive theories of sight both drew from and readapted the dominant Platonic and Aristotelian models. In his *Anatomy of Melancholy*, early modern physician-philosopher Robert Burton demonstrates a widely accepted middle ground between projective and receptive theories, as manifested in a tripartite brain. Burton claims that although *"there is nothing in the understanding, which was not first in the* [outer] *sense"* (158, emphasis in original), the three inner senses of common sense, "phantasie," and memory act to interpret sensory data (152). Francis Bacon, who famously positioned books as sensory objects in his essay, "Of Studies" – "Some bookes are to bee tasted, others to bee swallowed, and some few to bee chewed and digested" (sig. B2v) – responded to these visual controversies in his *Novum Organum* and *New Atlantis*. Bacon's *Novum Organum* is credited with the formation of inductive reasoning from visual and sensory observation, a model that is predicated on an epistemologically uncomplicated stance towards sight's relationship to perception and material reality. Bacon chooses to name common obstacles to this new, objective, and clear model of reasoning from observation *"idola,"* or idols (*Novum Organum* 79, aph. 38). This loaded term draws from early modern reformist concepts of visual idolatry, as well as from classical theories of vision. As Alistair Crombie outlines in *Science, Optics, and Music in Medieval and Early Modern Thought*, Plato, Aristotle, and Democritus believed that objects gave off "images, copies, or representations" of themselves; Democritus called these images *eidola* (177). Bacon's argument for induction from visual or sensory observation thus rather circularly counters the purportedly false visions or simulacra that mediate representation. Bacon more explicitly draws from Plato as he warns against "idols of the cave," a cave that "scatters and discolours the light of nature" (81, aph. 42).

Objective sight and internal prejudice, then, are oppositional in Bacon, yet sight itself is still a questionable, elusive path to knowledge. In the *New Atlantis*, Bacon creates an ideal model of specialized knowledge, Salomon's House, which serves as "the very Eye" of his utopian realm (9). Salomon's house has "Perspective Houses":

> *where we make* Demonstration *of all* Lights, *and* Radiations: *And of all* Colours: *And out of* Things uncoloured *and* Transparent ... *All* Delusions *and* Deceits *of the* Sight ... *We procure means of Seeing* Objects A-farr off; *As in the* Heaven, *and* Remote places: *And represent* Things Near *as* A-farr off; *And* Things A-farr off *as* Near ... *We have also* Glasses *and* Means *to see* Small *and* Minute Bodies, *perfectly and distinctly."* (30–1)

Mediation here comes in the form of clear glasses, telescopes, and microscopes. Mediums, in this passage, further and expand a telos-driven vision and observable knowledge. In another division, the "Houses of Deceits of the Senses,"

> *we represent all manner of* Feats *of* Jugling, False Apparitions, Impostures, *and* Illusions; *And their* Fallacies. *And surely you will easily beleeve that we that have so many* Things *truly* Natural, *which induce* Admiration, *could in a* World *of* Particulars *deceive the* Senses, *if we would disguise those* Things, *and labour to make them more* Miraculous. *But we do hate all* Impostures, *and* Lies: *Insomuch as we have severely forbidden it to all our* Fellows, *under pain of Ignominy and Fines, that they do not shew any* Natural Work *or* Thing, Adorned *or* Swelling; *but only* Pure *as it is, and without all* Affectation *of* Strangenesse. (32)

Here, representational delusion and fallacy are visually represented to the fellows of Salomon's House. The terminology of "juggling" and "disguise" echo the anti-Catholic, anti-miraculous stance of English reformers, as Catholicism and the Jesuit movement often implied idolatry, deceit, and false miracles in post-Reformation polemics. Reformation politics partially explain why visual delusions need to be forbidden, yet visually represented in this New Atlantis: the anti-spectacular movement in English Protestantism necessitated its own forms of political theatre. The "purity" and unaffected nature of the Fellows' representations are both a scientific and ideological value, evoked both by Bacon's epistemologically certain inductive model and its theologically "pure" and native English Protestantism.

Salomon's House parallels the longstanding model of inquiry and pedagogy in the modern academy: one of specialization, an anti-iconic ethos that seeks to remove cultural delusions with its own form of demonstrations, and a singular focus on clarity and precision in academic standards of writing that bespeaks a simplistic relationship among reading, perception, and politics.[9] Ryan J. Stark observes how rhetorical theory transitioned from a model of "entelechy," or phenomenologically "enchanted" forms, to an empirical model that favoured "clarity" or simplicity above all by the end of the seventeenth century. In this empirical model, rhetoric is ideally a clear glass that transparently reveals the matter or content beyond itself – as Stanley Fish would put it, texts are here "self-consuming artifacts" (xiii). This idealization of visual observation as a clear, unobtrusive path to a knowledge outside of itself can be encapsulated in the words of William Hinde, who, in the English post-Reformation context, sets the "dumbe and darke images" of stained glass, that "by their painted coates and colours, did both darken the light of the Church, and obscure the brightnesse of the Gospell" against the "white and bright glass" that replaced it in church windows (79). The clear glass becomes an episteme for a content that transcends its own form, rather than the formal, visual device of stained glass, whose images and patterns endlessly capture the gaze of its onlookers.

As Rayna Kalas explores, glass itself was an important metaphor as an episteme in the late medieval and Renaissance eras, signifying "poetry and the imagination" (106) and a material that linked macrocosm to microcosm. Glass, as discourse, was "instrument in shaping reality" (17). Glass frames became a figure for invention, as framed glass was a representation of "created matter" (28). As Hinde's sermon and Kalas's work demonstrate, the figurative meaning of glass constantly took on new shapes throughout the Renaissance as the technological and social aspects of its making changed throughout the era. While the change from stained to clear glass in Hinde's words signifies the social transformation of the Reformation, technical changes in glass transformed its metaphorical purchase. In the fourteenth and fifteenth centuries, convex or "pennyware" mirrors made of glass were available but distorted their reflections, minimizing their images; alongside these mirrors were reflective "steel and silver" that required upkeep but held a more accurate reflection (107). Nevertheless, glass became a metaphor for a necessarily inaccurate reflection of microcosm to macrocosm, much as the fallen world would not accurately reflect God's creation. By 1570, however, expensive and controversial crystal glass mirrors were imported to England and became a metaphorical reminder of vanity (108–9). Crystal versus older forms of mirrors demonstrated a conflict between an ontological mirror as a reflection of God (though imperfect) and a humanistic representation of material surroundings (108). Hence, my discussion of Caxton's 1481 *Mirrour and Description of the World* links rhetoric to metaphysics, while in chapter 4 mirrors, and the book itself, in the work of Francis Quarles become unwieldy and anxiety-ridden figures of representation.

The Fragmentation of Form: Whole and Part
in the Early Modern Book

With this changing material history of glass and its metaphorical senses in mind, the visual rhetoric (and rhetorical vision) of the early modern book is fungible, with the capability for transformation and illusion: while the authors I discuss hoped to employ their print texts for didactic, pedagogical, or political purposes, embedded within the visual patterns of their books is a vexed treatment of visuality. I track this troubling visual media through the period from 1481 to 1649. This range spans from the date of the first illustrated book printed in England, William Caxton's *Mirrour and Description of the World* (1481), to the (temporary) end of the monarchy and beginning of the commonwealth era in England, which witnessed a dramatic shift in the sociopolitical context of print publishing, distribution, and consumption. The texts I discuss each demonstrate a strong concern for the opposition of unity and fragmentation, a concern that is aesthetic, phenomenal, and political in nature. More commonly discussed illustrated books of the early modern era, such as John Foxe's *Acts and Monuments* (first ed. 1563) and William Camden's *Britannia* (1586), attempt an establishment of a nationalist and unified vision of England. Less canonized but aesthetically and culturally important works, such as Spenser's *Shepheardes Calender* (1579), Michael Drayton's *Poly-olbion* (1612), and Francis Quarles's *Emblemes* (1633), instead reveal fissures between ideological or aesthetic unity and fragmentation. The optical multiplicity of early illustrated books and the potentially divided gaze of their readers invite us to perceive such texts as spectacles: spectacles that mediate perception and spectacles that become shared events, inviting the participation of their spectators.

My treatment of the early modern book's perceptual crises revises the binary posed in the critically influential special issue of *Representations*, "The Way We Read Now," between the "surface"-style reading of current scholarship on material culture and the sedimented reading praxis championed by Jameson in *The Political Unconscious* (2). Leah Price argues against the more symptomatic scholarly methodology influenced by Jameson, where form is categorized as a symptom of hidden ideological messages to be exorcized by the critic-priest: "the way we read now" is that "we do not read at all" (120). Price contends that we should respect books' "it narratives," or the stories of their physical use, exchange, and collection (120). The problem with interpreting books as things and surfaces alone, however, is that this surface is also a medium that transmits, transforms, and mediates meaning. The opposition of a surface-level, object-based reading to a more sedimented, ideological reading is a false distinction. While symptomatic readings assume books to be an "opaque surface" (Best and Marcus 4) and surface readings assume clarity, these methods ignore the epistemological problem of sight and perception's relationship, neglecting the potential for meaning to be transformed by the very physiological, phenomenological, and cultural ways that readers look at books.

A respect for the book's objecthood in the new bibliography has indeed allowed our understanding of print to be revised, inviting us to appreciate print's multiplicity and readerly engagement. Nonetheless, this multiplicity is, again, not just material, but epistemic. In the emblem books, encyclopedias, pedagogical tracts, and engraved maps I discuss, the mediative structure of the book does not assume clarity but plays on the book's potential for optical illusions, broken materials, and false visions. This study responds to the call for a new "historical phenomenology" of early modern literature by Gail Kern Paster, Katherine Rowe, and Mary Floyd-Wilson (2). Paster poses the question of how early modern readers may have perceived or experienced emotions differently than we do. She argues that these different experiences of emotion and sensation may be brought to bear on how we understand early modern literary culture. I pose the question of how early modern readers' concepts and experiences of visual perception may be brought to bear on their books' visual and material design. These design features include, but are not limited to, woodcuts, engravings, page borders, arrangements, initials, inscriptions, and blank spaces. Such elements are often read as paratexts: features outside the text itself that shape the meaning of the work as a whole. However, this reading of design features as such discrete units, somehow existing beyond the textual matter, omits the rich interplay between text and image in early print. Instead, I read these features as full and integral components of the text itself.

This book broadly responds to the current call for both historical phenomenology and new ways of reading the surfaces of things in its analysis of the interaction between perception and material image in early modern print visuals. Although digital media has the potential to undermine empirical or as-is experiences of sight in our own historical moment, until quite recently we have lived in a "show-me" culture. What we see, we assume, is what we get – visual perception reflects reality. For those living in early modern England, what is seen was not, at all, assumed to necessarily indicate a clear path to knowledge or meaning. This ethos is reflected in early modern books' dually anxious and playful relationship with imagery and imagination. My combination of visual rhetoric, phenomenologies of sight, and early modern book history may at first seem a strange meld. I contend, though, that it is only when we place these approaches in conversation with one another that we can seek to understand how visual texts, the reading process, and the artefacts of material culture acted as a complex during the English print book's birth as a medium.

Of course, vision was not the only sense that would have interacted with the reading experience in a dually inventive and anxious fashion in the Renaissance. Touch, smell, taste, and hearing all played a role in a felt experience of the book; although, I will argue, sight played a particularly integral role in interfacing matter and mind. In recent scholarship, rich explorations of text and the senses, or sensation, have expanded our knowledge of the early modern reading experience.[10] Adam Smyth investigates the commonplace practice of touching and cutting texts as commonplace and as a method of invention ("'Reade in one age and understood i'th'next'" 71). In *Reading Sensations in Early Modern England*, Katherine A. Craik argues that the intense passions drawn by reading immersed early modern readers into an environment that "involved a heightened awareness and involvement of the embodied self" (7). Wendy Wall briefly explores food as a site for linking text with taste, as "aspiring non-elite women of means did indeed create food-letters and etch words onto tarts, often displaying their knowledge of socially meaningful fonts and penmanship styles" ("Letters, Characters, Roots" 19). Joe Moshenska focuses on touch in the Renaissance as a locus for debates on the body, the human, and the material world. Moshenska traces early modern humanist thought as perceiving touch and sight to be mutually corrective and in friendship (148); early modern readers would have used sight and touch in harmony to form a holistic interpretation of a book. Moshenska cites Paracelsus as an influential thinker who promoted the idea that touch collaborated with sight to create knowledge (218). In Aristotle's still-influential thought, though, touch is excluded from an experience of beauty (Moshenska 160), and too much touch could even, as with warnings against sight, cloud our reason (Moshenska 217). Matthew Milner claims that in late medieval and early modern thought, this inherited Aristotelianism meant that sight was distinguished from senses like touch at the top of a sense hierarchy (25) and was fully "the most debated and referenced sense in pre-modern European culture" (25). Sight transformed the body spiritually: "here visible spirit within the eye was altered by specie" (24). Hence, sight evoked connections to a spiritual and phenomenal field beyond the other senses in early modern thought and became a mediator to the other bodily functions. Vision's particular role as a mediative and uniquely phenomenal sense, when combined with the technology of visual print, is a primary reason for this book's focus on sight, although the ways in which sight merged with the other senses in early modern reading practices is a matter that warrants further study.

Because of vision's multifarious and controversial nature in the English Renaissance, I explore how philosophical, scientific, and rhetorical works and ideas intersected with the concerns of my primary texts. It is impossible to discuss the changing nature of visual perception from 1485 to 1650 without including the inherited philosophical and rhetorical theories of Aristotle, Plato, Cicero, and others, or the changing technologies of vision, including glasses, mirrors, optics, telescopes. The visual text, I argue, did not exist in a vacuum but rather connected with transformations in scientific and philosophical ideology – the Platonic gaze, for instance, in my discussion of Caxton's *Mirrour* becomes a telescopic insight in Francis Quarles's *Emblemes*. Through my research into visual perception, I have discovered that scientific and philosophical controversies were threaded throughout book visuals, even to the point of intending readers to choose a particular avenue or experiential attitude towards their text. While *Reading by Design*'s primary concern is with literary and rhetorical history, its connections between philosophies of sight, scientific theories such as the makeup of the eye organ and the nature of glass prism, and textuality do not restrict it to a single field. While we maintain a disciplinary structure to our own epistemologies in the university, the path to knowing in the Renaissance, and in the texts I study, was understood to be collective and overlapping, as the ultimate goal would be to link different forms of knowledge as a microcosm for creation. In many instances, the texts themselves refer to visual controversies in science, philosophy, and rhetoric, and there would be a certain amount of critical oversight without delving into these intersections. This multidisciplinary analysis of visual reading encourages a holistic framework within which to situate problems of perception alongside book materials. This study of perception's role in the composition of texts combines areas of study and historicizes how readers would have visually encountered books; I therefore draw from classical and early modern inquiries of the nature of sight to explore this encounter.

Glasses, Maps, and Mirrors: The Material Rhetorics of Books

Early modern visual culture's interfaces, of course, extend beyond the space of the book to the materials of daily life in the English Renaissance. As Juliet Fleming investigates in *Graffiti and the Writing Arts of Early Modern England*, writing on public walls, churches, domestic spaces, heraldry, and everyday objects created a sense of textual-visual ubiquity to the point where an empty wall signified an empty mind. While this study primarily focuses on the printed page, it traces how books' spatial features drew from parallel alterations to other visual technologies: mirrors, calendars, maps, telescopes and other optical glasses, and anatomies of the eye itself. The texts in each chapter have been chosen to illustrate how visual technologies, genres, and cognitive-perceptual functions combined in an intended interaction with a text or performance. The following chapters set these visual materials alongside the genres of the pedagogical tract, almanac, chorography, emblem book, and performance, respectively. These genres remediate rhetorical praxis from cognitive to print locations, particularly the methods of imagination and invention, memory, arrangement, and delivery. In addition, these genres, by inhabiting the space for learning and categorizing, timekeeping, spatial visualization, meditation, and spectation, call for readers who were active viewers and perceivers of their texts and who may have integrated reading into the rhythms of everyday life.

Each genre illustrated here also forms both text and viewer into a unique inhabitation and phenomenal field. Each genre calls for a particular cognitive shift and philosophical turn as we perceive it, whether entelechy in the case of Caxton's late-medieval encyclopedia *Mirrour and Description of the World* or a never-ending process of memorialization and forgetting in the chorography *Poly-olbion*. In the case of *The Shepheardes Calender*, I argue that readers would have approached this text with the almanac form already in mind, a genre that evoked memory, prophesy, and the inscription of visual space. Francis Quarles's *Emblemes* in chapter 4 asks readers to both meditate upon and evaluate the images alongside the text, creating a sense of double vision and constant vigilance. I turn to the performance *2 Henry VI* in my final chapter, a work that references bibliographical objects and John Foxe's visually magisterial *Acts and Monuments*. This play brings both books and eyes before the eyes and minds of its audience, as it adapts Foxe's *Acts* and interrogates the nature of sight. I analyse this play as a potential adaptation, and as such one that asks viewers to question what they are seeing and to call the visual nature of books to mind as they act as theatrical spectators. These genres demonstrate how the visual elements and composition of texts set up a cognitive and perceptual relationship between reader and text that is constantly interrogated and complicated by the thematics of the works themselves. While I've included canonical texts, such as Spenser's *Shepheardes Calender* and Shakespeare's *2 Henry VI*, my inclusion of non-canonical (but at times popular) sources such as Francis Quarles's *Emblemes* and almanac books alongside interrogates connections between what might have been "everyday" reading and what might have been interpretation. It is my argument that reading and visualization in itself may have called for a certain vigilance and participation in intellectual controversies, even with genres that tend to be uncanonized. The variety of texts and genres featured in this study demonstrate how crises of visual perception underpinned a wide swathe of the reading experience in the Renaissance. The key word here is experience. While Renaissance readers certainly interpreted and actively cut up, inscribed, and catalogued their texts, I will predominantly investigate how these works set up their visual interactions with readers to both create an experience and interrogate forms of knowing. My method throughout is thus one of material epistemology and phenomenology rather than pure historical materialism or reader response. Even with a compendium of material history at our hands about early modern reading practices larger than that assembled by this study and other scholarship, we may never fully grasp how early modern readers could have literally approached these texts in their time. Therefore, this book looks to histories of visual perception as well as the visual aspects of the texts themselves to imagine the kinds of epistemic and phenomenological frameworks these books would have placed readers within.

Chapter 1 investigates how print illustrations and spatial metaphors, such as mirrors, colours, and measurements, serve to mediate reader and image, cognitive perception and perceived object, and rhetorical invention and imagination in two early illustrated pedagogical texts, William Caxton's encyclopedic *Mirrour and Description of the World* (first edition 1481) and Stephen Hawes's allegorical *Pastime of Pleasure* (Tottel edition 1555). As Herbert Grabes explores in *The Mutable Glass*, mirror or glass metaphors for books had been a particularly English tradition since the late-medieval, preprint era (4). Mirrors were not the clear, two-dimensional objects we picture today but were often made of bronze or similar materials and formed in a convex shape that could only provide a partial or distorted reflection. Bronze mirrors date from the classical era, and were often handheld, featuring decorative motifs, vignettes, and designs.[11] The mirror as common metaphor for the book suggests reflection and refraction, mimesis and illusion. Through the symbolic language of their material images and visual metaphors, particularly the mirror, Caxton's *Mirrour* and Hawes's *Pastime* portray pedagogy, even rhetoric itself, as problematically dependent on the subjective visual imagination, or "fantasy," of the reader.

Chapter 2 locates Spenser's *Shepheardes Calender* (1579) and the annotated almanac genre it draws from as memory spaces. In the sixteenth century, readers used almanacs as a new, visual, and mnemonic media. Readers employed almanacs for inscription, accounting note taking, chronicling, and prognostication. As Frances Yates and Mary Carruthers famously detail, classical and early modern mnemonic practices shared a common technique: orators would often construct a memory palace or house in the mind, replete with intricately visualized rooms, cabinets, and spaces, to place ideas for later recollection (Yates 206; Carruthers 89). As Adam Smyth notes, annotated almanacs held specific spaces for the reader to inscribe reminders and commentaries, spaces that effectively operated as little rooms in a visual memory palace ("Alamanacs, Annotators, and Life Writing" 200–44). Early modern calendars and almanacs hence acted as memory machines; however, they were a highly ephemeral form, as readers used, discarded, and finally forgot them at the end of the year. I argue that the *Shepheardes Calender*, situated alongside this generic context, interrogates memory's dual prominence and ephemerality in print, particularly in its visual illustrations and layout.

In the sixteenth and early seventeenth centuries, early modern maps moved from a more ontological construction of space to an epistemological one, from a way to understand time to a means of conceiving space.[12] Engraved print books, like those of John Selden and William Camden, widely reproduced and distributed this early modern epistemological map, which sought to establish England's topographical features and political boundaries. New surveying techniques that could geometrically divide and enclose the English landscape, alongside the emergence of engraved maps, influenced how print spaces responded to problems of vision and knowledge.[13] Chapter 3's analysis of Michael Drayton's *Poly-olbion* (1612) demonstrates that the epistemic question of how to organize space on a map was concurrently a political problem of how to unite or subdivide the English landscape. As indicated by *Poly-olbion*'s title, the visual components of this book represent many competing "Albions" or Britains that, like the tiny figures that inhabit its regional maps, represent, contend, and point out a chaotic multiplicity of British identities. This chapter employs the concept of aporia, or a philosophical agon or boundary, to explore the many graphical and epistemic borders *Poly-olbion* presents to its readers: between vision and knowledge, reader and page, a unified Britain and multiple (poly) Albions. *Poly-olbion*'s aporia are both metaphysical and physical, displayed in its text and in its many graphical borders: maps of topographical spaces and watery rivers, elaborate page-border designs and vignettes, and the boundaries of the page itself.

Chapter 4 draws from a material history of telescopes and optical prisms to trace how the formal duplications of text and page create a sense of visual duplicity in the emblematic poetry and political rhetoric of Francis Quarles. Again, the print page reflects and even magnifies epistemic crisis. Quarles's *Emblemes* (1633) and political pamphlets set up dualistic visual and verbal structures, namely chiasmus, paradox, and mimesis. The duality between telos and trickery in these rhetorical and visual structures portrays sight – and the reading process itself – as potentially duplicitous, as we become lured by sensual visions and optical illusions. Quarles continues this concern with troubled vision in the rhetorical structures of his later political pamphlets. Through situating Quarles's seemingly more metaphysical emblem poems on a continuum with his representation of sight in his political works, such as *The Shepheards Oracle* (1644) and *The Whipper Whipt* (1644), this chapter uncovers the interconnected nature of phenomenal and political vision troubles in Quarles's historical moment.

In the final chapter, I turn my study of the early modern book's vision-perception agon to visual performance in Shakespeare's *2 Henry VI*. In *2 Henry VI*, the rebel Jack Cade's famous lament – that the "skin of an innocent lamb should be made parchment? that parchment, being scribbled o'er, should undo a man?" – has been interpreted by bibliographical scholars such as Roger Chartier as an eloquent, nostalgic, and ahistorical indictment of written culture, specifically print (4.2.79–81). My analysis of *2 Henry VI*'s "undone" materials instead situates this moment within the play's larger context of fractured, decomposable, and broken visual ecologies: optics, print, landscapes, and the performance itself. In this chapter, I analyse moments in *2 Henry VI*, such as the St Alban's "false miracle" scene, Jack Cade's debate with Lord Say, and Margaret's self-representation as an "alehouse sign," as instances of visual and material "undoing" (1.1.103). Simpcox, Cade, and Margaret of Anjou's performances act as metatheatrical – and metabibliographical – representations of visual uncertainty.

It is the aim of these chapters to reveal how previously understudied works such as annotated almanacs, illustrated, vernacular pedagogical texts, and emblems can instead become central to our understanding of rhetorical history and early modern culture, as well as the questions early print books raise about visuality as an episteme. We can trace the problem of vision and knowledge that runs through these materially complex texts as an important intellectual current in more canonized texts. Through this study, I argue that the early modern print book's visual interface and its readers dynamically engaged with one another. By connecting rhetorical and phenomenal history to how we look at early print books, we can view early modern print's visual features as more than unique decorative curiosities or concerns for collectors and bibliographers alone; instead, they are complex elements that defined the early modern book as a vibrant, unsettled, and unsettling medium.

Chapter One

Through a Looking-Glass: Rhetorical Vision and Imagination in William Caxton's *Mirrour and Description of the World* and Stephen Hawes's *Pastime of Pleasure*

William Caxton's *Mirrour and Description of the World* (first published 1481)[1] and Stephen Hawes's *Pastime of Pleasure* (first edition 1509; illustrated edition published 1555 by Richard Tottel), as early illustrated and pedagogical print texts, exemplify how an attention to the unique material and rhetorical features of early modern books can help to recover an understudied cultural history of visual rhetoric and, as I will soon discuss, rhetorical vision. In these texts, imagery and the imagination serve as crucial elements of rhetorical invention. Invention is co-produced by the material images of print and the imagination, or "fantasy," of the mind's eye. As Kalas argues, in late medieval and early modern thought, "the imagination is created matter" and not "spiritual essence" alone: it is "of this world" (2). As a metaphor, the mirror linked matter to spirit, macrocosm to microcosm, such that "innovations in framing, glassmaking, and poesy were perceived uniquely to mingle matter and meaning, the finite and the infinite, the natural and the artificial, the word and the image" (Kalas 3). Accordingly, Caxton's *Mirrour* and Hawes's *Pastime* present vivid woodcut illustrations alongside visual, optical metaphors, such as mirrors, colours, smoke, and geometrical measurements. Parallel transformations in optical and spatial technologies influenced the practice of visual rhetoric in the fifteenth and sixteenth centuries. As Catherine Hobbs observes, "breakthroughs in the science of optics and vision occurred in the same time frame as interest in the image and imagination intensified in language pedagogy" (28). These texts' visual figures, alongside their material illustrations, both produce and interrogate the transforming relationship between vision, rhetoric, and perception in early print.

My analysis of visual materials in these pedagogical tracts draws from recent histories of physical and material rhetoric, such as Debra Hawhee and Cory Holding's investigations of eighteenth century Enlightenment discourse, as well as Hawhee's discussion of a more phenomenologically oriented "rhetorical vision," to which Hawhee opposes a more material visual rhetoric.[2] More broadly, this chapter considers visual rhetoric in early print texts in light of the so-called new materialisms of Jane Bennett and Graham Harman. Bennett and Harman call for a renewed attention to material objects in their own right, as vital agents in a larger network or environment. Rhetoric's stylistic and visual tropes, by extension, can be seen to operate on both a material and a larger phenomenal or cosmological level, as things and as agents. This claim is far from new or radical. As Ryan J. Stark recounts, rhetorical style was "infused with cosmic purposes" and actively shaped reality (10). Indeed, a greater understanding of the "old materialisms" of rhetorical style and invention in late medieval and early modern discourse may connect material and phenomenal approaches to visual rhetoric/rhetorical vision, and, further, may historicize and inform new materialist approaches to rhetoric and the book.

The Cosmic Mirror

Visual materials, such as the book, the mirror, the eye, and the word itself, were intersecting and vital phenomena in early modern reading practices. As both a material and medium, the mirror appears as an overdetermined trope for the book itself in Caxton's *Mirror* and Hawes's *Pastime*. A mirror can reflect, transform, or even distort what is seen. In *The Mutable Glass*, Herbert Grabes outlines a number of mirror figures that appear in late medieval and early modern titles. Grabes concludes that the mirror acted as a "central image or metaphor" in the period (4): out of the "over three hundred *Speculum* titles, quite apart from vernacular titles," "approximately half of these can be substantiated easily for England" (29). More specifically, the *imago mundi* genre, or the book as mirror or image of the world, often describes a single-book encyclopedia, an attempt to classify and unite different arts and sciences.[3] Caxton's *Mirrour and Description of the World* adapts and translates Gossuin of Metz's illustrated Latin manuscript *Imago Mundi* (1245), which in turn is adapted from Honorius of Autun's own version of this text (ca. 1100). Honorius of Autun's text, a "collection of sermons" that was "known in England as the *Speculum Virginum*," was the "first 'secular' work employing a mirror-title" in late medieval English literature (4). Caxton's *Mirrour* can be traced back to English copies of Honorius's original *Speculum* as part of a secular, pedagogical tradition. This heritage shapes the *Mirrour* as an interactive pedagogical text for a new vernacular readership.

In addition to the *imago mundi* tradition, late medieval and early modern England witnessed a proliferation of texts within the genre of the *specula principis*, or mirrors for princes. This genre tends to be didactic, as the *speculum principis* holds an instructive mirror up to both political authorities and general readers. These *specula* could guide and caution kings through their images and instructions: they could thereby both authorize and limit kingship.[4] Mirrors for princes would often allegorize the virtues and vices of past rulers and historical figures, as they commented on their own political contexts. For instance, Władysław Witalisz employs the case of Troy's fall, a common exemplum in late medieval mirrors for princes, to examine how history operated as a collective mirror for present politics and mores in this genre (17–20).[5] John Gower and John Lydgate figure as perhaps the most influential authors of late medieval English *specula principis*, Gower for his *Speculum Meditantis* (also known by its French title, *Mirour de l'Omme*), *Vox Clamantis*, and *Confessio Amantis*, and Lydgate for his *Troy Book*, *Fall of Princes*, and *Temple of Glas*.[6] Late medieval *specula* could also broadly represent morality or amorality for readers' spiritual guidance. Lydgate's *Temple of Glas* and Gower's *Confessio Amantis* tend towards moral rather than political instruction. These texts are nevertheless important for an understanding of the genre, as their use of the mirror and glass metaphors form a complex representation of visual perception and the reading process.[7] Lydgate's *Temple* and its source, Chaucer's *House of Fame*, use an extended trope of a temple of glass, where reflective walls display allegorical images of lovers from history and myth.[8]

As Andrea Schutz argues, the metaphors of "book as mirror" and "sight as perception" are also crucial to interpretation in Gower's *Confessio* (107). According to David K. Coley, the glass and mirror imagery of these works draws from the way "glass was used in the Middle Ages, particularly in window cycles like those at the Sainte-Chapelle in Paris, Chartres Cathedral, and Canterbury Cathedral" (62). The production process for glass in medieval Europe, in which different raw materials were fused and transformed into a new medium, further inspired the use of glass as a metaphor for a work's "textual generativity" (63), as textual *specula* glean from disparate sources and materials to create a transformed, illuminative surface (83). As processes similar to glass production, William Kuskin notes that many of Caxton's texts, including the *Mirrour*, are infused with metaphorical language of goldsmithing and alchemy.[9] These practices refine materials and, in the practice of alchemy, purport to turn base metals into gold. The alchemical model of material amalgamation, Kuskin argues, influenced the ways books were produced and conceptualized in Caxton's era. Just as books' material images generated new meaning, imagination's own fusion of images and ideas often held an important role in *speculum* texts. For instance, Andrew Galloway explores visionary prophecy and dream visions as methods of claiming moral and political authority in the *speculum principis* genre, citing Gower's dream visions in Book 1 of *Vox Clamantis* and in the *Confessio Amantis* (291). Vision and imagination, on the part of the counsellor as well as, I will argue, on the part of the reader authorize these mirror genres' rhetorical and political ends.

Caxton's *Mirrour* largely focuses on geography, astronomy, and theology in addition to rhetoric, and falls within the broader *imago mundi* genre. Hawes's more civically focused text elevates rhetoric above its traditional situation within the seven sciences and forms an ideal image of the "man of action" (the rhetor-courtier or head of state).[10] Here, the mirror becomes less of a mirror of the cosmological world and more of the sociopolitical mirror found in *specula principis*. I have chosen an example each of an early print encyclopedia and a vernacular illustrated conduct book to analyse and compare two major pedagogical mirror genres of the early modern era. Pedagogical texts assume a position of interactivity and cognition on the part of their readers. In addition, both texts are unique for their publication in the vernacular and for their woodcut illustrations. For Caxton's text, the inclusion of illustrations in the incunable era would have been an expense, such that they would be important for the work's meaning and imagined readership. Hawes's *Pastime* precedes the more well-known vernacular conduct books of Henry Peacham the elder and George Puttenham and stands out for being printed in English. Both works, for their linguistic accessibility and connections between word and image, would assume a wider readership than texts published in Latin. They are therefore ambitious about their imagined audience and impact; their illustrations would not just be a selling point to readers but would also set up an economy of attention to promote their pedagogical aims. Caxton's work sets up his image of the world as a microcosm for all learning in its woodcuts' depiction of its subject matter, while Hawes's text includes images to create a state of admiration for its learning and imitation of its main character, the knight Amour. Both works' images guide readers by showing them how to read and navigate the text. By investigating the connections between text and image in these works, we can see how systems of observation such as deixis and active reception influenced the early modern reading process.

Changes to the mirror as a technology also wrought changes to the mirror genre and would influence the content of *Mirrour and Description* and Hawes's *Pastime*. Mirrors made of crystal glass that would accurately reflect an image without polishing would not have been in common use during either Caxton or Hawes's time – their use began around 1570 (Kalas 520). Classical mirrors were made of bronze and would give the viewer a hazy or partial reflection. Round, convex "pennyware mirrors" made of glass, available throughout the Middle Ages, both minimized and distorted their reflections (Kalas 519). Later medieval mirrors that came into vogue during the time of Caxton's publication of his *Mirrour* would have been made of polished metal and would have shown a clearer reflection. Metal mirrors were the superior technology to glass at the time (Schechner 146): the glass for early Northern European mirrors would have been forest glass: brownish-green and filled with air bubbles (Schechner 148). By the time of the Tottel *Pastime*, the popularity of Venetian mirrors with "backings of steel, lead, or silver" and "larger and flatter" mirrors would have spread from the Continent to England (Grabes 4). Caxton's work may refer to the mirror as a world or globe, a sense that reflects the use of rounded, convex mirrors in the classical and medieval eras. Hawes's discussion of reflection, as well as the illustrated woodcuts within the Tottel edition, situates rhetoric within a discourse of magnification, widespread usability, leisure, and ornament. This discourse is perhaps influenced by the clearer, more decorative mirrors emerging in the sixteenth century, as well as the potential ability of concave mirrors and glass reading lenses to magnify their images.[11]

The mirror imagery of medieval and early modern English books recalls similar phenomenological metaphors of mirrors in fifteenth and sixteenth century treatises on vision and cognition. For example, philosopher Nicholas of Cusa's *On the Beryl* (1458) combines epistemology and mathematics in its beryl or crystal metaphor. This crystal represents textual form as a recursively productive and receptive visual material. Nicholas of Cusa tells readers that he will "adduce a mirror and a symbolism by which each reader's frail intellect may be aided and guided at the outer limits of the knowable" (Hopkins 792). His symbolic conceit is the beryl: "Beryl stones are bright, white, and clear. To them are given both concave and convex forms. And someone who looks out through them apprehends that which previously was invisible" (Hopkins 792–3). His humanist contemporary Marsilio Ficino fashioned the mind itself as *speculum* or mirror in his description of perception. Ficino's use of the mirror-mind analogy emphasizes reception rather than production, as sensed images and "forms are received by the mind as in a mirror, that is, without intrinsic alteration" (Spruit 209). Whether recursive or receptive, these philosophical works suggest that the epistemological metaphor of the mirror united the perceiving mind and the material text in Caxton and Hawes's historical moment.

Caxton's own textual "mirror of the world" may best be described as illusory or shattered. Despite its aspirations to operate as a unified compendium of knowledge, Caxton's print *Mirrour* in its different editions and reader uses displays extraordinary visual and physical mutability. A bibliographic note to the Bodleian library's 1527 edition describes this text as an "extraordinary jumble of cuts from all sources" and a "victim of its own popularity."[12] By this third edition, print copies carried completely different versions of the original illustrations and were readapted, reused, and often reread to death. Rather than a united, authoritative compendium, Caxton's *Mirrour* ultimately became a "jumble," a miscellaneous assembly of movable visual parts and perhaps even a "shock, shaking, or jolting" of the encyclopedia into a physically mobile form.[13]

In the case of Caxton's *Mirrour*, print became *un*-fixed in its visual style. This *Mirrour*'s fractured editions counter the scholarly assumption of a fixed, linear, and uniform print culture outlined, for instance, in Jay Bolter's study of the print encyclopedia in *Writing Space* and in Walter J. Ong's famous claim in *Ramus, Method, and the Decay of Dialogue*: "reduction to spatial form fixes everything, even sound. *Verba Volant, script manent*" [spoken words fly away, written words remain] (Ong 109). Paul Zumthor's famous discussion of *mouvance* focuses on stylistic and inventive variability within a set, traditional genre in medieval literary culture that lent an attitude of incompleteness and polyvocality to manuscript texts ("Intertextualité et mouvance" 8–16). The print visuals of Caxton's text also display a sense of incompleteness and multiplicity: many remaining copies of the *Mirror* have different images in different orders. This *mouvance* of imagery reflects illustrated print books' transformation of rhetoric to a visual practice. Images can be visible, material, and held in reader's hands, rather than a more one-directional ekphrasis or amplification by the rhetor to an audience. Print visuals, at least in their early form, did not kill rhetoric but allowed it to flourish in a newly accessible setting.

Caxton's *Mirrour and Description* allows its wide body of knowledge to be used, reused, and recycled by a broad population of vernacular readers.[14] As Neil Rhodes and Jonathan Sawday argue in *The Renaissance Computer*, "the rhetorical programme of sixteenth-century pedagogy" involved dismembering and remembering texts; encyclopedias, in particular, appear "to be generated by a desire to 'remember' or retrieve a lost order" (12). The *Mirrour* demonstrates this dual pull towards both ephemerality and immortality, as it attempts to reflect a macrocosm, nonetheless becomes a vernacular and immanently exploitable text. For instance, the first woodblock image of the British Library's 1481 edition of Caxton's *Mirrour* appears to emblematize print's aspirations to permanence but demonstrates visual mobility in practice (Figure 1.1).

A figure sits in a bishop's chair and gestures to four kneeling men, three who present the priest with gifts and one who appears to hold a book. What we might call a speech bubble today reads, "[Vox] audita perit, literra scripta manet," or, "the heard word perishes, the written letter remains," a maxim repeated in the juxtaposed text (sig. A1r). The "vox" portion of the proverb, actually, is omitted: the speaker's mouth stands in for the written word "vox." The reader has substituted the voice of the orator for the spatial illustration of the mouth itself.[15] Caxton emphasizes the movement of perishable speech to permanent print in his text, where he claims to have printed this book "To th ende that science & artes lerned & founden of things passed myght be had in perpetuel memorye & remembraunce" (1481 edition, sig. A1r). In this passage, Caxton ambitiously wishes to encompass epistemology (as represented by the seven traditional arts and sciences) and cosmology in one perpetual handbook. This inscribed proverb, however, effectively disappears and reappears in other editions based on their readers' whims: Caxton's promise of permanence is not his book's material result. In uninscribed, blank editions of this woodcut, the speech bubble, with its maxim about the permanence of text, has passed away (1490 edition, sig. A3r) (Figure 1.2).

In another edition of this book, the maxim appears as an inscribed gloss, rather than a speech bubble (sig. A3r) (Figure 1.3).[16]

In other words, even a maxim about the permanence of the written word becomes an image or trace that is either invisible or visible

Figure 1.1. William Caxton, *Hier begynneth the book callid the Myrrour and Dyscrypcyon of the Worlde with Many Mervaylles …* (1481), sig. A1r, British Library

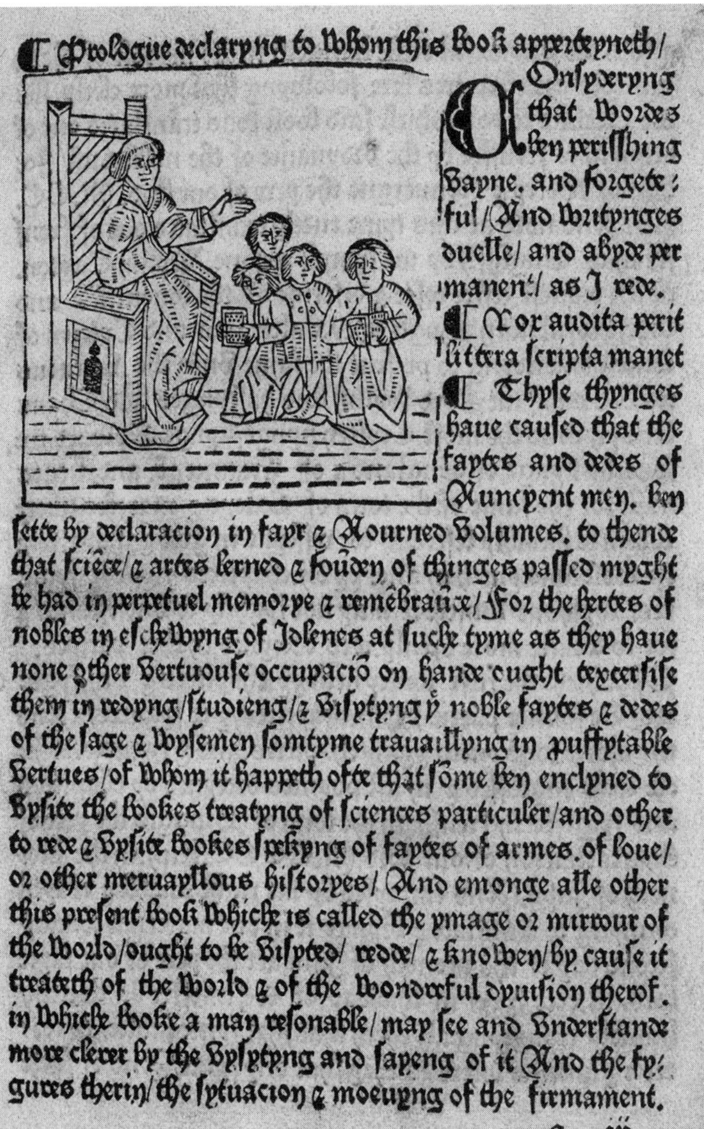

¶ Prologue declaryng to whom this book apperteyneth/

Onsperyng that wordes ben perisshing vayne, and forgete-ful/And writynges duelle/ and abyde permanent/ as I rede.

¶ For audita perit littera scripta manet

¶ Thyse thynges haue caused that the faytes and dedes of Auncyent men. ben sette by declaracion in fayr & aourned volumes. to thende that sciece/& artes lerned & fouden of thinges passed myght be had in perpetuel memorye & remembrauce/ For the sertes of nobles in eschewyng of Idlenes at suche tyme as they haue none other vertuouse occupacio on hande ought texercise them in redyng/studieng/& visytyng ye noble faytes & dedes of the sage & wysemen somtyme trauaillyng in puffytable vertues/of whom it happeth ofte that some ben enclyned to vysite the bookes tretyng of sciences particuler/and other to rede & vysite bookes spekyng of faytes of armes.of loue/ or other meruayllous historyes/ And emonge alle other this present book whiche is called the ymage or mirrour of the world/ought to be visyted/ rede/ & knowen/by cause it treateth of the world & of the wonderful dyuision therof. in whiche booke a man resonable/may see and vnderstande more clerer by the vysytyng and sayeng of it And the fy-gures therin/the sytuacion & moeuyng of the firmament.

a iij

Figure 1.2. William Caxton, *Mirrour and Description of the World* (1490), sig. A3r, British Library

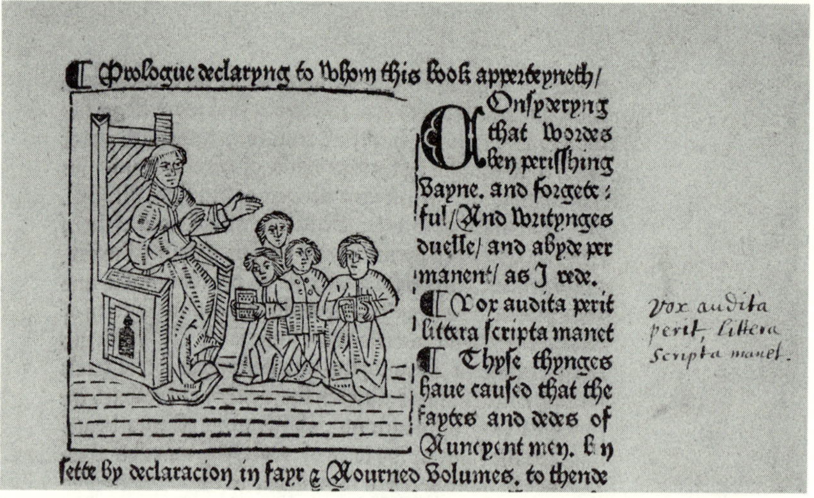

Figure 1.3. William Caxton, *Mirrour and Description of the World* (1490), sig. A3r, John Rylands Library

depending on reader use, not on visual or material stability. Each reader's interaction with Caxton's imagery transforms its meaning from copy to copy, in an impermanent and movable process. The encyclopedic nature of this text predisposes it towards a *mouvance* based an infinite range of reader interaction, even as it attempts to reflect the world. Fittingly, in the British Library's copy of the third 1527 edition, this maxim's reminder of the book's permanence disappears altogether. The maxim, whether inscribed by the reader's hand or Caxton's prologue, is omitted in favour of a direct discussion of God's creation, transferring the original text's focus on memory's permanence (or impermanence) to phenomenology. The first image of the 1527 edition, its title page, advertises the book's nature as a mirror and a microcosm, a self-reflective "little world" unto itself that reflects the macrocosm of the outer world. The mirror on the title page resembles a T-O map, a common form of cartography that depicted the world as a cross within a circle to demonstrate divine completion (Figure 1.4).

This edition's next illustration preserves the 1481 and 1490 editions' initial image of a holy man receiving gifts, but this time, the other figures are standing in a position of power in this exchange – a power symbolized in the gift of a book (Figure 1.5).

Figure 1.4. William Caxton, *The myrrour: [and] dyscrypcyon of the worlde with many meruaylles …* (1527), frontispiece, British Library

Figure 1.5. William Caxton, *The myrrour: [and] dyscrypcyon of the worlde with many meruaylles* … (1527), sig. A1v, British Library

The power of the print book to make the words permanent and to instruct a new, receptive audience in the first edition has become, instead, a power visible in the form of social and material exchange between what this illustration represents as the merchant and clerical classes, standing together as educational equals. The images of aspirational learners in the 1481 and 1490 editions has become one of empowered exchangers of knowledge. This image portrays the transference of book and literate culture from the clergy to a wider, middle-class reading public. The variability and *mouvance* among the different images in different editions of the *Mirror* reflects a class and educational mobility imagined and formed by early print pedagogies.

Movable texts like Caxton's *Mirrour* therefore invite readers to interact with its images, texts, and materials to uncover its meaning, in a process both subjective and inventive. This multimodal practice of reading among images, texts, and rhetorical figures recalls Linda Hutcheon's characterization of reading across media as a constant oscillation (xv). Hutcheon uses this term to describe the experience of encountering both an original and an adapted work at the same time. We can apply her description of an immersive, "interactive" reading process that "demands physical participation" across different media to the early modern process of reading among texts, images, and figures. Her description of oscillation as a retention of an afterimage (172) is particularly suggestive of these early illustrated print texts, which specifically adopt language of mirrors, fantasy, and perception to describe their material and cognitive effects. In addition, the visual ornamentation of both ekphrastic rhetoric and illustrated print incurs a multidirectional, active path of audience interpretation. In these visual rhetorics, figures and visual impressions merge with textual or allegorical content in the reader's creation of meaning. James A. Knapp argues that Caxton intended his *Mirrour* to form a combined system of word and image. The illustrations must be interpreted alongside the type "if the 'whole meaning' is to be revealed" ("Translating for Print" 76). Knapp here departs from the view advanced by N.F. Blake's reading of Caxton's illustrations and by Richard Lanham in his *Economics of Attention*. Blake and Lanham read visual imagery in early modern print as primarily a selling or advertising point. However, in Knapp's analysis, the inclusion of illustrations could present a "financial risk" ("Translating for Print" 76). By extension, Caxton's woodcuts also presented a technological risk, since this illustration process was new to English print (Knapp, "Translating for Print" 75).[17] Further, many of Caxton's woodcuts are incomprehensible without reading the juxtaposed text (Knapp 76–81). Caxton's illustrations, then, are not simply stylistic ornaments, but a systemic and purposeful co-production of meaning between image and reader.[18]

Visual Impressions in Caxton and Hawes: The Authorizing Afterimage

This visual and tactile practice of reading was both material and phenomenal. The status of Caxton's book as a mutable, movable mirror not only draws from the medieval *imago mundi* and *specula principis* genres, but also from classical thought. Vision is an integral feature of rhetorical invention in Aristotle, as Debra Hawhee argues in "Looking into Aristotle's Eyes." Aristotle's concept of *phantasia* informs what Hawhee calls "rhetorical vision," or a mode of perception that aids invention. She opposes this cognitive, epistemological model of rhetorical vision to visual rhetoric, which is dependent on a material index. Aristotelian *phantasia* "is activated when viewable matter is not immediately at hand ... as with dreams, delusions, and memories" (Hawhee 142). Hobbs describes classical rhetoric's positioning of the imagination as an "intermediary" between sensation and cognition (38). She cites Quintilian, who believed that "daydreamlike visions, hallucinations, in which absent experiences are revived in the imagination," was "a phenomenon common to all" (29). These partial visions reflect and simulate images and are not the things or images in themselves. Prominent metaphors for phantasia in the imaginative process include "a reflection in water or in a mirror; the bright trace that remains after staring at the sun and then closing the eyes; a hazy figure in the distance that may or may not be a man" (Hawhee 142–3). The mirrored or reflected nature of these images, then, impels both invention and an epistemological uncertainty as to the nature and form of the partial images themselves. Despite Hawhee's persuasive description of a phenomenological process of invention removed from a material medium, rhetorical vision and visual rhetoric, at least in early modern print, appear to inform one another. The perpetual compendium promised by Caxton's own *Mirrour*, with its adapted, altered, and reproduced images, forms just such an image of uncertainty. Its very physicality, in the trace of past editions and uses, creates a living memorial of previous images, yet this material trace is a mutable history plagued by constant movement, or jumbling.

In terms of perception, visual reflection was more of a precarious fun house than a simple model of clarity in early modern culture. A consideration of the ways that early modern readers may have perceived print impressions can further overturn our critical assumptions about print's material and epistemic fixity. One possible translation of *phantasia* is impression, a kind of pictorial impression on the soul or mind's eye (Hawhee 146). Hawhee claims, "this pressed in visual mode of self-perception is not metaphorical. It is material" (147). This material, ideal picture that is impressed on the mind parallels Stephen Hawes's use of visual allegory in his *Pastime of Pleasure*. Indeed, both Hawes and the compilers of the 1555 illustrated edition may have had Aristotelian *phantasia* in mind. Hawes describes the process of rhetorical invention in his poetic text as dependent on the images of "fantasye":

> For though a man, of hys proper mynde
> Be inventive, and he do not apply
> His fantasye, unto the besy kynde
> Of his connynge it maye not ratifye
> For fantasye, must nedes exemplify
> Hys newe invencion, and cause hym to entende
> Wyth hole desyre, to brynge it to an ende.   (sig. E1v)

Fantasy, or the formation of pictorial impressions in the mind, authorizes or "ratifyes" invention in this passage. This symbiosis of image impression and invention was both rhetorical and cognitive.

In early modern scientific and philosophical works, the visual impressions that aid memory and imagination were even thought to reside within the physiological matter of the brain itself. Medieval depictions of the brain generally show a tripartite structure, with imagination, reason, and memory as the main chambers or ventricles.[19] Imagination occupies the forefront of the brain; reason, which mediates perception and memory, lies in the middle; and memory is lodged in the hindmost section.[20] This shared concept of faculty psychology drew from the writings of Aristotle, Galen, Avicenna, and the early church fathers, and remained mostly unchanged until the late sixteenth century (Clarke and Dewhurst 8).[21] Several medieval illustrations of the brain display lines that intersect the optic nerves and these three chambers, demonstrating the importance of visual perception to cognition in late medieval philosophies of mind.[22] The imagination, or *vis imaginativa*, could both retain image impressions and create new images. In his thirteenth-century encyclopedia, *De Proprietatibus Rerum* ("On the Properties of Things"), scholar Bartholomaeus Anglicus calls the three ventricles of imagination, reason, and memory "small wombs" (Kemp 46),[23] a sense that captures their dually receptive and generative qualities. As Mary Carruthers establishes, the imagination was a phenomenal force, "an agent, a power, not just a receptacle" (*The Book of Memory* 68). In Aristotle, the "deliberative" part of the imagination could amalgamate or fuse different raw sense impressions into a new, unified image (Carruthers, *The Book of Memory* 65), much as a late-medieval artisan would make stained glass. Yet imagination was far from an untroubled chamber in classical and medieval understandings. The imaginative faculty was believed to cause "dream images," "phantasms," and hallucinations (Carruthers, *The Book of Memory* 73–4). Medical texts even blamed the imagination for nightmares and sleepwalking.[24] The imagination could act as a creative yet deceptive instigator in the brain.

As a component of the imagination, phantasia had the unique role of mediating among the three ventricles as a "comparing, uniting, and dividing faculty" in the work of Albertus Magnus.[25] In Roger Bacon's *Opus Maius*, phantasia retained the images produced in the imagination so that they could be processed by the brain's judgment, or reason (208). Phantasia could thus serve as a buffer for the imagination's wilder properties. This faculty allowed the brain to construct meaning from the images and impressions it received. In the Aristotelian "model of the soul," phantasia was thought to be "a faculty halfway between the (external) senses and (internal) powers of cognition," an intersection between the material and the cognitive that rendered invisible matter visible (Vogt-Spira 52; 64). Phantasia "gathered together" or "composed" sense data for cognition.[26] Hence, concepts of phantasia became crucial to how textual and rhetorical epistemologies were formed in late medieval and early modern thought, since it functioned as an essentially interpretive faculty. Cognitive perception, and phantasia more specifically, allows a text to interact with the eye and mind of the reader. As Gregor Vogt-Spira asserts, the concept of res-verba (form and matter) might be modified in studies of medieval rhetoric to a more triadic structure of "res-verba-nos," or form, matter, and us, to reflect the importance of perception as a "producer" or "audience" of a text (Vogt-Spira 62). By extension, this "nos" could alternatively be conceived of as the perceiving reader or viewer of a text, whose faculties of imagination, phantasia, reason, and memory retained, reproduced, and ultimately transformed its images and ideas.

Brain matter corresponded with book matter in late medieval and early modern metaphorical descriptions of cognitive perception. In the theories of Nicholas of Cusa, the mind acts as "a force or an energy-centre, capable of producing perception" (Spruit 205), a force that "may be compared to a wax tablet moulding itself" (Spruit 208). Here, the creation of mental impressions is a recursive process, as the mind itself acts as a sentient, self-replenishing material in cognition and invention. In late-medieval cognition, the species that objects gave off would imprint themselves – literally – on the brain matter: "it is this imprinting that gives 'ymaginativa' the capacity to make present something that was absent" (Walter 102).[27] In other words, imagination is materially crucial for the brain's receipt of impressions and its subsequent reproduction and recombination of images. Perception in the brain would later be attached to print metaphors. Bruce R. Smith observes that early modern "physiologists imagined memory in graphically physical terms" (107).[28] For example, Ambrose Paré and Levinus Lemnius describe cognitive perception with terms specific to imprinting and engraving. Following Galenic theory, Paré links the ability to retain sense impressions with the temperature of the brain matter itself: "Those who have a dry braine, are also slow to learne; for you shall not easily imprint any thing in dry bodyes, but they are most constant reteiners of those things they have once learned" (fol. 166, sig. P3v). Lemnius similarly contrasts slippery, overly liquid brains with overly hard brains, which "will not easely suffer the poynte of anye engravinge Toole to enter and pearce into it" (fol. 120v). Again, the perceptive processes necessary for learning take on a clearly material form here, in language that combines cognitive and book materials to form a metaphor of a reproductive image or impression on a physical form – an engraving or imprint on the book and brain.[29]

A "fantasye," which authorizes or "must nedes exemplify Hys newe invencion," and "brynge it to an ende," may seem unusual and even contradictory given the subjective nature of this imaginative process. In the historical moment of early print, however, both Caxton and Hawes combine authorizing impressions with cosmological authority through metaphors of "the word." Caxton and Hawes employ the same maxim as they introduce their sections on grammar and the trivium. Caxton begins his discussion of grammar with the proverb, "God made the world by worde & the word is to the world sentence" (*Mirrour*, 1481, sig. C5v). Hawes first sends his ideal knight, Amour, to grammar. Hawes situates grammar as the "fryst foundement / Of every science ... "; "By worde

the world, was made orygynally … to the world, the worde is sententious Judgement" (sig. D2v). Here, world reflects God's word, just as
the word is itself a mirror-image of that creation, in a doubly reflective
impression. The visual imprint of divine invention ratifies the word in a
larger world, and, as Stark argues, imbues grammar and style with cosmological significance. In late-medieval culture, texts, as impressed and
reproduced images of things, were thought to be already pictorial or
imitative in nature (Vogt-Spira 63). Words that are physically imprinted
on the book's page and reader's mind reflected the divine impression
of word on world (Stark 10).[30] Hawes employs the terms "sententiae"
and "sententious" not to indicate their current, more pretentious implications, but to indicate authority – intellectual, moral, and social. The
reflective imprint of word and world on one another, in addition to the
material imprint of the world's images through "fantasye" in cognition
and rhetoric, again authorizes meaning through visual invention and
impressed images. Invention is produced through the visual reading
process and through the imprint and engraving of images on the book,
eye, mind, and world.

Form and Matter in Visual Rhetoric: "Covert Coloures"
and Magnified Style

Visual perception, mediated by the materials of the book, brain, and
eye, thus produces a receptive, active, and, at times, uncertain process
of invention. Classical and early modern visual theories underscore this
fusion of a dually receptive and active observation. For example, the
first woodcut of the *Pastime*'s 1555 edition shows a vision of Fame (sig.
D1v) surrounded by fire (Figure 1.6).

Despite his status as a symbolic representation of the knight and protagonist Amour, ostensibly Hawes's ideal "man of action," the knight
in this illustration (on the bottom right) simply lies down and gazes at
this allegorical representation of Fame. The knight's main action here
is to passively receive a visual impression. In his discussion of image
reception, Alistair Crombie details the classical belief that objects gave
off replicas of themselves (177). Classical and early modern thinkers
apply a terminology of mirror-imagery and visual invention for these
object replicas: Democritus calls them *eidola*; Aristotle, Roger Bacon, and
Theophrastus, *imagines*; Leonardo da Vinci, *simulacra*; and Kepler, *pictu-
rae* and *illustrationes* (Crombie 177). The "passive reception of images"
given off by the object, according to Crombie, was at the same time an

Figure 1.6. Stephen Hawes, *Pastime of Pleasure* (1555), sig. D1v, Bodleian Library

active process in which "the eye by its own effort looked at the object and selected from among the images continually striking it those to which it paid attention" (178).

The apparent paradox of a reclining knight of action in this woodcut fits within this philosophical model of active reception. The adjoining woodcut's depiction of flames can be situated within Platonic and neo-Platonic models of vision. Empedocles and Plato use the image of fire and light issuing from the eyes to conceptualize sight. Plato imagines vision as a "current of fire issuing from the eyes, which, in the presence of daylight, met in the line of vision and united with a current of fire-particles streaming off the object seen" (Crombie 178). The Tottel *Pastime*'s portrayal of "tongues of fyre" that surround the woodcut image of Fame recalls this theory of disseminated fire (sig. A3v). Fire issues from the Lady Fame that is gazed upon. In the Platonic model, fire would also emanate from the eyes of the knight Amour, which readers would then receive in their own active visual impressions.[31] The woodcut's inclusion of fire in its depiction of vision may symbolize this theory of active reception in a context of visual reading. The illustration and text together model active reception as a reading process to Hawes's audience. The woodcut image appears before the poetic text in the Tottel *Pastime*. In the text, the knight first encounters "an ymage fayre and strong / With two fayre handes, stretched out along" (sig. A4v) who allegorizes Amour's choice between the active life and the way of contemplation. After Amour chooses the active life, in a description reminiscent of *phantasia*'s afterimages, the knight exclaims, "Me thought a farre, I had a vysion / Of a picture, of marveylous facion" (sig. B1v). This image is made of "fine copper" and carries the "sentence" to avoid sloth and be ruled by reason, after which the knight slumbers (sig. B1v). Then, the knight Amour has his vision of the fiery Fame (sig. B1r). In the woodcut, all of the figures' eyes and gestures mark Fame as the primary object of attention, demonstrating that other characters of the narrative are to guide the aspirational reader to this end goal. Unusually, there is a third female figure that is not present in the text. She stands above the knight and gazes at fame. Is she a representation of the copper emblem that advocates reason or a figure for the reader, who is progressing alongside the knight towards Fame? As a woman and one who leans towards Fame, if this emblem is indeed a figure for the reader, she represents the active role and broad audience envisioned by this vernacular treatise. After his vision, the knight progresses to a tower of learning, much as readers

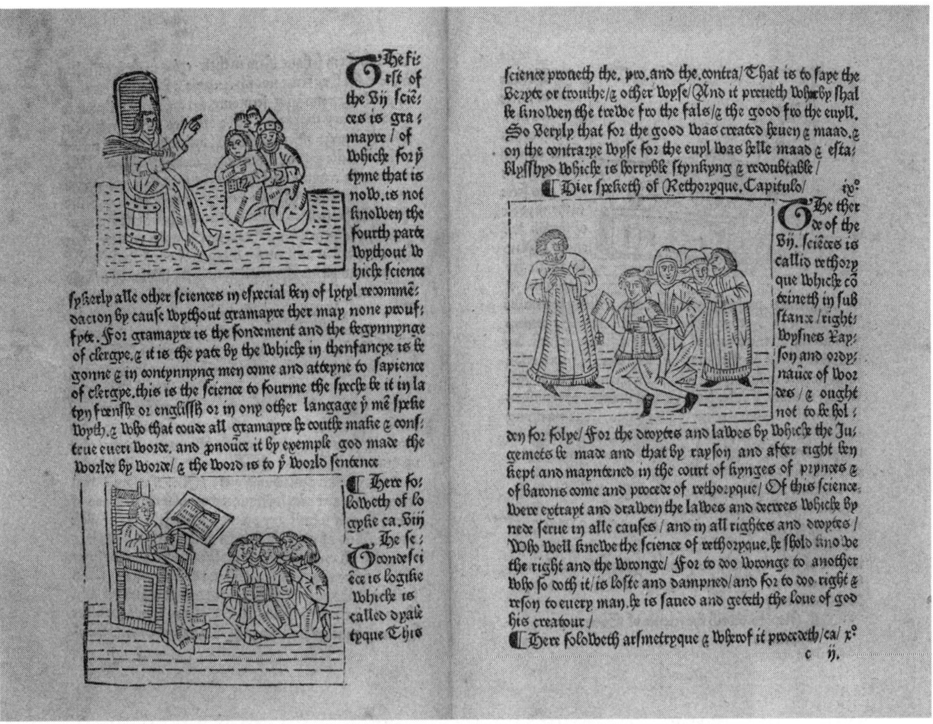

Figure 1.7. William Caxton, *Mirrour and Description of the World* (1490), sig. C2v–C2r, British Library

would marvel at the *Pastime*'s images to progress through the text. Hawes portrays visual pedagogy and active reception as necessary for a life of political action.

The *Mirrour* and *Pastime* authorize a new understanding of rhetoric for a popular audience through their images of pedagogy. The woodcuts of Caxton's *Mirrour* and Hawes's *Pastime* demonstrate the unique relationship of rhetorical instruction to the early print reader. In Caxton, rhetoric occupies a traditional "space" in the trivium, just as it literally occupies the same page as grammar and logic in the 1490 edition (Figure 1.7).

The figure of grammar holds a switch and gestures to a group of students in a subordinate pose. As Walter Ong and Brian Cummings argue, Latin grammar pedagogy in both the late-medieval scholastic and the early modern English grammar school models was a rite of male adolescent passage, replete with sometimes torturous physical punishment to suit the sometimes-torturous prose that developed from this process.[32] Carla Mazzio's *Inarticulate Renaissance* and Ian Smith's *Barbarian Errors* situate early modern anxieties of ineloquence as cultural and political anxieties: rhetorical inarticulateness and grammatical error could register as religious, racial, or political deviance. The physical position of the students in the *Mirrour*'s image of grammar portrays and furthers this model of linguistic and social instruction. In the woodcut representing Logic, too, the figures of the students kneel, with one student pointing back up to the instructor. Where grammatical pedagogy is aural and corporal in its illustration, logic's woodcut depicts its pedagogy as book learning.

Rhetoric's woodcut, in contrast, features students who have advanced to standing up. Where there is a visible gap of white space between the instructors and students in the grammar and logic woodcuts, the students are almost bearing down on the instructor in *The Mirrour*'s image of rhetoric, to a point where the instructor appears to be leaning back. The blank space between the instructor and students is the centre – and centralizing feature – of the previous two woodcuts of grammar and logic. Conversely, the centre space of rhetoric's image is taken up by an eager student who holds a book. The instructor stands alongside the students and appears to enumerate a point. One student follows behind the eager and central young man; two figures behind these two students appear to be engaged in a close discussion or disputation. Rita Copeland argues that Caxton does especially not elevate rhetorical pedagogy over the other liberal arts and sciences in his *Mirrour* (70), yet the rhetoric woodcut's dramatic break with the images of grammar and logic implies a sense of educational progress, from cowed adolescents to enthusiastic young men of action. Caxton's text also defends a vision of rhetoric as a crucial element in civic and political decisions: it "containeth in substance" the

> rayson and ordynaunce of wordes & ought not to be holden for folye. For the droytes and laws by whiche the Jugementes be made and that by rayson and after right ben kept and mayntened in the court of kynges & prynces ... Of this science were extrayct and drawen the laws and decrees whiche by nede serve in alle causes. (sig. ciir, 1490 edition)

The political world's laws and sentences are tied to rhetorical words and sententiae in Caxton and Hawes. The legal and political function of rhetoric, a Ciceronian model, appears to dominate in England's first illustrated print book. Although *The Mirrour* was commissioned by a patron, Lord Hugh Bryce, Caxton envisioned his adaptation for a wider audience (Knapp, "Translating for Print" 68). Knapp argues that the prose version of the French *L'Image* was set within a more popular tradition than its verse form (69). Caxton's choice to adapt his book from the prose anticipates a more egalitarian, participatory framework for rhetoric in the social sphere.

Tottel's 1555 edition of Hawes displays images of the trivium that respond to the conditions of rhetorical instruction in print. The three woodcut impressions of Hawes's own reorganization of the trivium are identical to one another, equalizing their importance (sig. dir, sig. diiiv, sig. eir) (Figure 1.8).

This repeated woodcut block is hierarchical, like Caxton's grammar and logic, yet interactive. Lady Grammar/Rhetoric/Logic, like the fiery Faerie of the Tottel *Pastime*'s first woodcut image, acts as a feminized and prominent allegorical symbol for the development of rhetoric and virtue. This depiction sets up rhetoric as an aspirational ideal: the actual plot of the *Pastime*, after the knight Amour's introduction to the seven sciences, resembles a medieval courtly romance genre, where knights are often shown serving aristocratic ladies. The book's title, *Pastime of Pleasure*, of course emphasizes leisure and sensuality. Further, the text's generic situation within a courtly romance genre accentuates the class context of its civic rhetoric. While an allegorical romance in genre, the *Pastime*'s vernacular and popular distribution, particularly with the additional illustrations of the 1555 Tottel version, locates itself as not a mirror for princes alone, but as an aspirational and ideal mirror for a literate general public. This edition shares the same printer (Richard Tottel) of *Tottel's Miscellany* (1557), the most popular and influential poetic collection of sixteenth-century England. This later poetic miscellany distributed court literature to a wide reading audience, just as the 1555 *Pastime* distributes its allegory of liberal education through its illustrations and textual content. This sense of aspiration and sensual pleasure informs the woodcut's image of instruction under a noble lady. We see her turn a book's page: this action emphasizes the Tottel edition's material context and physical mobility.

Unlike the specifically scholastic, clerical setting of Caxton's pedagogy in the *Mirrour*, the setting of Hawes's pedagogy could be clerical,

Figure 1.8. Stephen Hawes, *Pastime of Pleasure* (1555), sig. D1r, Bodleian Library

in a library, or even in a private home. The female figure's gaze turns to two (male) standing figures engaged in conversation. Another figure sits below the woman and reads yet another book. The scene appears busy with different modes of learning. The figures are engaged with a variety of different books and activities under the symbolic guidance of "Dame Trivium." Although a hierarchical image, readers participate with instruction in diverse ways. This interactivity points to a voluntary and more individualized model than the scholastic or clerical group setting of Caxton's pedagogical woodcuts. This image of rhetorical instruction imagines readers who will self-educate at their leisure, as a self-improving pastime, and who will later participate in the moral and civic rhetoric Hawes's text emphasizes. This scene corroborates Copeland's claim that vernacular rhetorical guides, such as Hawes's, effectively develop their own audiences – an audience, in Benedict Anderson's terms, that becomes an "imagined community" through the image-impressions of Tottel's edition.

The more individualized yet civic brand of rhetoric the *Pastime* displays later incurs a concept of rhetoric itself as a figure of subjectivity. In Hawes's description of Lady Rhetoric, the dominant metaphor is, perhaps unsurprisingly, the mirror. The pedagogical woodcut's third repetition corresponds with an elaborate textual ekphrasis of "Lady Rhetoric":

> Than above Logyke, up we went a starye
> In to a chambre, gayly glorified
> Strowed with floures, of all goodly ayre
> Where sate a lady, gretly magnified
> She had a garlande, of the laurell grene …
> Her goodly chambre, was set all about
> Wyth deputed myrrours, of speculation.　　　　　　　　　(sig. D4r)

Hawes reimagines rhetoric through a spatial, visual relocation, "up" the stairs "above" logic.[33] The laurel garland alludes to poetic achievement and military victory: the twofold model of rhetoric, aesthetic and political, that Hawes advances. The strewn "flowers" represent rhetoric's different stylistic ornaments and figures, a common metaphor that would later gain traction in both poetic and rhetorical miscellanies. These miscellanies employed a natural imagery of gardens and arbors to indicate an assortment of tropes arranged by the loose structure of a lightweight print handbook.[34] In Hawes's description, Lady Rhetoric is also "magnified" in its now-obsolete sense: honoured, as well as expanded.[35]

This passage's emphasis on magnification, of course, alludes back to the book as a mirror or *speculum*. Lady Rhetoric is magnified by the book, and the book in turn magnifies and reflects ideal political and civic virtue. Lady Rhetoric's "deputed" mirrors of speculation, in this passage, create an image of rhetoric as an arrangement of stylistic ornaments or "flowers." To "depute," in its late-medieval and early modern connotation, meant to ordain something for a particular purpose, a meaning that combines stylistic decoration with social decorum.[36] "Speculation" derives from the Latin *speculat-*, or *speculari* to examine/observe, *specula* a watch-tower or look-out, and *specere*, to look; it shares the same root (*specere*) as object species. The definition of speculation as the act of looking or observing has its first example in the *OED* with this very passage.[37] Hawes's *Pastime* may have been one of the first translations to adapt this term from its Latin meaning of watching/looking-out to its vernacular meaning of exploring, viewing, and learning. *OED* sense 4a defines speculation as a "profound study of some subject." The mirrors of speculation, again, ground rhetorical vision in some form of material mediation between object and replica, image and observer, perception and invention, visible matter and ontic meaning.

Magnification is also both an important stylistic property of rhetoric and a component of visual perception. As Peter Mack describes, the popular genres of romances and conduct manuals (both of which Hawes's *Pastime* incorporates) conventionally employed a rhetoric of amplification – in other words, magnification – for emphasis and emotional effect ("Ideas of Imagination" 149). The most common figures of amplification for these genres were comparisons, metaphors, and repetitions (149). Comparisons help to construct the nature of the conduct book as an epideictic "Socratic mirror," pointing out virtue and vice, praise and blame (Grabes 137). Repetitions recall the reflective figure of the book-as-mirror, as well as the Platonic simulacra of objects that connect a material thing to its perceiving onlooker. Hawes's own rhetoric of magnification emphasizes amplification, mediation, repetition, duplication, and reflexive ornamentation. The trope of the mirror combines form, matter, and the perceiver: a mirror could imply distortion, transversal, and transformation. By representing rhetoric as a deputed or arranged mirror, Hawes empowers it to act as a transformative medium as well as an aesthetic ornament. The book, mirror, and the rhetorical figure reinforce each material's ability to create and reflect meaning.

Given the mirror's potential for both amplification and visual distortion in its material history, however, the connection between rhetoric and vision is not untroubled in the *Pastime*. The nature of the *specula principis* genre, as a political rhetoric, necessitates a certain amount of dissembling and impeded visibility. Hawes self-consciously models his book after Lydgate and Gower's *specula principis*.[38] Hawes aims to mirror ideal political praxis and, at the same time, to refrain from the creation of so direct or clear a mirror-image as to cause offence. Hawes's images must therefore both reflect and refract. They must produce a rhetoric that conceals as it reveals – as Hawes terms it, a "covert coloure" (sig. A3v). The very partial or jumbled nature of images in phantasia and in book materials allows Hawes to maintain this contradiction. Hawes first actually dissembles his dissembling method: "The lyght of trouth, I lacke cunnyng to cloke / To drawe a curtayne, I dare not to presume / Nor hyde nty matter, With a misty smoke" (sig. A3v). The language of a cloak, curtain, and smoke that conceals "matter," brings forth a division between form and matter, or *res / verba*. This opposition often sets rhetorical or stylistic "ornamentation" apart from the logical and dialectical content of invention.[39] But directly after this profession of good faith, Hawes introduces alternative visual metaphors for political and moral allegory.[40] Hawes promises to

> ... blowe out a fume
> To hyde my mynde, underneth a fable
> By covert coloure, well and probable ...
> For under a coloure, a truthe may aryse
> As was the guyse, in olde antiquitie.   (sig. A3v)

The "covert coloure" paints, without painting over, a particular message. Hawes's covert colour is an illustration of truth, which is shaped by, and shapes, its matter/content. Hidden fable or allegory allows symbolic language to carry its matter without revealing its naked aim.[41] "Fume" could refer to our familiar definition of smoke, but "fumé" could also refer to a glass tinted with smoke or a glass that displays a smoky, hazy quality (similar to the forest glass of pennyware mirrors), as well as an "exhalation" that could produce "emotions, dreams, dullness," meanings that suit Hawes's clouded allegory and the hazy, subjective *phantasia* of invention.[42]

The foggy, curtained visual image of the "covert coloure" in Hawes's *Pastime* also recalls classical concepts of visual perception as a subjective impression/projection. In both Platonic and Aristotelian thought, "the proper object of vision was colours" (Crombie 178). These "colours" were thought to be created through the "interaction" between the perceiver and the "fire particles streaming off the coloured object" (Crombie 178). In *Theaetetus*, Plato discusses blackness, whiteness, and different colours. He believes that colours are created through the meeting of the eyes with the object's own motion:

> We will find that black, white, and so on are generated by the eyes meeting the movement for which they are adapted, and that what we call a colour is neither the thing which does the meeting, nor the thing which is met, but something generated in between, which is peculiar to the individual perceiver. (Oxford Ed., 134)

In the *Pastime*, rhetorical vision and visual ornament – in Hawes's terms, a covert colour – again connect the individual perceiver (or reader) to a material thing (or book). Perception, acting through a medium (an object of sight, an illustrated book), forms the basis for both pedagogical instruction and political action in the *Pastime*, even as the dispersed nature of this link allows the message to become conveniently scattered or hazy. These stylistic verbal and visual colours of Hawes's work, as allegorically "covert" or covered, carry a sense of disguise or veiling of a political meaning[43] and, at the same time, a sense of an authorizing or ratifying function.[44] "Covert," interpreted as a thicket or forest, suggests the covert colour's complex allegory and uncertain navigability – we may recall here Edmund Spenser's thicket of trees that introduces his allegorical *Faerie Queene*.[45] The connection that visual rhetoric makes between *verba* (stylistic, rhetorical form) and *res* (content and material thing) is subjective, disguised, and hazy by nature, yet it is this very mediated or uncertain perception that ratifies interpretation and invention.

The Epideictic and Deictic Function of Hawes's and Caxton's Mirrors

Deixis serves as an important component to Caxton and Hawes's visual rhetoric and rhetorical vision. In the Caxton and Hawes woodcuts, illustrated "fingerposts" and deictic gestures draw connections between symbolic content (*verba*) and the material medium (*res*) of print. Deixis serves to connect the reader's gaze to the material thing at hand. The

Figure 1.9. William Caxton, *Hier begynneth the book callid the Myrrour and Dyscrypcyon of the Worlde with Many Mervaylles …* (1481), sig. A3v–A4r, British Library

deictic signs of the *Mirrour*'s and *Pastime*'s woodcuts direct their readers' visual reception of the books. In his study of theatrical semiotics, Keir Elam situates deixis as drama's "most important linguistic component" (27). Deixis is part of the relationship of the "index," where the sign has a relationship of causality to a material object (22). Elam associates index deixis with fingerpost images in books (22). Although the figures in early print woodcuts are human, their different hand and physical positions are employed for emphasis, juxtaposition, and amplification. This stylistic structure implies their use as important markers for the reading process. The three editions of Caxton's *Mirror* demonstrate this deictic structure through their illustrations.[46] The 1481 edition portrays a solitary Christ as he holds his orb, a symbol that reflects this book's cosmological aspirations and operation as a reflective world-unto-itself (Figure 1.9).

The figure of Christ is presented with a stigmata and halo: his portrayal in the 1481 edition is late-medieval in form. The reference of the image to a material index is limited to the common symbol of the cross-bearing orb or *globus cruciger*, a figure of cosmological dominion. The 1481 image assumes a readership that seeks to understand ontology, to use the book to ultimately look outwards, as the book mirrors the world. The 1490 Christ appears as a heavenly, victorious, and risen Christ rather than the suffering servant and ruler of the 1481 edition. In the 1490 edition, Christ is surrounded by figures that gaze at or point towards him, deictically "framing" Christ's image (Figure 1.10).

Elam argues that the conspicuousness of "rhetorical figures, highly patterned syntax, phonetic repetitions and parallelisms" saturated early modern English culture (18). In theatrical semiotics, metatheatre and framing devices formed the symbolic language that magnified audience attention. In the *Mirrour*'s bibliographical semiotics, a structure of framing, conspicuous figures serve to foreground the divine Word. While the orb and stigmata signify the cosmological or metaphysical centre of the 1481 print, the 1490 edition centres its vision on the "IHS" symbol featured on Christ's chest, a visual figure for the Word that would become a commonplace in early modern English print. If the 1481 edition emphasizes the world, the 1490 edition self-references the Word. This self-conscious representation of the Word/world as image behaves as an "ostentation" that displays something that is referred to as a part of a class of objects (Elam 30). An ostentation affirms a meaning's context within (and reliance upon) a particular material structure, or matter's connection to form (Elam 30). The "IHS" symbol reminds readers that they are gazing at a material woodcut impression in a book, a book that aspires to mirror, as an impressed image, world and Word. By the 1527 *Mirrour*, the metaphysical content of Caxton's first edition has disappeared almost entirely in favour of material ostentation and self-reference.

Here, a monk inscribes a text in a scriptorium, surrounded by books (Figure 1.11). The theological content of Christ's image in the first and second editions becomes social and textual in the third, set within in a visible location of book production and reproduction. This ostentation of the book is one of a conspicuously medieval and manuscript culture. Caxton's previously "new media" print translation of the manuscript *L'Image* has now settled within a realm of textual tradition, even

¶ Wherfor god made and created the world/
Capitulo. ij.

God made and cre
ated al the world
of his only wille by cau
se that he myght haue so
me thynge that myght
be suche as myght deser-
ue of his wele and good
nes yf it were not in
his defaulte/ And ther
fore he establysshid this
world. Nothynge for þ
he shuld be the better/ ne
þ he had ony nede/ But
he dyde it for charyte and
by his grete debonayrte/
For as right charytable/ he wolde that other shold parte
wyth hym of his wele and goodnes. And that alle other
creatures euerich after his nature shold fele of his puyssau-
ce after that it myght apperteyne to hym. Thus wold god
establissssh this world. that suche thynge shold Issue þ might
vnderstande and knowe the noblesse of his power and of his sa-
ppence/ and also of the good that he made for the man erthely/
that he myght serue hym in suche maner. þ by hym he myght
deserue the grete wele and good that he had made for hym/then
ne ought we aboue alle other thynge to loue hym and than-
ke hym that made and fourmed vs/ Whan we haue suche
power and suche auctoryte by hym. That yf we wylt loue
him we shal be lordes of all goodes. Now loue we him the-
ne wyth all our myght. and thenne shal we do as wyse men

Figure 1.10. William Caxton, *Mirrour and Description of the World* (1490), sig. A4r, British Library

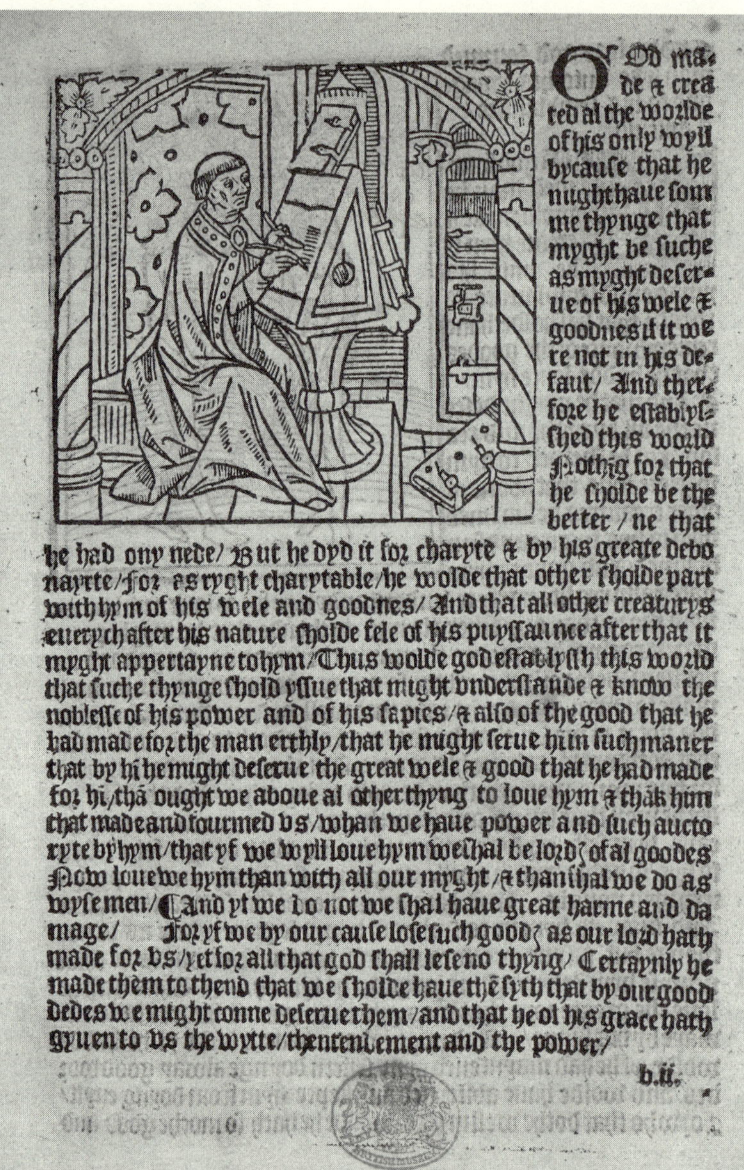

God made & created al the worlde of his only wyll bycause that he myght haue somme thynge that myght be suche as myght deserue of his wele & goodnes if it were not in his defaut / And therfore he estabysshed this world Nothig for that he wolde be the better / ne that he had ony nede / But he dyd it for charyte & by his greate debonayrte / for as ryght charytable / he wolde that other sholde part with hym of his wele and goodnes / And that all other creaturys euerych after his nature sholde fele of his puyssaunce after that it myght appertayne to hym / Thus wolde god establysh this world that suche thynge shold yssue that might vnderstande & know the noblesse of his power and of his sapies / & also of the good that he had made for the man erthly / that he might serue him such maner that by hi he might deserue the great wele & good that he had made for hi / thā ought we aboue al other thyng to loue hym & thāk him that made and tourmed vs / whan we haue power and such aucto ryte by hym / that yf we wyll loue hym we shal be lordz of al goodes Now loue we hym than with all our myght / & than shal we do as wyse men / And yf we do not we shal haue great harme and damage / For yf we by our cause lose such goodz as our lord hath made for vs / yet for all that god shall lese no thyng / Certaynly he made them to thend that we sholde haue thē syth that by our good dedes we might conne deserue them / and that he of his grace hath gyuen to vs the wytte / thentendement and the power /

b.ii.

Figure 1.11. William Caxton, *The myrrour: [and] dyscrypcyon of the worlde with many meruaylles …* (1527), sig. B2r, British Library

of nostalgia. The 1527 edition advertises its technological and visual novelty through ostentatious references to past textual media. The juxtaposition of a manuscript image in a print impression sets this edition within an established tradition of visual books, yet this edition makes a claim for its own innovativeness through that same process. This visual placement of "the word" within a scriptorium also highlights the *Mirrour*'s focus on pedagogy for a vernacular audience. Caxton's prologue to his 1481 and 1490 *Mirrours* hails an aspirational new audience that desires to imitate aristocratic leisure: he suggests this book "for the hertes of nobles in eschwying of Jolines at suche tyme as they have none other vertuouse occupation on hande ought exercise them in redying/ studieng/ & visytyng the noble faytes & dedes of the sage & wysemen" (sig. aiijr). In the 1527 edition, a wider imagined audience is invited to pick up the book by this woodcut's dual appeal to nostalgia and novelty.

Building the Book: Jacob's Ladder and the Tower of Babel

In the sixteenth and seventeenth centuries, the relationships among vision, rhetoric, and materiality extended beyond the popular book-as-mirror metaphor to newly prominent visual technologies and spatial systems of measurement, such as optics, geometry, and mapmaking. Sven Dupré outlines the relationship between geometrical diagrams and the science of optics in the late Middle Ages. These discoveries expanded to "the publication of perspectivistic treatise and the design of instruments," in addition to the practice of collecting "optical marvels, in particular mirrors" (16). Dupré describes the rhetorician Peter Ramus's library, filled with mirrors and instruments of design (16). Katherine Acheson argues that the "coupling of Aristotelian pedagogical values with geometrically based artistic practice" in drawing and handwriting manuals has been a neglected influence in early modern literary and rhetorical history (10). Drawing, handwriting, and developments in geometry and optics all depended "on complex and precise instruments" (Acheson 92), instruments that "disseminated the exotic, the ingenious, and the new" in their "promotion of classical values" and visual rhetoric (Acheson 111). Optics and cartography, in particular, shared technical instruments and geometrical methods. In addition, they shared a metaphorical relationship between microcosmic representation and macrocosmic space, the image and the larger world. For example, Henry Turner cites Arthur Hopton's 1611 *Speculum*

Topographicum or *Topographical Glasse* as a primary example for "an entire world" "reduced to graphic form" in a cartographical glass (7).[47] With the troubled phenomenological history of reflection in mind, however, I would pose the representation of rhetorical and visual devices in maps and mirrors as not reductive, but productive of discursive complexity. Indeed, Victor Stoichita groups "painting, map, and mirror" together as early modern forms of representation that produce an "intertextual discourse," "a dialogue aimed at the very status of the representation" (73).

In the *Pastime*, the knight Amour's entrance to a "tower of geometry" reflects the important cultural connection between visual rhetoric and new spatial technologies in its playful inclusion of mirroring and measurement tropes. A woodcut in the Tottel edition shows a figure that holds up a triangular prospecting and measuring device to a window of the "tower of geometry" (Figure 1.12).

The measurement device's interaction with the human figure and the tower's window models the relationship of reader to medium for the *Pastime*'s audience. The prospecting device this figure holds allowed English landscapes to be newly measured, laid out, and reproduced in print. This section on geometric "measurement" poses itself as a visual rhetoric centred in materiality. Measurement is not merely a science of geometry but a device for poetic "measure" and a stylistic device of magnification in Hawes's *Pastime*, for instance, in the following verse:

> Mesure, mesuring, mesurably taketh
> Mesure, mesuring, mesuratly dooth all
> Mesure, Mesuring mesuratly maketh
> Mesure, mesuring, mesuratly guyde shall
> Mesure mesuring, mesuratly doth call
> Mesure mesurynge, to right hye preemynence
> For alway, mesure is grounde of excellence.   (sig. N3r) (Figure 1.13)

Here, figures of repetition repeat, recur, and reflect one another. Repetition of these measurement terms creates a visual structure of recursion and mimesis on the page itself. Repetition in rhetorical practice also serves to magnify a figure or idea for stylistic amplification and discursive invention. Erasmus's *Copia* (1512) gives us a familiar example of the Renaissance practice of stylistically varied repetition and imitation (mimesis) in invention.[48] This passage includes mirror-like figures of

A.A quod I my loue and lykinge
Is now ferre hence on whome my hole delyght
Dayly was sette vpon her to haue sight

Fare well swete herte farwell, fareWell, farewell
Adieu, adieu I wold I were you by
God gyue me grace with you sone to dwell
Lyke ass I did for to se you dayly
your lowly chere and gentyll company
Reioysed my herte With fode most delycate
Myne eyen to se you were insaciate

Now good swete herte my lady and maystresse
I recommende me vnto your pyte
Besechyng you Wyth all my gentylnes
yet other whyle to thynke vpon me
What payne I suffer by great extrempte
And to pardon me of my rude Wrytyng
For With weful herte was myne endytynge

Figure 1.12. Stephen Hawes, *Pastime of Pleasure* (1555), sig. N1v, Bodleian Library

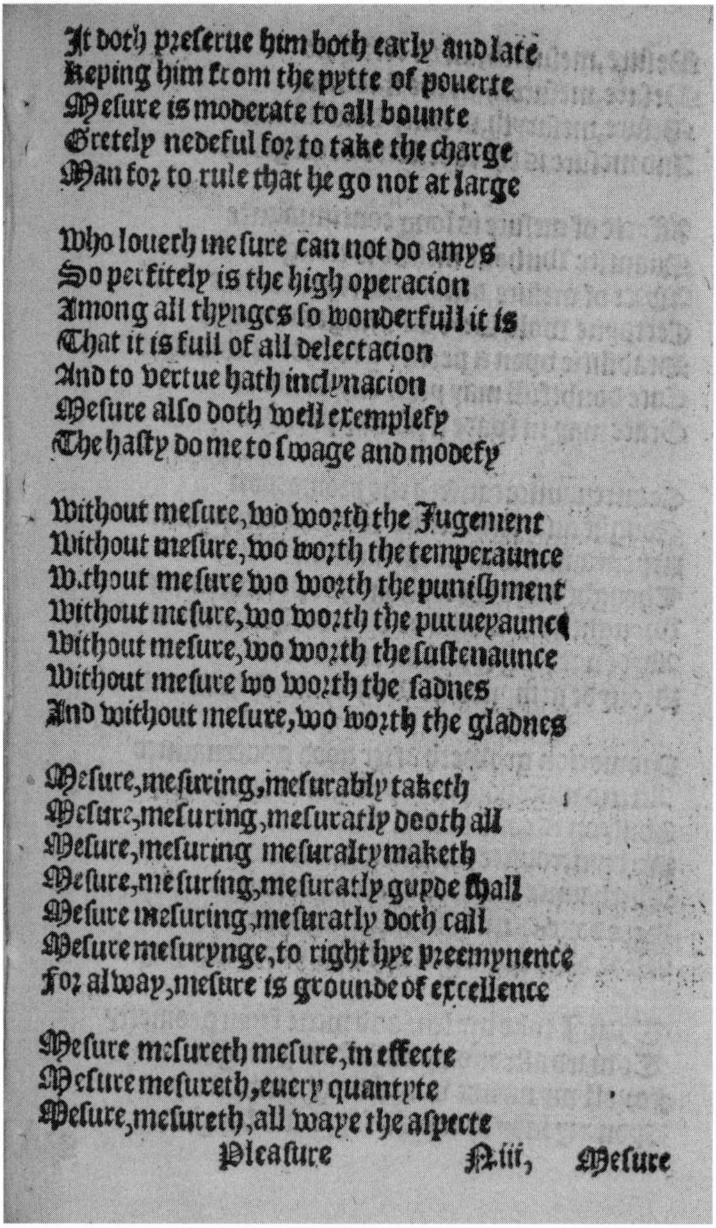

It doth preserue him both early and late
Keping him from the pytte of pouerte
Mesure is moderate to all bounte
Gretely nedeful for to take the charge
Man for to rule that he go not at large

Who loueth mesure can not do amys
So perfitely is the high operacion
Among all thynges so wonderfull it is
That it is full of all delectacion
And to vertue hath inclynacion
Mesure also doth well exemplefy
The hasty do me to swage and modefy

Without mesure, wo worth the Iugement
Without mesure, wo worth the temperaunce
W.thout mesure wo worth the punishment
Without mesure, wo worth the purueyaunce
Without mesure, wo worth the sustenaunce
Without mesure wo worth the sadnes
And without mesure, wo worth the gladnes

Mesure, mesuring, mesurably taketh
Mesure, mesuring, mesuratly deoth all
Mesure, mesuring mesuralty maketh
Mesure, mesuring, mesuratly guyde shall
Mesure mesuring, mesuratly doth call
Mesure mesurynge, to right hye preemynence
For alway, mesure is grounde of excellence

Mesure mesureth mesure, in effecte
Mesure mesureth, euery quantyte
Mesure, mesureth, all waye the aspecte
                Pleasure   N.iii,   Mesure

Figure 1.13. Stephen Hawes, *Pastime of Pleasure* (1555), sig. N3r, Bodleian Library

repetition: for instance, conduplicatio, the repetition of words (from the Latin term for doubling). Further, this doubling figure recalls the inventive reproduction of image impressions in cognitive perception and book production. The recursive, repetitive measure in this verse recalls Hawes's notion of fantasy's impressed, reproduced, and translated images; Nicholas of Cusa's concept of a self-moulding mind; and the phenomenal import of rhetorical forms in the early Renaissance. Hawes's verse appears to glorify order, precision, and measurement as a vital, nearly divine, instrument. Hawes's measurement verse employs traductio, repetition within a phrase or idea, a practice derived from the Latin term for transference. The device of traductio translates different images from one form to another, a process that could characterize both perception and visual print reproduction in Hawes's time. The figure of polyptoton, the repetition of similar words with slight alterations, also appears in Hawes's measurement verses. This celebration of measure parallels Hawes's description of rhetoric's purpose in the trivium as a rational arrangement and purification of speech that the man of action can use "prudently / His Wordes to ordre, his speche to purify" (sig. D4r). Hawes's definition of rhetoric evokes the values of a measured or plain style.

Yet the copious repetition and modulation of the "measure" repetition becomes an ornate stylistic ornament unto itself, even to the point of "barbarism" and echolalia, or a nonsense babble of meaningless repetition and cognitive disturbance. The "tower" of geometry in the text and woodcut evokes two competing allusions to Genesis that would have been familiar to early modern readers: Jacob's Ladder and the Tower of Babel. In the narrative of Jacob's ladder, Jacob flees his brother Esau and envisions a ladder extending from earth to heaven. God and several angels descend to promise him the nearby land. After Jacob rises, he exclaims, "'surely the Lord is in this place; and I did not know it.' And he was afraid, and said, 'This is none other than the house of God, and this the gate of heaven.'"[49] Jacob's ladder gives us a biblical model of *phantasia*: the ladder descends from heaven to earth, and, like Aristotle's dreams, hallucinations, and visions, is only partially materialized in Jacob's vision. "Jacob's staff," a metal rod that could be screwed into the ground and used to support a compass, was "designed to measure angles between the horizon and a star"[50] or the sun: a tower of observation. Jacob's staffs surveyed land and measured space for map production; they could be accompanied by a "suitably positioned mirror" to make geometrical measurements (Lindgren 483). Both Jacob's ladder and Jacob's staff attempt to ascend to heaven with visual images and reflections.[51] The word "Jacob" is also physically impressed on the measurement tower's woodcut image. The biblical Jacob himself presents a figure of measurement: he weighed and measured goats and sheep, separating the spotted or speckled livestock from the others.[52] This illustration's allusions to Jacob, his ladder, and his staff are amplified by Hawes's textual inclusion of measurement as an almost metaphysical force that takes, makes, gives, and guides in the poetic verse.

Hawes's copious, almost nonsensical description of measurement, however, also recalls a more troubling metaphor of measurement: the Tower of Babel. The Tower of Babel is a contrasting, negative model of bottom-up, monumental, and material measurement. In this narrative, God sees the attempt on the part of a united humanity to build a tower to heaven. He scatters them and their language as he proclaims, "Go to, let us go down, and there confound their language, that they may not understand one another's speech."[53] The desire to rationally and clearly measure space and speech in the "tower of geometry" lies precariously close to the vain attempt to build a tower to heaven in the Babel narrative. The *copia* concerning measurement appears at once an ordered mirror image, re-impressed and repeated across the page in figures of formal repetition (conduplicatio, traductio, polyptoton), and what sounds to the ear like a superfluous, tedious, and chaotic babble. Polyptoton, or the repetition of words across forms, derives from the Greek *poly* (many) plus *ptotos* (falling): a descending multiplicity. The most prominent metaphors used to describe early modern print books – mirrors, maps, and monuments of the world – reflect a macrocosmic and material permanence that symbolizes eternity. Caxton's unified, vernacular, illustrated book that aspires to timelessness and Hawes's allegorical colours of rhetoric seek to unify and symbolize rhetoric's situation within all human knowledge and virtue and to impress that theory upon an imagined popular audience. Yet as the mobility of Caxton's visual structure across its editions and the echolalia of Hawes's geometrical tower indicate, this unifying pedagogical goal became, over time and over reader use, a polymorphic jumble.

Caxton's *Mirrour* and Hawes's *Pastime* are therefore riddled with epistemic and material contradiction. Their phenomenal and visual forms seem to figure a vital, almost metaphysical reflection of world and word, yet their diverse figures and materials impel a physical and cognitive *mouvance*, within which the meaning of the text can be literally transformed and reshaped by readers' eyes, hands, and brains. This contradiction may be understood through new phenomenologists Jane Bennett, Graham Harman, and Bruno Latour's terminology of object relations as assemblages, networks, and ecologies.[54] In these ecologies or assemblages, vital objects can both form a larger system and contend with one another more disjunctively, often at the same time. Indeed, Harman calls for the object's moments of fissure to be understood as, instead of Heidegger's famous binary of a working versus a broken tool, a *"duel between a thing and its parts"* (172, emphasis in original). In Caxton and Hawes, book imagery and figures present an unsettled tension between a more totalized meaning or reflection and the movable and constituent parts that assemble this "whole entent (Hawes sig. B1r). Visual perception in itself further complicates this tension. A compilation or transformation of the book's material and rhetorical properties will necessarily be unique to the viewer. As Maurice Merleau-Ponty states in his *Phenomenology of Perception*, "the visual field is that strange zone in which contradictory notions jostle each other," where an object is removed from an ontological, self-sufficient context to one of epistemic subjectivity (6). This productive tension among whole, part, and perceiver (or, to recall Vogt-Spira's configuration, form-matter-us), can perhaps be best understood, albeit not resolved, through the book-as-glass metaphor. Like a "covert colour" that may simultaneously clarify and obscure meaning, a mirror may be either fogged and distortive or clear and reflective. In the book as mirror, different raw materials are assembled together by the maker, viewer, and reader to produce a movable matter and marvel.

Chapter Two

Memory Machines or Ephemera? Early Modern Annotated Almanacs, Edmund Spenser's *Shepheardes Calender*, and the Problem of Recollection

Memory, often seen as the forgotten and lost canon of rhetoric,[1] has recently gained renewed interest in popular culture, at a moment where digital technologies promise to supplement cognitive memory – or threaten its destruction. Joshua Foer's *Moonwalking with Einstein* (2012) recently popularized ancient mnemonic techniques and explored their relation to memory, visuality, and cognition. Foer describes how he won memory championships by attaching an item he wanted to recall to a spectacular or lurid visual image and, ultimately, by building a structural "memory palace" of the spatial, visual places that contain these items.[2] Another recent book, *Memory Palace: Learn Anything and Everything (Starting With Shakespeare and Dickens) (Faking Smart)* (2012), describes a method by which one remembers items by placing them along a mental journey through a spatial location. Nicholas Carr's *The Shallows* warns us that the Internet is "reprogramming the memory" and destroying neural circuitry (5), even as cloud applications promise to serve as permanent online locations for storing reminders.

The idea that vivid imagery and spatial location define and enhance memory as a cognitive and rhetorical practice also characterized early modern treatments of memory. Frances Yates's foundational analysis of mnemonics in *The Art of Memory* situates early modern memory techniques within the context of the era's revival of classical rhetoric and the ability of print technology to visually represent memory in new ways. Early modern concepts of memory drew from the classical models of Aristotle, Cicero, Quintilian, and the anonymous *Ad Herennium* (Yates 17–41). These models emphasized *imagines,* or iconic, vivid images, and *loci,* or spatial locations for reminders, as fundamental elements in the process of collection and recollection. Memory, or the collection of images, tropes, and ideas, fostered invention or their recollection. This collection could often be an assembly of vivid mental images, drawn together for the purpose at hand. In the case of print, spaces and images could be shaped and reshaped by printers and readers as mnemonic technologies.

Memory was intensively material and visual in early modern culture. As Mary Carruthers argues in *The Book of Memory*, "the value of *memoria* persisted long after book technology itself had changed" (9). Carruthers investigates how rhetorical memory and the book coexisted, and even responded to one another, in medieval book illustrations of "grotesque creatures, comic images of monkeys and other animals," and other striking images that operated as physical memory devices (315). Drawing from Carruthers's study of memory images in medieval books, my analysis of memory spaces in Spenser's *Calender* and early modern almanacs explores how physical illustrations and other visual features may reconstitute and remediate memory within early modern print. On the printed page, memory is transformed from imagined, mental spaces to material, physical spaces: we can look to the material, spatial, and structural elements of early modern print books as *loci* and *imagines*.[3]

The importance of visual materials to memory informs the structure of Edmund Spenser's *Shepheardes Calender*, as it acts as both a memory device and an ephemeral material. Spenser's *Calender* evokes several different material and literary genres of sixteenth-century print: eclogue, pastoral, annotated treatise, book of hours, and, most principally, the almanac. In early modern almanacs, readers used the arrangement, symbolism, and imagery of their spaces for daily reminders and notes. Almanacs, which, as I will argue, deeply influenced the *Shepheardes Calender*, contained information on feast and fast days, how and when to care for one's body and land, and how to track the signs of the heavens. These everyday reminders become remediated by Spenser's *Calender*, whose memory spaces are pre-inscribed by the mysterious E.K. E.K.'s glosses track the allusive references of the poetic text and show us where the poems carry references to classical authors. In these almanacs, memory comes in the form of daily mnemonics, allusions to the past, and historiographical memory. At the same time, the material structure of the almanac genre implied ephemerality, disposability, even forgetting. Memory's implicit duality – as a treasury of images and as a degenerative space of forgetting – stems from memory's cognitive, phenomenal, and material features in early modern culture. As Grant Williams investigates, early modern concepts of memory heavily relied on Aristotle, who in *De Memoria et Reminiscentia* divided the "mnemonic image into two parts: it is something in its own right, an inscription or figure (phantasm); and it is simultaneously something 'other' insofar as it is a copy (icon) or reminder that gestures towards the external phenomenon" (314). This division between the phantasm, or the image-in-itself, and the icon, or the simulacra of the external material image, lent memory a "double materiality" that often threatened to disrupt the process of cognition itself, for the mnemonic image needed to be ultimately transformed and purged from the brain for understanding to occur (Williams, "The Transmateriality of Memory" 315–16). Because of its proximity to and reliance on *phantasia* and its image-making capabilities, memory could also be prone to the same sensory delusions and, as Williams puts it, "epistemological degeneration" as the imagination (318). Memory's materiality, then, could be both valuable to cognition and phenomenally suspect. Aristotle's metaphor of memory as an *imprint* qualifies memory as a productive impression on the brain that leads to the retention of an image. At the same time, the corporeal nature of this imprint metaphor potentially casts memory as an obstructive material, clouding reason. The early modern print texts of the calendar and almanac, which specifically address memory as a visual material, highlight memory's material fungibility and potential for erasure. More specifically, Spenser's *Calender*, read across the calendar and almanac form, both embodies and defies expectations of a unified and permanent memorial, complicating the relationships among perception, memory, and visual space.

In Spenser's *Calender*, memory is both historical and rhetorical. As Rebecca Helfer explores, the space of the ruin became a site of generative recollection in Spenser's works (*Spenser's Ruins* xii).[4] While Spenser fashions himself as the new Virgil (16), Helfer argues that Spenser also adopts a Ciceronian model as he "renovates the art of memory" as a means to "explore how to recollect the ruins of the past" (6).[5] In Spenser's work, these ruins operate "as mnemonic spaces for dialogue and recollection" (732), rather as part of a unified monumental reconstruction. Where Helfer locates this space of dialogue and recollection within the poetic text itself, as well as within the dialogic gloss of the annotator "E.K," I locate this dynamic process of collection and recollection primarily in the visual and material elements of the *Calender*'s interface.

The Antic/Antique Library of Eumnestes

As a pretext to this chapter's investigation of visual memory in the *Calender*, I will here turn to Spenser's notorious depiction of memory's library in *The Faerie Queene*'s Castle of Alma (Book 2, Canto 9). This passage allegorizes both the promise and perishability of cognitive and material memory. Spenser portrays this library as a room, which "seemed ruinous and old," with "right firme & strong" walls, "though somewhat they declind" (sig. Xl). Both the cognitive construction of *loci* and the material construction of the room disintegrate, or "decline," over time. The guardians and workers in this memory library are an "old old man, halfe blind," "of infinite remembraunce," named Eumnestes, whose name signifies memory. Anamnestes, his young assistant, signifies both remembrance and invention: he reaches for what is needed from the memory space, "oft when thinges were lost, or laid amis, / That boy them sought, and unto him [Eumnestes, or memory] did lend" (sig. X3r) (sig. X3). The relationship between Eumnestes and Anamnestes parallels the interaction between invention and memory, recollection and collection, in classical and early modern rhetoric.[6] Memory is "halfe blind," calling to mind its traditional oral associations and the mnemonic feats of legendary classical figures, such as Homer and Tiresias. Further, the objects and structure of the room itself emphasize memory's status as a material space. In this passage, memory is both eternal and fragile. Christopher Ivic reads Spenser's library as a meditation on memory's fallible nature.[7] Indeed, as Grant Williams observes, images of sensory and cognitive distortion frame the Castle of Alma passage and precede our reading of memory's library. The cell of Phantastes, symbolic of the imagination or *phantasia*, buzzes with flies. Williams reads Phantastes's buzzing flies as a critical reversal of a popular mnemonic symbol in medieval and early modern culture, industrious bees who gather honey from different flowers ("Phantastes's Flies" 244–5).[8] Mnemonic imagery here "has a horrific, agitated life of its own" ("Phantastes's Flies" 245), as it distorts rather than aids knowledge and perception.

Although the physical materiality of this library's room and books might seem like a corrective to the distortive visual, cognitive fantasy of Phantastes's cell, these materials exist in a liminal state between permanence and ephemerality, or dislocation. Eumnestes's record of "ages past" was "laid" "up in his immortall scrine, / Where they for ever incorrupted dweld" (sig. X3). A scrine is a "chest in which the relics of saints are preserved" (*OED*) or "a box, chest, or coffer in which valuables are kept" (*MED*).[9] Judith Anderson relates Spenser's "scrine" to a "shrine," as well as the Latin "scriniarrii," or a location where "books or treasure are protected" (80). A scrine can hold books or bones – important artefacts of remembrance. Spenser's scrine recalls the depiction of memory in the *Ad Herennium*, where memory is depicted as a physical treasury of things invented. The scrine metaphor connects the concept of memory as a rhetorical *techne* with material memory, although it is a trope that reminds readers of memory's destructability. Anderson highlights this passage's friction between the library's old, materially fragile records and Spenser's allegorical representation of memory's "infinite nature" (81). This same binary of memory's seeming permanence and its material frailty is also reflected in the passage's references to relics and shrines: these memory spaces would have potentially recalled images of material ruin to post-Reformation readers, some of whom may have witnessed the physical destruction of their local shrines and reliquaries.

In this passage, Spenser continuously illustrates material objects of memory, particularly as it is manifested in manuscripts and print books, as vulnerable: the "rolls" and "old records," "some made in books, some in long parchment scrolls," were "all worm-eaten, and full of canker-holes" (sig. X3r). This library's books are all in a state of disarray, again demonstrating the ephemerality of physical, textual memory.[10] Alan Stewart interprets the library's decomposed disarray as a conscious response to the changing role of memory in Spenser's time as it was displaced from the cognitive space of mental images to the printed space of the page (219). Jennifer Summit frames Book II of the *Faerie Queene* as predominantly concerned with "biblioclasm," or the cataclysmic destruction of books ("Monuments and Ruins" 21). For early modern Protestant collectors, the problem of library building and book assembly was a question of which texts and fragments from pre-Reformation culture needed to be culled and which preserved. Summit argues that Eumnestes's library becomes a "center of Protestant memory," in Book II, "dedicated to reshaping cultural memory from remnants salvaged from the ruined monastic past" (*Memory's Library* 106). The print book could represent an aid to, and metaphor for, memory, while also displaying memory's state of cultural crisis and flux in the English Renaissance. For instance, commonplace books became a lightning rod for cultural disputes about memory in early modern pedagogical works.[11] William H. Sherman argues that just as modern writing teachers fret over the adoption of digital and social media in their classrooms, early modern rhetoricians worried that "textual tools like commonplace books would lead to passive readers and partial perspectives" (*Used Books* 146).

Books therefore promised to act as both physical and visual storehouses (scrines) for memory and as contributing factors to memory's fragmentation and decline. The reference to "registers" in Spenser's memory library further troubles the relationship between memory and print space. The Red Cross Knight consults the library's resources, as he "gan his Library to vew, / And antique Regesters for to avise" (X3r). Although the antiquity of these "regesters," could be read as a straightforward reference to their long age, Margreta de Grazia notes that the term "antique" "shared the same spelling and pronunciation" as "antic" in early modern England: "antic" and "antique" were often used interchangeably (101).[12] Perhaps most readily recalled in the context of Hamlet's "antic disposition," the term "antic" was also the English term for a grotesque design in art and architecture, a fantastical, monstrous image. Grotesque designs appear in both manuscript books and early modern print visuals, on borders between sections, in initials, and on printers' devices. A "register" could refer to a ribbon or cloth attached to a book's spine to hold a place, a table of contents, a book of brief commentary, a list of printer's signatures at the end of an early print book to aid the binder, the accurate positioning of type in printing, or, most commonly, to merchant's manuscript books.[13] This passage hence progressively moves the reader from Eumnestes's personification of blind, cognitive memory to a sense of visual, material memory mediated by fantastical images in a book. The "antic"/ antique register, interpreted as a fantastical illustration, subtly echoes the (re)collective activity of Phantastes's flies, as readers view and consult various texts and images.[14] As Sir Guyon peruses the library, he chances on an

> auncient booke, hight *Briton monuments*,
> That of this lands first conquest did devize,
> An old division into Regiments
> Till it reduced was to one mans governements."   (sig. X4v)

The binary here between unity ("one man") and "old division" of course reflects the dominant allegorical contrast in the *Faerie Queene* between "Una," coded as Protestant and symbolic of Elizabeth, and

"Duessa," who allegorized the Catholic Church and religious divisions. Indeed, the act of "devizing" – or dividing the British nation into parts – is also an act of reinventing or restructuring Britain, in the sense that to "devize" could mean to create (*OED* 13a, 5a–b). Another, now forgotten sense of the term "devize" also connotes an act of visual representation and design, the construction of a device (*OED* 5d). Division, creation, and display here meld in the material framework of the book and its "devices."[15] In her reading of the *Faerie Queene*, Lisa Dickson explores how Spenser often plays with the concept of visual perspective in order to "refer to 'things' in such a way that ultimately transcends them," as an ontic vanishing point of sorts (18), even as the text remains embedded within the physical, sensual world of matter (23). This duality, Dickson argues, speaks to the sense of "epistemological crisis," as the early modern eye is a dubious medium of perception (23). In the mnemonic imagery of the Castle of Alma's library and of the *Shepheardes Calender*, icons appear to allegorize external, noncorporeal things – cognition, historical crisis, literary history – but recur onto themselves, to speak to their own situation within the physical matter of print. The book's images become sometimes-troubled perceptual media. The materially and epistemically incomplete nature of memory's library in the Castle of Alma parallels the divisiveness – the sense of creativity, fragmentation, and complex design – of visual memory in Spenser's *Shepheardes Calender*.

Starry Signals: Metaphysical Mnemonics and The *Calender*'s Astrological Imagery

In Spenser's visual memory spaces, the reader is called to make choices about how to read the *Calender*, choices stressed by the woodcuts' organization. In *Exemplary Spenser*, Jane Grogan unpacks the elements of visual didacticism and ekphrasis that Spenser employs in *The Faerie Queene*. Although Grogan does not analyse *The Shepheardes Calender* at length, her attention to visual cues and visual rhetoric in Spenser can help us situate the woodcuts' relationship to the *Calender*'s text. The movement of the reader's eye in an interpretation of each woodcut image reflects what E. Armstrong characterizes in *A Ciceronian Sunburn* as humanist rhetoric's aim "at moving bodies to act" in a "habit of *doing* or *feeling*" (23). As Armstrong outlines, Lodowick Bryskett, a friend and associate of Spenser and Gabriel Harvey, translated Baptista Giraldo's humanist rhetorical treatise, *A Discourse of Civil Life*. This translation is a potentially neglected influence on Spenser's works. In Bryskett's text, rhetoric or discourse mediates

> between the senses and the intellect. The infinite particulars of our sensed experience are generalized in the Imagination, the "highest" part of the sensitive soul, and collected (or re-collected) by Memory; this is a nonrational process ... Discourse (language, speech) "transfers" or "carries over" our sensed experience to the rational understanding. (Armstrong 87)

In the *Shepheardes Calender*, images perform this discursive function; they form a crucial link between readers' visual gaze and the page. These images are set in disruptive, contradictory patterns that make this discursive link between memory and the imagination idiosyncratic to the viewer at the same time that they recall classical and medieval memory *loci*. For example, late-medieval manuscripts tended to use visual illustrations as "placeholders" rather than tables of content to arrange different subject matter; in the *Calender*, the woodcuts similarly arrange the poetic text. Abigail Shinn connects the visual organization of Spenser's *Calender* to the popular English almanac tradition, an association that reframes traditional interpretations of *The Shepheardes Calender* as a collection of pastoral eclogues modelled directly from Virgil. Shinn disputes characterizations of *The Shepheardes Calender* as a formally innovative text, written for a sophisticated, elite audience: almanacs instead demonstrated, she argues, a "continuity of design," a visual stability that allowed a wide audience of readers to access information readily. The formal features of English almanacs included "verse and prognostication" for the purposes of "political and social comment" (142).

Indeed, my recent search of sixteenth- and early seventeenth-century English almanacs on *Early English Books Online* revealed a standard visual pattern that distinctly parallels Spenser's Calender: gothic or "black letter" type, occasional printed commentary in separate sections and typefaces, woodcuts of astrological symbols and parts of the human body, and even a thematic focus on memory as a *topos*. A printed almanac acted as "an early newssheet that informed its readers of the new developments in science and agriculture as well as proffering opinions" (Shinn 142). The popular form of these almanacs, in Shinn's view, necessitated woodcuts and diagrams for the easy comprehension of popular readers. While an elite audience might appreciate its adaptation of the Virgilian model, the formal features of the material print text would appeal to a wider group of readers. The *Calender* thus assembles and imagines disparate reading audiences in its material and generic forms: an elite audience familiar with a classical, pastoral aesthetic, and a popular audience of almanac readers. Jeffrey Todd Knight's discovery of "a 1611 copy of the *Shepheardes Calender*" that was formerly bound with Caxton's *Mirrour of the Worlde* in the Cambridge University Library (124), alongside a Bodleian library compilation of the *Calender* with "vernacular conduct and husbandry manuals for the seasons, a monthly prognostication, and a treatise on calendar reform, all together in a calf binding" (125), leads him to conclude that the *Calender* perhaps "evokes something closer to the vernacular folk resource than the classical edition" (125).[16] Shinn's, Knight's, and my own situation of Spenser's *Calender* in the English almanac tradition radically transforms common scholarly notions of its audience and purpose, as it adapts visual and material features that have been previously thought of as non-literary. I would add that the juxtaposition of Spenser's *Calender* with Caxton's *Mirrour* may represent a conscious situation of the *Calender*, by readers and perhaps by Spenser himself, within English visual print traditions. Spenser's self-proclaimed novelty as a vernacular poet may derive as much from the *Calender*'s visual images as its textual allusions.

The *Calender*'s woodcuts blend a familiar, even "old fashioned" aesthetic with intricate visual symbolism (Luborsky, "The Illustrations to *The Shepheardes Calender*" 3). Many woodcuts, whether for economic necessity, aesthetic preference, or topical references, were recycled and repeated through several early modern books. S.K. Heninger detects that much of the *Calender*'s interface – its arrangement of woodcut, argument, poem, annotation/gloss, and emblem – directly mirrors the Venetian Jacopo Sannazaro's *Arcadia*, a print pastoral. The design and style of the woodcuts themselves also demonstrate the significant influence of the Venetian *Arcadia*. Heninger emphasizes, "these are the same shepherds dressed in the same way ... the same landscapes: the same sheep, the same trees, the same background buildings, even the same skies" (36). Heninger concludes that the *Shepheardes Calender* has less in common with the native English almanac and emblem book traditions. The book as a whole in Heninger's interpretation becomes "a coterie poem in the best humanist tradition" (48). Taken together, Shinn and Heninger's analyses seem to present two mutually exclusive models for *The Shepheardes Calender*: coterie poetry versus popular almanac, classical and international influence versus the influence of a native national tradition. However, *The Shepheardes Calender*'s illustrations instead present readers with as a hybrid (re)collection of elements from a variety of genres, sources, and formats rather than a singular or fixed genre. It is a library of disparate texts and a recollection of images.

Elements of Sannazaro's *Arcadia* indeed form the visual background of the woodcuts; however, the astrological icons situated at the corner and/or top of each woodcut are an important addition that reflect classical and early modern memory aids, as well as the popular almanac genre's astrological tropes. These zodiac signs appear at the left or right corners of the *Calender*'s woodcuts, or, more usually, at the top centre. This position in the woodcut's visual structure may seem to situate them as marginalia that indeed merely add to the template of Spenser's book. Höltgen reads the astrological symbols in the elaborate charts of Robert Burton's *Anatomy of Melancholy* similarly, as structures or taxonomic placeholders for information because of limited space on the page: "they turn out to be nothing more than formal reference signs," with "no symbolic value of their own" ("Literary Art" 24). He ties Burton's charts and astrological symbols to Ramist logic trees, which, following the analysis of Walter Ong, he posits as reductions of "intellectual processes" to mere visual "topoi" ("Literary Art" 23). I argue, however, that no visual symbol acts in a simple or one-dimensional way in the early modern book: the astrological symbols of Burton and Spenser serve to direct the eye, and, therefore, the mind, and connect systems of memory, cognition, and sight for early modern readers in a complex reading process. If readers trace the shepherd figure's line of vision from the first woodcut of the month of "Januarye," they will notice that his eyes gaze towards the heavens in a diagonal line, directly to the sign of Aquarius, the water bearer (sig. A1r) (Figure 2.1).

The woodcut's livestock, situated to the right of the shepherd, contrast with the shepherd's heavenly gaze as they look downward to the earth and hills of the landscape in the background. While the shepherd remains the central focal point of this scene, he directs his own gaze towards the Aquarian sign. The illustration combines an earthly (animal) with a heavenly (human) gaze. This comic juxtaposition between his heavenly vision and the animals' earthly vision instructs the reader on how to perceive and interpret the structure of the woodcuts and of the calendar as a whole. The deliberate inclusion of the zodiac signs and the livestock to Sannazaro's landscape background emphasizes the calendar's mixture of the pastoral and almanac genres. Viewed as a representational structure for the *Calender* overall rather than a tonal

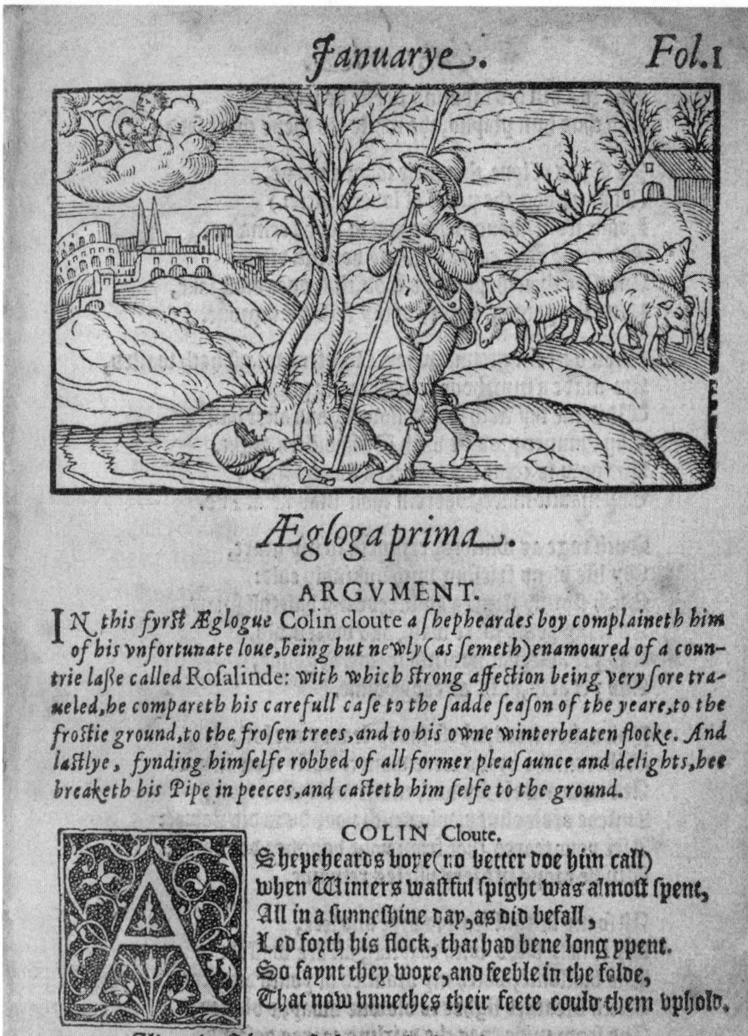

Figure 2.1. Edmund Spenser, *The Shepheardes Calender* (1579), sig. A1r, Huntington Library

or stylistic ornament, the woodcut loses its similarities to Sannazaro's *Arcadia*.

In each of Sannazaro's woodcuts, the human figures look at one another or across the vistas of the landscape. The situation and sight line of the human figures from the Venetian *Arcadia* are horizontal and earthbound, as opposed to the vertical, upward gaze of Januarye's shepherd. These woodcuts may emulate the style of Sannazaro's landscapes, but these are not the same skies, nor do the works' illustrations depict a similar systematic arrangement of meaning. This image instead represents a combination of Sannazaro's landscapes and a popular almanac's shepherd. The title page of Robert Copland's 1570 version of the *Kalender of Shepherds*, a widely reproduced almanac, shows a shepherd in a similar pose and heavenly gaze (Figure 2.2).

David Davis describes the *Kalender of Shepardes* as "perhaps the most convoluted and widespread example of how collections," as well as their images, "could change over time" and over religious and political contexts. He charts the surprising reproduction of seemingly Catholic images in its woodcuts, particularly those of the Virgin Mary, into new Protestant, Tudor book spaces (110). Spenser's *Calender* similarly melds poetic and visual forms from several genres, reproducing them as a dynamic palimpsest. In "The Illustrations to the *Shepheardes Calender*," Ruth Luborsky discusses how the *Calender*'s woodcuts both meet and disrupt generic expectations of a book of hours. Where, Luborsky observes, the flower at the bottom of April's woodcut stands in for the traditional depiction of "flower-bearing" in a book of hours' April scene (21), January's broken bagpipe and classical architecture are unique to this illustration (26). As Luborsky notes, this broken bagpipe does not appear at all in Spenser's poetic text and indeed contrasts with the broken "oaten pype" the poetic text describes (sig. A.iir.). Bagpipes are commonly made from animal skins, particularly those of sheep, a process that could previously be remediated, as parchment, into a manuscript text. Whether by the direction of Spenser himself or at the whim of the illustrator, the woodcut's bagpipe serves to emphasize the uniquely British context of the work and, potentially, its incomplete, fragmented state as a remediation and recollection of genres and images.

Spenser's inclusion of zodiac signs follows the calendrical form of almanacs and books of hours; these signs also recall classical memory techniques. Frances Yates discusses how allegorical images assisted the rhetor's movement from abstract ideas to concrete exempla (*Art of Memory* 53); for instance, the sign of Aquarius as a stand-in for a

Figure 2.2. Robert Copland, *The Shepardes Kalender* (1570), frontispiece, Folger Shakespeare Library

particular festival or prognostication. Metrodorus of Scepsis created one of the most famous, lauded memory systems in Cicero and the *Ad Herennium*. Metrodorus based his mnemonic structure on the "twelve signs of the zodiac" (39). His heavenly system for memory became a practical, ready-made system of *loci*. Early modern almanacs and memory treatises, sometimes claiming secret or occult knowledge, incorporated Metrodorus's zodiac system for their mnemonic techniques.[17] Quintilian shared with Cicero and later early modern humanists a belief that memory was inherently tied to vision. Quintilian states that memory is "in fact, like the eyesight, which turns to, and not away from, the objects which it contemplates" (217). This connection between memory and sight resembles a familiar comparison, also prominent in Aristotle and Plato, between memory and a wax impression: "certain impressions are made upon the mind, analogous to those which a signet-ring makes on wax" (215). In Quintilian's theory of memory, memory is again both material, connected to objects of contemplation, and mutable, an impression that is not set in stone but in wax. In *The Shepheardes Calender*, mnemonic signs are literally impressed upon the page by the technology of print and impressed subjectively upon the mind by visual cues.

The celestial memory system of Metrodorus, the *Calender*, and, more concretely, the astrologically oriented almanac genre is firmly rooted in Spenser's cultural moment, ranging from almanacs to memory treatises to, as Frances Yates asserts, an architectural model for the Globe Theater (342–67). One may recall Dr. Faustus's description of magical texts in Marlowe's play: "necromantic books are heavenly; / Lines, circles, scenes, letters, and characters" (1.1.53–4). In his "Defense of Poesy," Sir Philip Sidney also describes the ideal poet "freely ranging only within the zodiac of his own wit" (85). The rhetorical use of heavenly metaphors for memory, invention, and the transmission of knowledge did not end with the classical zodiac motif. Elizabeth A. Spiller convincingly argues that Galileo's *Starry Messenger* (1610) used print illustrations as "a kind of textual telescope for his readers so that his readers will experience this new way of observing as a new way of reading" (200). Richard G. Barlow frames Robert Burton's "Digression of Air" in the 1651 *Anatomy of Melancholy* as a form of rhetorical arrangement, where the organization of heavenly bodies are arrived at "by deliberate plan" in "the imaginative aerial journey by which the traveler reaches" the text's "heavenly bodies" (293). The use of heavenly imagery as a pedagogy, one that serves to shape and transform the visual reading process, thus extends from classical influences to seventeenth-century science in early modern discourse. Luborsky stresses the novelty of the zodiac inclusion in the *Shepheardes Calender*: the signs would have been unheard of in a primarily poetic, literary context at the time of its publication ("The Illustrations to the Shepheardes Calender II" 249). She argues that their placement shouts, "look at me, I'm new" ("The Illustrations to the Shepheardes Calender II" 250). The signs may alternatively be conceived of as Janus-faced, as they recollect mnemonic techniques of the classical past and appropriate the newer printed almanac genre as a visual memory system.

Meta-visuality, Accumulation, Disjunction: The *Calender's* Text-Illustration Relationships

In relation to the poetic text, many of the *Calender's* woodcut illustrations appear at first glance to either straightforwardly depict their adjoining poetic narrative or to correspond with their monthly theme, as an illustrated calendar. Yet their details form a complex relationship to the text, anticipating a readership that would potentially oscillate between word and image to pick up new images and new meanings. The woodcuts and text operate in relationships of meta-visuality, as the texts and images emphasize together the spectacular nature of the *Calender*: accumulation, as features are added to the woodcut that articulate matters beyond the poetic text alone; and disjunction, as certain woodcuts' features further a sense of ambivalence to the total eclogue by contrasting with the text.

In the February and August eclogues, the text displays Spenser's work as a distinctively visual (and meta-visual) work. February's argument posits its allegorical tale of the oak and briar "so lively, and so feelingly, as if the thing were set forth in some Picture before our eyes, more plainly could not appeare" (sig. a3v). Early modern rhetorical practices of enargeia, or lively visual descriptions, in the allegory itself here intersect with the illustrated nature of the *Calender*. February's woodcut puts enargeia into practice as it depicts the lively scene of the poetic text in motion: there is a sense of being frozen into place, mid-movement, in the stance of the illustration's shepherds and in the near blow to the oak by the husbandman on the right (Figure 2.3).

In the poem, an older Thenot allegorizes a tale of the oak and briar to the younger Cuddie, to bring about an appreciation of elderly wisdom. Cuddie's lack of appreciation for this moral is portrayed in the poem by him becoming trapped in the scenario itself: "so longe haue I listned to thy speche, / That graffed to the ground is my breache" (sig. b2v). This passage may reference the illustrated Cuddie, who is stuck in place by the lively woodcut. In the August eclogue, the poem references itself not as a picture but as an engraved mazer (a hardwood

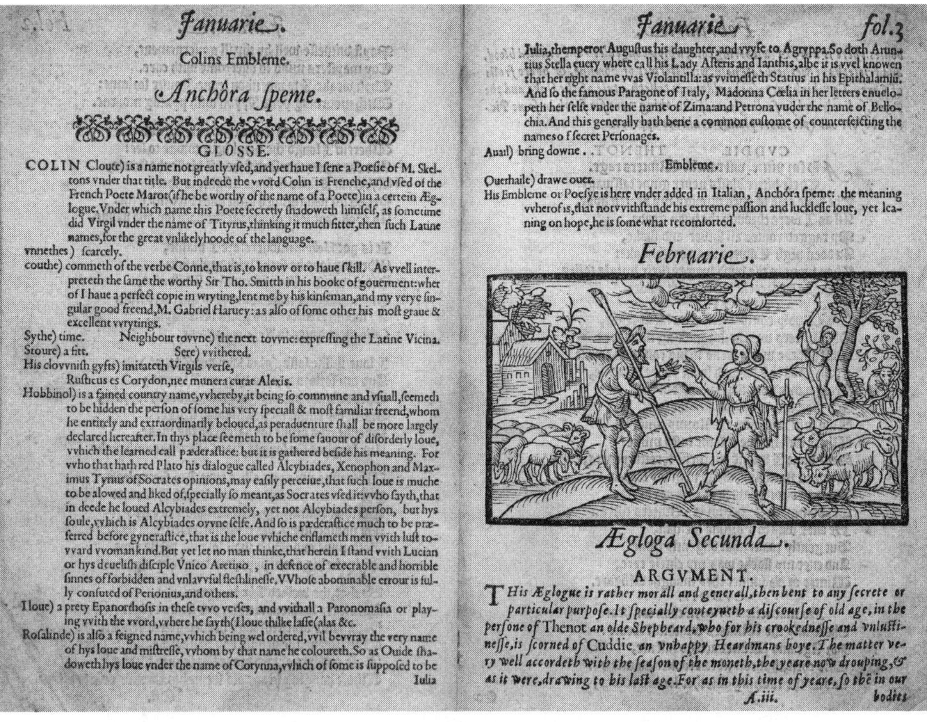

Figure 2.3. Edmund Spenser, *The Shepheardes Calender* (1579), sig. A3v–A3r, Huntington Library

drinking bowl), which lays at the centre and foreground of August's woodcut (Figure 2.4).

The mazer is a pledge by Wilye in a contest over music with the shepherd Perigot. Engraved or "enchased" on it is intricate designs of flora and fauna, "Beres and Tygres, that maken fiers warre: / And ouer them spred a goodly wild vine" (sig h3v). E.K.'s note on the word enchased, "engrauen. Such pretie descriptions euery where vseth Theocritus, to bring in his Idyllia. For which speciall cause indede he by that name termeth his Æglogues: for Idyllion in Greke signifieth the shape or picture of any thing, whereof his booke is ful," connects the mazer as object to the text of the *Calender* at large. Like the mazer, the *Calender* is book full of pictures, both literal and lyrical, with aspirations to imitate classic verse in a pastoral setting (sig i2v). The mazer is a microcosm for the book at large, a poetic exchange and gift for potential poetic imitators. Its illustrated nature in fact connects the *Shepheardes Calender*'s unique use of woodcuts

Figure 2.4. Edmund Spenser, *The Shepheardes Calender* (1579), sig. H3r, Huntington Library

to classical patterns, setting it within a poetic tradition while emphasizing the potentially popular draw of the illustrations in this note.

Hence, the woodcuts are promoted in the poetic text as an integral component of the book as a whole, illustrations that make the poetic text lively and complete. In some cases, the woodcuts go beyond featuring and capturing the narrative through adding elements that further the *Calender*'s thematic and generic concerns. March's eclogue discusses the dangers of Cupid. The woodcut shows two Cupids that appear in the narrative: one is supposed to be "shrouded" in "an yvie todde" (a "thick bush," according to E.K.) (sig. c1v) and the other "Entangled in a fowling net, / Which he for carrion Crowes had set" (sig. c2r). In the woodcut, the Cupid is not shrouded but featured, and a man to his right appears to be throwing a rock at him (Figure 2.5).

The man with the rock is not featured in the poetic narrative, but his presence perhaps highlights the vituperative nature of the eclogue, taken altogether, against romantic love. Since the Cupid in the poem is obscured to its characters but obvious to the reader, this scene also creates a sense of dramatic irony – we are in the know about Cupid's presence before the shepherds.

October's woodcut adds a classical structure to the left, as well as a shepherd crowned with leaves (perhaps laurel) who holds pipes (Figure 2.6).

In this eclogue, Piers and Cuddie – described as a "perfecte paterne of a Poete" in the argument – discuss the nature of poetry and Cuddie's need for a patron (sig. k4r). Piers advises a departure from the pastoral genre to the epic: "There may thy Muse display her fluttryng wing, / And stretch her selfe at large from East to West: / Whither thou list in fayre *Elisa* rest" (sig. l1r). Cuddie responds, "Indeede the Romish *Tityrus*, I heare, Through his *Mecænas* left his Oaten reede" (sig. l1r). This exchange informs us that Spenser, as personified by Cuddie, is aspiring to the grander genre. The "Romish Tityrus," as E.K.'s gloss informs us, is Virgil, Spenser's classical pattern, who also moved from the pastoral to the epic. October's woodcut of classical architecture and a laurel-crowned shepherd – who may either be Cuddie or Virgil himself – gives the reader a sense of the potential genre shift and the adoption of a classical pattern that Piers and Cuddie discuss. If the shepherd to the left is indeed meant to be Virgil, the image underscores Cuddie's (and Spenser's) mingling of old and new in its adoption of the Virgilian heritage within the English, pastoral setting of the *Calender*. The woodcut clues readers into the eclogue's genre and aspirations and adds to what the poetic text expresses on its own. November's woodcut also adds human and architectural features that are not present within the poetic text (Figure 2.7).

Februarie.   *fol.*8

at the firſt in cõtempt of old age generally,for it vvas an old opinion,and yet is
cõtinued in ſome mens conceipt,that mē of yeares haue no ſeare of god at al,
or not ſo much as younger folke.For that being rypened with long experience,
and hauing paſſed many bitter brunts and blaſtes of vengeaunce , they dread
no ſtormes of Fortune,nor wrathe of Gods,nor daunger of menne,as being
eyther by longe and ripe vviſedome armed againſt all miſchaunces and aduerſi-
tie,or vvith much trouble hardened againſt all troubleſome tydes: lyke vnto
the Ape,of which is ſayd in Æſops fables,that oftentimes meeting the Lyon,he
vvas at firſt ſore aghaſt & diſmayed at the grimnes and auſteritie of hys coun-
tenance,but at laſt being acquainted vvith his lookes,he vvas ſo furre from fea-
ring him,that he would familiarly gybe and ieſt with him : Suche longe experi
ence breedeth in ſome men ſecuritie.Although it pleaſe Eraſmus a great clerke
and good old father,more fatherly and fauourablye to conſtrue it in his Adages
for his own behoofe, That by the prouerbe Nemo Senex metuit Iouem,is not
meant,that old men haue no feare of God at al,but that they be furre from ſu-
perſtition and Idolatrous regard of falſe Gods,as is Iupiter.But his greate learning notwithſtanding,it is to plaine,to be gainſayd , that olde men are muche
more enclined to ſuch fond fooleries,then younger heades.

March.

Ægloga Tertia.
ARGVMENT.

IN this Æglogue two ſhepheards boyes taking occaſion of the ſeaſon,be-
ginne to make purpoſe of loue and other pleſaunce , which to ſpringtime
is moſt agreeable.The ſpeciall meaning hereof is, to giue certaine markes
                              B.4.   and

Figure 2.5. Edmund Spenser, *The Shepheardes Calender* (1579), sig. B4r, Huntington Library

September.   *fol.*39

vvorst, and through greate plentye vvas fallen into great penurie. This poesie I
knovve, to haue bene much vsed of the author, and to suche like effecte, as fyrste
Narcissus spake it.

October.

Ægloga decima.

ARGVMENT.

IN *Cuddie is set out the perfecte paterne of a Poete, whishe finding no
maintenaunce of his state and studies, complayneth of the contempte of
Poetrie, and the causes thereof: Specially hauing bene in all ages, and euen
amõgst the most barbarous alwayes of singular accounpt & honor, & being
indede so worthy and commendable an arte: or rather no arte, but a diuine
gift and heauenly instinct not to bee gotten by laboure and learning, but a-
dorned with both: and poured into the witte by a certaine* ἐνθουσιασμός. *and ce-
lestiall inspiration, as the Author hereof els where at large discourseth,
in his booke called the English Poete, which booke being lately come to
my hands, I mynde also by Gods grace vpon further aduisement to publish.*

Pierce.   Cuddie.

C Vddie, for shame hold vp thy heauye head,
       And let vs cast with what delight to chace:

K.4.   Ante

Figure 2.6. Edmund Spenser, *The Shepheardes Calender* (1579), sig. K4r, Huntington
Library

October   fol.44

Embleme.
Hereby is meant, as alfo in the vvhole courfe of this Æglogue, that Poetry is a diuine in
ftinct and vnnatural rage paffing the reache of comen reafon. VVhom Piers an-
fwereth Epiphonematicós as admiring the excellencye of the fkyll vvhereof
in Cuddie hee hadde alreadye hadde a tafte.

Nouember.

Ægloga vndecima.

ARGVMENT.

IN this xi. Æglogue he bewayleth the death of fome mayden of greate
bloud, whom he calleth Dido. The perfonage is fecrete, and to me altogether vnknowne, albe of him felfe I often required the fame. This Æglogue is made in imitation of Marot his fong, which he made vpon the death
of Loys the frenche Queene. But farre paffing his reache, and in myne opinion all other the Eglogues of this booke.

Thenot.   Colin.
COlin my deare, when fhall it pleafe thee fing,
As thou were wont fongs of fome touifaunce?
Thy Mufe to long flombreth in forrowing,
Lulled a fleepe through loues mifgouernaunce,
L.4.   Now

Figure 2.7. Edmund Spenser, *The Shepheardes Calender* (1579), sig. L4r, Huntington Library

The poem enacts Colin's lament for Dido. In the woodcut, one shepherd crowns another, who is playing the bagpipes, with laurel leaves. The shepherd playing music can safely be interpreted as a figure for Colin (who at times characterizes Spenser as poet), but nowhere in the text does this crowning occur: potentially, the genre shift here from pastoral to tragedy represents a sense of poetic accomplishment that had been discussed more theoretically in the October woodcut. Potentially, this image of poetic success could in part change our interpretation of the *Calender* as a whole: December's poem leaves us with a narrative of Colin as an elderly, failed poet, but November's woodcut opens up the possibility of at least momentary accolades for the Dido poem. The church and procession to the illustration's left are another addition, and one that represents the poetry's mingling of classical and Christian references. The church helps stress the Christian point stated in the emblem of a happy death, a death that "biteth not" (sig. m2r). In addition, the procession, shows communal mourning to depict this tragedy of Dido as a shared event.

In addition to accumulating and emphasizing certain meanings latent within the poetry, the woodcuts' images at times contradict the text, adding a sense of disjunction. For instance, July's narrative about ambitious and proud pastors with a "straying heard" (sig. g2r), which sets off humility versus ambition as a topic, shows in its illustration instead a herd that crowds around the pastor-shepherd on a hill, as if listening (Figure 2.8).

The hand gestures of the different shepherds, one with his palm stretched towards the earth, and the other with his finger pointed to heaven, also mirror the traditionally depicted figures of Plato, who points towards heaven, and Aristotle, who typically points to the earth, demonstrating a certain moral and philosophical equivalence between the two that is not always present in the poem. This woodcut ultimately sets off the ambivalence of the eclogue, which, in contrast to the straightforwardness of the opening argument, cannot decide in its final emblem whether the "lowly," "middest … mediocritie," or high way of "supremacie" is the best course (sig. h2v). In the December woodcut, broken pipes lay at the shepherd's feet, whereas in the poem he hangs them up on a tree (Figure 2.9).

In the final emblem, the eclogue's meaning is put forth as "all thinges perish and come to theyr last end, but workes of learned wits and monuments of Poetry abide for euer" (sig. n2v). Do the broken pipes signify a more lasting and final end to the poem – and poet – than the argument

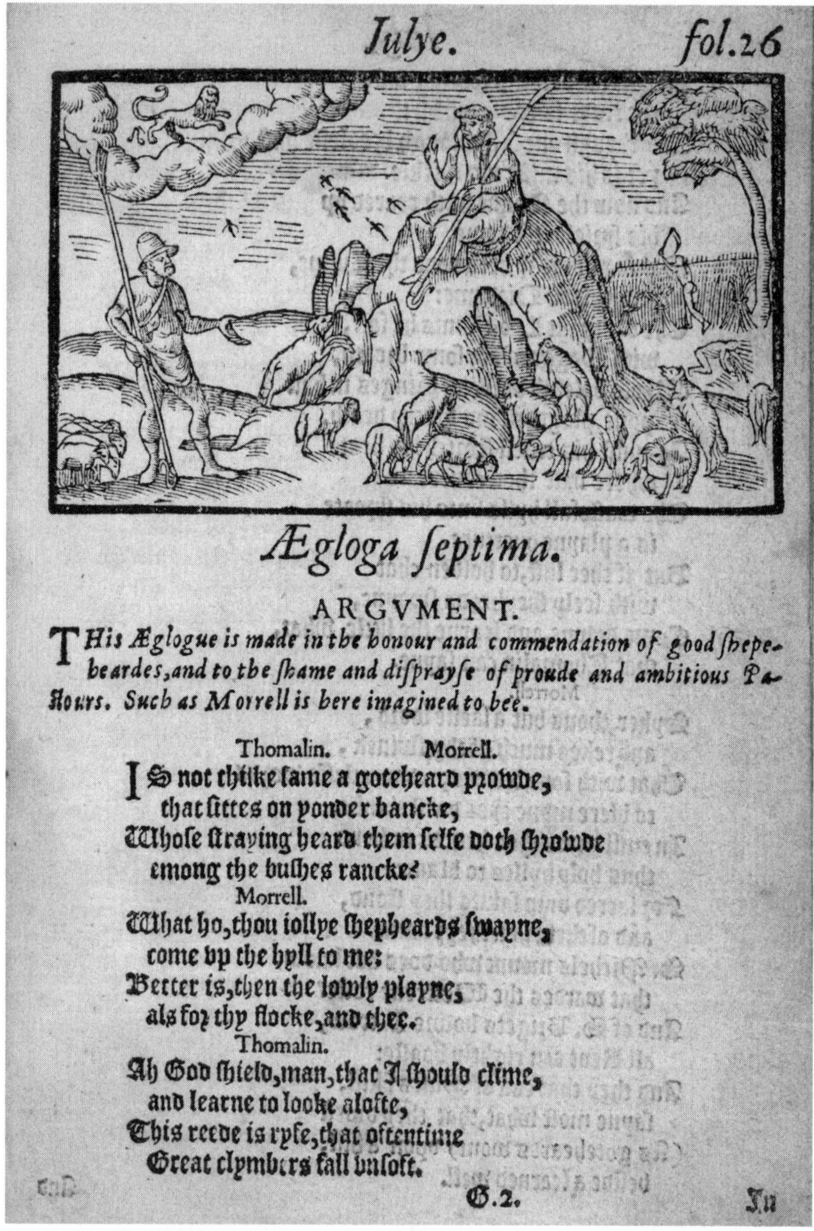

Figure 2.8. Edmund Spenser, *The Shepheardes Calender* (1579), sig. G2r, Huntington Library

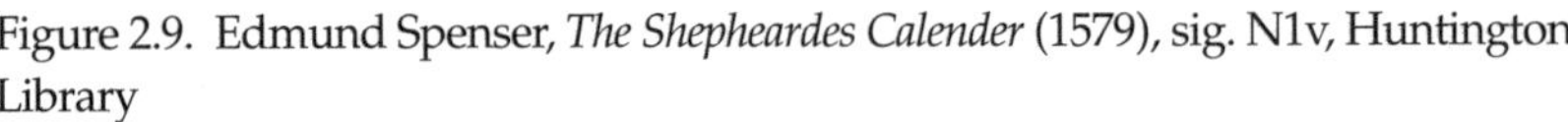

Figure 2.9. Edmund Spenser, *The Shepheardes Calender* (1579), sig. N1v, Huntington Library

or do they represent monuments that may be recollected and taken up by the reader? Perhaps either way, the music of the poetry is represented as lowly and accessible to the reader in the illustration, as the broken pipes in the woodcut are represented beneath the shepherd's feet rather than above him on a tree.

Politics and Religion: The April and May Woodcuts

May's woodcut combines accumulation, disjunction, and changes in perspective to deepen and complicate the meaning of its poetry's religiously controversial subject matter (Figure 2.10).

In the poem, the Protestant Piers and the Catholic Palinode debate forms, rituals, and traditions, including the May dance that is prominently featured in the illustration's foreground. In the text, Piers uses an allegory of the fox and the kid to warn against foxes in sheep's clothing that use visual manipulation to serve their ends. May and April are the only woodcuts where shepherds lie in the background of the image. Although the poetic text throughout seems to raise the religious debate and fable as the most important elements of the eclogue, the May dance itself takes over the image, jarring with the iconoclasm of Piers's argument and fable. We can also spot two churches, one at the centre and one towards the right, demonstrating (as perhaps appropriate in Gemini's month) a sense of doubled loyalties. The Gemini figure gestures towards the shepherds, indicating an attention that, in a reversal of January's woodcut, moves us from heaven to the earth. This woodcut is one of the busier of the *Calender*'s and ironically adjoins a text that appears to preach simplicity through the voice of Piers, who praises a time "When shepeheards had none inheritaunce, / Ne of land, nor fee in sufferaunce: / But what might arise of the bare sheepe" (sig e2r). Furthering the ironic disjunction between text and image, the visual doubling of the churches and divisions on our attention in the woodcut corresponds with a text that warns us that "deceitfull meaning is double eyed" (sig. e4r). In the woodcut as in the text, the reader's attention is pulled on as far as where to look: from the central figure of the May dance to the gesturing sign of Gemini to the debating shepherd, to the doubled kid goat, to the doubled churches. Like the reader's eye, in the text Piers and Palinodes' religious debates are far from settled. Indeed, while Piers complains of light Pastors who spend their time "In lustihede and wanton meryment" and let "their sheepe runne at large" (sig. e1r), in the woodcut both shepherds' attention lies on one another,

Aprill.   *fol.* 16

returneth all the thanck of hys laboure to the excellencie of her Maiestie.
VVhen Damsins] A base revvard of a clovvnish giuer.
Yblent] Y, is a poeticall addition. blent blinded.

Embleme.

This Poesye is taken out of Virgile, and there of him vsed in the person of Æneas to his mother Venus, appearing to him in likenesse of one of Dianaes damosells: being there most diuinely set forth. To vvhich similitude of diuinitie Hobbinoll comparing the excelency of Elisa, and being through the worthynes of Colins song, as it were, ouercome with the hugenesse of his imagination, brusteth out in great admiration, (O quàm te memorè virgo?) being otherwise vnhable, then by soddein silence, to expresse the vvorthinesse of his conceipt. VVhom Thenot answereth vvith another part of the like verse, as confirming by his graunt and approuaúnce, that Elisa is novvhit inferiour to the Maiestie of her, of vvhome that Poete so boldly pronounced, O dea certe,

Maye.

Ægloga Quinta.

ARGVMENT.

In this firste Æglogue, vnder the persons of two shepheards, Piers & Palinodie, be represented two formes of pastoures or Ministers, or the protestant and the Catholique: whose chiefe talke standeth in reasoning, whether the life of the one must be like the other. with whom hauing shevved, that it is daungerous to mainteine any felovvship, or giue too much credit to their co
                                              lourable

Figure 2.10. Edmund Spenser, *The Shepheardes Calender* (1579), sig. D4r, Huntington Library

the debate itself, rather than on their flocks. Ultimately, the poetic text expresses some ambivalence towards both shepherds, even while overall preferring Piers's ideology. Perhaps the woodcut demonstrates here that the reformist and Catholic religious debates with one another run the risk of ignoring the "flock" altogether. In addition, this intricately illustrated eclogue warns us of visual deceit and distraction, as the foxe uses "bells, and babes, and glasses in hys packe" (sig. e3v), or "the reliques and ragges of popish superstition" (sig. f2r), to trick the naive kid into emerging from his barn (sig. e3v).

Indeed, it is the act of looking at a glass that allows for the false fox to enter and capture the kid: "out of his packe a glasse he tooke: / Wherein while kiddie vnwares did looke" (sig. e4r). With common metaphors of the book as a glass in mind, the woodcut's centralization of the May dance here might consciously play into the thematics of visual deceit by idols, as the reader must attend to the heavens to see the shepherd's debate. Alternatively, the woodcut contrasts with this moral, as Piers's anti-iconic and anti-ritualistic rhetoric is countered by a sympathetic Palinode. Evan Gurney argues that both shepherds are shown to be equally negligent in this eclogue, as "Much like the kid's mother, Piers abandons his own flock to potential foxes as he tells Palinode his fable" (213) and as "readers face an interpretive conundrum, one that demonstrates how poetry participates in the fictive spectacle that enables the fox to capture the kid" (214). The shepherds of the image appear to be in fact neglecting the depicted fox and kid beneath them at the woodcut, again adding to this eclogue's sense of visual and moral uncertainty. Through looking at the woodcut itself, readers are in a similar position as the fable's kid, gazing at various visual objects and images to decide what message to let in. Ultimately, the gaze of the woodcut, like the argument, is both divided and circular, as the dance and debate distract readers from the flocks and the kid's dilemma.

April's woodcut (Figure 2.11) also plays into serious political debate as it functions as an unstable collection of political portent, historical memory, and visual mnemonics. April's eclogue responds to the potential, controversial engagement of Elizabeth I to the French Catholic Duke of Alençon. The text of the eclogue presents a discussion between two shepherds, Hobbinoll and Thenot, concerning the unrequited love of Colin for Rosalin (and Hobbinoll for Colin). This Petrarchan pastoral then moves into an epideictic song of praise for "fayre Elisa, Queene of shepheardes all" (sig. C.iir). This shift links the shepherd's love-longing to an encomium of Elizabeth, which situates the poem as a courtier's

Aprill.

Ægloga Quarta.
ARGVMENT.

THis Æglogue is purposely intended to the honor and prayse of our most
  gracious souereigne, Queene Elizabeth. The speakers herein be Hobbinoll and Thenott, two shepheardes: the which Hobbinoll being before men-
tioned, greatly to haue loued Colin, is here set forth more largely, complay-
ning him of that boyes great misaduenture in Loue, whereby his mynd was
alienate and with drawen not onely from him, who moste loued him, but also
from all former delightes and studies, aswell in pleasaunt pyping, as conning
ryming and singing, and other his laudable exercises. Whereby he taketh
occasion, for proofe of his more excellencie and skill in poetrie, to recorde a
songe, which the sayd Colin sometime made in honor of her Maiestie, whom
abruptely he termeth Elysa.

                    Thenot.   Hobbinoll.
T Ell me good Hobbinoll, what garres thee greete?
  What? hath some Wolfe thy tender Lambes ytorne?
Or is thy Bagpype broke, that soundes so sweete?
Or art thou of thy loued lasse forlorne?

Or bene thine eyes attempred to the yeare,
Quenching the gasping furrowes thirst with rayne?

                                                          Like

Figure 2.11. Edmund Spenser, *The Shepheardes Calender* (1579), sig. C4v, Huntington Library

praise and request for Elizabeth to read and listen to the message of the calendar. The following stanza displays the poem's celebratory tone:

> Tell me, have ye seene her angelick face,
> Like Phoebe fayre?
> Her heauenly haveour, her princely grace
> can you well compare?
> The Redde rose medled with the White yfere,
> In either cheeke depeincten liuely chere.
> Her modest eye,
> Her Maiestie,
> Where haue you seene the like, but there?   (sig. C.iiiiv)

The inclusion of Elizabethan and Tudor icons in the verse becomes a collection of mnemonic *imagines* (iconic, vivid images) that respond to the woodcut's vivid imagery of Elizabeth with her ladies. The red rose and the white emulate a conventional Petrarchan blazon of a fair beauty. They also symbolize the houses of Lancaster and York, which, in Tudor historiography, blended together in the Tudor line and brought a conclusion to the War of the Roses. Their "medled" nature depicts a mixture or combination of the blood lines and, in an inversion and double-meaning typical of Spenser, a conflict or struggle. The red rose and white both meld and meddle in this image: to "meddle" in Spenser's time could mean either to mix, to have intercourse, or to contend (*MED* def. 1a–d, 3, and 4; *OED* def. 1a and 1c). Both the woodcut flower and the textual imagery of the melded red rose and white evoke popular histories of Queen Elizabeth's 1558 royal entry into London, prior to her coronation. A 1558 pamphlet, printed anonymously, narrates the inclusion of a stage, upon which sat persons representing Henry VII and his wife, Elizabeth of York (sig. Aiiii.r). Henry VII was represented as "enclosed in a read rose," and Elizabeth of York "enclosed with a white" (sig. Aiiir):

> and the hole pageant garnished with redde roses and white and in the forefront of the same pageant in a faire wreathe was written the name, and title of the same, which was "The Uniting of the two howses of Lancastre and Yorke." … it was devised that like as Elizabeth was the first occasion of concorde, so the another Elizabeth myght maintaine the same among her subjectes, so that unitie was the ende whereat the whole devise shotte. (sig. Bir)

In her Royal Entry pageant, Elizabeth functioned as her own genealogical emblem, drawing the eye of her audience towards the political symbolism of the melded roses she embodied and fashioned. Here the creation of the Elizabethan image draws from or re-collects previous divisions in British historical memory and is transmitted through a visual device, a symbolic collection of red and white flowers. Like later emblematic terms in print culture, as well as in Spenser's later April woodcut, this visual device focused on clever visual and textual puns (the name Elizabeth that connects Elizabeth I and Elizabeth of York). The procession, as recounted in this pamphlet, combined written text with spectacle to create new meaning. Spenser's April eclogue therefore calls to mind a previous image from historical memory, Eliza's meddled roses in her royal procession. Spenser's *Calender* here unites memory practices with visual and historiographical memories.

April's verse represents an ekphrasis that typifies much of the calendar's poetry, lending a visual emphasis to the structure of the work as a whole alongside the woodcuts. Indeed, figures of sight repeat and pattern themselves across the verses of the song. Hobbinol states that he will "blaze" Elizabeth's "worthy praise," in a double entendre of both the love poem's "blazon," or enraptured description of a beloved's features, and a projection of brilliant light. He calls upon the audience to "See, where she sits vpon the grassie greene, / (O seemly sight)," and asks if we have "seene her angelick face / Like *Phoebe* fayre?" in the verse above (sig. Ciiiiv). This sight is both "seemly," lovely and appropriate for its occasion (suiting an ideal of decorum), and "seemly," or seemingly, a sight. This dual meaning of "seemly" combines a suitable spectacular ceremony with a covert element of mutability and doubt. He references the queen's own vision, asking, "Her modest eye, / Her Maiestie, / Where haue you seene the like, but there?" (sig. Ciiiiv). He enjoins Elizabeth/Phoebe to "Shewe thy selfe *Cynthia* with thy silver rayes, / and be not abasht: / When shee the beames of her beauty displayes" (sig. Dr). Light and vision become dominant motifs in April's verse, giving the book a sense of illumination.

Indeed, the verse and woodcuts combine to remediate the technological form of a pre-print manuscript illumination, just as the language of the verse is enlivened and innovated by Chaucerian diction and orthography. The material and literary collaboration of woodcut and verse recollects the visual form of medieval manuscript illuminations and liturgical calendars in early modern print. The reference to Cynthia's silver rays and Phoebus's "golden hedde" recall the dominant, brilliant colours of a manuscript illumination, silver and gold. The verse itself adds the colour, detail, individual craft, and visual complexity to the black-and-white, more roughly hewn, and reproducible woodcut. Illuminations in manuscripts helped readers to organize and synthesize the information of the written text; they also served as devotional icons. Like these illuminations in manuscript books of hours and devotionals, the woodcuts of Spenser's *Calender* help the reader to remember his or her place in the book.

Just as the Elizabethan Settlement formed a native English church from Catholic design and Protestant "content," Spenser's *Calender* assembles medieval Catholic mnemonic systems together with classical hermetic mnemonics. The Elizabethan Settlement describes the 1558 Act of Supremacy that broke the Church of England from that of Rome and re-established the English monarch as head of the church, as well as the 1559 Act of Uniformity that laid the groundwork for Anglican liturgical practices, including the institution of the Book of Common Prayer and the visual, architectural transformation of churches across England from a Catholic to a more Protestant appearance. The Elizabethan Settlement is conventionally deemed a politically savvy compromise between familiar Catholic tradition and more radical Protestant departures; however, as scholars Ian Archer and Eamon Duffy attest, this "Settlement" was far from actually settled in practice.[18] For example, while walls and ornaments of churches were often whitewashed, plastered over, or removed, materials such as "altar stones" and "holy water vats" were "resurrected" in the 1569 Northern Rebellion (Duffy 432). The stained-glass windows of churches, in particular, remained as a controversial material memory of the recently Catholic past: Elizabeth allowed stained-glass windows to remain if they served the practical function of keeping weather out (Duffy 440). English churches in Spenser's time would therefore have existed as doubly recollected spaces: plastered remediations and existing material reminders of the past. Nigel Yates notes that in 1566, "rood-screens" were to stay in place, "but everything above the beam, the loft and the figures of Christ on the cross with Our Lady and St. John, was to be removed and replaced with the Royal Arms" (73).

In other words, visual culture in Elizabethan Protestantism was not broken entirely but was reformed through the iconic centrality of the Elizabethan monarchy and its appeals to a British national consciousness. Alison Chapman argues that *"The Shepheardes Calender* symbolically remakes the Catholic liturgical calendar by substituting local

English figures for the traditional calendar saints, thus bringing a pointedly English history into the patterning of sacred time" (3).[19] Chapman ties the April woodcut to the traditional 23 April feast day of St George, the traditional patron saint of England, who featured prominently in pre- (and some post-) Reformation English calendars (14). Indeed, she argues that Elizabeth's "red and white" colours symbolized the traditional red and white associated with St George (14). Elizabeth is substituted for St George as a devotional and literary patron of Spenser and his readers, in addition to the iconic figure of Elizabeth as the former "virgin queen" of heaven, Mary. Like her memorial collection of flowers, the face and image of Elizabeth in the April eclogue appear to blend and unify divided ideological messages and historical conflicts.[20] Early modern readers would pick up on the common reference to "Phoebe," or the classical moon goddess Diana, to whom Elizabeth was often compared in the literature and culture of her reign. The reference to Phoebe reminds us of Elizabeth's own memorial "icon" as the classical virgin queen Diana (or, in a book-of-hours context, the Virgin Mary), and brings us back to the heavenly focus of the calendar, this time with the sign of Queen Elizabeth acting as a heavenly symbol.

In fact, the Taurus bull in the April woodcut is looking down at the image of Queen Elizabeth. Here, the mnemonic zodiac symbol instructs us on where to place our gaze. The circle of ladies who surround and look at the figure of Elizabeth underscore this emphasis on the central space where Queen Elizabeth holds court. In the next verse, Phoebus (the Greek sun god, counterpart to Phoebe, the moon goddess) "thrust out his golden hedde/ upon her to gaze … He blusht to see another Sunne belowe" (sig. Dr). The sun, like the Taurean symbol and the ladies, circles and supports rather than dominates the central figure of Elizabeth in the woodcut. Its phallocentrism is replaced by Queen Elizabeth's centrality. The bawdy potential of this verse's sexual politics are clear: the gazing Phoebus "thrusts" his "head" out to "gaze" upon her, is amazed by her "broad beams" and surprised to see "another Sunne below" (presumably, her maidenhead), which has the "overthrow" of him as a masculine cultural symbol.[21] Elizabeth, the moon goddess, becomes the masculine, dominant, present, bright, and phallic symbol in both verse and woodcut. The sun's position on the right-hand side of the woodcut perhaps depicts a rising sun, whereas the final stanza of the verse section, echoing the twilight imagery of Virgil's eclogues, depicts an absence of light: "night draweth on, / And twincling starres the daylight hence chase." The brilliance of the Elizabethan icon is perpetual: cyclical and even ephemeral, rather than wholly permanent and fixed.

The woodcut and verse's cumulative effect is one of "medling": both a construction of divergent, assembled textual and material elements, and a deconstruction of the unified effect of that assembly or collection. Elizabeth's brilliant light does not shine on the shepherds Hobbinol and Thenot in the woodcut or in the verse: they inhabit the illustration's left-hand corner, debating and looking at one another instead of at Elizabeth. Even the shepherds' flocks "graze about in sight," but the shepherds remain "shrowded" in "shade" (sig. Ciiiir). The absence of light in the verse and the spatial/optical reference to Elizabeth in the woodcut, on one hand, resembles a lover's and courtier's complaint about the lack of the beloved's (or monarch's) attention and grace, which resituates this eclogue as a lover's complaint. On the other hand, this separation of illuminated Elizabeth from shrouded shepherd also emphasizes a certain independent, objective distance of the singer from the song, author from text, (masculine) lover from (feminine) beloved, shepherd from court: the totalizing potential of Elizabeth's image becomes, from the shepherd's point of view, a removed and sexually objectified visual object. The divisions that appear unified by the iconic, illuminated device of Elizabeth disintegrate by the end of the verse (when "twinkling stars the daylight hence chase" [sig. Diir]) and on the shepherds' shrouded left-hand corner of the woodcut image. The removed position of the rustic shepherd allows him (and the non-aristocratic popular reader) the privilege of a (masculine) gaze at the Elizabethan centre of power. Indeed, Louis Montrose reads April as one of those "paradoxical celebrations of power that, in making the poem serve the queen, make the queen serve the poem" (332). April's woodcut and textual imagery remind readers that, after all, we are gazing on a paper pageant.

The *Shepheardes Calender*'s Mutable Type

Spenser's *Calender* also demonstrates different material collections and disjunctions through its typography. As D.F. McKenzie argues in his classic essay "Typography and Meaning," typefaces contain information on both a text's technological production and design and on that text's cultural and social position. Multiple typefaces are not unique to *The Shepheardes Calender*, yet the particular arrangement of type demonstrates strategic cultural associations in a text that is a (re)collection of parts. The *Calender*'s blackletter type in its poetic verse reveals several competing social implications. What bibliographers now call "blackletter" type was, during Spenser's time, called "English type" (Galbraith 14). At the time of the *Calender*'s publication, English type was often given to the English vernacular, just as Roman type would be used predominantly for books written in Latin. Italic type largely matched works written in Italian.[22] This typographical decision is a conventional one; it follows the tradition of the black letter "English" style that William Caxton lent to early modern print editions of Chaucer and Lydgate (Galbraith 16–26). Galbraith argues that this typographical layout asserts the *Calender* as a nationalist project. He contends that literacy in English blackletter was literacy in the English vernacular. Bland notes that "black-letter was the first dominant typeface in England" (93) and its continuing use could be explained by its cultural ties to English print production (93). Galbraith and Bland break with R.B. McKerrow's interpretation of this type choice as an "intentional bit of antiquarianism" (297n.). To take Galbraith's implications to their natural end, the *Calender*'s employment of English blackletter type functions as Protestant identity politics. Paul C. Gutjahr and Megan L. Benton associate blackletter with Protestant and specifically religious, biblical texts, including the Gutenberg bible (11–19): "in a sense, the eternal, changeless nature of God's words was reflected in the changeless nature of the type used to convey those words" (19). Nonetheless, they describe typefaces as always containing "multivalent" meanings (18). Blackletter was additionally, based on my search of texts with the term "almanac" in their title between 1530 and 1600, overwhelmingly the typeface of English almanacs, further connecting Spenser's *Calender* to this popular native genre. Blackletter type's disparate cultural connotations in *The Shepheardes Calender* – nationalism, eternality, religion, pastness – coexist as a collection of fragmentary cultural associations.[23]

In the *Calender*'s poetic text, certain words are italicized. These italics serve as "placeholders" for the reader who may wish to move between the terms and their gloss. They also serve as a system of names and references that builds towards the eclogues' artful and assembled construction of Elizabeth as national icon. The repetition, in italics, of moon and sun goddesses and gods takes us back to the role of manuscript illuminations as reminders of one's place while reading and the heavenly *loci* that serve as both ideology and techne. Italics also form the typeface of the "argument" section between the woodcut and the poems that appears to clarify and summarize the verse that follows it. Yet, like Thomas Nashe's accusations of so-called "termagant inkhorne tearmes," or recent Latin borrowings in the English language, the argument is written in an obfuscatory "official style," replete with dependent clauses: "whereby he taketh occasion, for proofe of his more excellencie and skill in poesie, to recorde a songe, which the sayde Colin sometimes made in honor her Majestie" (sig. C.iiiiv).[24] Such euphuisms are not a rare event in Spenser, but they serve here as a jarring, even humorous contrast to the antiquated rusticisms of the shepherd's verse. Where the verses plead for a view of "Colin" (or Spenser) as simple, humble shepherd, the argument and italics unveil his ambition and trumpet his accomplishment to an almost exaggerated level. This internal contradiction suits the pastoral and Virgilian convention of a cloaked sophistication in simple guise. The italic names and references, however, serve to disrupt the deceptively simple surface of the poetry's blackletter type. They also fulfil a mnemonic function. According to Mark Bland, italics were often associated with speech in the early modern era (100): the italicized names of Elizabeth visible throughout the text, then, could resemble a repeated litany of names as well as a visual cue.

To modern readers, the roman type of the gloss is the more accessible and visually familiar section of the calendar, one that would clarify and consolidate the poetry of the blackletter type. However, The *Faerie Queene*'s own roman typography, Bland argues, actually set the trend for the use of roman type in English print (107). The typeface of E.K.'s glosses would have been the most familiar to readers who read and encountered classical texts, while the blackletter type may have been more familiar to vernacular readers. Like many biblical glosses in manuscripts, E.K.'s roman gloss endlessly complicates, denaturalizes, and creates controversy. The glosses come off as exaggerated pedantry and are hard to read without irony.[25] For instance, a gloss on "ye daintie nymphs" reads as "Ye daintie) is, as it were an Exordium ad preparandos animos" (an exordium to prepare the emotions) (sig. D.2.v). The glosses interact with the italics to systematically divide the reader's focus. The glosses may satirize the tradition of Latin prose commentary on (Catholic) bibles, which, in Protestant polemics, purposefully obfuscated the already clear biblical verse itself. The defence of plain, native English against Latinate and international influence in the language (portrayed as a "gallimaufray or hodgepodge of al other speches" at the outset of the calendar) mirrors defences of an accessible, vernacular bible in Protestant pamphlets (Nashe sig. Ciij). At the same time, the glosses also call into question the simplicity and clarity of the blackletter verse of the calendar as it unpacks the layers of reference that underscore its pastoral form.

By highlighting the rhetorical, classical, and historical references of the verse, the Calender's multiplicity of typefaces unravels the aesthetic *and* cultural collection of meanings in the text. The *Shepheardes Calender* was printed by Hugh Singleton, who, prior to joining the Stationer's Register, was known for printing the Protestant polemics of John Knox and John Bale (Hadfield 127). Singleton also fled for political reasons to Strassburg, Germany, during the reign of Queen Mary. D.M. Loades cites Strassburg and Emden as important locations of the "illicit book trade" during this time (37). In September 1579, the same year of the *Shepheardes Calender*'s publication, Singleton gained even more notoriety by printing a pamphlet, *The Discoverie of a Gaping Gulf whereinto England is like to be Swallowed*, attacking the potential marriage of Queen Elizabeth to the Duke of Alençon (Cressy 365). After publication of this pamphlet, Singleton was sentenced to have his right hand cut off but was pardoned – although the author, the unfortunately named John Stubbs, and distributor, William Page, did experience this punishment (Cressy 365). This spectacle of censorship, David Cressy argues in "Book Burning in Tudor and Stuart England," was rare for Queen Elizabeth's rule, as she preferred more private methods of censorship, as seditious books were burnt in indoor Stationers Hall kitchens or quietly handed over to authorities (364). One month after his narrow reprieve, October 1579, Singleton printed the *Shepheardes Calender*. Galbraith indicates that the *Calender*'s typographical features indicate Hugh Singleton's "house style" (23), but the choice of Hugh Singleton in itself has political implications, as Galbraith and Paul E. McLane observe. McLane argues that "the selection of Hugh Singleton as printer, unless it was for political reasons, was most puzzling" (324). Singleton's typographical style may represent a conscious, ideological choice, as was Spenser's choice of printer. One may assume that Spenser knew the "house style" of his printer, decided to choose this particular printing house, and arranged his text with this knowledge in mind.

Yet within the potentially nationalist statement of the blackletter verse, the italic typography intervenes with a collection of classical, international associations. The words and names *Parnasse, Helicon, Elisa, Syrinx, Pan, Phoebe, Phoebus, Cynthia, Latonaes, Niobe, Colin*, and so on break with the black letter type – and English names – of the verse itself. The overall effect of the italics and roman type on the visual layout of the calendar is to weigh down and co-opt the comic pastoral verse.

The poems themselves seem to follow the early modern courtly ideal of *sprezzatura*, the ability to display a seemingly effortless, natural eloquence in carriage and rhetoric. *Sprezzatura* conceals effort and artistry behind a rhetorical articulation.[26] The italicized names and references unmask the studied art and effort that the verse sustains and reveal the more international and borrowed elements in the so-called English typeface. The italic typeface steals the spotlight from the effortless "plain English" style and type of the blackletter font to de-naturalize and disturb the dominant meaning of its text.

The *Shepheardes Calender* as a (pre)Annotated Almanac

Although the *Calender*'s visual arrangement, like its typeface, manifests a complex recollection of genres, it perhaps most specifically parallels the material form of a mock annotated almanac or "blank," with the space for annotation already inscribed by E.K. "Blanks," or annotated almanacs that featured the common almanac elements of astrological predictions, visual calendars, and reminders of holy, fast, and feast days, and included blank spaces for readers to include commentary, reminders, tables, and other inscriptions. By the *Shepheardes Calender*'s publication, annotated almanacs had begun to appear in early modern English print.[27] As Adam Smyth notes, approximately "one in seven" almanacs were annotated or inscribed by their readers by the seventeenth century ("Almanacs, Annotators" 204). Reader annotations in almanacs followed a non-linear, non-narrative form, and were miscellaneous and cumulative in nature, much like E.K.'s glosses. These non-linear annotations lent the genre, as Smyth puts it, "a sense of a resistant, unyielding text" ("Almanacs, Annotators" 218). The purpose of these annotations was never singular: many readers recorded daily events, used the blank spaces of their almanacs as diaries, or inscribed quotations and commonplaces onto the margins of the pages.[28] Although the almanacs themselves, Smyth claims, were an ephemeral, disposable form, readers used them to create their own personal histories and to serve as memory aids. Almanacs adapted to suit these readers' everyday mnemonic practices. Over the course of the sixteenth century, they began to include blank pages that invited the reader to participate in recording and prognosticating. According to Smyth, "almanacs with these inserted vacant pages were known as 'blanks'; regular almanacs were called 'sorts'" (204). While Smyth does not trace the specific derivation of the term "sort," early modern readers and printers may have had several of the following meanings in mind, which reflect the dynamic cultural role of almanacs as mnemonic systems: a "destiny" or "fortune" (*MED* 1a and obs., *OED* sense 1b); a more specific "divination" (*MED* 2a and obs., *OED*, sense 2b); a letter of type (*OED* sense 13b); or a "collection" of things (obs., *OED* sense 17e).

The earliest known surviving "blank" style almanac, printed by Thomas Purfoote in 1566, thirteen years prior to *The Shepheardes Calender*'s 1579 publication, demonstrates the simultaneously mnemonic, yet impermanent nature of the blank almanac. Its interface is simple and practical, and its title advertises its primary use as a record-keeping device for readers. The title page (Figure 2.12) contains the most complete textual and stylistic information in the entire book.

The anonymous author names this text a "blancke and perpetuall almanack, serving as a memoriall": the title seems to advertise its paradoxical permanence (memorial) and ephemerality (perpetual). The annotations readers could inscribe on this almanac could serve as a recording device, as the title page puts it, "for al marchauntes and occupiers, to note what debtes they have to paie or receive, in any moneth or daie of the yeare." It could also be used as a "memorial," a preservation of one's "actes, deedes, or thinges that passeth from time to time (worthy of memory, to be registered)": this sense would invite the reader to preserve and keep the almanac to remember the events of the year. Presumably, this almanac could act as a diary or note-taking device, where the items to be remembered would be personal and idiosyncratic to each reader, or, as Thomas Hill's almanac featured below (Figure 2.13), a book to keep accounts and records. This almanac reminds the reader of "thinges that passeth," things that are fleeting, yet recur from year to year – like the ephemeral form of the almanac, disposed of but returning, in a new year, like a perpetual, yearly flower or crop. The pages themselves appear as a blank chart with a table of dates. Blank almanacs perform a dually "perpetual and memorial" function in their blank spaces, spaces that call for the reader's mnemonic inscriptions and short-term, discardable use.

These blank almanacs consciously collected and transformed visual and cognitive memory spaces. Thomas Hill's 1571 almanac advertises itself as a "forme of a book of memorie necessary for all such, as have occasion daylie to note sundry affayres, eyther for receytes, payments, or such lyke" (frontispiece). Thomas Hill wrote two other almanacs, one published 1560, the other published 1572. Neither of these other

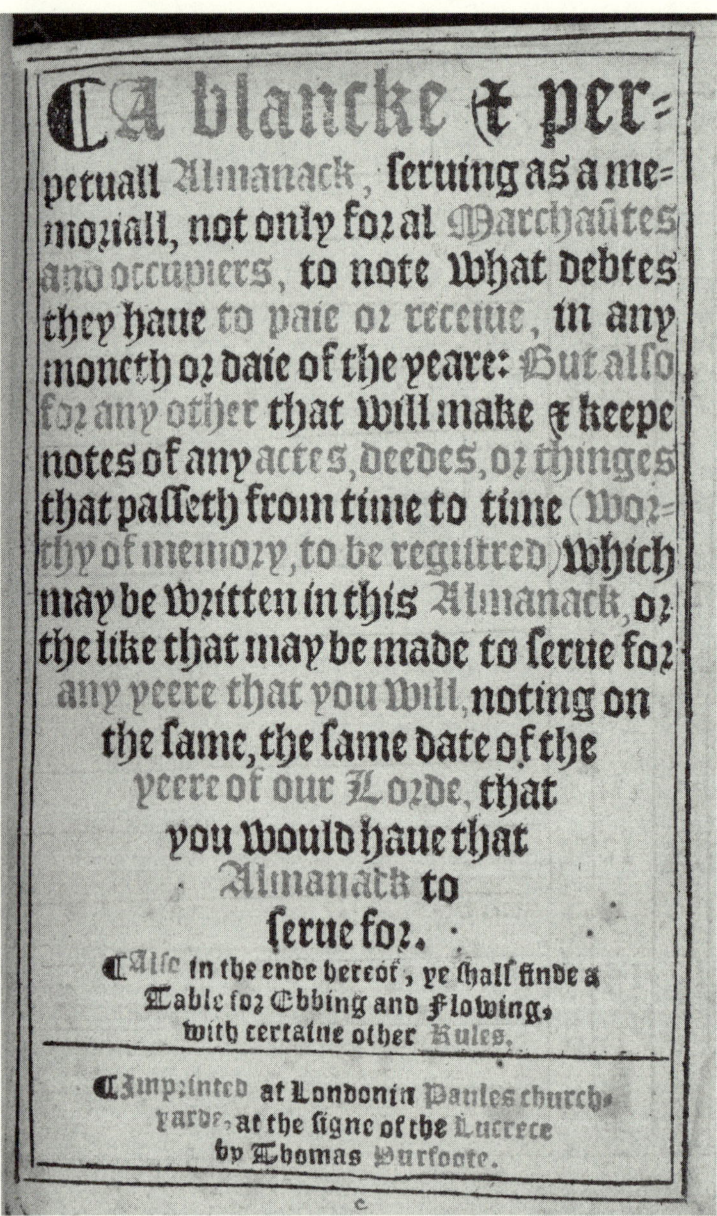

Figure 2.12. Anon., *A Blancke & Perpetuall Almanack* (1566), frontispiece, University of Glasgow Library

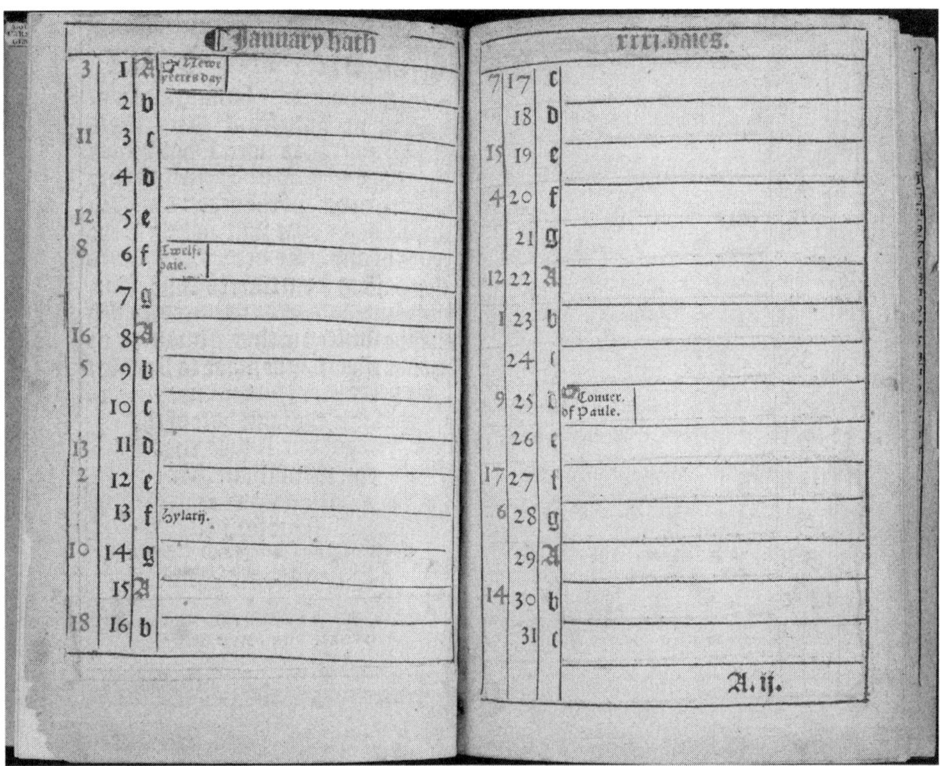

Figure 2.13. Anon., *A Blancke & Perpetuall Almanack* (1566), sig. A2v–A2r, University of Glasgow Library

almanacs were "blanks" nor did they advertise themselves as "memory books": the "blank" almanac, in particular, may have had a unique and specific tie to material practices of memory. The woodcut illustration on the 1571 blank almanac's title page (Figure 2.14) amplifies these mnemonic associations.

The woodcut displays a sun on the left-hand side of the page, and a moon on the right. One hand holds a globe, and another holds a divining rod. The astronomical imagery of this frontispiece, while of course reflecting the heavenly predictions of the almanac genre, also recalls the hermetic, metaphysical memory system of Metrodorus. Judith Anderson and Alastair Fowler argue for the presence of mystical Neoplatonic

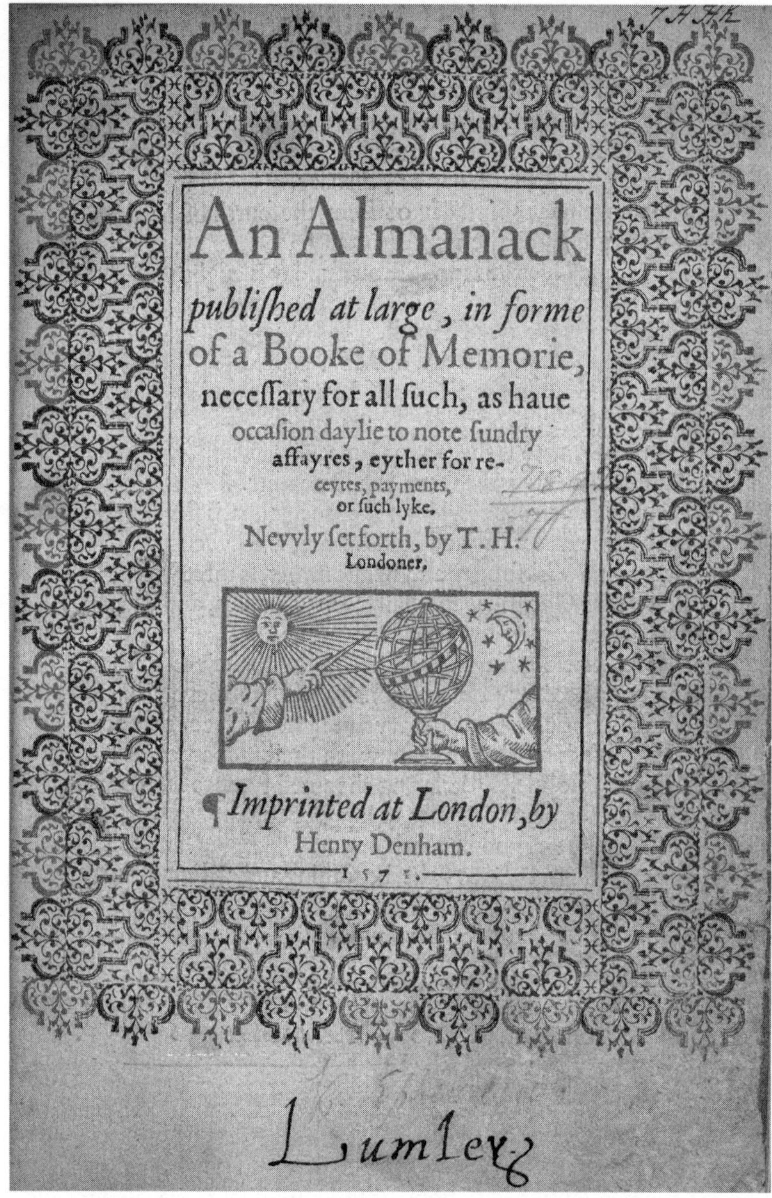

Figure 2.14. T. H., Londoner, *An Almanack Published at Large, in Forme of a Booke of Memorie* (1571), frontispiece, British Library

symbolism, based on astrology, in Spenser's *Faerie Queene* and *Shepheardes Calender*, specifically referencing his response to Microbius's commentary on Cicero's *Dream of Scipio*.[29] In Cicero's *Dream*, the departed Africanus appears to Scipio in a dream, and shows him the stars, planets, and Milky Way. Cicero specifically ties this heavenly vision to a discussion of memory's ephemerality. In this text, Africanus enjoins Scipio to "cast thine eyes alwaies toward these heavenly thinges, & contemne those mortall and humaine matter," and to remember the cyclical permanence of the planets to "beare" his vision in his "memorie" (sig. Fiiir).[30] This remembrance of heavenly things is difficult, Africanus states, since "no man is able to beare any thing in memorie, yᵉ space of one yere" (sig. Fiiir).

The planetary imagery of popular almanacs and Spenser's *Calender* respond to the same tension between memory's permanence and ephemerality that Scipio's dream recounts. In Cicero's *Dream*, memory's limitations are at least partially surmounted by visualization, as Scipio casts his eyes to the planets. Early printed almanacs, which include planetary symbolism and astrological prediction, contain memory and impermanence in the same material spaces. Reminders, in almanac blanks, were discardable and most likely erasable. Peter Stallybrass et. al discuss the important role of table books as material and even metaphorical spaces for commonplaces, reminders, and ciphering in the sixteenth and early seventeenth centuries. Stallybrass et al. track the use of erasable graphite, easily swiped by a sponge, for these tables: table books function as technologies of memory because they "make writing *impermanent*" (415, emphasis in original). Material memory was thus palimpsestic in early modern print culture, inducing "forgetfulness as much as remembrance" (414). This palimpsestic, dual nature of memory in the table book parallels and corresponds to that of the almanac genre at large, including Spenser's *Shepheardes Calender*. Memory is not simply plagued by forgetfulness, though: memory in the almanac genre is cyclical and recyclable, with many of the same images (the planets, parts of the body, the phases of the moon) and motifs recurring each year, across almanac types.

Although Stallybrass et al. use the example of Robert Triplet's and Frank Adams's writing tables to track their use as a memory device, they largely do not discuss the important visual and mnemonic roles of the almanacs and calendars that adjoin the writing tables of these texts. Frank Adams's *Writing tables with a kalender for xxiiii yeeres, with sundry necessarye rules* (1594) presents readers with directions for charting the phases or "chaunge of the Moone" and planets, and keeping track of

ona speranza, returned in
monethes, which was the 9...
This yeere in July. Babington with
...lifes were taken, and in September
...weare executed.
The same yeere 1586. the 29. of October, was
Parlament assembled, for ý trial of matters concerning Mary the Scottish Queene, and in the 6.
of December following, was solemly proclaimed
with ý sound of 4. Troumpets in seueral places
of London, 2 in Middlesex, the sentence giuen
by the Nobility against the saide Mary Queene
of Scots, to the wonderfull great reioising of all
the Godly, as apeared by their singing of psalms
ringing of Bells, and making of bonfires in the
Citye of London, and on ý 8. of February following, being wednesday in the forenoone, according
to the sentence giuen by the Nobilitye, the
sayde Mary Queene of Scots was beheaded, in
the Castell of Foddering haye. and in the first of
August, 1587. was as apertayned to a Queene,
most Royally buried at Peterborough.

FINIS.

Made at London by Frauncis Adams,
Stationer or Bookebinder, dwelling in
Distaffe lane, at the signe of the...

Figure 2.15. Frank Adams, *Writing Tables* (1594), final page, Cambridge University Library

important monthly dates, or "the mooveable feastes of the whole yeere" (sig. aiiir). As a whole, this text presents directions not just for inscribing and erasing items on tables, but also for keeping track of time, organized by such cyclical occurrences as feast and fast days, or local fairs. Between the calendar and table portion of this text, Adams includes a historical chronicle of England's monarchs and events. The final event that Adams witnesses, which precedes the blank tables, charts the 1587 beheading and burial of Mary, Queen of Scots (Figure 2.15).

The "finis" of the page marks the end of past events. Presumably, however, the chronicling of the years continues with reader inscriptions. The tables, then, may not be conceived as a space for daily reminders alone, but as an infinitely changeable continuation of political and cultural memorials, to which the reader might add and comment. As a text that, I argue, purposefully imitates the blank-almanac structure, memory in the *Shepherdes Calender* is not just a palimpsest, but a moving constellation and continual recollection of images and materials.

In a structure similar to the palimpsestic, yet continuous rendition of historical and material memory in Frank Adams's calendar, chronicle, and table, the 1570 *Almanack and prognostication* of Philip Moore contains the following: a table for feast days, a calendar, "brief remembraunces" for holy and fast days, a table for the "principall faires in England," "wherein any man havyng the booke, maie at his pleasure, adde therunto his owne knowledge," a chronicle of kings, "necessary for all menne" who deal with "evidence, or Lawe matters," signs of wind and waters, and, finally, predictions and portents for the next forty years, translated from the Bohemian mathematician and astrologer Cyprianus Leovitius, including "warre," "straunge sightes in the ayer," and "other miserable calamities" (sig. air–aiiv). Moore's juxtaposition of prosaic remembrances and eschatological events may seem bewildering, even chaotic, to modern readers. Yet this almanac's miscellaneous amalgamation of past, present, and future, the daily and the dire, in Moore's almanac typifies the genre. Moore's chronicle acts as both a macrocosmic chart of political events and as a common legal sourcebook. Like E.K.'s glosses in the *Shepheardes Calender*, Moore's almanac also includes pre-printed annotations that mimic reader inscriptions (Figure 2.16).

Such glosses add to a sense of memory's continuous yet contested nature within almanacs, as grand events worthy of chronicle or cataclysm meld with readers' (or glossers') brief remembrances. The printed gloss, in Leovitius's forty-year prognostication, serves to visually emphasize and reimpress the text's portents. Stallybrass et al. argue for the importance of "impressions" on the mind to supplement material inscriptions in early modern culture (416). In this paradigm, cognition is permanent; the material text, fleeting. Impressions, however, as outlined in the previous chapter, could be both mental and material in early modern phenomenology, often recalled the specific language of print itself, and could be uncertain or ambiguous in nature. In one passage from Moore's almanac, eschatological predictions are described in the language of uncanny visuality: as strange sights, such as a meteor,

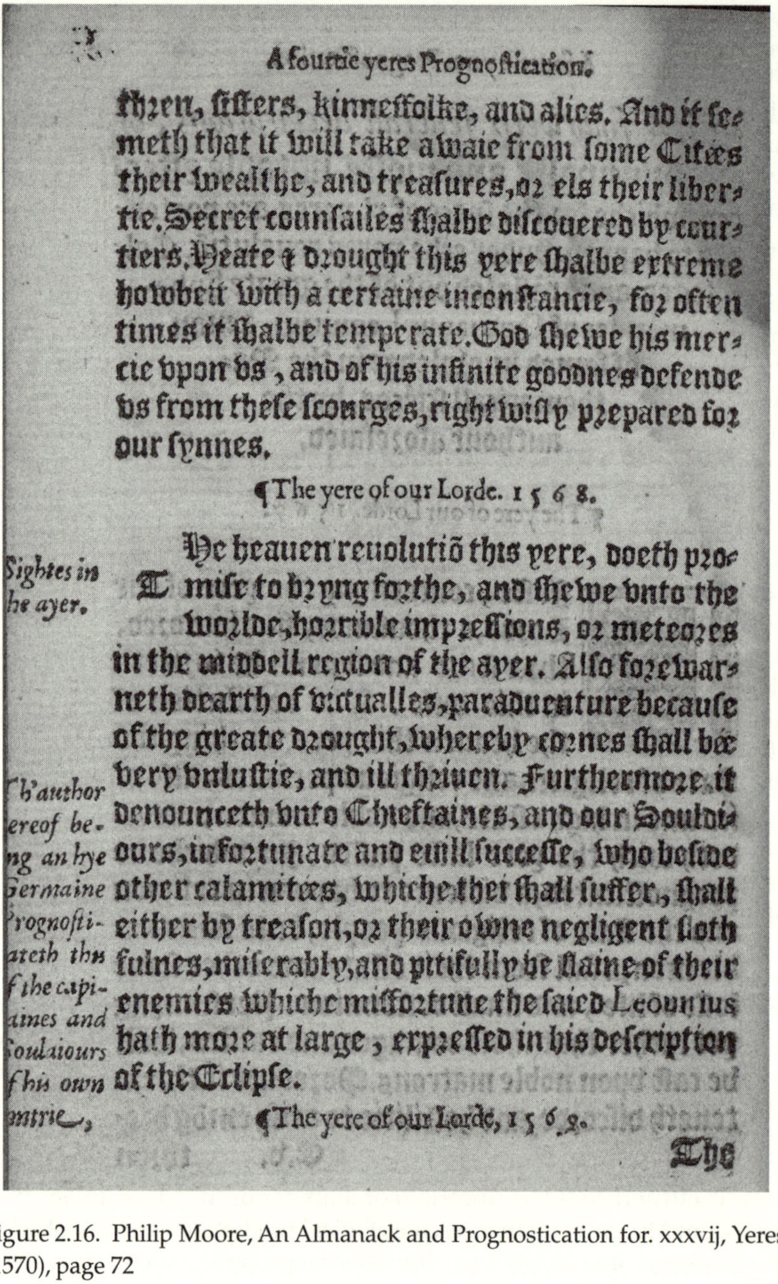

A fourtie yeres Prognostication.

thren, sisters, kinnessolke, and alies. And it seemeth that it will take awaie from some Citees
their wealthe, and treasures, or els their liber-
tie. Secret counsailes shalbe discouered by cour-
tiers. Heate & drought this yere shalbe extreme
howbeit with a certaine inconstancie, for often
times it shalbe temperate. God shewe his mer-
cie vpon vs, and of his infinite goodnes defende
vs from these scourges, rightwisly prepared for
our synnes.

¶The yere of our Lorde. 1 5 6 8.

Sightes in the ayer.

He heauen reuolutiõ this yere, doeth promise to bryng forthe, and shewe vnto the
worlde, horrible impressions, or meteores
in the middell region of the ayer. Also forewar-
neth dearth of victualles, paraduenture because
of the greate drought, whereby cornes shall bee
very vnlustie, and ill thriuen. Furthermore it
denounceth vnto Chieftaines, and our Souldiours, infortunate and euill successe, who beside
other calamitees, whiche thei shall suffer, shall
either by treason, or their owne negligent sloth
fulnes, miserably, and pitifully be slaine of their
enemies whiche misfortune the saied Leouinus
hath more at large, expressed in his description
of the Eclipse.

Th'author hereof be-ng an hye Germaine Prognosti-ateth this f the capi-aines and Souldiours f his own untrie,

¶The yere of our Lorde, 1 5 6 9.

The

Figure 2.16. Philip Moore, An Almanack and Prognostication for. xxxvij, Yeres (1570), page 72

an eclipse, or other "horrible impressions" (fol. 72; sig. E5v). These horrible impressions are enacted, presumably, in the future activity of the planets, as well as on the warnings impressed on the page and mind's eye. In keeping with the cyclical yet ephemeral, prosaic yet metaphysical nature of these sixteenth-century memory spaces, Moore's almanac does not end so much as briefly halt its text: "unto you verie many and sore Plagues seeme to be portended. Over your heades (I saie) shall hang extreme calamities. Here I could declare the significations of twoo yeres more yet ... But here Plato biddeth me make an ende" (sig. o1r).

The more practical, material uses of the almanac existed alongside, yet at times in tension with, their more enduring metaphysical attributes. Perhaps an indication of the increasingly disposable nature of printed timekeeping devices in early modern culture, the length of time for calendar and alamanac use began to shorten over the course of the sixteenth century. As Alison Chapman details, the calendar's material use "as a stable, enduring guide was fading by the beginning of the seventeenth century" in favour of the one-year perennial almanac form ("Marking Time" 1271). Further, astrological *loci* employed by the almanac genre created a particular historical tension in post-Reformation English culture. The notion that space and place could contain divine or phenomenal import had uneasy associations with Catholic, medieval superstition (Chapman 1266–7). Spenser's unique combination of astrological signs in each of his woodcuts and nationalist Protestant poetry reflects the importance of collecting forms from the past to (re)collect and remediate them into a new, post-Reformation form.

On the other hand, the visual and poetic texts of the *Shepheardes Calender* could also be interpreted as a site of material and historiographical tension. The inclusion of E.K.'s pre-inscribed print annotations and heavenly symbols outline the *Calender*'s aspirations to permanence, yet this permanence is predicated on the collection of tropes from the ephemeral form of the almanac. Anderson argues that Spenser's Neoplatonic treatment of memory appears in Spenser's "mystically charged diction in Eumnestes' chamber," but that "this reminiscence vanishes" and passes "into the demystified memory of an Aristotelian or more materialized system" (87). Anderson's division between mystical (Platonic) and material (Aristotelian) understandings of memory, though, is perhaps unnecessary within the early modern cultural context. In the language and imagery of almanacs, at least, metaphysical content was given an at-times jarring material and physical display. For example, Thomas Hill's frontispiece includes both the mystical symbolism of the

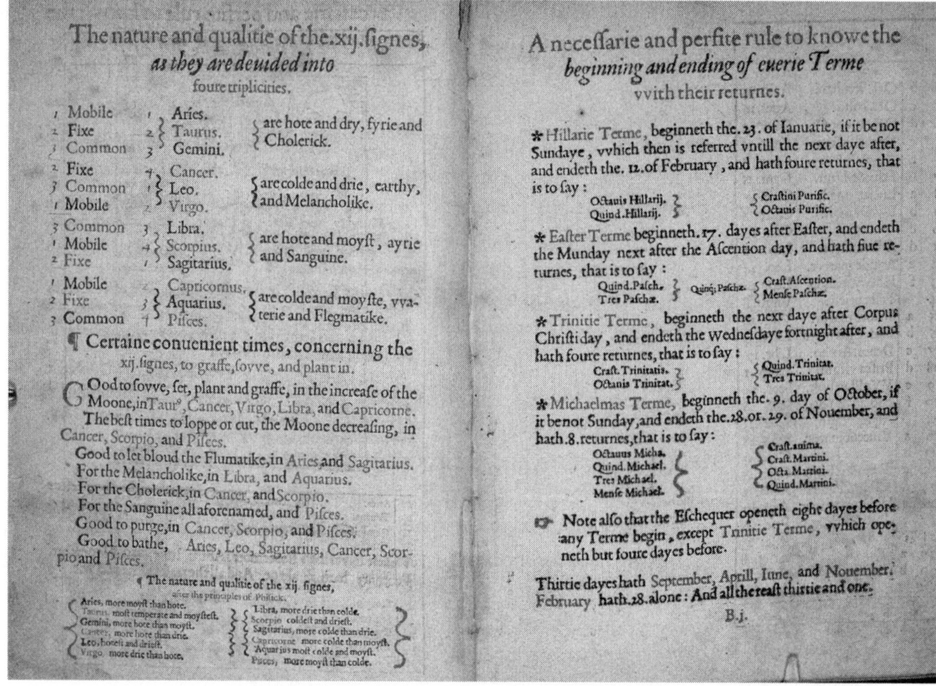

Figure 2.17. T. H., Londoner, *An Almanack Published at Large, in Forme of a Booke of Memorie* (1571), sig. Bjv–Bjr, British Library

stars and two disembodied hands that draw attention to the physicality of the blank almanac form, perhaps even the process of readers' physical inscription (see Figure 2.14). Philip Moore's almanac, too, includes an overwhelmingly cataclysmic, forty-year prognostication, yet advertises itself for the daily use of "phisicions, chyrurgians, men of lawe, marchauntes, mariners, husbande men, and handicraftes men" (title page). As a whole, these blank almanacs demonstrate how print technology and the ancient arts of memory could combine to organize everyday life in early modern culture, as they inform and remind the readers of the best times for baths and purges for the body, the planting and sowing of crops (see Figure 2.17).

Annotated almanacs, while containing empty spaces, were far from cultural blank slates in the sixteenth century and seventeenth centuries.

During this time, readers' inscription in almanacs came to symbolize early modern class anxieties. Smyth discusses the satirical treatment of almanacs and their readers in early modern England, to the point where "mock almanacs" that mimicked this textual form and "took particular delight in lampooning gullible annotating readers" began to appear in the seventeenth century (206).[31] Almanac readers and annotators were construed in popular culture as "provincial, uneducated, and hopelessly aspirational" (Smyth, "Almanacs, Annotators" 206). For instance, the "rude mechanicals" of *Midsummer Night's Dream* look to an almanac to forecast the weather of their opening night; Bottom exclaims, "A calendar, a calendar! Look in the almanac; find / out moonshine, find out moonshine" (3.1.46–7). The scene emphasizes their class status, superstition, and, in particular, Bottom's buffoonery. Prince Henry references almanacs in a comic conversation with Falstaff and his tavern friends in *2 Henry IV*. As Doll kisses Falstaff, Hal exclaims, "Saturn and Venus this year in conjunction! What says almanac to that?" (2.4.262–3). Poins replies, "And look whether the fiery Trigon, his man, be not lisping to his master's old tables, his note-book, his counsel-keeper" (2.4.265–7). "Trigon" refers to the arrangement of the four astrological elements (earth, air, fire, water) into three signs. The "fiery" Trigon represents Aries, Leo, and Sagittarius; the use of these heavenly signs comically echoes social and textual disruption (writing on a notebook, courting a master's wife) through metaphors of the almanac genre and almanac inscription. Hal uses both the cultural form of the almanac itself – again, associated with foolish upstarts who misread their social position – to poke fun at Falstaff. Poins's reply compares cuckoldry to inscribing in the "tables and note-book" of an almanac – in other words, cuckoldry as annotation. Lower-class almanac readers and annotators perform a disruptive social and rhetorical appropriation of the master text in this passage.

Almanac readers and their annotators, however, were not always destabilizing, lower-class inscribers in the early modern cultural imagination. Ben Jonson's depiction of almanacs in *Every Man Out of His Humour* instead emphasizes the connection between almanac use and the emerging capitalist class. The miser Sordido's main "recreation is reading of almanacks; and felicity, foul weath. One that never pray'd but for a lean dearth, and ever wept in a fat harvest" (106; cast of characters, 63–5). Sordido employs the almanac to make prognostications for his own predatory profit making: the space of his almanac is filled with financial calculations. In Jonson's text, both almanac and its annotating readers exacerbate emerging capital's worst excesses. The humour in Jonson's mock almanac reader comes from Sordido's upstart nature, and, more darkly, his growing power over the environmental and social life of his community, represented in his almanac consultation.

In Spenser's almanac, E.K.'s scholarly gloss potentially satirizes the socially and educationally aspirational nature of these new, ambitious lower- and middle-class readers.[32] The mix of satire, pedagogy, and random observation found in E.K.'s glosses reflects the practice of annotating almanacs, as well as popular, less-than-flattering depictions of almanac annotators. E.K.'s loquacious pedantry gives him the character of an educated fool. His gloss may lampoon an emerging class of readers who would wish to disassemble the latent meanings and allusions that underpin the verse. A couple of typically overwrought annotations by E.K. appear at the end of January's eclogue, "Neighbor towne) the nexte towne: expressing the Latine Vicina" and "his clownish gyfts) imitateth Virgil's verse" (sig. aiiv).[33] Technically speaking, *The Shepheardes Calender*, read with almanac conventions in mind, is a "sort" or fully typed, fully printed almanac: each page is filled with verse, argument, gloss, or woodcut. But the visual page border between the poetic text and its corresponding gloss sets the mysterious E.K.'s commentary off from the rest of the page (Figure 2.18).

Just as E.K.'s glosses transform the space of the *Shepheardes Calender*, his commentary transforms the structure of the calendar's memory space. The handwritten annotations in the blank pages of almanacs "maintain a consistent spatial system" (Smyth, "Almanacs, Annotators" 209), as do E.K's printed glosses in the *Calender*. E.K.'s obsession with classical influences and rhetorical devices mirrors the pedagogical approach emergent classes of ambitious readers took as they filled the pages of their almanacs. E.K.'s annotative glosses articulate the class and status anxieties of an era in which print technology upended the relationship between literacy and social position.

E.K.'s glosses also portray an active yet destabilizing interaction between reader and text. Adam Max Cohen notes that another common sixteenth-century usage of "gloss," aside from an annotation, could be a "sheen or glow emanating from the object" (74). If we consider this dual meaning, a printed or reader annotation parallels and recalls the concept of object species, wherein the object's own matter could serve to both mediate and disrupt the observer's perception of it. Written and printed glosses in almanacs often replicate, like species, the main points of a body of text, as in the case of the Moore almanac's

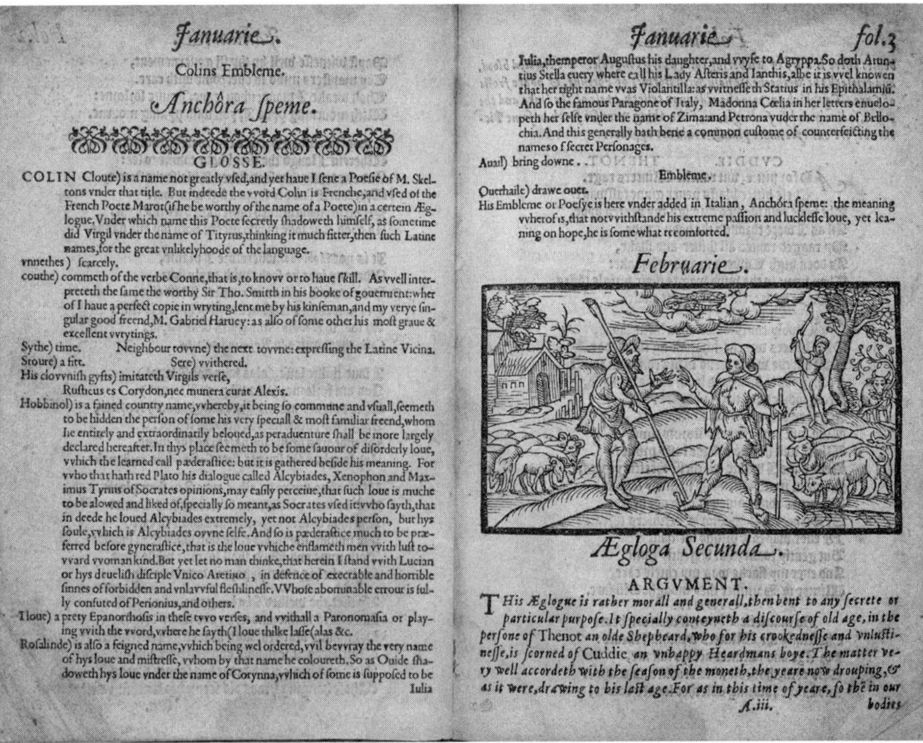

Ianuarie.

Colins Embleme.

Anchôra speme.

GLOSSE.

COLIN Cloute) is a name not greatly vsed, and yet haue I sene a Poesie of M. Skeltons vnder that title. But indeede the vvord Colin is Frenche, and vsed of the French Poete Marot (if he be worthy of the name of a Poete) in a certein Æglogue. Vnder which name this Poete secretly shadoweth himself, as sometime did Virgil vnder the name of Tityrus, thinking it much fitter, then such Latine names, for the great vnlikelyhoode of the language.

vnnethes) scarcely.

couthe) commeth of the verbe Conne, that is, to knovv or to haue skill. As vvell interpreteth the same the worthy Sir Tho. Smitth in his booke of gouerment: wher of I haue a perfect copie in wryting, lent me by his kinseman, and my verye singular good freend, M. Gabriel Haruey: as also of some other his most graue & excellent vvrytings.

Sythe) time.   Neighbour tovvne) the next tovvne: expressing the Latine Vicina.
Stoure) a fitt.   Sere) vvithered.
His clovvnish gyfts) imitateth Virgils verse,
    Rusticus es Corydon, nec munera curat Alexis.

Hobbinol) is a fained country name, vvhereby, it being so commune and vsuall, seemeth to be hidden the person of some his very speciall & most familiar freend, whom he entirely and extraordinarily beloued, as peraduenture shall be more largely declared hereafter. In thys place seemeth to be some sauour of disorderly loue, vvhich the learned call pæderastice: but it is gathered beside his meaning. For vvho that hath red Plato his dialogue called Alcybiades, Xenophon and Maximus Tyrius of Socrates opinions, may easily perceiue, that such loue is muche to be alowed and liked of, specially so meant, as Socrates vsed it: vvho sayth, that in deede he loued Alcybiades extremely, yet not Alcybiades person, but hys soule, vvhich is Alcybiades ovvne selfe. And so is pæderastice much to be præferred before gynerastice, that is the loue vvhiche enflameth men vvith lust tovvard vvoman kind. But yet let no man thinke, that herein I stand vvith Lucian or hys deuelish disciple Vnico Aretino, in defence of execrable and horrible sinnes of forbidden and vnlavvful fleshlinesse. VVhose abominable errour is fully confuted of Perionius, and others.

I loue) a prety Epanorthosis in these tvvo verses, and vvithall a Paronomasia or playing vvith the vvord, vvhere he sayth (I loue thilke lasse (alas &c.

Rosalinde) is also a feigned name, vvhich being wel ordered, vvil bevvray the very name of hys loue and mistresse, vvhom by that name he coloureth. So as Ouide shadoweth hys loue vnder the name of Corynna, vvhich of some is supposed to be
                                                                Iulia

Ianuarie   fol. 3

Iulia, themperor Augustus his daughter, and vvyfe to Agryppa. So doth Aruntius Stella euery where call his Lady Asteris and Ianthis, albe it is vvel knowen that her right name vvas Violantilla: as vvitnesseth Statius in his Epithalamiũ. And so the famous Paragone of Italy, Madonna Cœlia in her letters enuelopeth her selfe vnder the name of Zima: and Petrona vuder the name of Bellochia. And this generally hath bene a common custome of counterfeicting the names of secret Personages.

Auail) bring downe.

Embleme.

Ouerhaile) drawe ouer.
His Embleme or Poesye is here vnder added in Italian, Anchôra speme: the meaning vvherof is, that notvvithstande his extreme passion and lucklesse loue, yet leaning on hope, he is some what recomforted.

Februarie.

Ægloga Secunda.

ARGVMENT.

THis Æglogue is rather morall and generall, then bent to any secrete or particular purpose. It specially conteyueth a discourse of old age, in the persone of Thenot an olde Shepbeard, who for his crookednesse and vnlustinesse, is scorned of Cuddie an vnhappy Heardmans boye. The matter very well accordeth with the season of the moneth, the yeare now drouping, & as it were, drawing to his last age. For as in this time of yeare, so thẽ in our
                A.iii.   bodies

Figure 2.18. Edmund Spenser, *The Shepheardes Calender* (1579), sig. A3v–A3r, Huntington Library

forty-year predictions. At other moments, such as with the glosses of *Shepheardes Calender*'s E.K., the annotations interrupt a totalized reading of the book. A "gloss" could also indicate "a deceptive appearance, fair semblance, plausible pretext" (*OED*, sense 1b), like fair Eliza in April's eclogue, a "seemly" – fair, or *seeming* – "sight" (*OED*, senses 1a and 5b) (sig. Ciiiiv).[34] This sense potentially unsettles the link between glosses' use as visual markers and reminders and an unfalsified, permanent sense of memory in these calendrical texts. E.K.'s annotations invite the reader to toggle between the two spaces of poet and commentator, prohibiting the unified vision or permanent memorial the *Calender*'s epilogue appears to promise: "if I marked well the starres revolution / It shall continewe till the worlds dissolution" (fol. 52, sig. niir). In Spenser's time, "marking well," could in fact mean to observe, prognosticate an omen, memorialize with an object, display a device, impress, and inscribe – collective and ongoing ventures for early modern almanacs' authors, illustrators, printers, and readers.[35] A "mark" could also indicate a "trace" or "vestige," a ruins or remnant from a past material. The *Calender*'s continuity thus depends on its necessarily fragmentary recollection of materials and images.[36] Indeed, this promise of permanence appears in italic script, culturally associated with the written or spoken rather than printed word (Bland 100), visually simulating a readers' trace. As a memorial object and mnemonic space, this *Calender*'s meaning must be (re)collected and gathered from among its woodcuts, glosses, and generic echoes, as readers assemble and add to memory's perpetual disintegrating library with their eyes, hands, and minds.

Chapter Three

Devising the Page: *Poly-olbion's* Troubled Boundaries

Much like the memory spaces of Spenser's *Calender* and the almanac genre, Michael Drayton's *Poly-olbion* (first edition 1612) is an intricate collection of texts and images that invite viewers to co-create their meaning. As Michael Drayton promises in his introductory letter to the reader, *Poly-olbion's* engraved maps, intricate page borders, and detailed portrait of Prince Henry of Wales abundantly display both the technological and rhetorical potential of engraving in English print. *Poly-olbion's* engravings help us "in artificiall caves, cut out of the most naturall Rock," to

> see the ancient people of this Ile delivered thee in their lively images: from whose height thou maist behold both old and later times, as in thy pros-pect, lying farre under thee; then convaying thee downe by a soule-pleasing Descent through delicate embroidered meadowes. (sig. Ar)

Despite its delightful aesthetics and status as Drayton's lifework, *Poly-olbion* failed to stir much interest in its own time.[1] In the nineteenth century, *Poly-olbion* received some attention from antiquarians and liter-ary scholars for its unique poetic text and material attributes. Empha-sis on its poetic text and bibliographical features, however, has more recently given way to an engagement with *Poly-olbion's* historiographi-cal potential as a unique window into seventeenth-century transfor-mations of English landscapes – literary, material, and political. John Kerrigan, Angus Vine, and Alexandra Walsham connect the work to controversies of seventeenth-century English nationhood.[2] *Poly-olbion,* as indicated by its title, portrays the regions of Britain as vital, complex, and conflicted through its imagery and poetic text, a diversity that has led to a recent ecocritical recovery of this visually and intellectually rich text. Sukanya Dasgupta, Andrew McCrae, and Sara Trevisan have recently taken an ecocritical approach to *Poly-olbion*'s object-oriented and even activist depiction of the English landscape in its text and maps.[3] Taken together, these political and ecological readings of what *Poly-olbion*'s title page indicates as a "topo-chrono-graphicall" work thoughtfully connect this work's spatial topography, or survey of the material features of the British landscape, with its temporal chronology, or historiography.

Yet a close analysis of its "graphical" elements – and their troubled recollection of British spaces – has yet to be undertaken. To look at *Poly-olbion*'s maps and visual spaces and to take them seriously is to counter certain critical assumptions about both early modern maps and their inclusion in this book. The idea that printed maps necessarily fixed or codified visual space, an entrenched view since Marshall McLuhan's argument of print's hegemony and fixity in his analysis of *King Lear*'s map, unduly influences current analyses of *Poly-olbion*'s own diverse spaces.[4] As Benedict Anderson, Helen Smith, and Brian Stock observe, seeing space translated to reading space during the production of early modern print maps (Smith 25); reading implies interpretation, playfulness, complexity. In visual print texts, graphical elements and printer's devices forged a system of navigation, as they acted as markers, symbols, and gateways for readers (Smith 25–7; Fleming 57–8). While Vine situates *Poly-olbion*'s visual materials as important elements of its "polyphony" (171), he still privileges Drayton's poetic text in the bulk of his analysis. As Drayton puts forth in his letter to readers, however, "lively images" actively populate and interfuse his text. This chapter will give equal interpretive weight to *Poly-olbion*'s visual composition – particularly its engraved maps and woodcut designs – as its poetic text. As Helen Smith and Louise Wilson contend in their introduction to *Renaissance Paratexts*, it is such so-called paratextual elements that actually make a book what it is (4). While we may be able to safely assume collaboration among Michael Drayton, John Selden, and William Hole for the book's poetry, annotations, and engravings respectively, paratextual elements such as *Poly-olbion*'s woodcut borders, which I will discuss at length in this chapter, would have been produced by craftsmen and compiled by printers in a collaborative setting. We cannot know whether the arrangement and style of such features was fully intentional. Nevertheless, I argue that these elements are crucial for an understanding of the work's total composition and meaning.

I am here less interested in authorial intentionality, or whether Drayton or Selden commissioned each visual element, than in the potential co-creation of meaning between the visual interfaces of this text and the reader. I will therefore explore several interpretive possibilities for *Poly-olbion*'s visual paratexts, with the caveat that there are certainly more potential meanings than I have set forward. In a work that consciously sets up vision as an episteme and controversy, it is valuable to fully explore the potential of these visual features.

Such elements in *Poly-olbion* construct its meaning and the process of visual-verbal interpretation the work sets forth. As the previous chapters outline, the process of beholding and becoming moved (or, as Drayton puts it, "convayed") by images was a crucial component of invention, or recollection, in classical and early modern rhetoric.[5] Peter Mack ties the classical theory that "the cultivation of *fantasiai* or visions was an essential aid to manipulating the emotions" in a rhetorical situation ("Early Modern Ideas of Imagination" 59) to the early modern practice of enargeia, or a vital, visual description (63). Mack comments on the sheer frequency of discourse surrounding images and the imagination in sixteenth-century pedagogy (69). Although Sidney and other early modern poets do not frequently use the term fantasy/phantasia, Mack observes that Sidney uses the term "invention" where we might expect "imagination" (70). Mack concludes that invention might "share tasks" with the cognitive faculty of imagination in early modern rhetoric and phenomenology (70).[6] Heinrich F. Plett connects the method of enargeia to the imagination as well, a technique shared by both poets and rhetoricians as a "means to create a fictive world" (25).[7] *Poly-olbion* draws from the classical method of epideictic rhetoric that Catherine Hobbs posits as an innately visual rhetoric. In particular, *Poly-olbion*'s ornate poetic descriptions and elaborately crafted visual images of the English landscape evoke classical topographies. In Roman antiquity, epideictic oratory became "especially important" after Virgil's Arcadian eclogues: epideictic descriptions were "filled with pleasurable topography (*topoi*) such as springs, hills, and animals" (Hobbs 31). *Poly-olbion*'s material structure and Drayton's message to the reader underscore this book's status as a shared space for visual invention: this book's images guide readers through *Poly-olbion*'s many locations, where readers are called upon to behold, imagine, invent, and (re)collect Albion.

The collective vision of *Poly-olbion* paradoxically (and problematically) relies on negative material and visual space: these negative spaces are crucial to an interpretation of *Poly-olbion*'s mutable borders.

On its maps, the negative spaces of oceans and rivers define and divide political and topographical regions, just as the processes of woodcut and engraving used to create these maps carve out images from blank material. The visual interface of *Poly-olbion*, like Spenser's *Shepheardes Calender*, invites an oscillation between whole and part, totality and multiplicity. Yet this divided sight is even more consciously represented as an epistemic crisis in *Poly-olbion*. As Plett explains, the practice of enargeia itself paradoxically emphasizes part over whole, detail over message, to more effectively move the listener: "the unified whole (*totum*) of an utterance is less relevant than the multiplicity of its parts (*omnia*), because only the latter make the subject of description directly palpable (*manifesta*)" (9). In *Poly-olbion*, the lively and co-created spaces of its maps, page borders, and introductory engraving form conspicuously troubled boundaries. In *Poly-olbion*, the act of devising, or inventing/devicing, British space incurs a concurrent poetics/politics of division.

This constant movement between a unified and divided space parallels the interwoven relationship of memory and invention in early modern culture. As I discussed in my reading of the *Shepheardes Calender*, memory, or the collection of phrases, ideas, and images, was closely related to invention, or the re-assembly of these stored items for a particular context. This dynamic relationship pervaded early modern theories of cognition, in addition to rhetoric. In his *Anatomy of Melancholy*, Robert Burton distinguishes the outer (five) senses from the inner senses, "three in number": "common sense, phantasie," and "memory" (152). The three inner senses retain and interpret the sense data received from the five external senses (158). Memory, invention, and judgment combine in Burton's theory of the mind to create human cognitive perception. These three inner senses, each with a different location in the brain, coordinate to give us our powers of apprehension, by which we "perceive the Species of Sensible things present, or absent, and retaine them as waxe doth the print of a Seale" (150). These three inner senses allow cognition to range backward and forward in time in the absence of external sense data. Burton gives cognitive perception the metaphor of imprinting or impression, a metaphor drawn in part from Plato's discussion of memory in *Theaetetus*. Memory is fundamentally visual yet fragile in Plato's metaphor of memory as wax impression: "whatever is imprinted, we remember and know, as long as its image is present: but whatever is smudged out or proves unable to be imprinted, we've forgotten and don't know" (78). With this metaphor of impressed images in mind, *Poly-olbion*'s own graphical imprints are a crucial way of remembering, inventing, and perceiving British space.

The connection between memory and invention at the time of *Poly-olbion*'s publication was not limited to cognitive or rhetorical theory. Rhonda Sanford, citing Castiglione, argues that maps themselves functioned as memory aids and spatially represented mnemonic *loci* (18–22). Further, the technologies of measuring space in the practices of land surveying and map making were the same technologies used to measure time in astronomical observations, observations that would make their way to the memory places of print almanacs. These shared technologies, popularized in sixteenth century "teaching manuals," included "the magnetic compass, the plane table, the ephemerides, and the surveyors' assistants" (Lindgren 492). These tools helped the astronomer, cartographer, and surveyor to draw and calculate angles. Angle measurements allowed the landscape and the heavens to become geometrically divided and spatially represented on the visual page.

The division of space and the impression of images were crucial to visual representation in print. Visual illustrations in print production relied on two primary methods: woodcut impression and intaglio engravings, usually on copper plates. *Poly-olbion*'s woodcut page borders, as they divide and arrange the different sections of its text, employ negative spaces as visual and perceptual boundaries, or *aporia*. Drayton's specific description of embroidered meadows and his promise to the reader to "see the ancient people of this Ile delivered thee in their lively images" "in artificiall caves, cut out of the most naturall Rock" evokes through the figure of "cutting" the technology of print illustrations (sig. A.r). To produce a woodcut image, such as those of *Poly-olbion*'s page and section borders, a specialized craftsman, often working with a template, cuts away wood from a block. This relief block is then set against and impressed on the page. The resulting image is actually a negative (artificial) space of the image cut upon a natural object (wood). In other words, woodcut impression, the type of image prominent in *Poly-olbion*'s page borders and decorative initials, is inherently based on negative space: an artificial image, like Drayton's cave images, "cut out" from natural material. The image that would result from print in the hand-press period would be the reverse of the original block. Similarly, regarding the "lively images" of the woodblock's artificial carvings, it was the belief in early modern medicine that the eye would reverse and receive a "negative" of the object of sight, which the mind then sets aright. In a woodcut, the press itself performs the same operation.

Intaglio copper engravings make up *Poly-olbion*'s maps and its elaborate portrait of Henry Frederick Stuart, the Prince of Wales and older brother to Charles I. In the intaglio techniques that shape engraved print images, an engraver cuts an incision into the surface. The ink then sits on top of the incisions; the paper picks up the excess ink to form the printed impression. The original engraving, like a woodcut, is a "mirror image" or negative of the final print illustration. In general, a woodcut results in a simpler, more iconic image: a carving in a rock. Intaglio copper engravings, in Drayton's era, were becoming technically more advanced, to the point where an artful engraving may just resemble delicate embroidery. Drayton's description of readers who behold lively images and navigate their way to embroidered meadows sets forth the material features of the land and the page of Albion, and their reader's visual perception of these images, as vital and infinitely diverse.

This interaction of the reader with the visual elements of *Poly-olbion*'s print illustrations and epideictic poetry is troubled by the complex relationship between sight and perception in classical and early modern thought. Drayton's language of images beheld in artificial caves recalls Plato's famous allegory of cave dwellers who see only artificial, mediated, and shadowy reflections of true forms on rocky walls. Drayton's potential allusion to the Platonic cave points to a treatment of visual representations as flawed, derivative, "artificial" images that delude viewers. John Selden, whose annotative comments in *Poly-olbion*'s margins are called "illustrations" in the text, expresses scepticism towards both vision and recollection. In his own letter to the reader, he remarks, "nor can any conversant in letters bee ignorant what error is oftimes fallen into, by trusting Authorities at second hand, and rash collecting (as it were) from visuall beam's [sic] refracted through another's eye" (sig. A3.v). This description of sight as a shadowy impression or secondhand refraction and historiography as a "rash collecting" from unreliable authorities expresses scepticism towards the entire project of *Poly-olbion*, with its emphasis on historiographical recollection and visual inventiveness. Selden's mistrust of "refraction" parallels Stuart Clark's discussion of visual refractions as simulacra or phantoms in the seventeenth-century imagination (292–3). Paradoxically, visual perception was described as a process of multiple refractions in early modern medical and phenomenal texts, such as the works of Helkiah Crooke and Ambroise Paré (Clark 19). Selden therefore expresses mistrust towards the very act of looking and reading as a recollective process, a scepticism that undermines the antiquarian project of *Poly-olbion* itself. In her discussion of early modern maps, Sanford observes that the terminology and concept of the visual "spectacle" "was also used or implied in titles of maps such as Norden's *Speculum Britanniae,* and works about surveying such as William Cuningham's *The Cosmographical Glass* (1559)" (60). This metaphor of the map as spectacle, while implying a totalizing reflection of the world, in Selden's letter implies constant visual division. To continue Selden's metaphor of visual refraction, what we see on *Poly-olbion*'s printed maps may be a continuously mediated, fragmented vision, refracted by secondhand accounts and dubious memories. The interwoven yet troubled connection between memory and sight runs as an aporia, or uncertain boundary, through *Poly-olbion*'s textual matter, maps, page borders, and dedicatory engraving.

Murky Waters: The Contested Borders of *Poly-olbion*'s Engraved Maps

Selden's description of a refracted, divided gaze is made visible in *Poly-olbion*'s first map (Figure 3.1).

In this map of Cornwall, Britain's external borders are unified and limned by the sea, yet its internal boundaries divide the reader's vision. Tiny figures of spirits and nymphs populate Cornwall's rivers and regions, as their physical gestures pull the eye towards different focal points. The visually descriptive epideictic rhetoric of Drayton's poetic text is already rich with images of Albion's multiplicity. Song One begins, "Of *Albions* glorious Ile the Wonders whilst I write / The sundry varying soyles, the pleasures infinite" (sig. B.r). This epideictic song is further complicated by its map's competing deictic figures, which literally point in altogether different directions, dividing our visual attention. The rivers, forests, mountains, and streams are inhabited by nymphs and spirits, whose pointing fingers and arms in this map indicate conflicting directions and aims. With its many nymphs who inhabit sundry rivers and streams, the overall visual impression of this map is of the waters' circulation through space; generally, the nymphs' arms and hands mirror the flowing tides between the rivers and the sea.

Alongside the visually striking nature of Cornwall's deictic spirits, it was also perhaps conspicuous to early modern readers that *Poly-olbion*'s first map is that of Cornwall, part of the so-called Celtic fringe, rather than the more spatially and politically central space of southern England or London. Different regional aims, symbolized by the myriad river nymphs, conflict with the sense of British unity established by the

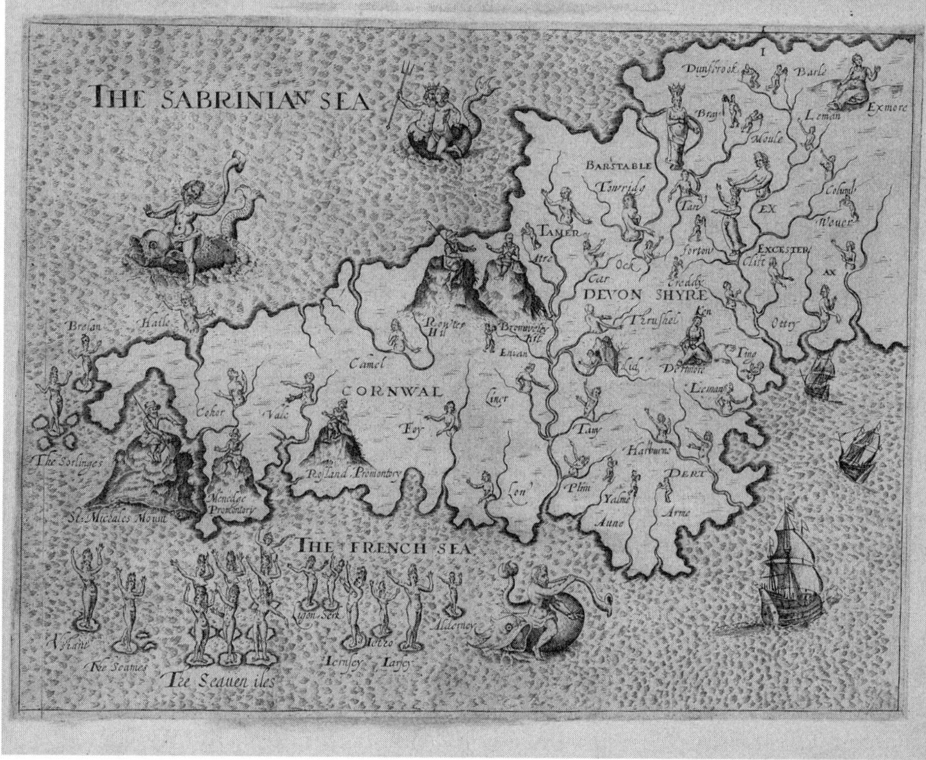

Figure 3.1. Michael Drayton, *Poly-Olbion* (1622), sig. A4v–A4r, Bodleian Library

oceanic images of *Poly-olbion*'s frontispiece (Figure 3.2), where the portrait of "Great Britannia" shows a female figure of Britain wearing a map of its lands, with the sea to her background.

In Cornwall's map, visual perspective is subjective and variable, and the seemingly unified space of mapped topography becomes both epistemically and visually divided. Following McLuhan's theoretical assumption of visual unity within early modern maps and early modern culture, Bernard Klein claims that *Poly-olbion*'s maps create a unified, utopic vision of "Albion," as "attempts to capture in mythological imagery an eternal and original truth about land" (158). In Klein's view, the unified, eternal vision of *Poly-olbion*'s maps opposes the more complex text of its songs, which portray a "historical reality of continuous political factionalism" (158). According to this framework, the visual

Figure 3.2. Michael Drayton, *Poly-Olbion* (1622), frontispiece, Bodleian Library

aspects of *Poly-olbion* are more simple, constructive, and unified, a "project of national synthesis based on cartographic homogenization," while the poems remain complex, deconstructive, and fragmented (158).

This reading of *Poly-olbion* privileges a sensibility towards the visual that assumes sight to be a simple matter of immediate sense perception and the visual image or icon to be totalizing – a far simpler perspective on the relationship between memory, invention, and sight than I argue to be the case in early modern culture. David Woodward, a contemporary cartographic scholar, traces the multiplicity of early modern printed maps' spatial features and technological practices. He recounts that early modern print maps incorporated both engraving and woodcut, in addition to both typography and manuscript lettering. He argues that printing did not standardize maps' spatial representations as much as might be expected, but rather the main effect of early print on maps was to popularize their use in the late sixteenth and early seventeenth centuries (610). In contrast, Stephen Speed contends for a more nostalgic and unified reading of both text and map in *Poly-olbion*. Speed claims that "Drayton wants to keep Britain as it is" and is reluctant to question "finality and authenticity" (123). In Speed's reading, Drayton divides Britain to reclaim or invent a past totality.

Drayton often casts as much doubt on the chorographic text's memorializing project as Selden does on secondhand visual beams.[8] The reading of *Poly-olbion* as a nostalgic text leads Speed to claim that the lively, deictic figures on its maps are mere "byproducts of cartography," totalized and harmonious figurations of an ideal landscape (124). If we look at the map of Cornwall, however, we see that the visual deixis of Drayton's map and nymphs prompt us to divide our attention between different regions and to choose how to navigate this divided space. This reading of the divided visual attention invited by Cornwall's maps draws from Angus Vine's argument that *Poly-olbion* emphasizes "polyphony" (or multiplicity) and "incompleteness" in its visual and material structures, "as the reader's gaze shifts back and forth from text block to margin, and also from song to song" (193). As Vine observes, the maps of this book often depart from the text itself, enjoining readers to closely look at them as competing regions of a varied whole (194). This co-creation and co-division of space invites the reader to try to visually manoeuvre between competing regional aims.

Even Vine's reading of the playful aesthetic "circularity" of the visual reading process in this text (193), however, in part belies the serious political and historical conflicts that *Poly-olbion*'s visual boundaries represent. For example, its map of the England-Wales border (Figure 3.3),

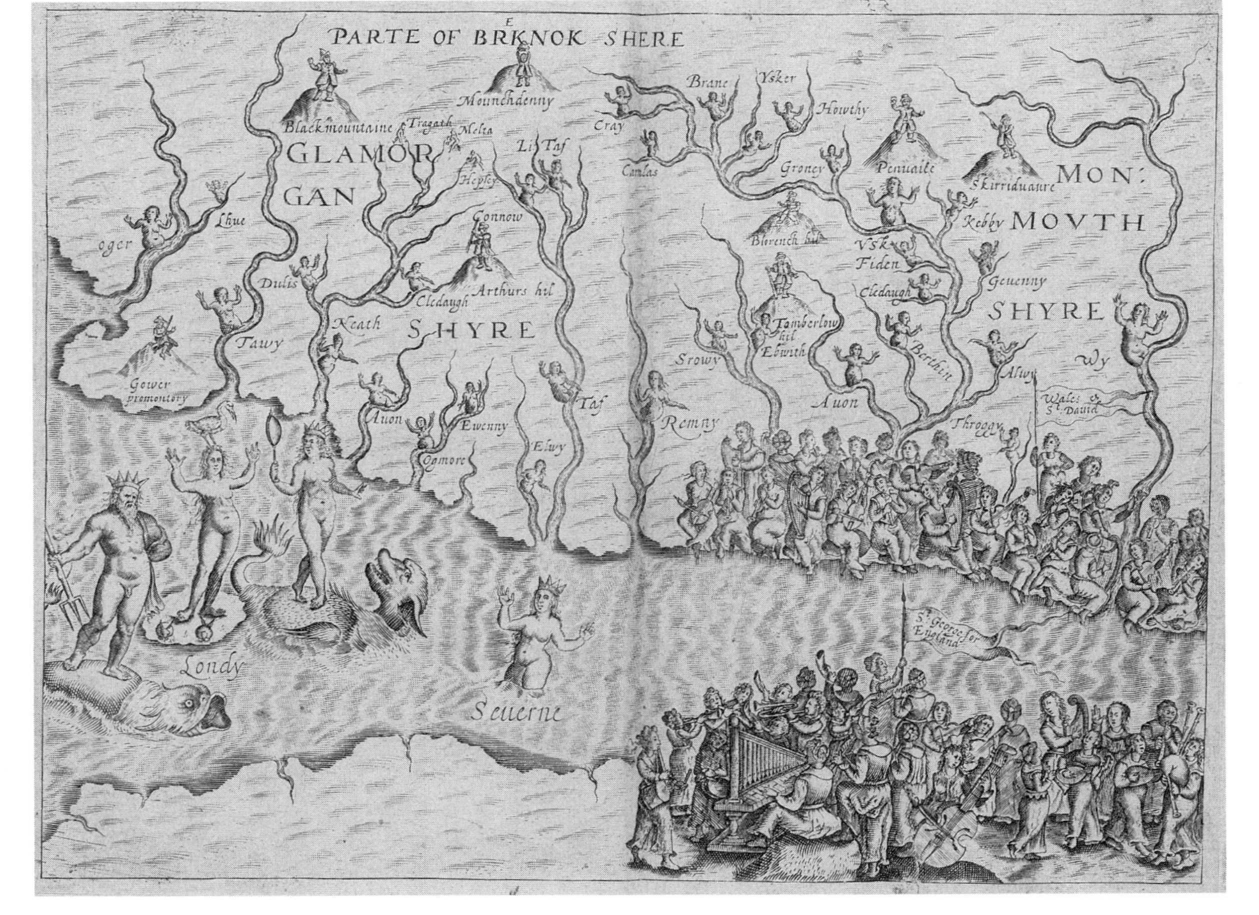

Figure 3.3. Michael Drayton, *Poly-Olbion* (1622), page 55, Bodleian Library

prefacing Song Four, surpasses the competing deictic signals of Cornwall's map to depict outright regional conflict (sig. F3).

The nymphs of the two lands contend over the River Lundy, whose spirit is personified as a nymph with her arms outspread, as if to judge and weigh the dispute. The two "camps" of nymphs, for England and for Wales, are divided by the River Severn and the Lundy (both an island and sea area), a historically contested border between the two regions. Drayton frames this dispute as fundamentally aesthetic as well as political: the battling nymphs sing or play a musical instrument. One nymph from each side holds a flag: "St. George for England" on England's side, "Wales & St. David" on the Welsh. Song Four's corresponding poetic text enacts a bardic, historiographical contest between the glories of the British, Celtic King Arthur and those of a particularly "Saxon" or English cultural memory. The Welsh "marches," or mountain-men as they are portrayed on the map, take an even more aggressive, warlike stance towards England than the musically competitive nymphs: the figures of the mountains Blackmountaine, Mounchdenny, and Penuaile hold up rocks, ready to pummel the English nymphs away from the Lundy. Philip Schwyzer argues that national consciousness moved from an Elizabethan identification with British history and Welsh mythology, due to the connection of the Tudor line to Wales, to an emergently English sense in the seventeenth century (173). *Poly-olbion*'s publication in the early seventeenth century situated its spatial and historical border disputes within a context where both senses of national identity were in competition.

The concept that the geographical, spatial features of the land itself may represent a contested historical memory is not unique to *Poly-olbion* but pervaded early modern cultural perceptions of visual space. In the *Reformation of the Landscape*, Alexandra Walsham discusses the specifically spatial and ecological politics of early modern religious upheaval. For instance, Rogationtide or "beating of the bounds" processions during Ascension week became a controversial marker of visual and ecological space. In these yearly rituals, priests (and later, Anglican ministers) blessed the fields and villagers "beat the bounds," perambulating through landscape boundaries and local landmarks, such as "ditches, at springs and over prominent stones" (256). These perambulations effectively operated as memorized, walkable maps for communities that did not historically have access to visual maps. This practice was both controversial to some Reformers as an idolatrous superstition and preserved by others, including Elizabeth I, as a tradition with practical value for impressing local boundaries on the minds of community members (252–6).[9] In such controversial border rituals, landscape spaces became "sites of contention" over religious ideology and historical memory (260). Walsham argues that early modern concepts of the past were significantly "shaped by the visible world": "historical consciousness was intimately connected with topography," and "space rather than time often provided the most significant fillip to the task of remembering" (7). The visual materials of the landscape provided a collective yet conflicting storehouse of historical memory. As Drayton characterizes the song of the Welsh nymphs in his poetic text, "To tell each various Straine and turning of their Rimes," "Even Memorie her selfe, though striving, would come up short: / But the materiall things Muse help me to report" (sig. F.iiiiv). Drayton here substitutes the visual materials of the landscape for Memory's ability to capture song.

Recent ecocritical approaches to *Poly-olbion* attempt to situate the vivid figuration of its landscape features alongside seventeenth-century Britain's ecological crisis and transformation. Sukanya Dasgupta emphasizes the "near-complete absence of human characters" in this text, as Albion's topographical features "become the most articulate local historians who recollect the past but also prophesy the future" (160–1). *Poly-olbion*'s visual and ecological spaces serve as active visual imagines/loci in a dynamic, conflicted process of memorial recollection. Ecological readings, such as Dasgupta's analysis of *Poly-olbion*'s enchanted ecological materials and Andrew McCrae's specific contextualization of Drayton's description of tree felling with seventeenth-century debates about deforestation, focus on *Poly-olbion*'s figuration of the land.[10]

Yet as the book's oceanic frontispiece, the population of its rivers and streams with nymphs, and the specific contest over the River Lundy as a crucial boundary in book four demonstrate, watery spaces become perhaps the most dominant and uneasy visual borders of *Poly-olbion*'s maps and texts.[11] The watery boundaries of *Poly-olbion*'s streams, rivers, and seas are literally and conceptually fluid. As with the contested river Lundy in Song Four, water forms and divides the regional spaces of Albion, even as water is an innately negative visual space, a not-Britain, that sets off these maps' topographical features. The watery ocean surrounds Britain as a unified island, an "office of a wall" or "moat defensive" in John of Gaunt's famous description of "this blessed plot, this earth, this realm, this England" (*Richard II* 2.1.47–8; 50). Yet watery rivers and streams divide *Poly-olbion*'s different mapped regions.

Poly-olbion's watery boundaries, as divisive, negative, yet productive spaces, are overdetermined by their illustration techniques. As described earlier, to create an intaglio engraving, such as these illustrated maps, a copper plate would first need to be etched in with incisions and grooves, then covered with ink. This liquid ink would fill the grooves of the plate and become imprinted on the page by the pressure of the press. In other words, a liquid (ink) filled in the negative, engraved lines of a plate to produce the mapped, impressed images of *Poly-olbion*. Like the watery rivers and seas that fill this text's images of Albion, the negative, inky, engraved spaces of the plate both divide the space of the material and produce the resulting image. Moreover, the process of boundary drawing in cartography was historically and materially associated with print engraving: engraving and maritime navigation shared tools and techniques by the seventeenth century. Katherine Acheson outlines naval technology's relationship to drawing and engraving techniques. Both relied on "the same sort of instruments and knowledge of geometry" (93); for instance, the "sector" that allowed for lines to be measured and divided proportionally in "surveying, navigation, and drawing" (96). Again, the process of dividing regions and spaces is a process of devising/device-ing them.

Poly-olbion's oceanic divisions and devices are also tied to Britain's status as an island, as well as the troubled status of its archipelagic marginal spaces, from Ireland to Cornwall. Song Four's contest over the Lundy, as well as the sheer multiplicity of embodied waters throughout this book's maps, may be situated within the seventeenth-century spatial-political context of what John Kerrigan calls "archipelagic" British identity: an identity that lends itself to the sea's centrality of the sea in Britain's (divided) national consciousness. "Stuart writing," Kerrigan notes, "is full of islands" (49). As he details, "the standard route from Edinburgh (Leith) to London was through coastal waters, not along horseback on difficult roads" (48). Drayton's description of the river Severn's course reflects the unifying, yet divisive nature of Britain's watery boundaries:

> *Severne* finds no Flood so great, nor poorelie meane,
> But that the naturall spring (her force which doth maintaine)
> From this or that shee takes; so from this Faction free
> (Begun about this Ile) not one was like to bee.   (sig. F.iiiir)

In this passage, the river Severn's powerfully accumulative – even collective – nature also entrenches its regional factionalism. This characterization of the Severn dramatically contrasts with Milton's later depiction of the Severn as a nymph, "Sabrina fair," who rescues a besieged Lady in his *Comus* (859). In Milton's masque, this river nymph is a daughter of Locrine and a descendant of Brutus, the mythic Trojan founder of Britain. Sabrina is invoked in "In name of great Oceanus, / By the earth-shaking Neptune's mace" (868–9). The Severn's Trojan and oceanic allusions, in Milton's *Comus,* represent a far more mythological and unified Britishness than in Drayton. In Drayton's Song Four, the Severn's watery fluidity creates tension among the regions it runs through. As accumulative, yet divisive spaces, the personified "bodies of water" on *Poly-olbion*'s maps both re-member and dis-member Britain.

Drayton's project presents itself, spatially and rhetorically, as a sort of memory chambers, a storage house of collected regional histories from which to invent ("from this or that") the idea of a manifold Albion. At the book's outset, however, Drayton appears to treat *Poly-olbion*'s own accumulative project of material (re)collection with considerable uncertainty. In his letter to the reader, Drayton laments that

> [i]n publishing this Essay of my Poeme, there is this great disadvantage against me; that it commeth out at this time, when verses are wholly deduc't to Chambers, and nothing esteem'd in this lunatique Age, but what is kept in cabinets, and must only passe by Transcription; In such a season, when the Idle, Humorous world must have of Nothing, that ... savors of Antiquity. (sig. A)

One of the first visual-material spaces Drayton refers to, then, is that of a manuscript in his reference to transcription. Scepticism of the written text, and the (re)collection of an alternative history through oral, bardic memory, recur throughout this book. The parallel between "chambers" and "cabinets" in Drayton's letter also seems to invoke a private reading space or library in a household, an escritoire or writing desk, or, perhaps, a curiosity cabinet filled with collected relics and written records for a spectator to peruse. The reduction of poetic "verses" to a linear, private exposition in a chamber hints at an anxiety that a private memory wholly dependent on "transcription" via text will be the private property of a little room rather than a living, shared public memory, as the library or study walls close in on his book. He appears to mistrust the written book's ability to transmit a true sense of British identity or history. However, the reference to manuscript practice also blurs with allusions to print culture, specifically visual print culture, in this passage. The allusion to "chambers" and "cabinets" plays on his own advertisement of "antiquities" for the general, "idle" reader to draw from in his printed book. "Chambers" in a house or room of course also recall early modern association of castles, rooms, and libraries with memory spaces. Indeed, the situation of memorized material and visual objects in various rooms and nooks of a house places print culture on a continuum with classical memory and invention practices. As historical antiquities fill the mind of the listener, literal books (such as Drayton's) fill up a room or curio. Drayton's chambers, however, negatively operate as a private space rather than as a location for a public memory of historical "antiquity."

This concept of "chambers" as spatial and mnemonic boundaries may also draw from the specifically oceanic meaning of the term "chambers" as a watery boundary in the early seventeenth century. In the years directly prior to *Poly-olbion*'s publication, King James I broke with the Elizabethan policy of *mare liberum*, or the freedom of the seas. This policy left the seas around England and Wales free for international travel and trade, whereas *mare clausum*, or enclosed seas, was a policy favoured by James I as an establishment of maritime territorial sovereignty (Fulton 118). On 4 March 1604, thirteen men were commissioned under the "Court of Admiraltie" to "set downe the bounds and limits, how farre the Kings Chambers, havens, or ports, on the Sea coasts do extend." The pamphlet that lists these borders, *A Note of the Head-Lands of England* (Figure 3.4), represents the coasts of England and Wales as a primary and defining topographical boundary of the Jacobean state.

With a compass placed towards the upper middle of the page, its lines radiating out through the island, and a large blackletter label, "England," spread across the represented spaces of England, Wales, and the Scottish lowlands, empirical cartography accompanies imperial expansion in this map, both across the lands of Wales/Scotland and previously international waters. The spatial boundaries and "headlands" that make up this geographical representation of "England," determined by James's maritime "cabinet," would be termed the "King's Chambers" for another couple of centuries, as if the whole island territory of Britain were the sovereign's household, and, by extension, its coasts and ports his own private rooms. Drayton's "verses deduced to chambers" may parallel his book's descriptions and mapped illustrations of Albion's watery spaces. *Poly-olbion*'s illustrator John Selden later wrote a defence of territorial seas, *Mare Clausum* (1635), which contains a very similar illustration of "Anglia's" "chambers" and headlands, with the local coasts and ports of England and Wales labelled in a striking visual parallel to the 1604 pamphlet (Figure 3.5).[12]

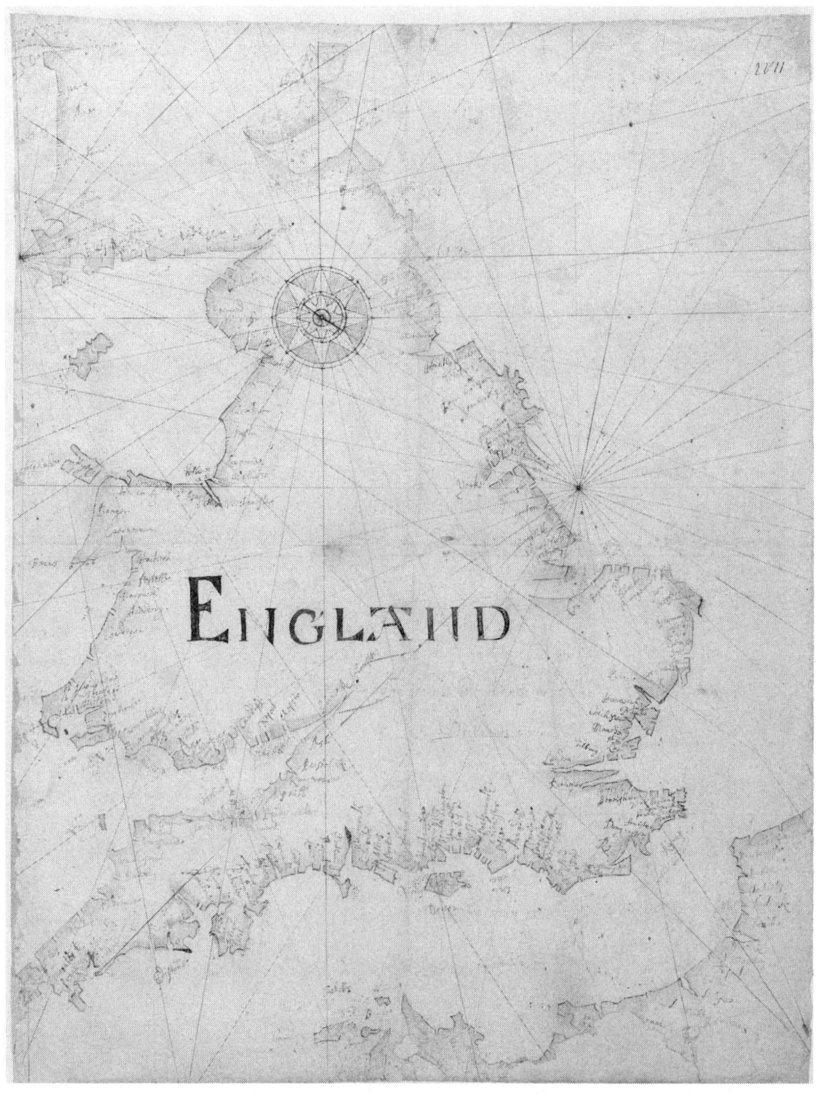

Figure 3.4. Anon., *A note of the head-lands of England [as] they [beare] one from another …* (1605), second page, Bodleian Library

Figure 3.5. John Selden, *Mare Clausum* (1635), page 239, British Library

Print affords the mass reproduction of this particular image of "England," one which *Poly-olbion*'s collaborating "illustrator" John Selden would later imitate. Yet Drayton expresses doubt with a transcription of Britain to political "chambers" as a legal document and charted map alone.[13] The watery boundaries of the king's oceanic chambers incur a political and epistemic problem: how far do these fluid boundaries expand and how can these limits be set or known?

Memory's Limits: The Page Borders of *Poly-olbion*

Poly-olbion's decorative page borders serve to further complicate this text's thematic concern with the fluid, mutable boundaries that define/divide its spaces. Unlike the book's copper-engraved maps, the page borders are created from carved woodcut blocks. Woodcut page borders often appear to be merely ornamental in early modern books. In print production, these decorated blocks were often recycled and placed at random several times in the course of one book, then reused later in different books produced by the same printer.[14] By contrast, copper engravings such as *Poly-olbion*'s maps tended to be more "bespoke." They advertised their importance and expense: it was difficult, if not impossible, to create a copper engraving on the same page as a text. Some printers even created faux-copper engravings by printing detailed woodcuts on an opposite page from the printed text. The greater ephemerality and reuse of woodcuts lends the decorated borders on the pages of *Poly-olbion* a sense of mannerism and play, where their placement and design suggest – but do not solidify – a meaningful "framework" for the book's sections.

In a text that overwhelmingly focuses on conflicting spatial and regional boundaries, however, the visual design of *Poly-olbion*'s woodcut borders should not be neglected. In his discussion of early modern English map making, Peter Barber tracks engraved print maps of the late sixteenth century. These maps featured elaborate decorations and came from Flemish mapmakers to London (1659). "The most striking feature" of these maps was "their border decoration" which often conveyed "sociopolitical messages": the print maps themselves would often be "derivative" copies of previous maps, whereas their borders would be original to the engraver or printer (1659).

Border marginalia on print maps produced spaces that would feature significant aesthetic novelty and social meaning for late sixteenth and early seventeenth-century readers. As a book filled with engraved maps and border concerns, *Poly-olbion*'s page borders help to structure the reader's interpretation and visual-material experience of the entire work. Most of *Poly-olbion*'s page borders have arabesque (flowing and curling lines), flora (flower/plant), and fauna (animal) designs. In addition, they often feature a circular "IHS" (the monograph that figures Christ) appearing in their centre or the Hebrew script of "Yahweh" (the Hebrew name for the Judeo-Christian God). The inclusion of religious symbolism creates material boundaries that signal a spiritual meaning beyond the boundaries of the page. *Poly-olbion*'s first border includes this Hebrew script, in addition to winged armillary spheres that frame it on either side (Figure 3.6).

As round structures topped with crosses, these spheres visually imitate the Sovereign's Orb, a component of traditional British royal regalia that signifies Christian (and monarchical) dominion. Armillary spheres represent lines of latitude and longitude on a globe and could be used to measure geographic distance, to measure time, and to make astronomical calculations. They could symbolically represent wisdom as well as global dominion. Peter Barber observes that Elizabeth I wears a "jeweled armillary sphere" as an earring in her Ditchley portrait, where she stands over a map of England, as a symbol of her "mastery over nature" (1665).

Poly-olbion's combination of a page border featuring winged armillary spheres and a frontispiece of a personified female "Albion" framed by the ocean perhaps draws from this Elizabethan iconography, in addition to the sea and armillary sphere's associations with naval dominance. The armillary spheres of this page border are also winged with feathers. Even as they establish a reference to the spatial boundaries of maritime and landscape navigation, these spheres' wings may also suggest an extension or expansion beyond navigational or even visual page borders.

While *Poly-olbion*'s different page borders repeat the devices of Hebrew script, arabesque designs, hearts, flowers, and birds, the winged armillary sphere on a border design reappears only once more in the text of its first edition. These spheres recur before *Poly-olbion*'s third song, which warns us, "In this third song, great threatenings are / tending all to Nymphish war":

Cleere Avon and faire Willy strive,
Each pleading her prerogative.
The Plaine the Forrests doth distaine:
The Forrests raile upon the Plaine.   (sig. E2, Figure 3.8)

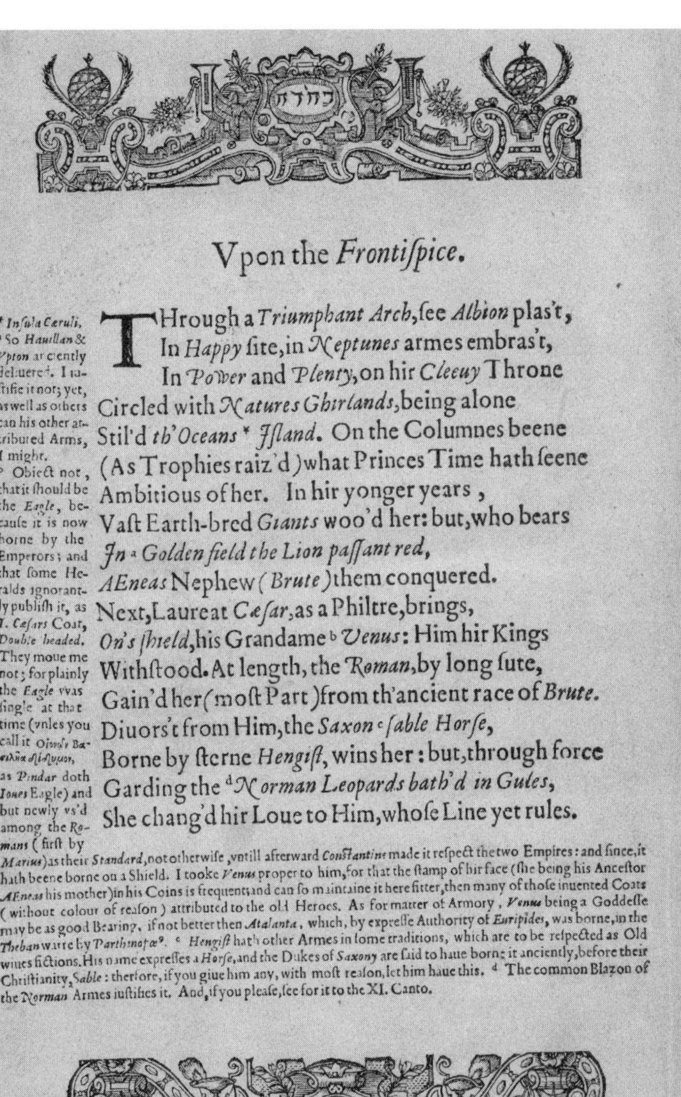

Figure 3.6. Michael Drayton, *Poly-Olbion* (1622), poem adjoining frontispiece, Bodleian Library

Figure 3.7. Ditchley Portrait, National Portrait Gallery

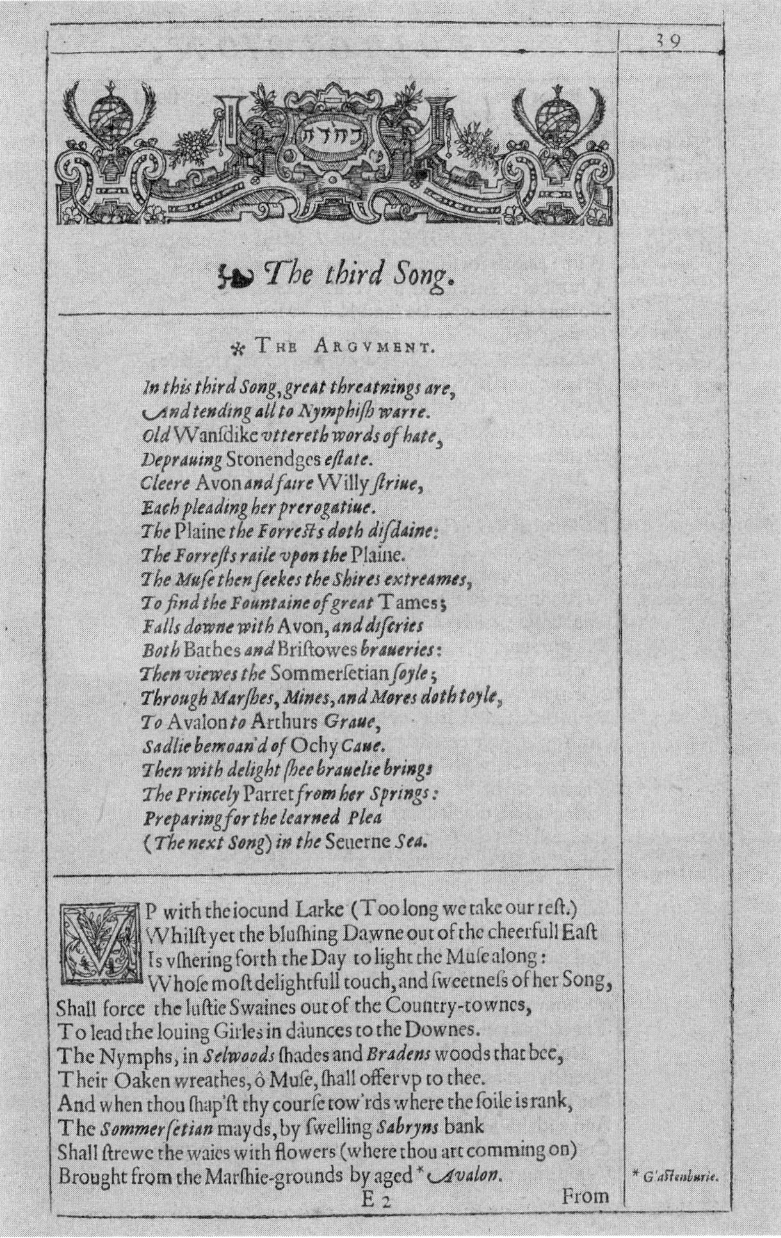

The third Song.

* THE ARGVMENT.

In this third Song, great threatnings are,
And tending all to Nymphish warre.
Old Wansdike *vttereth words of hate,*
Deprauing Stonendges *estate.*
Cleere Avon *and faire* Willy *striue,*
Each pleading her prerogatiue.
The Plaine *the* Forrests *doth disdaine:*
The Forrests *raile vpon the* Plaine.
The Muse then seekes the Shires extreames,
To find the Fountaine of great Tames;
Falls downe with Avon, *and discries*
Both Bathes *and* Bristowes *braueries:*
Then viewes the Sommersetian *soyle;*
Through Marshes, Mines, and Mores doth toyle,
To Avalon *to* Arthurs *Graue,*
Sadlie bemoan'd of Ochy Caue.
Then with delight shee brauelie brings
The Princely Parret *from her Springs:*
Preparing for the learned Plea
(*The next Song*) *in the* Seuerne Sea.

VP with the iocund Larke (Too long we take our rest.)
Whilst yet the blushing Dawne out of the cheerfull East
Is vshering forth the Day to light the Muse along:
Whose most delightfull touch, and sweetnes of her Song,
Shall force the lustie Swaines out of the Country-townes,
To lead the louing Girles in daunces to the Downes.
The Nymphs, in *Selwoods* shades and *Bradens* woods that bee,
Their Oaken wreathes, ô Muse, shall offer vp to thee.
And when thou shap'st thy course tow'rds where the soile is rank,
The *Sommersetian* mayds, by swelling *Sabryns* bank
Shall strewe the waies with flowers (where thou art comming on)
Brought from the Marshie-grounds by aged * *Avalon.*

* *Glastenburie.*

E 2   From

Figure 3.8. Michael Drayton, *Poly-Olbion* (1622), page 39, Bodleian Library

The song thus begins with a cacophony of divided, competing regions, even as the winged spheres appear to signify dominion or transcendence over material boundaries. This song portrays Salisbury plain as a literal and figurative battlefield for contested claims to the throne (such as the Celtic King Arthur and the invading Saxons) and claims to historical memory. While the stories and monuments of King Arthur, Avalon, and Stonehenge figure as unifying and "once and future" (continuously remembered and reinvented) British mythologies, the land of Salisbury itself bears a conflicted material memory. As the nymph of Salisbury plain details, there is "not a foughten Field, / Where Kingdoms rights have laine upon the speare and shield, / But *Plaines* have been the place; And all those Trophies hie/ That ancient times have rear'd to noble memorie" (sig. E3.v). The land itself carries the memories and monuments (trophies) of conquest, as Drayton depicts the contested nature of the plain through turmoil between the rivers Willy and Avon. This section, however, soon settles into harmony as the Parret River gathers strength and flows down to "Arthurs ancient seat," "where as at Carlion, oft, hee kept the Table-Round" (sig. E4.v). The Parret River grows in strength, "wallowing in excesse, / Whilst like a Prince she vaunts amid the watery presse" (sig. Fr). This description looks back to a mythical Arthurian Britain: the connection between the round table and maritime sovereignty via a pax Britannia, envisioned by James I, illustrates a harmonious, united England with its power based on water. An imperial monarchy based on the ocean, rather than the land, neutralizes the regional, land-based confrontations remembered by the Salisbury plain. The plains, in Song Three, are transcended by the round, maritime, and vaunting globe. But like Drayton's accumulative yet divisive rivers, Spenser's paean to the rivers carries a sense of ambiguity regarding the ability to merge Britain's fluid bodies of water into a unified collective memory:

> How can they all in this so narrow verse
> Contayned be, and in small compasse hild?
> Let them record them, that are better skild,
> And know the moniments of passed times.   (161)

Spenser's rivers overflow beyond the boundaries of "compassed" space, recorded time, and his own poetic "skill." The inability for the poet to fully remember or contain Britain's watery monuments echoes Spenser's dual inclusion and occlusion of the Irish river nymphs into this harmonious flood. The Irish rivers are present at the wedding of the Thames – "They saw it all, and present were in place" – but the verse cannot describe and recount them, as "I them all according their degree, / Cannot recount, nor tell their hidden race, / Nor read the saluage cũtreis, thorough which they pace" (167). The Irish rivers' ambivalent presence and silence at Spenser's river wedding parallels the uncomfortable ambiguity of Ireland's "place" and situation within the British archipelago and its historical memory.

Likewise, many of *Poly-olbion* page borders spatially and symbolically represent the division rather than unification of memory spaces. The border at the end of Song Ten features a skull at its central focal point, a convention of *memento mori* or reminders of death (Figure 3.9).

This exact woodcut design is not repeated in any other section of Drayton's book, although a border with a central skull also appears on page borders at the end of Songs Twelve, Thirteen, and Eighteen, *Poly-olbio*n's final song. Songs Twelve, Thirteen, and Eighteen all share the same design and all act as a lower, second border underneath a top border with a central "IHS" symbol (Figures 3.10, 3.11, and 3.12).

Each of the song sections that feature the dual IHS and skull borders substantially represents fissures between beginnings and endings. Song Twelve chronicles the Saxon kingdom and Edmond Ironside's battles with the Danish King Knut; this section outlines the fall of the Saxon line before the Norman invasion, which created a new line of kings. Song Thirteen displays a scene of the Forest of Arden's decline, in a narrative that parallels the loss of Eden through this forest's loss of territory: people began "to spoyle / My tall and goodly woods, and did my grounds inclose: / By which, in little time my bounds I came to lose" (sig. T3.v). Nevertheless, the song hopes to reinvent Arden by renewing its borders through verse: "This song our Shire of Warwick sounds; / Revives old Ardens ancient bounds" (sig. T3.r). Finally, Song Eighteen draws *Poly-olbion* as a book to a close in its first edition. This double boundary of skull/memento mori and IHS symbol remains between *Poly-olbion*'s old and new material, between its first and second part or "continuance," in its subsequent editions. The page borders of *Poly-olbion* generally cross between past and future, what is material and what is mythical. As Peter Stallybrass argues, visual paratexts such as page borders become material forms that beckon but do not fix our visual range of perception, creating "a reading that doesn't see and a seeing that doesn't read, of a visual paratext that moves in and out of focus" ("Afterword" 210).

the tenth Song.   169

ding to their custome)in a banquet by *Gyptis* the Kings daughter for her husband; Hereto successe grew so fortunat, that honorable respect on both sides ioyn'd with imitation o' *Greeke* Ciuility (after this Citie built neere their arriue)it seem'd, as my author [a] sayes, as if *Gaule* had beene turnd into *Greece*, rather then *Greece* to haue trauailed into *Gaule*. Wonder not then why, about *Marsilles*, *Greeke* was so respected, nor why in the *Romaunt-French* now such Hellenismes are: here you see apparant Originall of it; yet conclude, vpon the former reasons, that the *Druids* and *Gaules* vsed a peculiar tongue, and very likely the same with the now *Welsh*, as Most learned *Camden* hath euen demonstrated; although I know some great Scholars there are, which still suspend their iudgement, and make it a doubt, as euer things of such antiquity will be. But(if you will)adde heereto that of the famous and great Lawier [b] *Hotoman*, who presumes that the word [*] *Græcis* in *Cæsars* text is crept in by ignorance of transcribers, as he well might, seeing those Commentaries, titled with name of *I. Cæsar*, commonly published, & in diuers *Mss.* with *I. Celsus*, are very vnperfect, now and then abrupt, different in stile, and so variable in their owne forme, that it hath beene much feared by that great [c] Critique *Lipsius*, lest some more impolite hand hath sow'd many patches of base cloth into that more rich web, as his owne Metaphore expresses it. And if those Characters which are in the pillars at *Y-Voellas* in *Denbighshire*, are of the *Druids*, as some imagine (yet seeming very strange and vncouth)then might you more confidently coucurre in opinion with *Hotoman*. In summe, I know that *Græcis literis* may be taken as wel for the language(as in [d] *Iustin* I remember, and elsewhere) as for the Character: but here I can neuer thinke it to be vnderstood in any but the last sense, although you admit *Cæsars* copie to be therein not interpolated. It is very iustifiable which the author here implies, by slighting *Cæsars* authority in *British* Originals, in respect that hee neuer came further into the Isle then a little beyond *Thames* towards [e] *Barkeshire*; although some of Ours idly talke of his making the *Bath*, and being at *Chester*, as the *Scotish* Historians most senslesly of their 𝔍𝔲𝔩𝔦𝔰 𝔥𝔬𝔣𝔣 built by him, which others referre [f] to *Vespasian*, some affirme it a Temple [g] of God *Terminus*; whereas it seemes expressly to be built by *Carausius*, in time of *Dioclesian*, if *Nennius* deceiue vs not. But, this out of my way.

[a] *Trog. Pomp. Hist.* 43.

[b] *Franco-Gall. cap.* 2. *quem v. etiam ad Cæsar. Com.*
[*] Greeke.

[c] *Elect.* 2. *cap.* 7. *Epistolic. quæst.* 2 *cap.* 2.

[d] *Hist. lib.* 20. *in extrema.*

[e] *Cæsarem si legas, tibi ipsi satisfacias, verum & ita Leland. ad Cyg. Cant. in Baln.*
[f] *Veremund. ap. Hect. Boet. hist.* 3.
[g] *Buchanan. hist.* 4. *in Donaldo.*

Q   (THE

Figure 3.9. Michael Drayton, *Poly-Olbion* (1622), page 169, Bodleian Library

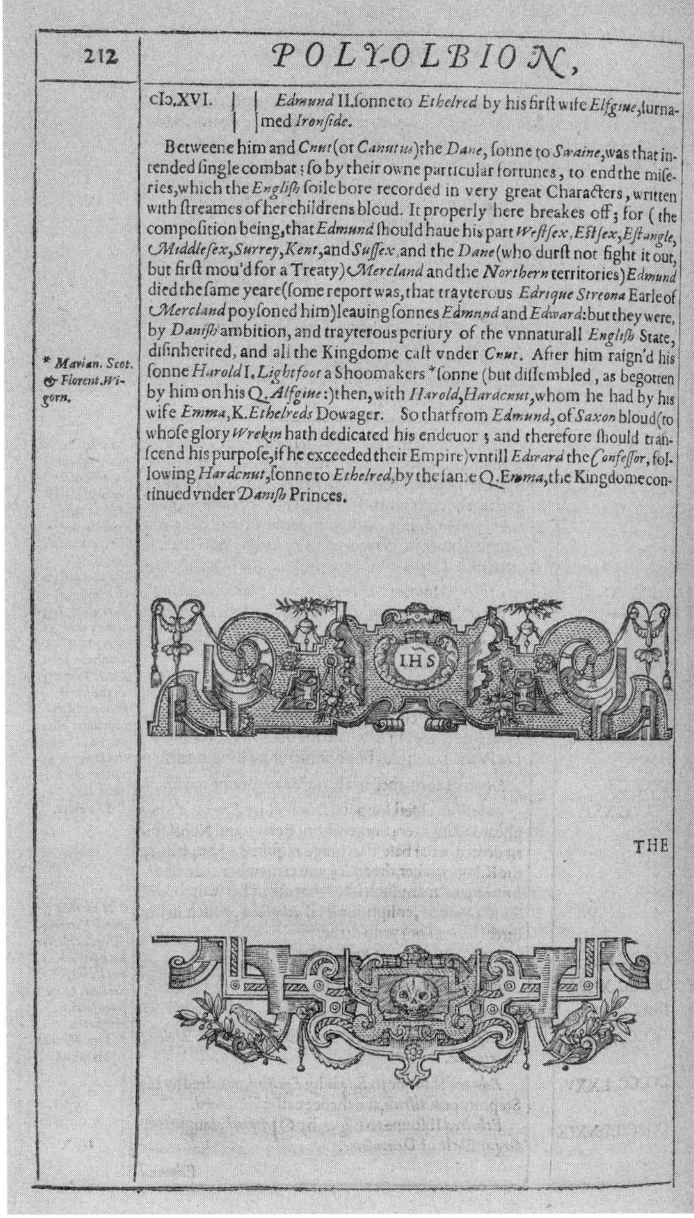

212

POLY-OLBION,

cIↄ.XVI. | | *Edmund* II. ſonne to *Ethelred* by his firſt wife *Elfgiue*, ſurna-
med *Ironſide.*

Betweene him and *Cnut* (or *Canutus*) the *Dane*, ſonne to *Swaine*, was that intended ſingle combat : ſo by their owne particular fortunes, to end the miſe-
ries, which the *Engliſh* ſoile bore recorded in very great Characters, written
with ſtreames of her childrens bloud. It properly here breakes off ; for (the
compoſition being, that *Edmund* ſhould haue his part *Weſtſex*, *Eſtſex*, *Eſtangle*,
Middleſex, *Surrey*, *Kent*, and *Suſſex*, and the *Dane* (who durſt not fight it out,
but firſt mou'd for a Treaty) *Mercland* and the *Northern* territories) *Edmund*
died the ſame yeare (ſome report was, that trayterous *Edrique Streona* Earle of
Mercland poyſoned him) leauing ſonnes *Edmund* and *Edward*: but they were,
by *Daniſh* ambition, and trayterous periury of the vnnaturall *Engliſh* State,
diſinherited, and all the Kingdome caſt vnder *Cnut*. After him raign'd his
ſonne *Harold* I. *Lightfoot* a Shoomakers *ſonne (but diſſembled, as begotten
by him on his Q. *Alfgine*:) then, with *Harold*, *Hardcnut*, whom he had by his
wife *Emma*, K. *Ethelreds* Dowager.   So that from *Edmund*, of *Saxon* bloud (to
whoſe glory *Wrekin* hath dedicated his endeuor ; and therefore ſhould tran-
ſcend his purpoſe, if he exceeded their Empire) vntill *Edward* the *Confeſſor*, following *Hardcnut*, ſonne to *Ethelred*, by the ſame Q. *Emma*, the Kingdome continued vnder *Daniſh* Princes.

Figure 3.10. Michael Drayton, *Poly-Olbion* (1622), page 212, Bodleian Library

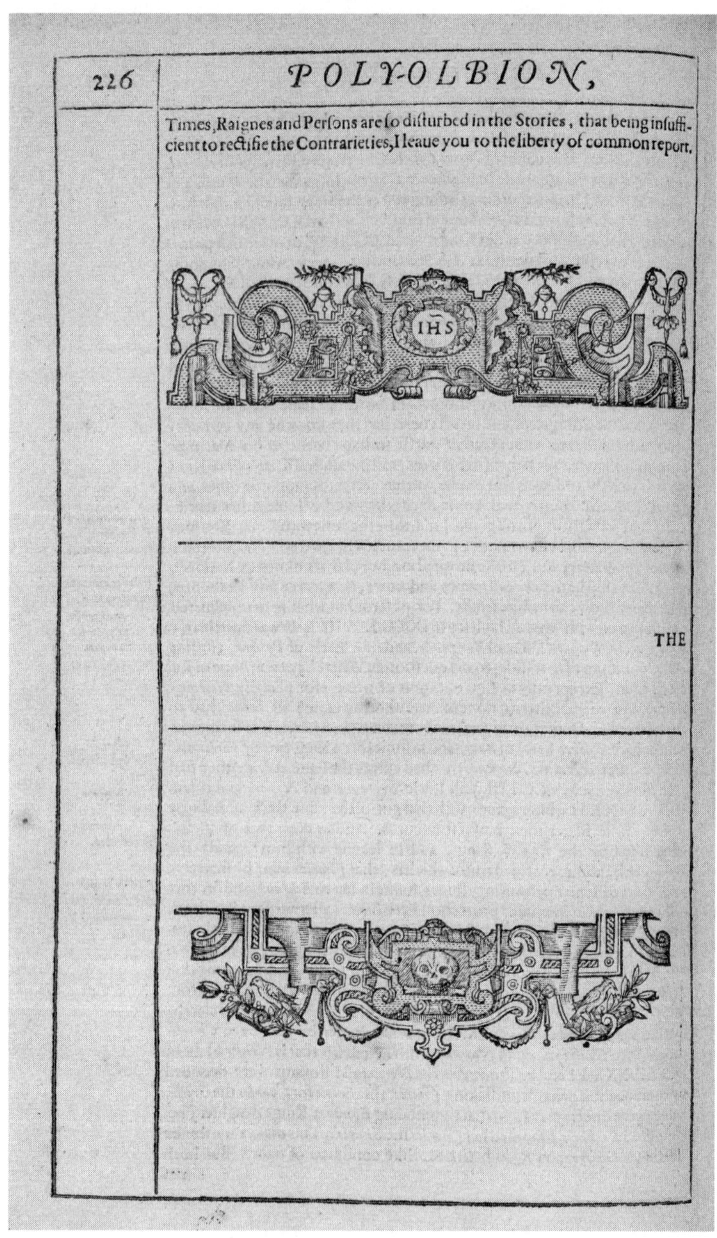

Figure 3.11. Michael Drayton, *Poly-Olbion* (1622), page 226, Bodleian Library

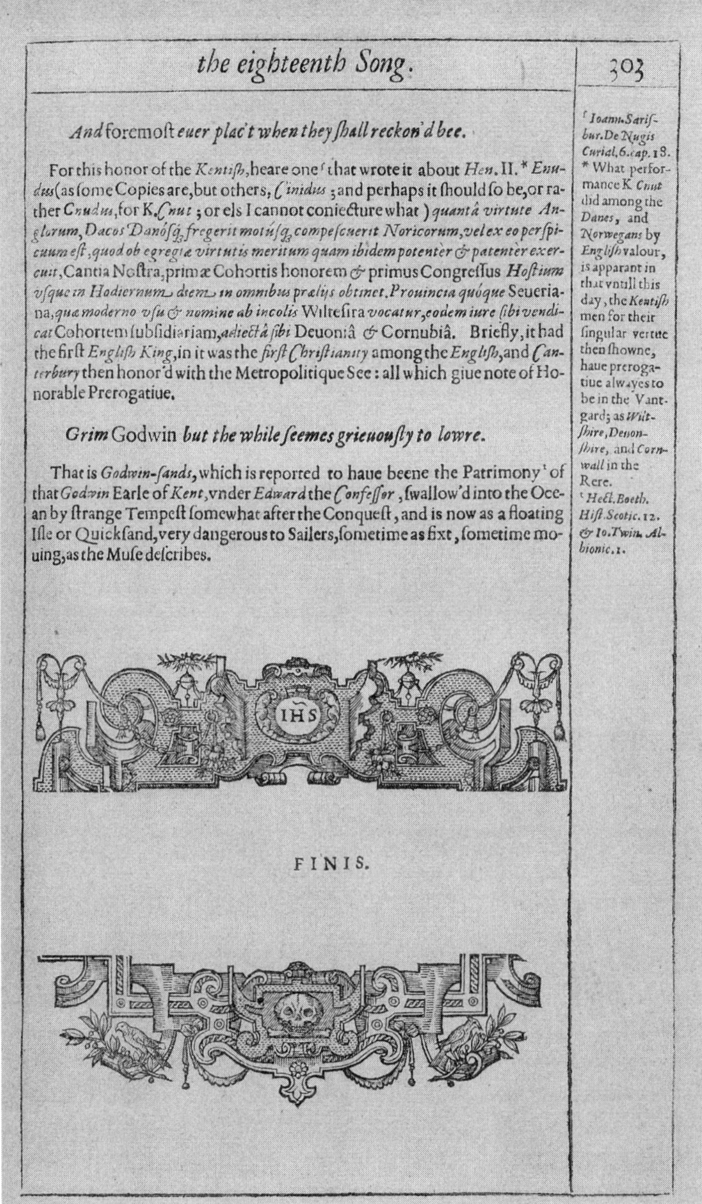

Figure 3.12. Michael Drayton, *Poly-Olbion* (1622), page 303, Bodleian Library

The singular design of Song Ten's page border, in which the skull stands alone without a separate IHS woodblock on top, appears to reflect this song's more sceptical attitude towards a recollection of historical memory through verse and visual boundaries. In this song, Drayton figures the River Dee as yet another troubled watery border "twixt Wales and England," whose changes and floods bespoke prophecy "of eithers warre, or peace, / The sicknes, or the health, the dearth, or the increase" for both regions (sig. P3r). Dee becomes a Druidic mouthpiece for a specifically Celtic or Welsh British historiography. This more marginal history interrogates the connection between recollection and sight in *Poly-olbion*. In his description of a ship sailing by a cliff, neither memory nor sight can reliably illuminate the past:

> But, in things past so long (for all the world) we are
> Like to a man embarqu't, and travelling the Deepe:
> Who sayling by some hill, or promontory steepe
> Which juts into the Sea, with an amazed eye
> Beholds the Cleeves thrust up into the lofty skie.
> And th'more that hee doth looke, the more it drawes his sight;
> Now at the craggy front, then at the wondrous weight:
> But, from the passed shore still as the swelling saile
> (Thrust forward by the wind) the floating Barque doth haile,
> The mightie Giant-heape, so lesser and lesser still
> Appeareth to the eye, untill the monstrous hill
> At length shewes like a cloud; and further beeing cast,
> Is out of kenning quite: so, of the Ages past;
> Those things that in their Age much to be wondred were,
> Still as wing-footed time them farther off doth beare,
> Doe lessen every howre.   (sig. P3.v)

The River Dee's speech renders the past incommensurable to our visual perception. This passage limits our sight of the past by a horizon or boundary both spatial and temporal, as the ship sails across both time and distance. A "craggy front" can seem fantastical and faraway the more space lies between it and the viewer, just as a significant historical event can seem ever more legendary or dubious as time passes. The topographical feature of the cliff in Dee's narration becomes mutable and reliant on the subjective, limited nature of memory and sight. In this vignette, the geology of the visual object transforms from "some hill, or promontory steepe," to a "mightie Giant-heape," to a "monstrous hill," to a mere "cloud," until it passes out of our knowledge ("kenning") entirely. At first, the mountain could be any hill, a mere exemplum for Dee's argument. Then, it is a legendary feature, large and imposing, in our mind's eye, with its own mythical narrative. This mythic giant heap recalls both the Ovidian tale of a giants' war and the biblical stone giants Gog and Magog. In Ovid's *Metamorphoses*, a race of giants "to win the gods' domain, / Mountain on mountain reared and reached the stars" (66). Zeus strikes the heap with a thunderbolt, so that "High Pelion piled on Ossa" (66). Gog and Magog appear through the bible, sometimes as giants, sometimes as priests, and sometimes as features of the landscape (cf. Ezekiel 38–9, Revelations 20:8). Drayton references these apocalyptic giants in his new mythology of Britain. Giants fight the first settlers of Britain, who arrive from Troy, and bring "great *Gogmagog*" into this conflict (sig. B3r).[15] A Trojan Corineus fights Gogmagog and tosses him into the ocean, after which the mountains jut up and form Cornwall, named for Corineus (sig. B4v). In his reading of Caliban as a mythic and uniquely British monster, Rowland Wymer turns to the legendary figures of Gog and Magog as a visual emblem for primordial Britishness. Wymer recounts the practice of carrying the "giant images" of Gogmagog and Corineus in London pageants; these figures were "kept at the Guildhall as symbolic guardians of the City of London and survived till the early eighteenth century" (7). The images of Gogmagog and Corineus, rather than remembered solely as "conquerer and conquered," were employed as icons of London pride and British power (8). Dee's narrative about the rock that becomes remembered as a giant heap indicates the process of mnemonic and historical erasure necessary for British unity. John Selden discounts the mythological memory evoked by these British giants by, like Dee, interrogating visual perception. Selden sceptically glosses this fabulous tale of a British giant's heap as follows: "as Monsters rather then naturall, such proofe hath bin; but withall, that both now and of ancient, time, the eyes iudgement in such like hath beene, and is, subiect to much imposture; mistaking bones of huge beasts for humane" (sig. C3r). To the mapped space of Cornwall and Drayton's fabulous epideictic description of this conflict, Selden responds with an interpretation of these tales as "impostures" or as deceptive optical illusions. The term "monster/monstrous" could refer to a visual display or marvel in early modern usage (*MED* "mŏustre" sense a, *OED* def. A.1a, A.2).[16] The Dee's giant heap is both "monstrous" in a legendary sense, relating back to the connection with Ovid's, the bible's, and Cornwall's "Giants," and an inherently visual display, subject to illusion.

The way in which we remember this rocky hill, then, depends on how we see it. Finally, this giant heap has diminished to a cloud: the monument of the hill, then, transforms in our interior perception over time, just as our external sight of the hill transforms over space. As the mind ranges from direct historical experience (crag) to legend (giant heap), from legend to a vanishing point, the sailor's "amazed eye" ranges across different vantage points in space. In the connection he draws between visual and temporal perception, the River Dee casts doubt on the ability to know the past, to navigate space, or to recollect Britain's monuments. Paradoxically, the River Dee employs a vivid ekphrasis of the disappearing cliff to suggest invisibility and absence. In his depiction of the insurmountable horizon between past and present, distance and proximity, truth and myth, Dee (and Drayton) visualize these boundaries while clouding them over. As with *Poly-olbion*'s striking watery maps and ornamented page borders, the River Dee uses a visual device to suggest negative spaces (water, historical memory, the end of a book section) and epistemic boundaries (aporia).

Many of *Poly-olbion*'s visual and ekphrastic devices, as its rivers, lands, and forgotten "giant-heaps" attest, indicate epistemic divisions between visual perception and knowledge. More specifically, the River Dee's scepticism towards visual memory recalls the sight-perception aporia Plato advances in his dialogues, dialogues that heavily influenced discussions of vision and epistemology in classical, medieval, and early modern intellectual contexts. In *Theaetetus*, Plato complicates several "common sense" understandings of the relationships among knowledge, perception, memory, and sight. Theaetetus at first defines knowledge as perception, with the underlying assumption of sight (external sense) as the dominant mode of human perception. However, Socrates casts doubt on this implicit syllogism – sight is perception, perception is knowledge, therefore, knowledge is sight – through the example of internal memory. Socrates queries, "[I]s it possible that, at the very time when" someone remembers something, "he might fail to know the very thing which he remembers?" (34). Socrates thus reduces the relationship Theaetetus draws between sight, perception, and knowledge to an aporia. One cannot, conceivably, both remember, and therefore know something, and at the same time not see (and therefore not know) something: "because we agreed that sight, or perception, and knowledge are the same thing. But if someone shuts their eyes, they can still remember something and have knowledge of something they have seen without seeing it" (34–5). Socrates later criticizes this move, in which he concluded that knowledge could not be perception, as logic chopping. The aporia he reached did not arise from the link between knowledge and perception but from the assumption of external sight as the basis for cognitive perception. Knowledge and perception can be linked, according to Plato, but only if that perception is internally rather than externally derived.

To take Socrates's aporia a step further, the link between knowledge and perception may stand only with an a priori assumption of Plato's own: knowledge in Plato's dialogue is internal and is a memory or remembrance. Using Socrates's example, knowledge can either be visual/external or mnemonic/internal, but not both at the same time. This epistemic boundary influenced early modern philosophies of memory and sight, such as Robert Burton's. Does external sight create a memory impression, and therefore knowledge, or does an internal memory project outward, creating a subjective "vision" of the external world? Or, as in Burton's combination of external/Aristotelian and internal/Platonic sense models, do they form a relationship to one another through the use of reason? In *Theaetetus*, Plato connects the ability to know and remember to the ability to receive impressions: Socrates tells Theaetetus to imagine an "imprint-receiving piece of wax in our mind" as a metaphor for the ability to gain knowledge, and then for that knowledge to remain in the memory (78). With this metaphor in mind, the visual materials of print impressions could conceivably be set forth as a path between visual perception and memory or knowing.

Selden and Drayton reference Platonic philosophy at the outset of this text. The cave imagery of artificial visuals cut out of natural rock in Drayton's letter to his reader returns with his poetic text's first chorographical description of the area around Cornwall. This area is filled with caves inhabited by Druid nuns: "To Ushant and the Seames, whereas those Nunnes of yore / Gave answers from their Caves, and took what shapes they please" (sig. B.v). These Druidic nuns seem to be humanoid and protean images, like those of the engraved maps' variable nymphs, flickering in front of caves. Before these shape-shifting nuns appear, Drayton describes priests who held the belief that "When these our soules by death our bodies doe forsake, / They instantlie againe doe other bodies take" (sig. Bv). This passage outlines the Platonic concept of metempsychosis, the idea that souls migrate to other bodies after death. This idea is prominent in Plato's *Republic* and in his dialogues. In his *Republic*, Plato vividly recounts how different souls choose new bodies after death, both human and animal: "among wild animals there were moves into human beings, and into one another … Every kind of intermingling was taking place" (343–4). After choosing their bodies, all souls then travel to the "plain of Forgetting," and drink from the "river of Lost Cares," or Lethe (344). Although the soul inhabits or trans-animates (drawing from the word *anima*, or soul) the new body, the soul cannot recall its previous state.[17]

Poly-olbion's maps of humanoid bodies who figure the landscape may fit within this model of animated bodies enchanted with variable souls, as the maps' chorographical and graphical materials are given lively animation and "revived" by the text's visual materials. Nevertheless, the Platonic concept of transanimation or re-inhabited bodies is predicated on forgetting, or memory's loss. As in Dee's description, again, visual materials may act to figure a loss rather than a recollection of memory. In his illustration to Drayton's description of Druidic priests, Selden specifically comments on the ideas of "trans-animation" (sig. C.v). Selden refers to Plato's "Phadon" (*Phaedon*) and "Phadrus" (*Phaedrus*), along with the Druids, as proponents of this belief (sig. C.v). Of trans-animation, Selden claims, "The Author, with pitie, imputes to them their being led away in blindnes of the time, and errors of their fancies" (sig. C2r). Selden's "illustrations" seek to erase blindness, error, and fancy, as components of faulty imagination, sight, and memory, even as *Poly-olbion*'s peopled maps and Drayton's poetic visions emulate a process of trans-animate material embodiment.

Material embodiment that coexists with mnemonic failure appears again in Plato's "birdcage" metaphor, perhaps the most evocative section of the *Theaetetus* dialogue. Theaetetus compares memory (and knowledge) with an aviary full of wild birds: one may possess fragments of knowledge without having them. In this metaphor, one may recall different "birds of knowledge," and sometimes have them at hand for the purposes of invention/recollection, but they may not always come when we call. In the birdcage metaphor, memory and sight are unreliable sources of knowledge; Socrates claims that it is

> possible not to have one's knowledge of that thing, but to have some other piece of knowledge instead of it. That happens when, in trying to catch some piece of knowledge or other, among those that are flying about, one misses, and gets hold of the one instead of the other … as one might get hold of a dove instead of a pigeon. (199)

Recollection is here a fundamentally troubling task: memories or collected bits of knowledge themselves have the agency to distort or alter our perceptions. Theaetetus takes this problem a step further, arguing that "perhaps we ought to have also imagined pieces of unknowing flying about in the mind with them. When one tries to catch them, one sometimes gets hold of a piece of knowledge and sometimes of a piece of unknowing about the same thing" (199). In the texts and images of *Poly-olbion*, the process of recalling and inventing a national consciousness is unreliable.

Different "birds of memory," and different regional "nymphs," compete to voice their historical narratives. Dee's description of a "giant-heap" that becomes a "cloud," or a historical event that becomes a legend, then forgotten, parallels Plato's metaphors of a smudged imprint and a disobedient bird. Oral history and visual impression, in other words, are both unreliable conduits for a unified or totalizing recollection of the past. *Poly-olbion* very much resembles Plato's birdcage. Multiple voices and competing deictic images fly about its page image, beguiling and dividing the eye of the reader. Song Ten's unique page border of a skull, a *memento mori*, reminds us of the limits of memory.

Another unique page border in *Poly-olbion*, an image of a skeleton that sits on a throne, advances its concern with uneasy historical and spatial boundaries. This woodcut design recurs in three significant places, perhaps as a deliberate thematic choice on the part of *Poly-olbion*'s collaborators. The first instance appears at the opposite page from *Poly-olbion*'s frontispiece, beneath the woodcut of armillary spheres. The poem "Upon the Frontispiece" signals to the title page's placement of Albion in a "triumphant arch," and chronicles the line of Albion's conquerers and kings – giants, Trojans, Romans, Saxons, and Normans, "whose line yet rules" – each conqueror displaced by the next. The continuance of a ruling line through different external conquerors and the establishment of royal continuity sit ambivalently with the "*yet* rules" of this poem's last line (emphasis mine). As chapter 2 mentions, a visual grotesque was described as an "antic" or antique design in early modern culture. This title page's throned skeleton beneath the poem's catalogue of conquerers and kings recalls Richard II's lament, "within the hollow crown / that rounds the mortal temples of a king / keeps death his court and there the antic sits" (3.2.160–2). Whether this description draws from a previous emblematic tradition or this page border draws from *Richard II*, the throned antic/antique of *Poly-olbion*'s title page forms a dramatic reminder of empire's graveyards, even across from the opposite page's engraving of the map-wearing Britannia. The skeleton on a throne appears as a dynastic *memento mori*, signalling both the continuity and the impermanence of British rulership.

Two winged hearts frame the central skeleton on either side of this same border. Frances Yates describes the symbol of a winged heart in

Jesuit emblematic poet Giordano Bruno's *De Gli Eroici Furori*, translated and published in England in 1575.[18] In Bruno's emblem, this winged heart escapes from a cage as if it were a bird: the cage symbolizes worldly entrapments and the wings symbolize the soul, in a reference to Plato's description of the soul in winged flight (Yates 107–8). Plato's winged soul in his *Phaedrus* appears in his description of the soul's recollection of ideal beauty (92:249D). In this recollection,

> By the sight of a beautiful object the Soul is reminded of the true Beauty, and seeks to wing its flight upward thereto. This love of Beauty is the fourth and highest type of divine madness. But recollection is not always easy: some souls saw little of the vision, and some forgot what they saw, being corrupted by evil associations. Yet the Form of Beauty may be more readily recollected by the other Forms, since its image is discerned by sight, the keenest of our senses. (92)

The winged hearts that frame the throned skeleton, then, draw from an emblematic tradition, where the wings symbolized an escape from or transcendence of earthly boundaries (a birdcage) and, again, appear beneath the winged armillary spheres on the upper border of the page, amplifying a sense of feathery flight. These winged hearts, positioned oppositionally from the book's visually detailed frontispiece of Albion, suggestively parallel Plato's recollection of ideal beauty through sight. Again, the process of recollection or invention by the Platonic soul and the early modern rhetorician occurred through visual impressions and audience imagination (enargeia). These winged hearts bespeak a transcendent recollection or invention of Albion through a detailed visual recollection of its spaces, as the engravings interact with readers' imaginations. Yet as in Plato's description of recollection's limited visual scope (some souls see a partial vision, some souls forget it), this border's throned skeleton and corresponding poetic text invite a sense of recollective ambiguity. In the poem to the frontispiece, the earliest events of British history have slipped into myth (Brutus and the giants) and its future seems uncertain (a lineage that "*yet* rules").

The second instance of the throned skeleton on a page border marks the end of Song Seven. Here, books frame the central image rather than winged hearts (Figure 3.13).

This replacement of winged hearts with books suggests a connection between the symbols of escape from boundaries and the book's page borders. Fittingly, this song begins as a border resolution, as the

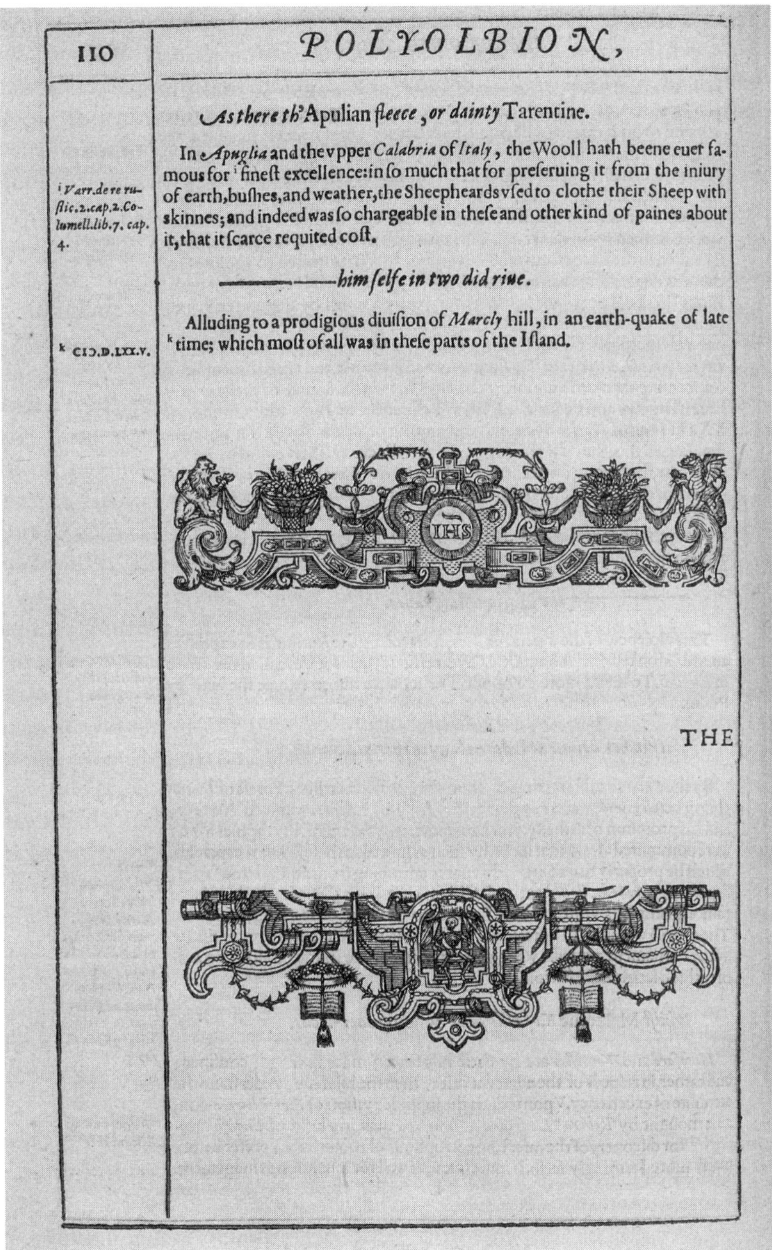

Figure 3.13. Michael Drayton, *Poly-Olbion* (1622), page 110, Bodleian Library

spirits of the River Lug and the River Wye are allegorically married at a "wedding" (drawn together as river courses) near the border of England and Wales (sig. K3r). Yet the song concludes with what the ecocritical readings of Dasgupta, McCrae, and Trevisan frame as a scene of environmental devastation, voiced by the animated forest of Wyre: "whole Forests" "decay," their "spoyle unpunisht goes," "their Trunkes (like aged folks) now bare and naked stand, / As for revenge to heaven each held a withered hand" (sig. K4v). The forest Wyre ends her song in silence and grief, flooded by the Salopian River. In other words, a song that begins with a resolution of borders ends with their diminishment and silence. While it may be tempting for modern readers to view this scene as a direct meta-criticism of print's use of tree pulp, paper in the seventeenth century was formed from a greater variety of natural materials, such as flax, scraps and rags of cloth, and wool, as Joshua Calhoun traces (333). Calhoun observes these vegetable and animal materials' visibility in early modern books: he has seen feathers, hairs, and vegetal fibres woven into the paper page itself (334). Books with printed paper would not have directly contributed to the forest of Wyre's decomposition, but they did visibly recompose and recollect natural materials, physically binding them. In addition, as Leah Knight catalogues in *Reading Green in Early Modern England*, greenness itself was associated with the acts of reading and visual observation: the book as garden or arboreum operated as a familiar early modern trope (17), the glass of domestic windows was known as "'forest glass,' a substance that appeared, owing to impurities in the materials and the manufacturing process, distinctly greenish" (21), and readers habitually used green eyeglasses (24), green screens (26), and the location of the garden itself (25) to reduce eyestrain from whitish paper. In this song, then, green spaces are bound within – yet distinctly frame and mediate – book spaces. Song Seven's page border, with its display of skeleton and book, both reinforces and reframes the forest's lament, as the forest and page become intersecting locations of both decomposition and regeneration. *Poly-olbion* allows the forest to speak anew through its poetic text, while binding together and enclosing natural materials – a vegetal graveyard reanimated by engraved nymphs.

The third and final throned skeleton reminds us further of death, memory, and recollection; this time, as with the frontispiece, within the context of the monarchy. This page border (Figure 3.14), a recycling of Song Seven's woodblock, appears at the end of John Selden's annotations to Song Seventeen (Figure 3.15) and before his chronicle of English kings.

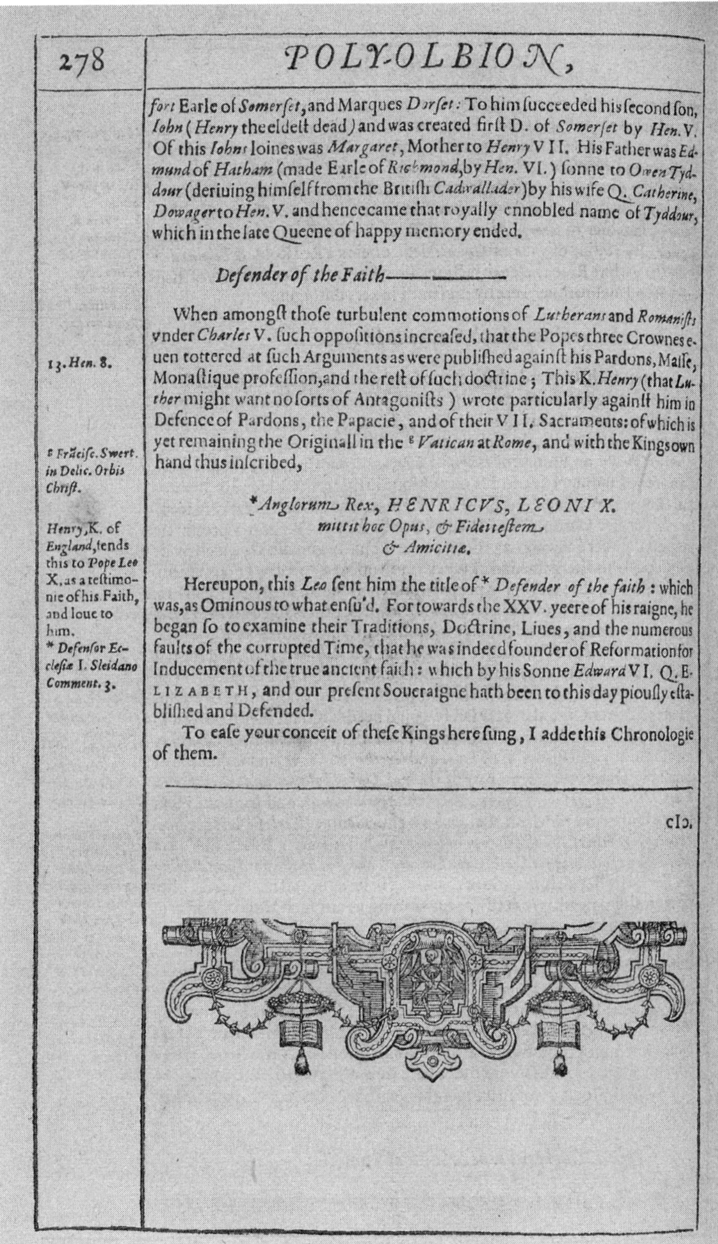

fort Earle of *Somerset*, and Marques *Dorset:* To him succeeded his second son, *Iohn* (*Henry* the eldest dead) and was created first D. of *Somerset* by *Hen.* V. Of this *Iohns* loines was *Margaret*, Mother to *Henry* VII. His Father was *Edmund* of *Hatham* (made Earle of *Richmond*, by *Hen.* VI.) sonne to *Owen Tyddour* (deriuing himselfe from the British *Cadwallader*) by his wife Q. *Catherine*, Dowager to *Hen.* V. and hence came that royally ennobled name of *Tyddour*, which in the late Queene of happy memory ended.

Defender of the Faith———

When amongst those turbulent commotions of *Lutherans* and *Romanists* vnder *Charles* V. such oppositions increased, that the Popes three Crownes euen tottered at such Arguments as were published against his Pardons, Masse, Monastique profession, and the rest of such doctrine; This K. *Henry* (that *Luther* might want no sorts of Antagonists) wrote particularly against him in Defence of Pardons, the Papacie, and of their VII. Sacraments: of which is yet remaining the Originall in the ᵍ *Vatican* at *Rome*, and with the Kings own hand thus inscribed,

* *Anglorum Rex*, *HENRICVS, LEO NI X.*
mittit hoc Opus, & Fidei testem,
& Amicitiæ.

Hereupon, this *Leo* sent him the title of * *Defender of the faith*: which was, as Ominous to what ensu'd. For towards the XXV. yeere of his raigne, he began so to examine their Traditions, Doctrine, Liues, and the numerous faults of the corrupted Time, that he was indeed founder of Reformation for Inducement of the true ancient faith: which by his Sonne *Edward* VI. Q. ELIZABETH, and our present Soueraigne hath been to this day piously established and Defended.

To ease your conceit of these Kings here sung, I adde this Chronologie of them.

Margin notes:
13. *Hen.* 8.

ᵍ *Fräcisc. Swert. in Delic. Orbis Christ.*

Henry, K. of *England*, sends this to *Pope Leo* X, as a testimonie of his Faith, and loue to him. * *Defensor Ecclesiæ* I. *Sleidano Comment.* 3.

cIɔ.

Figure 3.14. Michael Drayton, *Poly-Olbion* (1622), page 278, Bodleian Library

the ſeuenteenth Song.   279

cIↃ. L X V I.	*William* I. conquered *England*.
CIↃ. LXXXVII.	*William* the *Red* (*Rufus*) ſecond Sonne to the Conqueror.
cIↃ. C.	*Henry* I. ſurnamed *Beuclere*, third ſonne to the firſt *William*.
cIↃ. C. XXXV.	*Stephen* Earle of *Moreton*, and *Bologne*, ſonne to *Stephen* Earle of *Blois* by *Adela* daughter to the Conqueror. In both the prints of *Math. Paris*, (*An*. cIↃ. LXXXVI.) You muſt mend *Beccenſis Comitis*, and read *Bleſenſis Comitis*; and howſoeuer it coms to paſſe, he is, in the ſame Author, made Son to *Tedbald* Earle of *Blois*, which indeed was his brother.
cIↃ. C. LIV.	*Henry* II. Sonne to *Geffery Plantageneſt* Earle of *Aniou*, and *Maude* the Empres, daughter to *Henry Beuclere*.
cIↃ. C. LXXXIX.	*Richard* I. *Ceur de Lion*, Sonne to *Henry* I I.
cIↃ. C. CXIX.	*Iohn*, Brother to *Ceur de Lion*.
cIↃ. CC. XVI.	*Hen*. III. Sonne to K. *Iohn*.
cIↃ. CC. LXXIII.	*Edward* I. *Longſhanks*, Sonne to *Hen*. III.
cIↃ. CCC. VIII.	*Edward* II. of *Caernaruan*, Sonne to *Ed*. I. depoſed by his Wife and Sonne.
cIↃ. CCC. XXVI.	*Edward* III. Sonne to *Edward*. II.

In Matth. Paris diſputation.

Bb 2   *Richard*

Figure 3.15. Michael Drayton, *Poly-Olbion* (1622), page 279, Bodleian Library

This image directly follows John Selden's account of the English Reformation under Henry VIII: Henry "began so to examine their Traditions, Doctrine, Lives, and the numerous faults of corrupted Time, that he was indeed founder of Reformation for Inducement of the true ancient faith" (sig. Bb.v). Here, the phrase "corrupted Time" presents a concept of memory and the past that demands re-formation and recollection. The skeletal image that follows this praise of Henry VIII's reformation and prefaces the forthcoming royal lineage is more ambiguous: it reminds us of potential lost, forgotten, or destroyed traditions following such reforms. However, the skeleton's presence on a throne may conversely imply what Ernst Kantorowicz famously recounts as "the king's two bodies": the physical, decomposable body of the king and the immortal and continual aspect of kings in a dynastic succession. These kingly bodies are collected together in Selden's chronology. This genealogy emphasizes the "once and future" aspect of the king's mortal/physical and immortal/spiritual bodies. Each page border of *Poly-olbion* forms a threshold, a space that mediates and binds what has come before it (the past) and frames what will come after. These border thresholds alternately seem to escape or dominate material boundaries (winged hearts and spheres, IHS letters) and, at the same time, reemphasize them (skulls, skeletons, books).

Prince Henry's Pike

The engraving of Henry Stuart, Prince of Wales (Figure 3.16), that adjoins the book's dedication, arguably presents the most visually striking instance of a threshold effect in *Poly-olbion*.

In this image, Henry wears an elaborate suit of armour that shows off the skill of William Hole and the aesthetic properties of copper engravings. He poses facing to the right (forward, assuming a left-to-right reading) in a military stance and holds a pike that appears to be literally thrust into (or beyond) the borders of the page. Henry's pose and pike emphasize the ambivalence of *Poly-olbion*'s boundaries. The pike either pushes beyond or is pushed back by the boundary of the page itself. The possible movement of Henry's pike past the page boundary corresponds to the dedicatory poem's comparison of Henry to "great Neptune," who "on the three seas shall rove, / And rule three Realms." In his illustration and poem, Henry is a figure who may be uniquely capable of mastering the watery borders of Albion and unifying the three contentious regions of Britain (Scotland, England, and Wales),

Figure 3.16. Michael Drayton, *Poly-Olbion* (1622), Portrait of Prince Henry, Bodleian Library

despite the local border disputes that fill this book's maps and texts. Henry's pike and gaze also point eastward, towards the Continent, in an aggressive and expansionist posture. This pose suggests a militaristic stance towards the European Continent to the east. Jason C. White examines Henry Frederick's cultivation of a militaristic, nationalist, and Protestant image that had been "heaped" upon him since birth (169). Henry was held up as an antithetical figure to his more pacifist, internationalist father, James VI and I.

This self-cultivated image made its way to Henry's symbolic representation in print visuals. As White observes, portraits often "depicted the prince as an active warrior, sword at the ready to engage in combat" and "popular woodcuts often depicted him practising his arms" (169). This engraving fits within this warlike representation of Henry, but, as Timothy Wilks argues, this specific image uniquely depicts Henry as a foot soldier, an association unusual in an era when the aristocratic and royal classes would have remained in the cavalry (181). Henry often performed military practices on foot with a pike, an aristocratic weapon that nevertheless bespoke "humility," "self-sacrifice," and "comradeship" with his men (Wilks 193, 196). Wilks makes the convincing case that this engraving was imitated from a portrait by court painter Isaac Oliver, in turn copied from an illustrated, textless manual for military drills, *The Exercise of Arms for Calivres, Muskettes and Pikes*, published 1608 (186; see Figure 3.17).

This drill book almost seems like a flip book of poses, with its pages of soldiers' physical movements perhaps being physically moved around by readers.

Henry's stance as a foot soldier symbolizes his willingness to stand with his men on the field, demonstrating egalitarianism and brotherhood in the portrait's military context. This mutuality between the prince and common foot soldiers extends to the mutuality of image and reader in this engraving. The possible extension of Henry's pike beyond the page's boundaries depends on the reader's visual extension of the pike in the "gutters" of the page, his forward motion imagined, and invented, by the image's readers and viewers.[19] The first lines of *Poly-olbion*'s dedication to Henry, "Britaine, behold here portray'd to thy sight, / Henry, thy best hope, and the world's delight," invents an "imagined Britain" to gaze on Henry, to cite Benedict Anderson's theory of "imagined communities" of readers who began to see themselves as part of a shared nation. To animate this ideal image of Albion, readers must collectively invent and imagine movement between and

Figure 3.17. Jacob de Gheyn, *The Exercise of Armes for Caliures, Muskettes, and Pikes* (1608), J9, Cambridge University Library

beyond its borders, and drink from the River Lethe to forget its historical conflicts.

Taken as a whole, *Poly-olbion*'s visual eclecticism and epistemic uncertainty counters other, more popular chorographical works of Drayton's time, such as William Camden's *Britannia*. Its less-than-celebratory nature perhaps led to its unpopularity in its own time, even as current scholarship now acknowledges its fascinating complexities of British identity, landscape, and vision-text intersections. Indeed, *Poly-olbion* anticipates a reading pattern that is perhaps more postmodern than early modern: any attempt to read the voluminous work from front to cover will ultimately be frustrated. Instead, this work rewards flipping through, skimming, and toggling between image and text: this method asks us to compose, and decompose, its landscapes and features together with the text. To help us discover its thematics, icons, and borders, *Poly-olbion* gives us visual markers and "tags" from its woodcut borders to its italic script for place names and certain figures, to navigate it as if it were a map in itself. This map, however, can be (even possibly, intentionally) disorienting and disconcerting, as it interrogates its own construction and situation within British historiography. We become part of Albion's history and chorography in our navigations of this work, even as Albion's history – and our own abilities to glimpse and view history with any consistency – is often contested within the text. In *Poly-olbion*, "Albion" is an unsettled landscape, with a history that we can only remember in hazy, uncertain, and multifarious fragments, like Dee's giant heap turned to a mysterious, whimsical cloud.

Image and Illusion in Francis Quarles's Emblems and Pamphlets: Duplication, Duality, Duplicity

Unlike Drayton's *Poly-olbion*, which ultimately failed to capture the imaginations of most seventeenth-century readers, Quarles's emblem books and political polemics enjoyed a broad popular readership in his own time and the next two centuries.[1] His critical reception and inclusion in the traditional literary canon, however, has been ambivalent at best. As Alexander Pope acidly assesses in *The Dunciad*: "pictures for the page atone / And Quarles is saved by beauties not his own" (118). Pope's contempt for Quarles anticipates the values and biases that have long characterized literary production and criticism as books gradually began to assume their structural conventions: single authorship, single modality, and clarity of arrangement and formatting. Quarles's works are instead collaborative and dialogic in their arrangement of text, image, and icon, even as they often treat visuality as morally and politically suspect. Quarles's *Emblemes* (1634) and later political works perform an extended meditation on early modern cultural anxieties of sight, even as they construct an elaborate, arresting visual structure.

Patterned Hieroglyphics

While Quarles's political and religious stance is that of a moderate Royalist Anglican, his *Emblemes* appropriate the Jesuit emblem books *Typus Mundi* (1627) and *Pia Desideria* (1624). When the engravers of the *Emblemes* alter their Jesuit sources, it is generally to add a *memento mori*, to create a dualistic symbol that mirrors the one already present, or to indicate visual perspective. Since most of Quarles's emblems reproduce or alter Jesuit sources, his text continuously refers to both popular visual culture and political debate. Protestant print's reproduction of Catholic visual motifs was both common and controversial. For example, the adoption of the "IHS" textual icon, "used by Jesuits and seen as Jesuitical" due to its Eucharistic associations, sparked polemical response yet proliferated as a visual commonplace in Protestant books, such as *Poly-olbion* and the *Emblemes* (Aston 32). Consciously leaping into the fray of religious controversy, Quarles justifies his employment of visual emblems in his apologia to the reader. He argues,

> An emblem is but a silent Parable. Let not the tender Eye checke, to see the allusion to our blessed SAVIOUR figured, in these Types ... why not presented so, as well to the eye, as to the eare? Before the knowledge of letters, GOD was knowne by *Hierogliphicks*; And, indeede, what are the heavens, the Earth, nay every Creature, but *Hierogliphicks* and *Emblemes* of his glory?" (sig. A3r)

The term "type" here denotes a symbol, figure, or emblem, as well as the raised block used to print letters. A "type" also signifies allegory in the context of biblical exegesis, where Old Testament events would prefigure or "type" New Testament fulfilments of those events, or "archetypes." Late-medieval popular illustrated typologies, such as the *Speculum Humanae Salvationis* or *Mirror of Human Salvation* (1309) and the so-called Pauper's Bible, which underwent multiple manuscript and print editions, form a material history of illustrated "typology" from which Quarles's *Emblemes* and his Jesuit emblem book sources drew.[2]

Like allegories of biblical typology, Quarles's own "types," anticipate an end point, whether the soul's salvation on the personal, devotional level or the second coming on the widely eschatological level. His typographical capitalizations of GOD and SAVIOUR act as visual emblems that mirror the visual commonplace "YHWH" or "IHS" stamped by woodcuts on so many printed page borders (Aston 24–32).[3] Types, as well as "hieroglyphs," a term adopted from Egyptian symbols in early modern emblematic literature, self-consciously treated visual motifs as a patterned system of meaning. Barbara Lewalski interprets Quarles's hieroglyphs as a way to distinguish *Emblemes* from Catholic metaphysics in his focus on "symbols and allegories found, not made," "grounded in the divine order of things" (185). Karl Josef Höltgen criticizes Lewalski's interpretation of the *Emblemes* as an emphatic contrast to Catholic theology and iconicity: Höltgen emphasizes continuity with a Continental, Catholic tradition and with Quarles's Jesuit sources. He cites the influence of a "Jacobean revival of art" in Quarles's lifetime, when "the older Reformation iconoclasm had been overcome to some extent and when the Court, travellers, and virtuosi opened England to the influence of the Continental art world" (*Aspects of the Emblem* 32). The controversial influence of Caroline-era Laudianism, too, re-invested Anglican practice and theology with an emphasis on form, ceremony, and image as a path to salvation. William Laud, archbishop of Canterbury from 1633 to his beheading in 1645, opposed more radical, iconoclastic strains of Puritanism and established a counter-Reformist, high-church policy that embraced visual ornament, ritual, and ceremony.

Quarles's own theological and ideological sympathies may be best described as militant moderation. As Robert Wilcher notes, "Quarles's position was typical of a conforming member of the pre-Laudian Church of England, antagonistic not only to Roman Catholicism but also to both the Arminian and Separatist factions within English Protestantism" (255).[4] His *Emblemes* were printed during Charles I's personal rule following the dissolution of Parliament and reflect that political situation. Quarles's anti-Laudianism, opposition to both sectarianism and Catholicism, and defence of the divine right of kings were lifetime beliefs (Christopher Hill 192; Haight 159). His main works, following his emblem books, were politically driven pamphlets that actively took part in pre-Civil War controversies. In his political works, he defended a system of "mixed monarchy," or a combination of monarchical, aristocratic, and democratic power, following the 1641 concessions of Charles I to Parliament (187). His *Enchiridion* (1641) and *Shepheards Oracle* (1646) plead for an ideal state under a benevolent monarch and warn of the dangers of social fragmentation. In his pamphlet, *The Loyall Convert* (1644), Quarles "explains how he stood 'amazed' at the 'Riddle' of two opposed parties" (Parliament and Charles I), "each claiming to preserve the true Protestant religion," but he ultimately chooses Royalism (Wilcher 254). It is safe to say that this Royalism was ideological rather than opportunistic: Lorraine M. Roberts notes that his "advocacy" for Charles I led "to the taking of his property, the burning of his manuscripts, and the assassination of his character" as a crypto-Catholic (229). However, the wide popular audience of the *Emblemes*, of which there were forty-four editions produced, would mean that different audiences would potentially use and read them for purposes beyond Quarles's own ideological ends. As Michael Bath and Betty Willsher investigate, gravestone engravings of Quarles's emblems in Britain and the United States from the mid-seventeenth through mid-eighteenth centuries "testify to Quarles's continuing popularity," and suggest a meditative, devotional context for this work (169). The *Emblemes* were "popular with Puritan readers" (Roberts 228) – the very sectarians that Quarles argued against in his lifetime – after his death and experienced a revival among Evangelical communities (as well as literary circles) in the nineteenth century (Höltgen, *Aspects of the Emblem*, 31–2). The *Emblemes'* adaptation of Jesuit images with a mainstream Protestant poetic text and ultimate Puritan readership demonstrates the contested middle ground in which Quarles and his works aimed, as well as the polyvocality of different religious symbolisms and arguments in Quarles's time. Situated within its own mid-seventeenth century religious and political context, though, Quarles's work follows an ethos of moral instruction through readers' own visual vigilance: in an era when different "truths" competed in the civic and religious sphere, Quarles's *Emblemes* and political works demand that readers figure out truths for themselves among competing aims and signs. The heated political context of Quarles's era informs his works, as they demonstrate an ethos of moral scrutiny in the midst of conflicting narratives and symbols. As in Quarles's more ostensibly political books, his *Emblemes* is neither iconoclastic nor iconophilic but assertively responds to the visual controversies and problematics of Quarles's time, presenting vision as both potentially divine and potentially duplicitous. His emblems' visual elements set hallucinatory delusions and divine visions side-by-side as dual, duplicative paths. Quarles justifies his symbols as patterns of God's creation in his apologia; however, his emblems portray this creation as a complex, conflicting system of visual cues.

Fool's Paradises and Windows to Heaven:
The *Emblemes'* Visual Mediation

Moral progress in Quarles depends on a successful interpretation of these types, hieroglyphics, and emblems of creation, a difficult process for which his book positions itself as a guide. Book Three, Emblem XIV in the 1634/5 edition of *Emblemes* ("The Entertainment") cites Deuteronomy: "*O that men men were wise, and that they understood this, that they would consider their latter end*" (sig. M4r) (Figure 4.1). The engraver of this emblem, John Payne, adds to Quarles's Jesuit source, *Pia Desideria* (1624) (Figure 4.2), a nude, seated woman opposite the older woman (Figure 4.3).

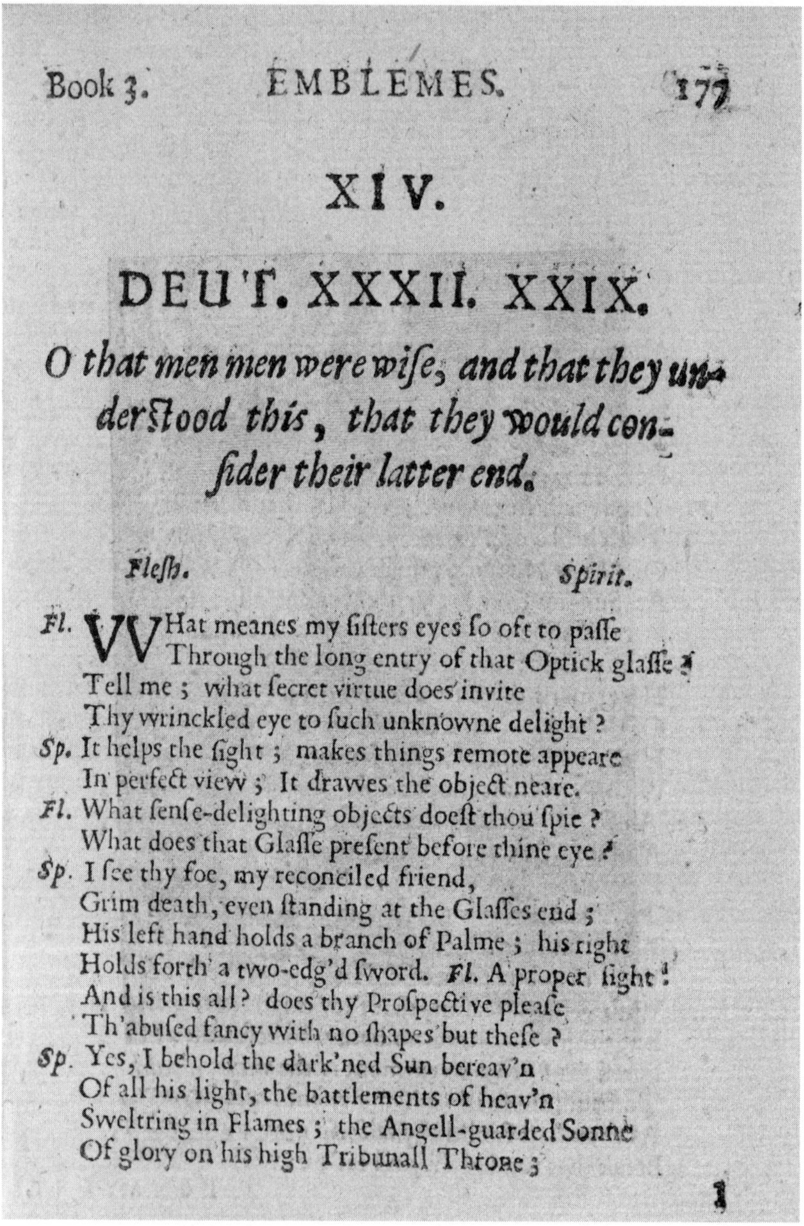

Book 3. EMBLEMES. 177

XIV.

DEUT. XXXII. XXIX.

O that men men were wiſe, and that they understood this, that they would conſider their latter end.

Fleſh. *Spirit.*

Fl. WHat meanes my ſiſters eyes ſo oft to paſſe
Through the long entry of that Optick glaſſe?
Tell me; what ſecret virtue does invite
Thy wrinckled eye to ſuch unknowne delight?
Sp. It helps the ſight; makes things remote appeare
In perfect view; It drawes the object neare.
Fl. What ſenſe-delighting objects doeſt thou ſpie?
What does that Glaſſe preſent before thine eye?
Sp. I ſee thy foe, my reconciled friend,
Grim death, even ſtanding at the Glaſſes end;
His left hand holds a branch of Palme; his right
Holds forth a two-edg'd ſword. *Fl.* A proper ſight!
And is this all? does thy Proſpective pleaſe
Th'abuſed fancy with no ſhapes but theſe?
Sp. Yes, I behold the dark'ned Sun bereav'n
Of all his light, the battlements of heav'n
Sweltring in Flames; the Angell-guarded Sonne
Of glory on his high Tribunall Throne;

Figure 4.1. Francis Quarles, *Emblemes* (1635), page 177, Bodleian Library

Figure 4.2. Herman Hugo, *Pia Desideria* (1624), page 72, Bodleian Library

Figure 4.3. Francis Quarles, *Emblemes* (1635), page 176, Bodleian Library

The duplication of "men" here is most likely an erratum (subsequent editions omit this repetition), yet it well suits an emblem that contemplates truth and error in sight. The engraving shows an elderly woman who gazes at the heavens with an "Optick glasse." The woman appears ecstatic in her gaze: her sight (and the reader's) focuses on Christ descending from the clouds, which encircle the sun. Two angels frame either side of the sun, which has multiple spots and a triangle at its centre. Beneath this sun and Son lie hellfire and a skeletal *memento mori* in front holding chaff in one hand and a sickle in another. This addition appears to be the same visual and allegorical "type" as Eve in Book 1, Emblem 1.This added figure sits beside the elderly woman and holds a triangular glass in her hand, beseeching her to gaze upon it.

The unified, beatific vision of the Jesuit source becomes, in the *Emblemes'* appropriation, a disputed, double vision over what is actually being seen. In Quarles's text, the two women are Flesh and Spirit. Flesh and Spirit dispute different methods of visual perception in this emblem. Flesh asks,

> What meanes my sisters eye so oft to passe
> Through the long entry of that Optick glasse?
> Tell me; what secret virtue does invite
> Thy wrinckled eye to such unknowne delight?   (sig. M4r)

Spirit responds, "[I]t helps the sight: makes things remote appeare / in perfect view: It drawes the object neare." This "optic glass," which draws distant objects near, resembles the early telescope. Prior to the *Emblemes* publication, Galileo's discoveries of sunspots with his telescope (1610), Kepler's *Catoptrics* (1611), and Christoph Scheiner's *Rosa Ursina* (1630) – the first detailed description of a refracting telescope – destabilized and expanded an already problematic early modern gaze. Spirit's own "Optick glasse," an expansion of her visual capabilities, acts as both a *tele*scope (for seeing far into the heavens) and a *telos*-scope for seeing the end and aim of life (the afterlife). Quarles's verse here recalls George Herbert's treatment of an optic glass in "The Elixir," which similarly posits a heavenly gaze against more distracted, material sight:

> A man that looks on glasse,
> On it may stay his eye;
> Or if he pleaseth, through it passe,
> And then the heav'n espie.   (sig. H4r)

This poem's publication in the consciously visual work of Herbert's *Temple* displays a similar paradox as Quarles's emblematics: a use of visual, material form to represent an aim that surpasses it. Flesh, however, casts doubt on Spirit's heavenly vision: in her argument, the ability to see beyond a physical and immediate reality is the delusional projection of a "wrinkled eye." As Stuart Clark outlines, cataracts in early modern science were thought to cause motes, mites, and "clouds of small flies" to disturb normal vision; the cause could either be physiological (from age or disease) or psychological, imagined by a disturbed mind (41), as Flesh implies. The sunspots and heavenly visions of Spirit and her glass are instead, in Flesh's response, the "shapes" of an "abused fancy" drawn from a "prospective." A "prospective" in early modern usage could mean a prospective glass used to see a distance, an object (like a prospective stone) used for looking into the future, a "magic glass revealing distant or future events" (*MED* def. d), or an image that makes cunning use of visual perspective.[5]

Again, visual perception and visual reading were both complex and problematic activities in early modern culture. Quarles's poems, as textual companions to the engraved emblems, parallel their representations of duplication and inversion. This process, in addition to the emblems' literal, controversial duplication of the Jesuit sources, establishes a rhetorical pattern of doubling and paradox throughout the book. This duplication process evokes seventeenth-century agons over sight itself: as Clark explores in *Vanities of the Eye*, physiological, psychological, and diabolical forces constantly threatened accurate sight. According to Clark, the use of "perspective" "rests on the ultimate visual paradox: complete deception in the service of utter veracity," presenting "an ambiguous and irresolvable combination of the false and the true" (83–4). Good and evil, false sight and true, both contrast with and mirror one another in the emblems. The engravings and their corresponding poetic texts perform a visual and rhetorical double vision that draws and instructs the eye of the reader.

These popular renderings of spots or motes that disturb the eye further respond to early modern intellectual debates over sight as projection versus sight as reception. These small particles that alter vision, potentially cataracts or mites, also potentially reference Democritus's atomic theory, which he discussed in terms more phenomenological than scientific (Taylor 83–4). C.C.W. Taylor articulates in his commentary on Democritus's atoms that "it is not the case that atoms are imperceptible because they are too small to be perceived ... the atom is not transparent; it blocks off the atomic films from the objects behind it" (178). If a larger atom came across one's field of vision, "a temporary blind spot passes across it ... And if I were confronted with an atom big enough to blot out all but the edges of my visual field, it would be like having only peripheral vision" (178). Atomic particles, in classical, medieval, and early modern phenomenology, could cause perceptual distortion, like the sunspots or motes on the visual engraving of the sun, and perhaps within the Soul's wrinkled eye. In this emblem, Flesh acts as an empirical or Aristotelian sceptic in her response to Spirit's projective sight. The vision of sun and Son the reader sees on the page, in her perspective, is a figment of Spirit's "fancy." The sun's spots, represented on the page, are delusions or mites of Spirit's cataracted eye in Flesh's dialogue; however, they could alternatively resemble sunspots – a new, far vision recently achievable with Spirit's telescope.[6]

This engraving's use of visual perspective, however, seems to encourage readers to share Spirit's far vision and to "remember the end" (sig. M4). The engraving achieves its perspective through its framing images: the hedges on either side of the hellfire/skeleton symbols, the angels on either side of the clouds, the women on either side of the page, and the spotted sun situated at the top/centre of the illustration. Flesh construes Spirit's far vision as a fantastical delusion: "can thy distemper'd fancie take delight / in view of Tortures? These are showes t'affright" (sig. M4). Flesh argues that an imbalance of humours or psychological disturbance, implied by the terms "distemper," which would cause a physiological visual delusion, and "fancie," a psychological visual delusion of the imagination, could be the true cause of Spirit's far (or false) sight. Yet Flesh does not dismiss sight altogether as a means of perceiving truth; she instead presents an alternative "glasse-triangular" that "will ravish" our "eyes" (sig. M4). Sight itself is triangular in the classical and Islamic sources from which early modern understandings of sight drew. Objects send the eye "species" or light along a "visual pyramid," and the image/impression of the two-dimensional object then reaches into the eye and brain (Clark 16). This triangular concept of sight also informs the use of perspective in representational art. Triangular perspective paradoxically deceived the eye to represent a more realistic image. The triangle also appears in the sun itself, to which the Christ figure points. A triangle could visually represent the divine trinity in medieval and early modern theological allegory.

Flesh's triangular glass therefore mixes truth with deception, blurring the boundary between the two: the "optic glass" or telescope competes with the colourful optical illusions of the prism. This prism is kaleidoscope-like, as it refracts and captures different, varied colours for the sensory delight of the eye. A "prism" in Quarles's time could mean both a geometrical shape and an object for refracting light.[7] The *OED* cites Henry Peacham's *Gentleman's Exercise*, a book that included its own emblems alongside specific techniques for engraved illustrations, as its first citation for the optical prism. Peacham introduces this optical glass alongside manipulations of colour, as the prism refracts red and blue light: "as by a most pleasant and delightfull experiment wee may perceiue in a three square cristal prisme, wherin you shal perceiue the blew to be outmost next to that the red" (150). An English translation of educator Johann Amos Comenius's dictionary, *The Gate of the Latin Tongue Unlocked* (1656), includes a definition of prisms in its section "The Delights of the Eyes" situated as painting, embroidery, and "especially Gravers cutting most curious little images in brass, and imprinting them on paper" (137, def. 478). Visual delights and illusions, optical technology, and seventeenth-century discussions of prisms are adjacently situated alongside print illustration techniques in Peacham and this translation of Comenius. This association between glass prisms and copper engravings may draw from a late-medieval association of books with mirrors, as chapter 1 discusses, and from their status as concurrent visual technologies in the seventeenth century. Flesh's deceptive prism therefore recursively reflects the engraving technologies of the emblem itself. Under the term "specularium," Comenius's translator discusses telescopes, prisms, and optical technologies:

> The Glass-man provideth looking-glasses, wherein men may behold themselves, and spectacles, wherewith they may perceive things more sharply; and perspective-glasses, whereby they may view things a far off, as if they were near at hand; and multiplying-glasses, wherewith they may see little dusts as it were mountains; and prisms, (called fools paradises) which transform the colours of things into a thousand shapes, and burning-glasses, &c. (139 def. 480)

This definition of the prism or triangular glass as a "fool's paradise" may have been in common use by the time of the *Emblemes'* publication. If so, Flesh's colourful glass-triangular gives us a paradise of folly juxtaposed with the competing alternatives of Spirit's heavenly sun and the hellish skeleton, even as Comenius defines the perspective glass or telescope as one of many optical distortions.[8] As Catherine Gimelli

Martin observes, Galilean, optical language suffuses *Paradise Lost*'s "heliocentric" and "epic cosmos" (245), as Satan becomes a sunspot that Galileo "through his glaz'd Optic Tube yet never saw" (Milton 3.590). To extend this analysis, Milton juxtaposes his far-seeing Tube with a potential reference to the illusory prism as a fool's paradise: as Satan walks the "round World, whose first convex divides / The luminous inferior Orbs" (3.419–42), he encounters Limbo, a "Paradise of Fools, to few unknown" (3.496). The green spectacles that, as chapter 3 mentions, may have aided early modern readers' eyesight, also led in early modern texts to a fear of their "simultaneous distortion of vision" (Leah Knight 32): this tool for assisting sight could just as easily delude it. As Knight notes, these green spectacles became a metaphor for unruly passion and imagination, cast in early modern texts as a projective visual delusion. In one text, "passions are green spectacles that make all things look green" (Samuel Clarke 23); in another, "The imagination putteth greene spectacles before the eyes of the witte, to make it see nothing but greene" (Wright 92).[9]

The dialogue between Spirit and Flesh therefore contrasts the unity and far sight of the telescope with the aesthetic multiplicity and visual seductiveness of the glass prism. Through the triangular glass, Flesh presents "the world in colours; colours that distaine / The cheeks of *Proteus*, or the silken traine / Of *Floras* nymphs" (sig. M4v). The figures of shape-shifting Proteus and seductive Flora are classical types for aesthetic mutability and sensuality. The term "distaine" amplifies the troubling nature of Flesh's earthly vision. "Distaine" could mean, in Quarles's time, to colour, to discolour, to dim, to defame, or to defile.[10] This emblem's inclusion of a glass (and word) that could both create and dim colour reinforces visuality's association with optical illusion and paradox in the *Emblemes*. The connection between Flesh's glass and defilement through the term "distaine" additionally associates vision, with its sensory, sensual aspects, with sin, even as this message is transmitted in the form of a visual emblem. As a figure for wordly sight, Flesh seems to make the case for a more objective correspondence between vision and the external world. However, as Clark states, early modern "vision *itself* was pictorial" and already representational (16) – and, if we remember Quarles's apologia at the beginning of his text, sight is figured as a partial representation, though fractured, of God's own representational hieroglyphs. The triangular structure enables Flesh to make vision "scant" or "widen" by the force of "thine owne will / make short or long, at pleasure," as she enjoins Spirit to "tyre thy fancie": imagination, instead of projecting outwards with the help of the "Optick Glasse," indulges itself with visual delights in Flesh's "glasse-triangular." Quarles's description of Flesh's colourful prism resembles the classical philosopher Anaxagoras's concept of the rainbow as a "reflection of the sun in the clouds" (Curd 29, B19): the distained colours of the prism mediate and reflect light, rather than draw it closer. Through Flesh's prism, we are trapped by pleasurable chimeras, and, like Plato's cave dwellers, we substitute these delusions for end or telos-driven sight. In her analysis of Margaret Cavendish's *Blazing Worlds* (1666), Elizabeth A. Spiller argues that "the unreliability of telescopic vision becomes a dominant metaphor for the unreliability of reading printed texts" (192). Here, though, it is the glassy prism, or "fool's paradise," that delights and deceives the eye, a spectacle that reflexively parallels the "curious little engraving" of the emblem itself.

The poetic text's criticism of Flesh's triangular glass rests uneasily with the overall triangular representational structure of the engraving, which duplicates Flesh's false triangular prism. The duplicity of the "glasse triangular" in this emblem rests not in the use of sight or perspective itself, which can operate as a partial, mediative form – as a spiritual telos-scope – but the use of that perspective for visual delights alone. After all, the heavenly sun/Son is imprinted with a triangle of its own in the emblem. Ernest B. Gilman reads this emblem as an exploration of the "problem of vision": "the condition of sight has become a kind of agon between Flesh and Spirit for the eye of the viewer, who is made to feel the pull on him from two directions" (393). A visual rhetoric of duplication in Quarles's emblems complicates Gilman's observation of the duality between Spirit and Flesh, earthly/sensual vision and heavenly/spiritual vision. The Flesh figure duplicates the Eve figure of the *Emblemes'* first engraving, and Flesh's triangular glass duplicates the triangle at the centre of the sun. Spirit tells Flesh to "break that fond glasse, and let's be wise together" (sig. M4), but no form of sight in this engraving is unmediated through some visual-material object of representation: the optic glass, the triangular glass, the engraving, and the book itself. The emblem does not present any vision that is objective or unmediated; rather, it offers us a moral and metaphysical choice on how to look at it, a choice that becomes complicated by the duplication of images and motifs across the page.

Visual perspective, then, is both a potential deception and a medium for divine sight in this emblem. The use of depth or a vanishing point in perspective art both beguiles the viewer's eye and draws the sight to a high or distant plane. The engraving itself, which sets Spirit, Flesh, and the sun/Son as points that compose a triangle on the picture plane, both promises telos and uses the duplicitous nature of triangular visual perspective itself to draw our eye to the sun/Son. The process of employing material, visual form for divine content has its dangers: the inclusion of Flesh endangers the eye, tempting it to rove permanently away from the sun/Son. The metaphor of the book as a glass or mirror, as chapter 1 discusses, also drew from metaphors of the bible as a mediative glass for the divine: this concept of book or bible as dark glass emerges from a passage in Corinthians, which promises that we will see the divine end/aim only "through a glass darkly" (KJV 13:12). Eve's prism metaphorically speaks to the anxiety that readers will be distracted by the form of the book itself as a spectacle, that print visuals could be duplicitous, deceptive shadows and colours of a prism rather than a clear glass. The book of the *Emblemes* itself, in this structure of duality, becomes either a partial, translucent glass with which to access glimpses of truth or an errata-filled, distortive prism. Even this emblem's print errata may be situated within its troubling representation of vision: will men become wise or will "men men" become wise after reading this emblem?

Crossed Eyes: Figures of Chiasmus and Paradox

Quarles's other emblems further complicate the visual reading process through their use of optical illusion and paradox. Book Two, Emblem Six reproduces an image from *Typus Mundi* and shows an image of Cupid, who points towards his own reflection in a globe mirror (Figure 4.4).

The globe or "world as bubble" motif repeats itself throughout the *Typus Mundi* and Quarles's *Emblemes*: fittingly, the poem accompanying this image is a sententious polemic against vanity: "her Glasse diffuses / False Portraitures ... it scatters / Deceitful beames" (sig. F4r). Cupid's duplication in the world/bubble/mirror, which stretches him to be slightly larger than his normal size, seems to deliver a fairly uncomplicated message on the errors of vanity and worldly sight. The good angel who holds up this globe/mirror complicates this maxim: he visually "mirrors" Cupid as he stands on the opposite side of the engraving and holds the false glass. The labour conditions of engraving encouraged (and necessitated) the

Figure 4.4. Francis Quarles, *Emblemes* (1635), page 84, Bodleian Library

repetition of several imitated visual "types" across different print texts or, as in this case, within the same text. Good and bad Cupid are drawn from the same type, literally and metaphorically, then repeated across several different emblems. Thematic concerns and technological processes thus work together to present a philosophical and aesthetic context of conflicting and multiplying signs. The text itself of this emblem draws on the metaphor of a print book. This mediative mirror contains the ability to erase aesthetic error, portrayed as print errata:

> had surfeits, or th'ungratious Starre
> Conspir'd to make one Common place
> Of all deformities, that are
> Within the Volume of thy face
> Shee'd lend thee savour.   (sig. F4v)

The mirror obfuscates a necessary meditation on error/sin, while the face, as book, is a compendium of errata/error. Again, Quarles and his engravers set up competing symbols of mediation side by side, or within the same metaphorical conceit, as they demonstrate the vexed relationship between sight and perception. Further, the *Emblemes'* engravings literally reverse those of Quarles's Jesuit sources: a direct copy of an engraving always ends as a reversed "mirror image" of the original after printing, so that Marshall's direct imitation of his sources also created a literal reversal or "negative" of those copies on the page. This process of mirroring (inverse mimesis) is both a duplication/imitation and a reversal: reproduced form has the ability to transpose content. In stanza seven of the emblem's text, Cupid's image is a "shadow" that declines when heaven's "bright beames" fall on him and grows when the beams move away: the shadow metaphor presents a paradox of a dark, negative, yet visible image, one that is both mimetic and inverse (sig. F4v). A shadow, like Marshall's print copies of the Jesuit emblems, is a reverse mimesis. The ability for (little) Cupid to grow larger in the false mirror (or for his shadow to grow larger in refracted light) parallels, diabolically, book engraving's own ability to alter and invert images.

The rhetorical duplication of this biblical reference and the visual duplication of bad Cupid/mirrored Cupid/good angel make use of two common rhetorical devices that commonly appeared in early modern English visual and rhetorical tropes: paradox and chiasmus.

For example, paradox and chiasmus figure in this emblem's concluding epigram, "[T]he least is greatest; and who shall / Appeare the greatest, are the least of all" (sig. F4v). Rosalie L. Colie's *Paradoxica Epidemica* famously explores the ubiquity of paradox as an early modern rhetorical form. Paradox, she argues, has "duplicity built into it"; "its duplicitous intent, honestly proclaimed, imposed an antic decorum encouraging, in many ways, to novelty and trickery" (5). Paradox and chiasmus are devices that can transpose and reverse visual and verbal forms to construct new meanings. A paradox contains both truth and not-truth, or two different statements that necessarily cancel one another. Paradox calls attention to itself as a form. Visual duplicity in representation is doubly duplicitous by the cunning reality effect of representational perspective and the necessary visual trickery this reality effect entails. This emblem, alongside the text, performs paradox on multiple levels. Mediative representation, and the visual capabilities of that representation, acts as both error and the solution to error. Cupid expands in the mirror, yet without our perception of that expansion (or the Cupid-like good angel who holds the mirror), we do not have an instructive mirror held up onto our own vanities. Perceptual distortion is both "vanity" and the tool of a divinity that makes the greatest the least; and the least, greatest. The trope of the mirror itself, too, makes the demonstration of distortion into a spiritual instruction. Unlike steel mirrors or glasses used in devotionals as spiritual heuristics (Kalas, *Frame, Glass, Verse* 48), the later Renaissance glass mirror was a technology that signified vanity and was an object that "accrues meaning incontinently as it is exchanged" (117): much as the wearing or exchange of glass mirrors as status symbols, the Cupid gets falsely larger in his reflection, through a process of mediation. The perceptual distortion caused by the beams of vanity in this emblem negatively parallels the more benevolent distortion caused by divine beams. Again, truth and error in Quarles's *Emblemes* reproduce themselves via the same visual-material forms of mediation.

The emblem's epigram, "least greatest and greatest least," is also a figure of chiasmus. William Engel's *Chiastic Designs* outlines the use of chiasmus as a rhetorical technique in early modern poetry, including "emblematic conceits" that "function as memorial triggers," such as Quarles's poems on King David in his *Divine Fancies* (1624) (1, 15–40). Chiasmus, as Engels explains, forms an "ABBA" structure in language and connotes a sense of veiled truth (3–7). The term chiasmus derives from the letter "chi" (X in Greek) (Engels 5), and is the first letter of Christ, represented in the "chi rho" figure, ☧. Peter McCullough explores Lancelot Andrewes's employment of verbal chiastic figures in his Good Friday sermons, as he erected rhetorical crosses before Protestant audiences still suspicious of the iconic, visual cross. McCullough claims that "Andrewes's strategy of erasing" the very "iconography that had been tainted as popish superstition, only to re-inscribe the very same iconography, but in ways that articulate" Protestant theology (574). McCullough's analysis of Andrewes's sermon, as well as seventeenth-century English emblem books' adoption of Jesuit iconography, presents us with a dialectical process of iconoclasm and mirroring: a destruction of image and form to rearrange and transpose new meaning. Cupid, the mirror, and the good angel form a visual chiasmus on the emblematic page: Cupid mirrors the good angel, who holds a mirror up to the vain Cupid. Chiasmus here symbolizes duplication and, in the context of Anglicanism's rearrangement of Catholic iconography, appropriation.

Vanity's visual distortion and the chiasmus of the epigram portray the vexed, yet potentially instructive role of duplicative sight. Book 3's first emblem, *"my soul hath desired Thee in the night,"* shows the good angel with a lamp pointing to the heavens, leading the woman/soul figure who, in the hatching techniques of this chiaroscuro engraving, is shrouded in darkness (Figure 4.5).

The technique of cross-hatching gives an engraving or woodcut in print the technical ability to portray darkness and light, or chiaroscuro, and literally replicates a cross or "X" figure multiple times across the engraved plate or woodblock. The final lines of Quarles's poem that accompany the engraving, spoken with the voice of Soul, form a textual, rhetorical chiasmus that meditates on a thematic use of light: "lend the Twilight of thine Eye: / If I must want those Beames I wish, yet grant, / That I, at least, may wish those Beames I want" (sig. I3). "Wish" and "want" in these lines form the ABBA structure of a chiasmus (want/wish/wish/want) in these lines. The very lack of light in the "eye" of the soul creates a desire for God's heavenly beams. Quarles's and Marshall's use of shadow, light, and reflection as a visual, technical motif and metaphysical metaphor performs both an illusionary and instructive role.

Figure 4.5. Francis Quarles, *Emblemes* (1635), page 128, Bodleian Library

Black Snow: Visual and Political Inversion

The *Emblemes'* visual and rhetorical figures hence perform an extended meditation on the problem of visual perception, knowledge, and truth. Their duplications and paradoxical reversals potentially draw from the thought of Anaxagoras, popular in seventeenth-century print debates. Anaxagoras's work, which now exists only in fragments, focused on issues of phenomenology, perception, and the natural world; he studies rainbows, eclipses, meteors, the sun, and snow. He boldly claimed that "appearances are a sight of the unseen," a paradoxical statement that conveys a sense that reality is "unavailable to perception, but graspable by understanding" (Curd 75). This sense that reality is a matter of interpretation and discernment rather than visual perception parallels the telos-driven (yet visually mediated) messages of Quarles's emblems. Visual paradox is also prominent in Anaxagoras's existing fragments. His claim that the colours of the rainbow were created through reflection found a similar explanation in solar reflection, as he describes "mock suns that are said to occur near the Black Sea" (Curd 223n.49), or parahelia, which are seen as "bright spots" that "appear in pairs, one on either side of the sun" (Curd 223). Anaxagoras enjoyed some popularity – or, perhaps more accurately, notoriety – in mid-seventeenth-century texts.[11] References to Anaxagoras proliferated in mid-seventeenth-century philosophical,[12] scientific,[13] and, especially, religious, devotional, and polemical publications.[14] Anaxagoras's claim of visual paradox, that snow is actually black despite its white appearance, again opposed visual perception to material reality: he believed that "snow is frozen water, water is black, and therefore snow is black" (Curd 121). Anaxagoras's opposition of vision to matter in his paradox of black snow paralleled the Catholic belief in transubstantiation, where the host appears as bread, but is Christ's body in actual matter. Anaxagoras's black snow therefore became a trope of foolishness and deceit in Protestant polemics contemporary to Quarles's *Emblemes*. This trope of black snow appeared to operate as a rhetorical figure deeply embedded in seventeenth-century sermons and pamphlets that discuss sight, deception, and revealed truth. John Downe's *Treatise of the true nature and definition of justifying faith* (1635) uses this figure to counter "Skepticks" who do not believe in Scriptural plainness or clarity:

> neither are all satisfied with these plaine places, neither are all places of Scripture plaine. True. Yet haue you no reason to doubt of that which is plaine, because some through frowardnesse will not vnderstand: no more then you haue of the snow whether it be white, because *Anaxagoras* thought

that it was blacke. If nothing can be certaine but that which is unquestioned, we must all turne Scepticks, and neuer beleeue any thing. (sig. Nn1v)

In a 1627 sermon and exposition against non-believers, Puritan clergyman William Sclater asks us,

What if a man held as *Anaxagoras,* that the Snow is blacke; could he not be induced to belieue it white: or as *Copernicus,* that the heavens stand still without motion; the earth moues, and were refractary to all contrary perswasion. Heretiques or Infidels you might call such in Philosophy. (171)

As in Quarles's emblem, metaphors of refraction ("refractary") parallel figures of false or deluded sight. In Richard Montagu's anti-Catholic *A gagg for the new Gospell? No: a new gagg for an old goose Who would needes undertake to stop all Protestants mouths for euer* (1624), Anaxagoras features as a co-deluder of souls: "honest good Catholiques must belieue what their *Instructors* say, though they teach that the Snow is blacke: so are they hood-wincked in implicite *Faith*" (sig. Niiir). Anaxagoras's theorems feature in these religious polemics as optical illusions for misguided heretics, sceptics, and Catholics, in metaphors of refracted or altogether blocked sight ("refractory," "hood-winked"). In these allusions, Anaxagoras's black snow symbolizes an unnecessary complication of the plain and visible truth. In contrast, Quarles's *Emblemes* returns us to Anaxagoras's original sight-perception problem, while appearing to draw inspiration from the new visual technologies of Copernican and astronomical science. Quarles's own visual rhetoric complicates rather than simplifies. His work, unlike these seventeenth-century Protestant polemics, instead parallels Anaxagoras's argument that interior perception should be privileged over external vision. Both Quarles and the polemicists who appropriate Anaxagoras's black snow, however, are responding to visual controversies – transubstantiation, phenomenological perception, the heliocentric Copernican universe – that were still uncertain grey matters in the seventeenth century.

Truth and error, light and shadow, therefore criss-cross, parallel, and duplicate one another in the work of Francis Quarles. The most well-known engraving of *Emblemes,* Eve's conversation with the serpent in Emblem One (Figure 4.6), again indicates the pitfalls of vexed sight.

Ernest B. Gilman explicates the emblem's ability to subvert "the authority of all the engravings by making us realize both their covertly lustful appearance and our complicity in that lust" (401): William Marshall's engraving of paradise serves as a tempting visual snare. Marshall

Figure 4.6. Francis Quarles, *Emblemes* (1635), page 4, Bodleian Library

radically transforms the corresponding emblem of *Typus Mundi*: Eve rather than Adam is the protagonist of the emblem as she displays her body to the reader with her arms apart. Her hand wards off Adam, whom Marshall adds to the original Jesuit engraving as he stands in the distance. His parallel posture at the tree of life duplicates Eve's temptation at the tree of knowledge.

Like polemical references to Anaxagoras's black snow, Quarles's and Marshall's visual and textual treatment of paradox, duality, and deception is not purely a metaphysical or theological allegory but a religious and political argument. The *Emblemes* were published during Charles I's personal rule following his dissolution of Parliament in 1629. Although Quarles had Puritan family connections and sympathies, he remained a staunch royalist throughout the personal rule and Civil War periods, even as his personal poverty increased. We can safely assume that Quarles was a Royalist for ideological and not practical reasons.[15] As Eve resists the cunning arguments of the serpent, she claims, "'Tis true, we are immortall; death is yet / Unborne; and, till Rebellion make it debt, / Undue'" (sig. A3v). The epigram concluding this section laments,

> Unluckie Parliament! Wherein, at last,
> Both Houses are agreed, and firmely past
> An Act of death, confirm'd by higher Powers:
> O had it had but such successe as Ours.   (sig. A3r)

In this analogy, Eve and Adam are the two "Houses" of Parliament. Parliament's attempt to curb the royal privilege of Charles I led to its dissolution. At the moment of the *Emblemes'* publication, Parliament had been unsuccessful at its own form of "Rebellion," so that Quarles's "such successe as Ours" represents a wish that the rebellion of Adam and Eve had failed. The epigram allegorizes the Houses of Lords and the House of Commons as Adam and Eve and God himself stands in for King Charles. The visual duality and duplication of Adam and Eve, as they stand in similar poses, promises their mutual fall: had God asserted a unified royal authority, to follow Quarles's logic, they (and England) may have remained in a Royalist paradise.

Visual Duality and Discernment in Quarles's Political Pamphlets: "Many Heads, Many Eyes"

Quarles ended his career as an emblematic poet with his *Hieroglyphicks* (1639), after which he turned to political poetry and prose. Intriguingly, the *Emblemes'* main engraver, William Marshall, who would illustrate the famous portrait of Charles I as martyr in *Eikon Basilike*, also began to illustrate religious, political, and polemical texts soon after his emblematic collaborations with Quarles. Quarles structures his pamphlet *The Whipper Whipt* (1644) as a Socratic trilogue. He excerpts the text of Dr Burges from his own pamphlet (1625), the text of "Calumnator" who wrote *The Whip* (presented in italic type), and casts himself as the Replyer. He allows Dr Burges – an influential anti-Laudian and Calvinist-leading minister who nonetheless opposed the Solemn League and Covenant of 1643 and the trial of Charles I – and the Calumnator to speak for themselves. In his note to the readers at the end of the book, he tells us

> If you look on this skirmish with a generall eye, you wil see nothing but (as in a Battail) smoak and confusion: But if you mark every ones particular behaviour, you wil easily distinguish betwixt a rash fieire spirit, and a truly valiant. (sig. A)

In other words, the eye that tries to unite the "many and too many Pamphlets which have abscured the Truth" will fail to discern it, where the eye that looks more particularly at the multiple, competing claims, arguments, and debates surrounding the issues of Parliamentary rebellion and Puritan uprising will be better able to judge the situation (sig. A). Daniel S. Russell argues that in viewing emblems and pages, the early modern reader as part of an audio-tactile culture would "scan" a frame for objects and symbols before viewing the emblem or sign as a whole. Readers emphasized "particular objects" "at the expense of the whole picture" as "mosaic-like" visual compositions flourished in early print culture (84). Both Quarles's pamphlet and the visual details of his *Emblemes'* engravings encourage a visual reading process focused on patterns of detail as a necessary component of political and moral discernment. As Höltgen and Horden observe together, "Quarles's emblem verse very often begins with demonstrative or deictic phrases," that call attention to the "details of the pictorial composition" (Introduction, *Francis Quarles' Emblemes (1635) and Hieroglyphikes of the Life of Man (1638)* 16). Marshall's inclusion of several small, particular symbols and alterations of the Jesuit emblems – a skeleton/ death figure with a bow and arrow in Emblem Seven of Book One (sig. C2v, Figure 4.7), a tiny dot in the hand of an angel, symbolizing the divine eye in Book Three, Emblem Two (sig. I3v, Figure 4.8) – encourages this ethos of visual vigilance.

This ethos of visual discernment was carried forward by a later reader and compiler of Quarles's political pamphlets. In the Bodleian Library,

Figure 4.7. Francis Quarles, *Emblemes* (1635), page 28, Bodleian Library

Figure 4.8. Francis Quarles, *Emblemes* (1635), page 132, Bodleian Library

a version of Quarles's *Shepheards Oracle, delivered in an eglogue* (1644) and his *Argulus and Parthenia* (1629) are bound together in a miscellany by a collector, most likely Royalist in political sympathies, with several other works concerning the role of kings and of state organization.[16] Adam Smyth discusses the importance of the miscellany as both a literary and political form in the mid-seventeenth century: miscellanies often expressed moral commonplaces, world-weariness, and religious devotion, but were often implicated in the era's political crisis. Royalist miscellanies often carried a sense of the political elegiac.[17] This miscellany is both poetic and political: its component parts are mostly poetic and dramatic texts, yet they share a thematic concern with the English state. An inscription marks a date of 1666/7, but a name that was once on the first blank page has been scored out with black ink. The note to the reader, not written by Quarles himself, gives the work both anonymity and publicity: *"Whose soever these Lines were, Readers they are now yours ... The Sense of this Eglogue is covered with a vaile, but so thin that an easie eye may Transpect it"* (sig. A). The term "transpect" appears to be a usage unique to the inscriber; however, it may share a close relationship to the word "transpeciate," which shares the root word "spec" or "species" (*OED*). To transpeciate means to transform, a change in appearance or kind that might take, at its origin, a phenomenal cast from its etymology. Transpect, in this context, appears as an idiosyncratic term for looking or reading. Transpection may also imply a sense of visual, phenomenal transformation, from the eye to the page. In their transpection of this miscellany, readers both observe and transform the material within.

These political pamphlets' aesthetic properties operate, in this metaphor of transpection, as mediative *species* that allow perception and political action to take place. *Argulus and Parthenia*, which is included with alterations in the miscellany, presents a frontispiece, engraved by Thomas Cecill, of a stage or architectural structure with a curtain drawn over an italic text (sig. A). A poem, "The minde of the Frontispiece," adjoins it:

> *Reader, behinde this silken Frontispiece lyes*
> *The argument of our Booke: which to your eye:*
> *Our Muse (for serious causes, and best knowne*
> *Unto her selfe) commands should be unshowne:*
> *And therefore, to that end, she hath thought fair*
> *To draw this Curtaine, 'twixt your eye and it.*   (sig. A)

The veil of Zeuxis, alongside the grapes of Zeuxis, were classical commonplaces of visual duplicity and representational perspective in early modern discourse. Zeuxis painted grapes so accurately that birds began to peck at them. His rival Parrhasius later painted a veil so lifelike that someone attempted to pull it back. The grapes and veil represented the paradox of a natural artifice, or a lifelike representational object (Colie 276). The act of reading the "sense" (i.e., the political sense) of these political texts resembles the act of pulling back a representational curtain: the reader is invited to look through the veil to understand the political message underneath. This veil, like a dark glass, allows for a partial understanding through the mediation of print visuals.

As in *The Shepeards Oracle*, the symbolic uncovering of political meaning references Zeuxis's substitution of an artificial curtain for a real one – generic and aesthetic form in Quarles's political writings conceals, yet reveals, political function. Mid-seventeenth-century political crises threatened pamphleteering and visual display. Fear of censorship or persecution on every side of these disputes imbued its print culture. Yet this danger could also act as an advertisement and intrigue for the reading public. This pamphlet, and its adjoining frontispiece, emblematize Quarles's pamphlets as political peepshows: they form an aesthetic cover that draws the gaze and advertises the pamphlets' underlying political aims.[18] The blotting out of this collection owner's name and its curtained title page conceals, even as it reveals a material and aesthetic system of concealment.

Although literal visual engravings are absent in his pamphlets, Quarles still creates a rhetorical structure of vexed emblematics. In *The Shepheards Oracle*, Philarchus the royalist argues with Philorthus the Parliamentarian, and the undecided Philarthus responds in kind to both. Philorthus argues to the other two shepherds to trust in the vision of Parliament:

> ... their great Assembly's wise;
> Has many Heads, and twice as many Eyes,
> Eyes bright as day, that view both things and times
> Fast closd to Persons, open to their Crimes:
> Judgement, not Fancy, moves in that bright Sphere.   (sig. A3)

The "bright Sphere" of Parliament's "judgement" recalls the Star Chamber, the room where the court of Chancellors, sympathetic to Charles I, met. The Star Chamber was actually abolished by Parliament in 1641, prior to the *Oracle*'s publication. Philorthus's description of

Parliament recalls the image of Argus (from classical texts, the many-eyed monster who never slept), the image of the Greek Hydra, and the many-headed beast of Revelation. Marc Bensimon discusses the use of eye imagery in the early modern period as a "means of visualizing abstractions"; he cites Janus and Argus as popular figures for representing visuality and sight (274). Argus, "sometimes called bifrons and represented with two heads," paradoxically represented both sleep and wakefulness, as well as emblematic visuality in itself (276). These associations draw from Ovid's *Metamorphoses*, in which the watchful hundred-eyed Argus is lulled to sleep and slain by Mercury. According to Ovid, Hera preserved Argus's eyes in a peacock's tail. Argus displays what rhetoricians might recognize as *conduplicatio*, an organized repetition (eyes, visual symbolism), a figure based on duality.

Parliament's sight and multiplicity in this passage therefore form a meta-visual reference to the emblematic Argus. Whether that allusion lends itself to keen perception or slumbering deception, of course, depends on readers' political perspectives. Ironically, while Philorthus depicts the Star Chamber as a figure of judgment, not fancy, his description of a multi-headed, all-seeing political body is entirely fantastical and imaginative. The Assembly-as-Argus, like the Eve and Adam of Quarles's *Emblemes*, presents readers with an image of monstrously divided "heads," or authorities, a fitting rhetorical tactic for one with Royalist sympathies. Argus's situation alongside the "Star chamber" in this passage may, further, figure visual debates of observational judgment versus fancy, or the imagination, in astronomy. Volker R. Remmert analyses the anti-Copernican emblematic frontispiece of the Jesuit astronomical pamphlet *Almagestum Novum* (1651) (Figure 4.9), where the "virgin Astraea" (a classical goddess of justice) "representing theoretical and cosmological astronomy" is set alongside Argus, representing "practical and observational astronomy" (29).

While this Italian text postdates Quarles's *Shepheards Oracle*, Argus as a figure for both watchful observation and folly in this frontispiece parallels Argus's employment by Quarles as a metavisual figure for the assembly's own starry chamber.

The paradoxical role and emblematic nature of Argus lent itself to radical religious and political rhetoric in Quarles's cultural moment. Baptist radical Henry Adis, whose "opposition to the violent removal of King Charles I from power resulted in his being jailed in 1648" (Durso 144), uses Argus primarily as a symbol of watchful justice in his 1648 pamphlet *A Spie, Sent out of the Tower-Chamber in the Fleet* (Figure 4.10).

Figure 4.9. Giovanni Battista Riccioli, *Almagestum Novum* (1651), frontispiece, University of Ghent Library

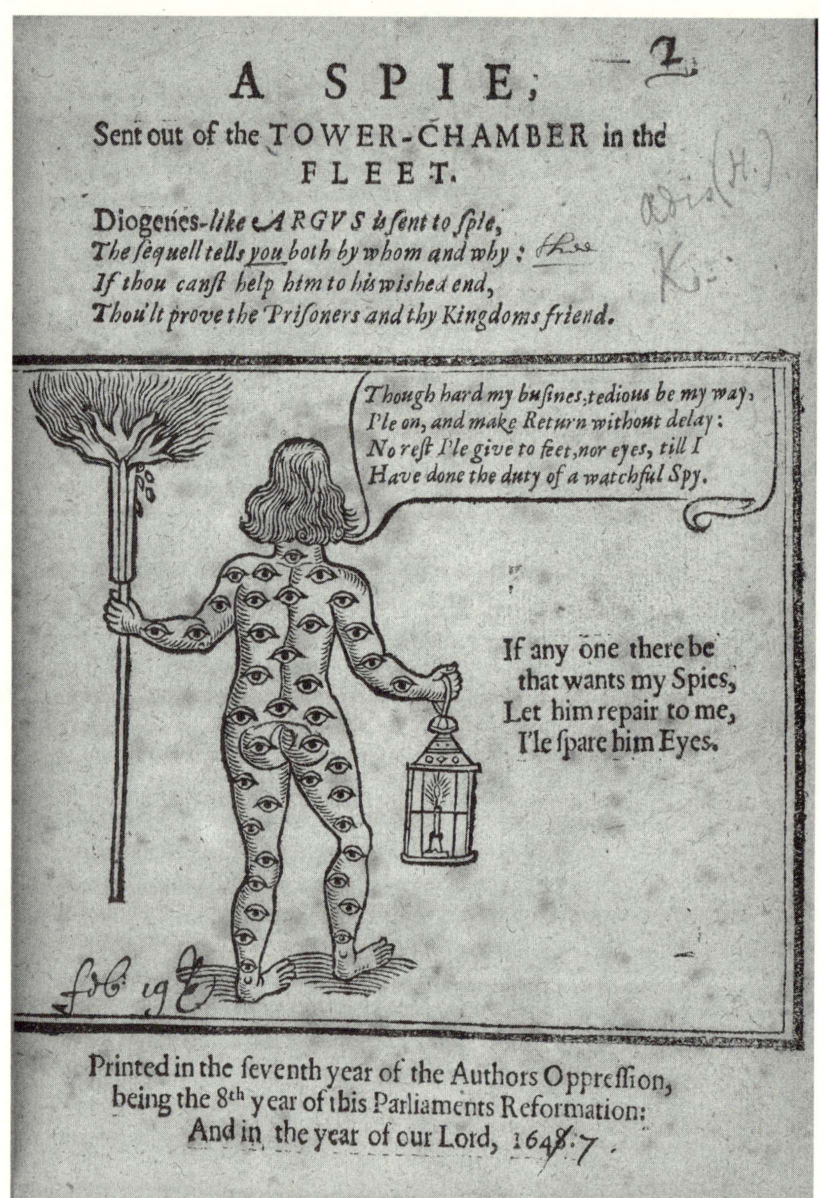

Figure 4.10. Henry Adis, *A Spie, Sent out of the Tower-Chamber in the Fleet* (1648), frontispiece, British Library

The title page of this pamphlet shows a naked Argus who holds both torch and lantern, as this figure exclaims "No rest I'le give to feet, nor eyes, till I / Have done the duty of a watchful Spy." The "spy" here is both Argus and the emblematic pamphlet itself. Adis's many-eyed *Spie* attacks William Lenthall, that year's house speaker, for his imprisonment (Durso 146). The watchful, optical elements of Argus, like Quarles's own adoption of the Argus figure, carry political and eschatological associations in this historical context of crisis and division; Adis's next pamphlet, *A Cup for the Citie* (1648), prophesies the cataclysmic destruction of London (Durso 144).[19] In Quarles's own trope of Parliamentary judgment as many-eyed Argus, observational judgment and imaginative fancy are again hard to distinguish.

Up Go We! The Mobile Figure of Anarchus

The emblematic figure of "Anarchus" plays a monstrous role similar to Argus in Quarles's *Shepheards Oracle*. He appears as a sign in the heavens to the three shepherds in an eschatological, Antichrist-like reversal of the star of Christ's nativity. The *Oracle*'s three shepherds literally "see" Anarchus differently. Philorthus the parliamentarian exclaims, "How like a *Meteor* made of Zeale and flame / The man appeares?" (sig. B). Philarchus the monarchist responds, "Or like a blazing *Star* / Portending change of State, or some sad Warre / Or death of some good Prince" (sig. B). Finally, Philarthus bemoans, "He is the *trouble* of three sad Kingdomes" (sig. B). The text's italicization of *Meteor*, *Star*, and *trouble* create three different images of Anarchus. Anarchus is then transformed in the trialogue into a textual, self-referential icon:

PHILORTHUS: Hee's a *Page* / Fill'd with Errata's of the present Age
PHILARCHUS: The Churches Scourge
PHILARTHUS: The devils *Enchiridion*.   (sig. B2)

In 1640/1, Quarles published his own *Enchiridion*, containing miscellaneous moral and political aphorisms. An enchiridion is a lightweight book popular in the sixteenth and early seventeenth centuries. The term derives from the Greek term for handbook. Early modern enchiridions were often employed as devotionals, quotation books of sententiae, or miscellanies. Quarles's *Enchiridion* operates as a "conduct book" for state organization (the king, his subjects, and Parliament). In his own *Enchiridion*, Quarles makes diplomatic plea for all sides to follow his advice and prevent the war that soon followed its publication. For example, in the fourth chapter of his first "century," he warns, "Let no price nor promise of Honour bribe thee to take part with the Enemy of thy naturall Prince ... He that loves the Treason hates the Traytor" (sig. B2). Anarchus, as "the devil's *Enchiridion*," both parallels and inverts Quarles's attempt at state stability in his own print text. Again, print's visual-material construction has the potential to both divine truths and delude spectators. Anarchus or political chaos in this passage functions as an icon of errors in print culture – perhaps referencing, like Quarles's *Whipper Whipt*, the hydra-headed multiplicity of political expression in print, spurred by the Civil War. This passage presents the print page itself as a potential emblem of anarchy and social discord.

Anarchus also diabolically fulfils the visual and rhetorical practices of duplication, chiasmus, and paradox we see in the *Emblemes*. Anarchus, an iconic figure steeped in metaphors of print culture and emblematics (as meteor, star, trouble, errata-filled page, scourge, and enchiridion), acts as a figure of extreme Protestant/Puritan iconoclasm. In a section of *The Shepheards Oracle*, Anarchus recites his own cataclysmic ballad: "Wee'l breake the windowes which the / Whore of Babilon hath painted" (sig. B3). Anarchus, an icon of destruction, is a destroyer of icons. As an Antichrist-like, negative mirror image of divinity, Anarchus also parallels the chiastic, utopian promise in *Emblemes* to make the least the greatest and the greatest, least through divine sight. Anarchus's comrades mistake false, chaotic, political levelling with spiritual, heavenly levelling:

> Wee'l breake their Pipes and burne their Copes
> And pull downe Churches too:
> Wee'l exercise within the Groves,
> And teach beneath a Tree,
> Wee'l make a Pulpit of a Cart,
> And hey! Then up go we.   (sig. B3)

The ballad's refrain portrays an act pulling what is up down in order to make the low go up in a figure of chiasmus that mirrors, antithetically, the Parables' famous reversal of social hierarchy. The visual distortion that the rhetorical figures paradox and chiasmus create transforms into a social distortion in this passage.

The ballad form for Anarchus places his song in a popular, mass-print context: a suitable genre for his song of social levelling. The pamphlet then concludes with a note to the reader that tracks a popular adoption of the Anarchus ballad: *"The Author ... was made bold with, concerning the speech of* Anarchus," as it *"hath been nois'd by the Balad-singers about the streets of* London, *with some additions of their owne, to make up a full penny worth"* (sig. B3). The public's appropriation of Anarchus's speech for popular Royalist ballads on the streets of London inverts and adopts the figures of paradox and chiasmus yet again, as they pull the levellers down to pull the monarchy back up.[20] This ballad's first seven stanzas had their first publication as "The Round-heads Race" in the anonymous *Distractions of Our Times* (Roberts 237). After the *Shepheards Oracle*'s publication, Royalist and Tory pamphlets, alongside broadside ballads, appropriated Quarles's emblematic satire of social disorder. For instance, the broadsides "The Whig Rampant" (1682) and "The Whig's Exaltation" (1682) are published to the score and tune of "Up Go We," a line that is repeated over the course of these ballads (Figure 4.11).

The "Whig's Exaltation" advertises itself as "A Pleasant New Song of 82 To an Old Tune of 41." Although Quarles's 1645 *Oracle* was the first use of "up go we" in a ballad, according to my search, this advertisement raises two possibilities: that Quarles himself drew from a popular ballad motif to construct his polemic, or that the "Whig's Exaltation," while misdating the reference, captures the popularity of Quarles's original "Up Go We."

The nearest reference of "up go we" following Quarles's ballad that I found exists in a 1648 pamphlet publication of the Lord Mayor of London's against Oliver Cromwell and his army:

Follow then the Thrust (Victorious Soules) dispatch *Charles Stewart,* then downe goes monarchy: and then streight way those rigg-widgeon Traytorly *Don-quket-sotts* of *Westminster,* (most of them as meane and mechanick as our selves) will tumble after, and vanish like their owne Ordinances or a morning Cloud. Heye then up goe wee. (6)

The mayor's use of the "up go we" phrase in reference to Cromwell's army may have further popularized the phrase in broadside ballads. The repetition and popularity of this phrase after Quarles's *Oracle* demonstrates the popular use of chiasmus and inversion to represent political upheaval. As Joshua B. Fisher examines, the broadside ballad form experienced significant mobility across different classes and across different material forms in the seventeenth century (9). Ballads' appropriation by a wide participatory audience paralleled their

Figure 4.11. Anon., "A Whig's Exaltation" (1682), broadside, Pepys Library Cambridge

physical re-uses. For example, "the woodcut images that frequently adorn printed broadsides were often recycled" and "the tune designed to accompany a ballad was similarly vagrant, often reused in numerous ballads" (3). Eric Nebeker marks ballads' social and technological mobility, as well as their role in forming a public sphere. Early modern broadsides were "multimedia" and were characterized by "cheap production, wide distribution, and a varied means of consumption" (3–4). The phrase "up go we" could be fairly stated to represent the mobile, popular, and often querulous form of the broadside ballad itself. As philosopher-activist Cornelius Castoriadis claims, "Representation is precisely that by which 'us' can never be closed up within itself, that by which it overflows on all sides, constantly makes itself other than it 'is,' posits itself in and through the positioning of figures and exceeds every given figure" (331). Here, chiasmus and inversion, both textual and visual, are reproduced and overturned in each iteration of the "Up Go We" ballads, in a way that exceeds Quarles's original context and intention, as new readers and new publications appropriate these representational figures in a public and participatory spectacle.[21]

Conclusion: Milking the Press

In perhaps the most bizarre instance of visual duplication and paradox in Quarles's work, the act of milking the breast of the world in Book One, Emblem Seven of the *Emblemes* (sig. D4, Figure 4.12) parallels that of the printing press in the final engraving of the 1635 edition of *Emblemes* that introduces Edward Benlowes's *Quarleis* (sig. X3v).

Both engravings are original to the 1635 *Emblemes*. Book One, Emblem Seven, a jeremiad against the dangers of indulging in earthly, sensual pleasures ("Ah foole, forbeare," it warns, "thou drawst both milk & death"), shows a giant globe with breasts and a cornucopia sprouting from its top; one fool sucks straight from its left breast, another fool pulls its milk from a sieve to a ladle beneath. *Quarleis*'s initial engraving has a large wreath with the name of "Quarles" inside, framed by two angels. One angel holds a magnifying glass, the other a triangular musical cymbal, representing the two modalities of sound and sight that have enriched the book. The right side of the page shows angels feeding on the honey of bees, and the left portrays a book being pressed with a hammer: hammering the cover of a book was a necessary process for attaching the cover in the hand-press era. As the book is hammered

Figure 4.12. Francis Quarles, *Emblemes* (1635), page 48, Bodleian Library

in this image, ink drains from it into a ladle from which the angels are feeding. This image of angels who feed from the ink of Quarles's book mirrors the image fools who drink from the breast of earthly delights. Wendy Wall describes milk as an "exchangeable secretion" in early modern English culture (134). Sujata Iyengar observes that milk was conceived of as "whitened blood" that influenced the nature of the child in early modern medicine: these fluids, milk and blood, were fungible liquids (223). This fungibility of form was also a fungibility of practice: the social and economic, exchange-based activities of wetnursing and dairying established images of milk and milking as "part of" the world of "work, transaction, and business" (Wall, *Staging Domesticity* 134). Milking also had sensual undertones: Wall describes the sexualized imagery of milkmaids in aristocratic pastorals (138). Again, the worldliness and sensuality Quarles's emblems warn readers against are embedded in the very structure of the book as a visual, sensory form, as heavenly ink mimics earthly milk. The sensual appetite represented in the Emblem Seven's image of breastfeeding finds its metaphorical parallel in the final engraving's idealized image of book production. At the same time, this visual parallel also establishes the creation of these emblems as a productive exchange between author, printer, and reader.

In the work of Francis Quarles, sight and sense perception can thus equally lead to folly and wisdom, angelic and demonic forces, truth and error: gazing on the world's tempting images is not after all so different from gazing on the images of the moral emblem. The engravings of the book medium directly mirror the coloured, prismatic, sensual deceptions of the flesh against which it is juxtaposed. Sin and salvation, and, in political terms, anarchy and the utopian establishment of the kingdom of heaven on earth act as chiasmic, paradoxical doubles of one another. In Quarles's works, moral discernment and political stability invite a troubled, error-filled process of sight and reading, in which duplicative, duplicitous hieroglyphics and figures alternately reveal and conceal their aims.

Chapter Five

Dead Lambs, False Miracles, and "Taintured Nests": The Crisis of Visual Ecologies in Shakespeare's *2 Henry VI*

In this chapter, I turn to visual ecologies in *2 Henry VI* as a means by which we may see the wider scope of book materials' problems of perception. With its specific adaptation from John Foxe's *Acts and Monuments* and staged rebellion against writing itself, books and their visual materials in mind emerge as important thematic concerns in Shakespeare's *2 Henry VI*. I will explore how book materials are consciously deployed as metaphors for the instability of visuality in *2 Henry VI*. Jack Cade's rebellion against textuality, a false miracle scene's adaptation of the *Acts*, and allusions to print visuals demonstrate the interwoven nature of book and performance conditions as mutually troubled visual ecologies. *2 Henry VI* is both metatheatrical and metabibliographical: its multiple references to visual perspective demonstrate the play's concerns with material destruction and visual indeterminacy. *2 Henry VI* consciously reminds its audience of the dangers and controversies of observation, setting the page alongside the stage on a continuum for its examination of visual crisis.

Reading and performance were often intertwined in early modern drama, particularly in moments that highlight the contours of vision troubles. One may recall Dr Faustus's burning of the Quran onstage preceding his damnation as a moment that illustrates the power – and danger – of the very visual icons that audiences are observing. Shakespeare's Richard II examines his face in a looking glass as if it were a book: "I'll read enough, / When I do see the very book indeed / Where all my sins are writ" (4.1.273–5). This passage emphasizes, as I will further examine, the actor's function as a readable, legible sign-system onstage, as Richard's face is "read" in his mirror. Theatre-going also paralleled early modern visual reading in its material structures.

Although theatrical spaces like the Swan and Globe were visually decorous, with hangings and statues (Kiefer 10), Anthony B. Dawson observes that early modern stages held a "relative paucity" of props and stage décor (139). The structure of three-dimensional theatres in the round, such as the Globe and the Rose, where many of Shakespeare's plays were performed, emphasized hearing over spectation (Gurr, *The Shakespearean Stage* 139). The Rose Theatre was the most likely venue for *2 Henry VI* (237). In such a space, prime seats were located behind the stage, where the sound would be best, and no one audience member would have a perfect sight line (139). Hence, audiences would in part imagine and project imagery onto the stage, much as the early modern reading process required a combination of projection and reception in the reader's imagination to co-create a book's meaning. As I argue in this chapter, performance, like reading, necessitated a collective, though fragile, construction of what was seen that operated through modes of refraction and alteration. Since the stage was not a separate space, the audience of a play were "as visible as the players," as they "completely surrounded the plays on their platform" (Gurr 179). The system of observation predicated by the Rose's physical structure thus relied on mutuality between performers and their audiences and predisposed metatheatricality – a conscious, collective awareness of theatrical illusion as illusion. The function of early modern audiences as readers – and, indeed, as legible texts themselves – is perhaps best illustrated in *The Roaring Girl*:

> As many faces there, filled with blithe looks,
> Show like the promising titles of new books
> Writ merrily, the readers being their own eyes,
> Which seem to move and to give plaudities   (1.2.21–4)

Like this passage, *2 Henry IV* interrogates and collapses boundaries between theatrical spectation and reading, between texts and iconic images. This passage, and the following analysis, suggests that play going was influenced by the practices of reading and print culture, carrying with it a sense of self-reflexivity and visual crisis as audiences both scanned and spanned the stage. As it draws from the images and processes of book production, Shakespeare's *2 Henry VI* situates performance as every bit as mediated, unsettling, and transformative as setting eyes on a book. The vision trouble described in previous chapters pervades *2 Henry VI*, especially through the characters of the lower-class upstart Jack Cade, the falsely blind Simpcox, and the aggressive warrior queen Margaret. For each of these characters, references to visual materials – particularly book materials – deconstruct the boundaries between sight and perception, actor and audience, and book and reader.

"My Mouth Shall be the Parliament of England": Jack Cade's Anti-Bibliographical Prejudice

Through Jack Cade's rebellion, *2 Henry VI* deliberately puts print, writing, and their educational apparatuses on trial. Cade accuses Lord Say of corrupting the realm with book materials:

> Thou has most traitorously corrupted the youth of the realm in erecting a grammar school; and whereas, before, our forefathers had no other books but the score and tally, thou hast caus'd printing to be us'd, and, contrary to the King, his crown, and dignity, thou has built a paper-mill. (4.7.32–7)

Cade's rebellion is presented as a hatred for written, educated culture that overlapped with class conflict. While this antipathy has its roots in popular uprisings and an exploitive use of literacy in late-medieval England, the Cade rebellion's specific terms of accounting and grammar schools in the text of *2 Henry VI* indicate a conscious anachronism that portrayed class and education-based anxieties of print literacy and widespread state education. Grammar schools founded after the Reformation, within which Shakespeare would have been educated, offered a more universal book learning to young males and promoted a wider literacy than before. This education included English and Latin grammar, the catechism in English, and the Book of Common Prayer, all of which codified and universalized a religious and state ideology as an "engine of change" (Cummings, *The Book of Common Prayer* 12).[1] Cade sets antipathy towards print up as a rebellion against state power, private property, and the educational system that upheld them. Cade and his followers attack a clerk for the "seting of boys' copies" (4.2.88) and having a book with "red letters" (4.2.90), most likely a primer for the education of boys. This clerk is hung with a "pen and inkhorn about his neck" (4.2.110). While scholars such as Stuart Hampton-Reeves have tied Shakespeare's historiography of Cade to the historical Jack Cade, as well as with peasant rebel figures such as Wat Tyler and Jack Straw, another recent analogue could be the 1549 Prayer Book rebellion of

Cornwall. This rebellion – alongside socioeconomic pressure that followed land enclosures and rising food prices – was fomented by the English Book of Common Prayer, meant to unify liturgy across England. The Cornish rebels' slogan, "kill all the gentlemen" (Carlton 17) parallels Dick the butcher's injunction, "The first thing we do, let's kill all the lawyers" (4.2.68). The primer and prayer book, as symbols of national unity, are under attack in a play that interrogates British political power. Further, the first paper mill to manufacture high-quality white paper and make a profit was completed in 1588, in Dartford, Kent, not long before *2 Henry VI*'s estimated writing (1591–2) and publication (1594) (Dard Hunter 119). Cade's rebellion thus assembles a historical memory of enmity towards print and makes book materials themselves a main figure within the play.

By attacking writing, Cade metabibliographically attempts to destroy the historical apparatus that characterizes him as an enemy of the state: "writing, signatures, legal bonds, lineage, and property" (Hampton-Reeves 67). Cade also specifically speaks against wax seals: "some say the bee stings, but I say, 'tis the bees wax, for I did but seal once to a thing, and I was never mine own man since" (4.2.81–3). Green wax for documents became a marker of textual destruction for the historical Kentish commoners Shakespeare drew from. As Roger Chartier traces,

> [T]he historical Kentish rebels were also aware of the unjust authority imposed by the misuses of the royal seal. In the bill of petition they gave to the royal delegation they met on June 1450, when they were encamped under the walls of London, one of their demands was 'that all the extorcions may be leid down, that is to sey, the grete extorcion of grene wax that is falsly used to the perpetuall destruccion of the Kynges liege men and the Comons of Kent without provision of our Souvraigne lorde and his trewe Counsell.' This bill of complaint of the rebels, known by a fifteenth-century copy and printed in John Stow's *Chronicles of England* published in 1580, which was a major source for Shakespeare's play. (79)

The play's references to writing show the materials that construct history as malleable, threatening, and under threat. This situation is best summed up by Cade's infamous plea, "Is not this a lamentable thing, that of the skin of an innocent lamb should be made parchment? That parchment, being scribbled o'er, should undo a man?" (4.2.77–83). Skin marks a visible, visual text in Shakespeare's works. Katherine Knowles analyses Philip's description of Arthur as a "little abstract" in *King John*. She interprets this reference as an inscription of his character as a "as a historical text in the process of being written, the 'abstract' that will eventually become a 'volume'" (3). In "Take Five," Patricia Cahill notes a recurring appearance of skin, particularly animal skins, in Shakespeare, a trope which sets sensation and textuality together "uneasily" (1025). Skin in early modern culture was, according to both Elizabeth Harvey and Sujata Iyengar, paradoxically "surface" and "interior," "porous" yet "impermeable" (Harvey 2; Iyengar 312). Cade's description illuminates this culturally porous yet demarcated role of skin. In his portrayal of a parchment made of a dead lamb that undoes men, the socioeconomic and ecological crises of the commons permeate textual production, yet the skin of a page divides an illiterate, displaced public from a literate elite as an impermeable barrier.

The skin of a lamb resonates as a visual marker of class in its textual role and as a material marker of enclosure in its ecological role. The wool and cloth trade, also produced from the skin of sheep, accelerated enclosure of common lands. As Thomas More famously puts it in *Utopia*, "The increase of pasture," "by which your sheep are naturally mild, and easily kept in order, may be said now to devour men and unpeople, not only villages, but towns" (23). The movement from increasingly enclosed lands to lambs, from lamb to parchment, from parchment to print text, and from text to legal or social oppression in Cade's speech shows the dynamic, interwoven, and here mutually destructive relationship between the changing material culture of text and the changing material ecology of the English landscape, particularly in an era that fixed property lines and physical common places through textual documentation. Cade's response – "Burn all of the records of the realm, my mouth shall be the parliament of England" (4.7.14–15) – threatens national destruction through textual obliteration. Queen Margaret and her lover Suffolk's treatment of traditional common property laws and paper petitions highlights their own contributions to ecological and textual instability. In a scene where Suffolk and Margaret treat with petitioners, Suffolk is accused of "enclosing the commons of Melford" (1.3.21–2). Margaret, in this scene's stage directions, tears the paper of these commoner's supplications: the violence of enclosing the commons parallels the textual violence of tearing up the commoner's paper petition. Textual destruction becomes an emblem of Britain's destruction in *2 Henry VI*.

Gloucester's Prophecy: Visual and Material "Undoing"

The Duke of Gloucester's warning to his nephew Henry VI at the outset of the play about his hasty marriage to Margaret also links the destruction of the British state to emblems of book destruction, as it alludes to several different fragile or decomposed book materials. He condemns Henry VI's marriage to Margaret of Anjou, an unfavourable match that initiates the war between Lancaster and York:

> Fatal is this marriage, cancelling your fame,
> Blotting your names from the books of memory,
> Rasing the characters of your renown,
> Defacing monuments of conquer'd France,
> Undoing all, as all had never been!   (1.1.99–103)

Gloucester's warning presents several processes of destruction, each one a more vivid image than the next: first, to blot, next, to rase, then, to deface, and finally, to undo. To cancel, blot, rase, deface, and undo are destructive actions done to a particular material: an account-book, a commonplace, a monument or church, or a text. In a paradox typical of how the play represents visual materials, "rased characters" could signify razing, or destruction, as well as book production: the word "raised" could imply print's raised letters, or type. A blot could become either an inscription of ink as one writes, or an inking over of a previous script. The language of blotting and rasing implies a continuum of material composition and decomposition, implying a historiographical book of memory that is palimpsestic, whereas the final line's language of "undoing all, as if all had never been" portrays a material that is ultimately perishable. Monuments in early modern English culture could signify either physical markers of history, such as churches, landscape features, or artefacts, or the books themselves that marked and situated these material monuments' existence (such as John Foxe's *Acts and Monuments*, William Camden's *Britannia*, and Michael Drayton's *Poly-olbion*).

This passage places such books on a continuum with other textual practices. For instance, the first line's concept of a "marriage" "cancelling your fame" recalls the sixteenth century's emergent system of double-entry bookkeeping. Thomas Keith charts the rise of arithmetic, Arabic numerals, and a new attention to written calculations in the trades over the sixteenth and seventeenth centuries.[2] This new mode of numeracy paralleled the rise of print media as a visual structure: the arrangement of the balance sheets and numerical ledgers on the page enabled economic transactions to be made visible and physical. The double-entry reference in Gloucester's first line sets marriage (deficit) against fame (credit), a visual reminder or tally of the marriage's financial drain on the kingdom. Arithmetic implied divination, just as almanacs predicted both natural and eschatological events. As Keith notes, would-be diviners carried books of arithmetic with them as a matter of course: in early modern discourse, "mathematician was a synonym for astrologer" (121). Commoner Jack Cade and his followers present accounting and literacy as mutually diabolical in their attack on a Clerk. One follower of Cade, Smith, frames the ability to "cast accompt," or to record accounts on the written page, as malfeasance (4.2.86). Jack Cade's responds to the clerk's book "with red letters in't" (4.2.90) with "then he is a conjurer" (4.2.91). Red was the most common colour to be inked on a printed page, and capital letters were the most common location for this extra decoration. Cade's condemnation of this red-lettered book as a conjuration, as well as Gloucester's characterization of the Henry-Margaret marriage as a table-book, unites emerging economic practices of numeracy and accompt with book visuals and print culture.

These passage's references to book visuals and markers additionally envision the theatre as a visible, readable space. As Jerome Mazzaro claims of *2 Henry VI*'s reference to books, the theatre itself constructed a collective book of memory for its audience (398). The audience could presumably fill this book with their imaginations and witness its permeability and fragility. In addition to representing economic crisis and diabolical vision, this passage's reference to accounting practices situates the actors, props, and visual signs of performance as both visual markers and as ephemeral, erasable ciphers. The sixteenth-century term for inscribed arithmetic with the use of Arabic numerals was "ciphering" (Keith 106), referring to the Arabic "zero" (*OED* < Arabic *çifr*). *Henry V*'s prologue enjoins the audience to invent and visualize its action on the stage as it employs this cipher metaphor:

> O, pardon! Since a crooked figure may
> Attest in little place a million;
> And let us, ciphers to this great accompt,
> On your imaginary forces work.   (Prologue 19–22)

The actors in this passage here become "figures," both visual and numerical. Ciphers were also associated with the act of impression or engraving. The *OED* cites the impression of letters and/or figures on "linen" or "plates" on a device as a definition for "cipher." By extension, ciphering recalls the practice of print engraving, the impression of type, and, as discussed in previous chapters, visual emblematics and impressions on the early modern imagination.[3] Cipher could also signify a note or abbreviation in Shakespeare's time, which would imply that the actors of *Henry V*'s prologue behave as a conceptual and visual shorthand for the audience's imagination.[4] In her discussion of rape as a "kind of violent printing press" in Shakespeare's *Lucrece*, Miriam Jacobson traces the association between the cipher or figure of zero and print reproduction, including engraving (337). Shakespeare's Lucrece, whom Jacobson convincingly links to the sign of zero/0/cipher, compares herself to an engraved book illustration (354); additionally, woodcuts, engravings, and illustrations of Lucrece as a cipher figure were popular in Shakespeare's time (354–5). The reification of actors into "ciphers" in a great ledger book (or exchange) situates early modern book illustrations, bookkeeping, and stagecraft as intensely visual, material, and even destructive practices. Accounting (or ciphering/numeracy), theatrical performance, and print production were therefore connected through their emphasis on visual signs or ciphers. *Henry V*'s reference to actors as "ciphers" alludes to their symbolic potential as empty visual signifiers, in need of an audience to deliver their meaning – meaning that is contingent on audience invention and actor delivery, in threat of being undone or erased at any moment.

This passage's blotted "books of memory" pose questions of visuality and exchange in the play. This book of memory could indicate a book of monuments, such as John Foxe's materially prodigious *Acts and Monuments*, an important source for *2 Henry VI*. Further, the image of a blotted line in a book of memory evokes the important biblical metaphor of the Book of Life and the book of remembrance, prominent in Daniel, Malachi, and Revelations. Daniel prophecies that "there shall be a time of trouble, such as never was since there was a nation to that same time: and at that time thy people shall be delivered, every one that shall be found written in the book" (KJV 12:1). In Malachi, this book of the saved is a memory book, "a book of remembrance" that "was written before for them that feared the Lord, and that thought upon his name" (KJV 3:16). Damnation or salvation is here situated in the language of chronicling or recording. In typological readings of the bible, where the Old Testament prefigures Christ's first and second coming, Daniel's prophecy of the "Book of Life" and Malachi's Book of Remembrance prefigure Revelations' "book of life," where "the dead were judged out of those things which were written in the books, according to their works" (KJV 20:12). After the Hebrew exiles from Egypt make a golden calf, Moses pleads, "Yet now, if thou wilt forgive their sin – ; and if not, blot me, I pray thee, out of thy book which thou hast written," to which God replies, "Whosoever hath sinned against me, him will I blot out of my book" (KJV, Exodus 32:32–3). The speaker of Psalm 69 pleas that his enemies "be blotted out of the book of the living, and not be written with the righteous" (Psalms 69:28). John in Revelation proclaims, "He that overcometh, the same shall be clothed in white raiment; and I will not blot out his name out of the book of life, but I will confess his name before my Father, and before his angels" (3:5). The specific biblical language of blotting out a name from the Book of Life, alluded to in Gloucester's warning, ties the play's civil conflict to a more eschatological narrative of apocalyptic reckoning – weighed, measured, and accounted in the form of the book. Memory, prophecy, and materiality are joined in this figure of a Book of Memory. The blotting out of a name ties eschatological turmoil to a visual marker of textual fragility.

"Memory books" or "books of memory" in early modern English culture could additionally indicate portable handbooks or ledgers for reminders, a genre that included account books, almanacs, and commonplace books. Early modern commonplace books integrated famous or important quotations, rhetorical devices, witticisms, fables, and personal reminders in a single codex that would be ready-to-hand and promised a unified mnemonic structure. Commonplace books served an important pedagogical function in the English grammar school system that formed Shakespeare's own education. These books provided a physical space within which to integrate and remember fragments of knowledge.[5] In his *Consolation for Our Grammar Schooles* (1622), the radical Puritan pedagogue John Brinsley refers to specific printed commonplace books to be used in rhetorical instruction:

> For the helpe of Memorie, besides all directions for briefe summes of euery matter, as are set downe in their places in the Grammar schoole and others; and besides diuers good rules and precepts for memorie in a little booke called *The Castle of Memorie* ... Maister *Willies* his booke of Memorie, called *Mnemonica siue Reminiscendi,* are gathered out of the best who have

written thereof: out of which the most profitable things may be selected and used by them who are judicious. (sig. Niiiiv)

Commonplace books were also used to collect medical treatments and receipts. Guglielmo Gratarolo named his print receipt book *The castel of memorie wherein is conteyned the restoring, augmenting, and conseruinge of the memorie and remembrance, with the safest remedies* (published 1562 and 1573). Konrad Gesner writes of a receipt for "A Lyniment or thynne oyntment, as *M. Michael Angelus Blondus* wryteth in his booke of memorie, which in vertue may bee compared to a Baulme choose" (134); this balm could be used for "ulcers," "canker," or "the quickning and helping of memory" (135). Here, a potion written in a memory book acts as a cognitive memory aid, demonstrating the conceptual slippage among materiality, rhetoric, and cognitive perception in early modern books' discourse. The term "memory" in early modern print seems to indicate a more everyday, lightweight book, as opposed to the term "monument," which referenced a materially and generically vast and heavy book of historiography.

Gloucester's passage hence focuses on the "blots," deletions, and subtractions from a book of memory, symbolizing the apocalyptic nature of England's War of the Roses (as in the biblical Book of Remembrance), an omission from a historiographical record or book of monuments, and the material disunity that the practice of reader commonplacing often encouraged. To delete or omit a section from a book, readers could tear a page or blot over a previous inscription with ink. Similarly, early modern printers could use pieces of blank paper to place over misprints. Commonplace books could also be recycled and reused, passing from owner to owner. As Heidi Brayman Hackel argues, these books "are often palimpsests reflecting the use of a series of owners, many of whom did not restrict themselves to commentary on their reading" (148). Commonplace books fused print and manuscript media, as print pages could be removed from their original sources and become interwoven together as a reader's own compilation (143).

Commonplace books could therefore operate as material and mnemonic palimpsests, where the old material could exist, albeit perhaps blotted out, re-inscribed, or glossed by each new hand. This practice of blotting, overwriting, and glossing, as Hackel describes, also extended to the visible adaptations, additions, and destructions readers made to print texts (142). The material and rhetorical practice of commonplacing integrated visual and kinetic learning, as well as the canons of memory, invention, arrangement, and style. These common-place passages, whether in daily life, in the grammar school, or on the Elizabethan stage, made their way to practices of delivery: recitations, elocutions, and performances. The book of memory promised by the commonplacing practice could become a function of theatricality, in yet another re-compilation and recycling of its material structure. Fame or history itself, characterized by Gloucester as a "book of memory," is therefore figured as palimpsestic, recyclable, and an ephemeral unification of fragments.

In his vision of history as malleable and material, Gloucester's metaphor of "rase[d]" characters becomes clearer. We tend to associate the term "character" to be that of the alphabet or of typography: the modern reader may question how, after all, type or a letter could be destroyed so violently. A character, though, can also imply an "engraved" or "impressed" mark (on a page or material object), or even a visual symbol (*OED* sense 1a); "to character" meant "to write" as well.[6] The impressed symbol recalls the *impresa* of aristocratic houses on armour or emblematic devices in early print books. The destruction of Henry's "characters" symbolizes the fall of his royal lineage over the course of the *Henry VI* trilogy. "Rased" or destroyed characters in a book of memory could refer to modifications to its visual structure if we take the meaning of character to be an emblem, graphic design, impresa, or a visual design in a print book, "rased" or torn out, perhaps, to be recompiled into a new commonplace book of memory. This rasing of characters/images can be situated within the play's portrayal of overturned gender, class, and monarchical hierarchies, as the author's production becomes, as Cade would put it, "in common," the collective and physically mobile property of different readers (4.7.19). The word "rase" in Gloucester's speech implies the etymologically related "erase" and "arace": erase would convey a scratching or rubbing out of text in an early modern manuscript, and the earlier term "arace," meant "to pull up by the roots; to tear up or away; pull or snatch away; to tear" (*OED*).[7] The *OED*'s first use of "erase" dates to the early seventeenth century and it marks the last use of "arace" in the mid-sixteenth century: it follows that these two terms may have overlapped around the time of *2 Henry VI*'s performance. These terms of material destruction – "Erase," "arase," and "rase" – connect the play's motifs of historical and ecological crisis to the fragility of visual materials in book and performance. The mobile interactivity of memory books, account books, and visual devices in early modern reading practices becomes a source of crisis in Gloucester's warning, as it undermines a larger sense of British historical fame. In turn, the connection between book visuals and theatrical delivery in this passage and throughout *2 Henry VI* situates the theatre as a site of uneasy visual and material exchange between actors and their audience, books and their readers.

"A Miracle, A Miracle"! False Sight in the St Alban's Scene

2 Henry VI's St Alban's scene exhibits this vision trouble through a (falsely) blind pilgrim, Simpcox. Soon after Margaret tears the commoner's petition, Gloucester interrogates a "false miracle" at St Alban's shrine, a location that was purported to cure blindness in pre-Reformation English culture. Gloucester questions and then punishes this counterfeit blind pilgrim who claims to have been cured at this shrine. This scene poses complex philosophical questions of how we see what we see and, more specifically, how to name and distinguish the colour spectrum. While this focus on the relationships among language, perception, and sight may at first seem removed from *2 Henry VI*'s portrayal of fragile material ecologies, the location of these questions alongside the conditions of book production and performance demonstrates the interrelated nature of visual materials to problems of visual delivery. As Lindsey Row-Heyveld argues, disability in early modern English culture was seen as a potentially troubled form of performance. Post-Reformation narratives of "counterfeiters," beggars, and false miracles replaced pre-Reformation conditions of spiritual exchange between the able-bodied and disabled ("The lying'st knave in Christendom"). Simone Chess convincingly argues that this scene "disrupts the audiences' intuitive sight, drawing attention to the act of looking and seeing, and potentially casting doubt on the efficacy of all sightedness" (109). Gloucester's interrogation of Simpcox's vision serves as an interrogation of sight itself – this scene captures the "early modern wonder at how it is that *anyone* can tell the difference between colors, or how any color can be a definitive thing, since even functioning eyes can deceive us" (Turner 109).

Simpcox claims to have been cured of lameness and blindness at St Alban's shrine. Gloucester's responds to Simpcox's cure by sceptically interrogating his new vision. He questions Simpcox about the colours of his wardrobe, which Simpcox names with metaphorical language – "red as blood" (2.1.108) and "coal-black as jet" (2.1.110). Gloucester responds with an apparently unusual conclusion: "Sight may distinguish of colors; but suddenly / To nominate them all, it is impossible" (2.1.126–7). Why does Gloucester believe that Simpcox can distinguish or see colours but not name them? Simpcox's potential act of "distinguishing" colours implies an act of perception or judgment. "Distinguishing" in the sixteenth century also conferred a more literal, physiological division or separation of colours by the eye.[8] The act of nominating or naming the colours, rather than distinguishing or separating them, may be the moment at which sight approaches cognitive perception in Gloucester's own visual theory. The moment that sight is transposed into speech, then, defines simple classification from perception in Gloucester's philosophical response – a concept that recalls Hawes's, Puttenham's, and other early modern rhetoricians' terminology of rhetoric as a "colour," or an ornamentation of language in which visual imagery and communication meet.

The problem of "nominating" colours, then, is both cognitive and rhetorical: Simpcox, in Gloucester's interpretation, should have problems with rhetorical invention if he had been blind prior to the miracle. Indeed, Simpcox does not merely say "red" or "black," but amplifies them through common figures and associations. He employs figures of amplification to nominate the colours: simile, metaphor, *exergasia* (repetition of similar words or images in a delivery), and synonymia (the repetition of synonyms, such as coal and jet, for emotional force). Simpcox's naming of Gloucester's gown "coal-black as jet" is not just a matter of designating the robe's appearance. The comparison and juxtaposition of "coal" to "black" relies on what early modernists would have thought of as the inventive and perceptual faculties. Simpcox's nomination of colours, as he compares black to coal and jet, is an interpretive and inventive process, as he locates these three terms within the same recalled mental image. This cognitive process would be impossible for a previously blind man. Simpcox performs another method of invention as he names Gloucester's cloak "red as blood" (2.1.108). "Coal-black" and "red as blood" are, even to the modern ear, "dead metaphors," connections that are so obvious as to be unconscious, hidden in plain speech. These comparisons speak to an immediate association of images, already processed through *phantasia*.

The controversy over sight, perception, and speech featured in this scene also recalls Plato and Aristotle's focus on sight and perception's mediation through colours. In both Platonic and Aristotelian visual theory, internal cognition and external object interact to form perception and interpretation. Todd Stuart Ganson claims that the object-perception relationship in Platonic theory to be such that "our sensory cognition of what is outside *depends on* our awareness of the body" (3). A perception of external objects, in other words, depends on the cognitive interaction between the eye, body, and mind. N. Gulley cites Plato's comparison of colour images with the alphabet's letters in *Theaetetus* to explain the mind's movement from simple colour images to an understanding of what these images communicate (99).[9] In *Aristotle on Perception*, Stephen Everson summates Aristotle's belief in *De Anima* that "it is an object's colour which grounds its capacity to affect the organ" (29). T.W. Bynum cites *De Anima*'s conviction that sight does not err when reporting the presence of its perceived object – the sense organ knows that "'what is before it is colour'" – but that it "'may err as to what it is that is colored or where that is'" (166). According to Aristotelian theories of sensation, Simpcox's ability to distinguish colour would be more immediate, but his ability to perceive and "nominate" it in a more precise fashion would be more likely to "err" directly after gaining his sight. Bynum cites Aristotle's belief that the sense organs "passively take in the appropriate forms when acted upon by" the objects themselves (166). The eye, for example, would immediately receive the imprint of an external object as an image, for example, the "coal black" Simpcox identifies in Gloucester's gown (2.1.110). However, this form must reach the heart and the faculty of *phantasia* must be employed for this perception, image, and form to be interpreted fully (166). In Bynum's reading of *phantasia*, the faculty is not one of glimpsing images or imagination alone, but a fundamental process of perception and interpretation (171).

In addition to its interrogation of sight, this scene also underscores the relationship between book emblematics and performance through its adaptation of John Foxe's *Acts and Monuments*, otherwise known as the *Book of Martyrs*. Foxe chronicles Protestant martyrdom under Queen Mary's reign and, in its second edition, warned Elizabeth from drifting off the reformed path. Throughout this text, elaborate woodcut engravings illustrate Protestant martyrs going to their deaths in different ways, as each becomes a material emblem for the Reformist cause. The *Acts'* large size had the effect of marking itself, and not just its tales of martyrdom, as an iconic monument. As David Scott Kastan puts it in *Shakespeare and the Book*, Foxe's book is "as much a material accomplishment as a literary one" (150). Kastan notes that *Acts and Monuments* was heavily purchased by parish churches, "chained next to the Holy Bible" (150), and a Canon Law of 1571 required that the book be placed in cathedral churches (Knapp, *Illustrating the Past* 126): this book acted as both object and institution. James A. Knapp argues that the *Acts'* method of woodcut illustration sought to both reactivate the "spectacle" (*Illustrating the Past* 149) of martyrdom and – to avoid the "temptation to idolatry" that its visuals may have led to – to construct a "narrative, which urges reflection on the martyr's conceptual existence – the symbolic ideal for which this person might be remembered as well as the beliefs that led to his or her martyrdom" (144). Conversely, Shakespeare's adaptation would bring this symbolic narrative to life.

While there are no illustrations of the Duke of Gloucester, he acts as a symbolic martyr in the text, and the *Acts'* St Alban's passage marks him as a noble character. Its marginalia marks "[t]he cruel death or martyrdome of the good Duke of Glocester" (706), and sets up the scene to "note, not only the craftye working of false miracles in the clergye, but also that the prudent discretion of this high and mighty prince, the foresayd Duke Humfrey, may geue vs better to vnderstand what man he was" (705). Therefore, Gloucester can be placed on a continuum with the *Acts'* other martyrs, a role he also fills in *2 Henry VI*. While the scene paints Gloucester's wisdom for not believing false miraculousness, it also uses visual language to uphold the Duke. Gloucester carries "noble prowesse & vertues, ioyned with the like ornamentes of knowledge, & literature shining in this Princely duke" (705): the Duke himself is a visual ornament in this description. Foxe's *Acts and Monuments* countervails and displaces miraculous and medieval notions of sight in order to reimagine an ideologically Reformist but highly visualized English historiography. Lindsey Row-Heyveld reads Shakespeare's adaptation of St Alban's scene as a Protestant repudiation of medieval iconicity, with Gloucester playing the idealized part of a reformist sceptic ("Lying'st knave in Christendom"). But it is important to note that the source for this scene was itself a material icon. Foxe gives Gloucester a benevolent response to Simpcox, as he first becomes "joyous of Gods glory" at the miracle (705). After his fall from power, Foxe makes Gloucester an icon or illustration of virtue: "whether it was that the nature of true vertue commonly is suche, that as the flame ever beareth his smoke, and the body his shadow: so the brightnes of vertue never blaseth, but has some disdayne or envy wayting upon it" (705). The references to smoke and flames, light and dark, brightness and "disdayne," resemble both the visual repetitions of Foxe's woodcuts throughout this work (Protestant martyrs burning at the stake in the illustrations) and the contrast of light and dark colours enabled by the craft technique of woodcut etching. This association of Gloucester's visual image with smoke, flames, and shadow elicits both the form of the woodcut illustration itself and the Platonic concept of visual mediation through colours and flames. The act of observing the iconic shadows and flames of Gloucester's character in the St Alban's passage, and of looking at the burning martyrs of the woodcuts, is one of active interpretation of and interaction with these images, one that relies on the visual delivery of the book's materials and on the inventive imagination of the viewer.

2 Henry VI's rendition of the St Alban's false miracle sets Foxe's iconic portrayal of Gloucester as martyr in his book against the theatrical conditions of the play, complicating Foxe's narrative. As Simpcox's miraculous sight and counterfeit delivery is interrogated in this scene, so is his audience's response. Gloucester's command to nominate colours and discern images obliquely refers to the audience's own visual observation of the play. The reactions of Henry VI, Margaret, and Simpcox's wife show competing responses to the false miracle that represent their own roles as audience members in this scene. Simpcox's wife's and Henry's response to the scene effectually undercut Shakespeare's source material in *Acts and Monuments*. Henry VI cries, "O God, seest thou this, and bearest so long?" (2.1.151). Margaret responds with "It made me laugh to see the villain run" (2.1.152). Between them, Henry and Margaret reflect the ambivalence of this scene's delivery. The Simpcox scene could either be seen as a slapstick, anti-clerical comedy or as a cruel punishment. Henry's reference to divine sight categorizes this scene as a tragedy, where Margaret's laughter perhaps reinforces the audience's own if we view Simpcox's punishment as comedy. The choice between travesty or tragedy in this scene, in turn, responds to vision's religious and classed nature in Shakespeare's time. Margaret's response appears to be a post-Reformation reaction to a false miracle, where Henry's reaction counteracts this interpretation and points out the cruelty of that laughter. This sense of cruelty in the scene's comic potential is furthered by Simpcox's wife's plain yet eloquent appeal: "Alas, sir, we did it for pure need" (2.1.154). Simpcox's wife reminds us that the philosophical disputes and comic relief in this scene also must be placed alongside the play's depiction of enclosure, class revolt, and famine.

By adapting the *Acts*, Shakespeare complicates Foxe's iconology and potentially controversializes his source's full embrace of Reform. Bringing every false miracle to light, after all, would mean that those who would resort to them out of need would go without. Cade's own lament at his death, "Famine and no other hath slain me" (4.10.60), parallels the simple response of Simpcox's wife. Both responses undermine assumptions of retributive justice in the punishment of Simpcox and Cade. Interestingly, directly after his portrayal of Gloucester's life and death, John Foxe discusses the invention of printing. He portrays print as "diuine and miraculous" (707), ordained by God, a way towards truth and out of ignorance: "through the light of printing, the worlde beginneth nowe to haue eyes to see, and heades to iudge" (707). Where Foxe praises Gloucester's judgment for outing the false miracle and upholds the miraculousness of print, 2 *Henry VI*'s portrayal of Cade's hatred for writing and the potential cruelty of the St Alban's scene's comedy complicates the notion of a straightforward visual mode. Instead, the audience must make choices about what is seen in this scene and potentially toggle between Shakespeare's theatrical representation and Foxe's *Acts*. If the *Acts* is effectually onstage with the characters, it is also put under scrutiny. Again, textual materials in 2 *Henry VI* serve to complicate and unravel its dramatic and political theatre. 2 *Henry VI*'s audience could "read" the St Alban's scene as an anti-recusant comedy, a philosophical controversy of sight, a tragedy of the commons as exemplified by the plight of Simpcox and his wife, or as a visual icon or monument, constantly oscillating between Foxe's iconic Gloucester and Shakespeare's phenomenally and socially troubling portrayal of visual observation and audience response.

Alehouse Sign and Dusky Eye: Margaret as Spectacle

Like the Simpcox scene's troubling depiction of vision, Queen Margaret's emblematic characterization further destabilizes the audience's act of observation. Directly after his interrogation of Simpcox's vision, Margaret interrogates Gloucester's guardianship of Henry. Gloucester is ultimately ousted by Margaret and his court rivals as they use his wife's ambition against him. To this end, Margaret threatens, "Gloucester, see here the tainture of thy nest, / And look thyself be faultless, thou wert best" (2.1.184–5). "Tainture" can imply a stain or degradation, a meaning that is fully at play in this scene (*OED* sense 2). Another, earlier meaning of tainture is "colouring" (*OED* sense 1). Margaret commands Gloucester to examine himself for flaws and to himself gaze on the colours of his own "nest." Margaret portrays Gloucester himself as blind and lacking in the perception necessary to discern colours and images.

Just as the colour controversies of Simpcox's false blindness interrogate visual perception and appropriate book materials, so does Margaret's reference to "taintures." The *OED* locates the first use of the term "tainture" in Caxton's English translation of the *Aeneid, Eneydos* (1490). Caxton employs the term in a discussion of the Phoenician alphabet and its capability to retain historiographical memory with its "letters cronykes [chronicles] and historyes" (sig. Biiiir), things that would otherwise "have be forgoten it and put in oublyaunce" (sig. Biiiir). Caxton claims that the Phoenicians were fond to

> note wyth rede colour or ynke firste the sayd lettres of which our bokes ben gretely decorated soucured & made fayr. We wryte the grete and firste capytall lettres of our volumes bookes and chapytres wyth the taynture of reed coloure. (sig. Biiiir)

Here, Caxton claims a heritage of book ornamentation – the red colours of capital letters in a book – from the Phoenicians, who both developed the alphabet and, in his account, allowed ancient history to be later remembered. In Caxton's account, the remembrance of history relies on the arrangement and colouring of letters in books. Here, the colour (image) and the nomination (letter, language) combine to form historical memory and cognitive perception. Like Gloucester's earlier reference to the book of memory, Margaret's threat ties political destruction to degraded textual materials; in a history play, the potentially decomposable nature of taintures and memory books remind us of history's palimpsestic, interpretable nature as it is displayed and performed.

Again, the metatheatrical is metabibliographical in *2 Henry VI*. Margaret, in particular, unites these strands in the scene of Suffolk's departure. She yearns to transcend the ephemeral nature of the visual image by impressing herself onto Suffolk, as a seal upon a book:

> Nor let the rain of heaven wet this place
> To wash away my woeful monuments.
> O, could this kiss be printed in thy hand,
> That thou mightst think upon these by the seal,
> Through whom a thousand sighs are breath'd for thee!   (3.2.341–5)

Margaret's connection of her own "woes" to "monuments" refers back, again, to books as monuments. Here Margaret wishes to invest her farewell to Suffolk with a sense of iconic permanence and materiality, as she compares the imprint of their "kiss" to the physical, kinetic imprint of a book's wax seal. She sighs and kisses the "book" that, metaphorically, stands in for Suffolk's hand, employing this book monument as a holy relic or object of worship in itself. Margaret construes this book/ hand as a permanent, miraculous, and affective material object. In this scene, Shakespeare presents the book as iconic and, more problematically, idolatrous. Her kiss in this scene, as the "seal" of the book, acts as both a token of her love and as an impressed wax stamp or device.[10] Such seals were often emblematic and visual in nature, as they portrayed visual devices. Her lips are impressed like a wax seal that closes letters or documents. The sign or emblem of Margaret is impressed on Suffolk's body and mind, as she describes herself in the visual terms of sign, seal, and device. This description resituates Margaret's mouth, which signifies both oral delivery and material imprinting, as a liminal space or medium (wax seal) between reader/viewer and book/performance, as she becomes a medium of visual observation.

Margaret's emblematic self-representation becomes more emphatic as this scene progresses. Margaret demands of Henry, "I am no loathsome leper, look on me" (3.2.73). Margaret reinforces the visual emphasis of the play as she berates Henry for his sadness following Gloucester's death: "Erect his statue and worship it, / And make my image but an alehouse sign" (3.2.80–1). In "'If My Sign Could Speak': The Signboard and the Visual Culture of Early Modern London," Andrew Gordon delineates the ubiquity and importance of inn, alehouse, and tavern signs in early modern England (35–51). These signs therefore portray the interconnectedness of visual and textual reference during the time of *2 Henry VI*. This scene represents the emblematic nature of performance itself, as Margaret's delivery draws from metaphors of the book's visual materials: actors of the political and theatrical stages, again, were often figured as devices, ciphers, and illustrations, to be interpreted and (re)invented by their audience of spectators. In his "Defense of Poesy," Philip Sidney alludes to the use of emblematic signs in theatrical practice: "What child is there that, coming to a play, and seeing *Thebes* written in great letters upon an old door, doth believe that it is Thebes?" (103). In this same passage, he characterizes poetics as "pictures" of "what should be" (103). Shakespeare's allusions to characters as "signs" or "ciphers," as well as Sidney's textual prop, indicates the cultural intersections among visual representations, textual reading, and the delivery of a theatrical performance, despite the lasting critical tendency to think of stage and page as separate, self-sufficient media.

In a performance context, actors' bodies, as well as their own self-references as visual objects in *2 Henry VI*, form a system of interpretive visual navigation. Gordon outlines the role of alehouse signs as a "key resource in negotiating and deciphering the spaces" of Shakespeare's London ("'If My Sign Could Speak'" 38). These signs also transformed according to religious and cultural upheavals: Gordon cites the transformation of a "common tavern sign" depicting the Annunciation "into two gallants," as well as Puritan polemics against the supposed idolatry of these signs ("If My Sign Could Speak," 42). The early modern theatres outside London, of course, were also located by their signs ("the Rose, the Curtain, the Swan," etc., 43). The surviving copy of Johannes De Witt's sketch of the Swan (Figure 5.1), for example, shows a flag of a swan flown at the pinnacle of the theatre, in addition to a flag with a swan emblem descending from a trumpeter's horn.

Gordon interprets Margaret's position as an alehouse sign as an indicator of her dually textual and performative visuality. To extend Gordon's point, this passage describes Margaret in terms of low culture and visual delivery, which, in combination with her gender, provides a dichotomy with the virtuous, monumental image of Gloucester, which is now fixed (like a statue) by his death, his masculinity, and his virtue. If Gloucester is a monument of history – an authoritative text and book of memory – then Margaret is reduced here to a visual marker or sign, a cipher to be read or impressed.

This passage additionally links Margaret's role as visual marker to visual uncertainty, as the Queen recounts her sea journey to England. First, "the dusky sky began to rob" her "earnest-gaping sight of thy land's view" (3.2.104–5), after which she loses view of the shore, "And bid mine eyes be packing with my heart, / And call'd them blind and dusky spectacles, / For losing ken of Albion's wished coast" (111–13). Her eyes, as "spectacles," are objects of sight, now dusky. First, the sky itself or natural landscape creates the partiality and haziness of vision in this passage. Margaret then refers to the eye itself as a partial, dark mirror or window reflecting this scene.[11] Shakespeare was not alone in describing the eye itself as a spectacle. This metaphor drew from late-medieval and early modern technologies of eyeglasses and optic lenses that aided the sight. Eyeglasses were invented in thirteenth-century Italy, "associated with the Venetian glass industry" (Crombie 204) and eventually became objects of discussion in medical and scientific texts.[12]

Figure 5.1. Arnoldus Buchelius, Sketch of Swan Theatre (c. 1596), University of Utrecht Library

The material extension of the eye's purview through the glass became a dominant metaphor for the eye itself in early modern cultural and medical texts. Leonardo da Vinci drew several sketches of restorative lenses in his attempts to understand eyesight (209). Later, Kepler in *Ad Vitellionem Paralipomena* (1603) and physician Felix Plater in *De corporis humani structure et usu* (1583) described the retina itself as an eyeglass. Plater "held that the lens stood to the retina as a convex spectacle lens stood to an eye with weak sight: both magnified the object seen" (Crombie 289). Rayna Kalas cites sixteenth-century astronomer Franciscus Maurolycus's comparison of "the glass lens to the crystalline humor of the eye"; the "pupil" of the eye itself operated as a "lens of nature and conversely the glass lens as the pupil of art" (*Frame, Glass, Verse* 160n78).

Helkiah Crooke's *Microkosmographia* (1615) employs glassy metaphors at length in its discussion of the eye's anatomy and how the eye processes images.[13] Crooke describes the eye's membranes as four refractions or humours through a comparison with the glass spectacle, which makes "the object both larger and brighter" by means of its six refractions (570). Crooke calls these four refractions or humours – from most to least solid and external – the horny membrane, the watery humour or "Diaphanum," the "cristalline" humour, and the glassy humour. Crooke's visceral description of the "crystalline" membrane specifically links the eye-as-spectacle metaphor to the visual reading process:

> [I]f you take out the cristalline humour compassed with his Membrane and lay it upon a written paper, the letters under it will appeare much greater then indeed they are, from whence haply came the invention of Spectacles, and indeed this humour is a very spectacle to the Opticke nerve. (571)

Crooke tells readers to take the disembodied reflective membrane of the eye itself and attach it to the page for an extended magnification of readers' sight. The process of reading, with the mediative spectacles of eyeglasses, the eye, and the eye's glassy and crystalline membranes, magnifies the reader's sight. At the same time, this magnification takes place through a process of multiple refractions, as the glassy and crystalline membranes each refract the image within the glassy spectacle of the eye itself in an indirect, multiplied, and even visually uncertain process – a hall of mirrors. Perception depends on the refractive, viscous quality of the eye, "not so thicke or hard that the species or formes could not be imprinted therein, but soft like unto waxe and viscid that they might cleave faster thereto" (571). The image impressions of visual perception are (again) described in the metaphor of a material impression that is malleable yet absorbent, permanent yet impermanent, like ink on paper, or a parchment skin. The eye conceived as a glass, also found in the work of Francis Bacon and George Puttenham (Kalas, *Frame, Glass, Verse* 145), links the material to the sensible. Yet the permanence and magnification of the visual and material impression in Crooke is followed by a description of the crystalline humour's necessary ephemerality, as it describes a disconnection among sensation, perception, and the visual materials themselves. "Naturally," Crooke argues, "the image of visible things are no longer retained in the Cristalline then is necessary for their perception, but give way to others … for before the former images be vanished the succeeding cannot bee admitted" (571). Once the image has passed through this spectacular, crystalline membrane, "the alteration" or impressed image "vanisheth together with it, and so there is way made for a new alteration" (571).

Crooke's description of the image as it passes through the crystal membrane as an "alteration" shows the visual image's multiple refractions through the eye's membranes. Yet "alteration" could also suggest a "disease or disorder":[14] the process of perceiving images in a healthy eye suggestively intimates a language of disability, even, in the context of an image's vanishing, blindness. "Alteration," too, could imply expansion and doubling, a sense that most often appears in early modern music.[15] In his 1609 translation of *Micrologus, or The Art of Singing*, early modern composer John Dowland describes an alteration as a "doubling of a lesser Note in respect of a greater," "the doubling of the proper value" of a note, or a repetition of "one," "self-same Note" by two voices (sig. Rr).We may also recall here the contrast between the permanent, material "fixed mark" and a love that is "not love," "which alters when it alteration finds," in Shakespeare's sonnet 116 (90) or Polixenes's confrontation of Camillo in the *Winter's Tale*:

> Good Camillo,
> Your chang'd complexions are to me a mirror
> Which shows me mine chang'd too; for I must be
> A party in this alteration, finding
> Myself thus alter'd with 't.   (1.2.380–4)

In Crooke's description of visual perception, the image must pass through the eye's crystalline membrane, pass from the eye to the mind, and vanish. The spectacle of the eye's cyrstalline humour works to undo the image, to paraphrase Gloucester, as if it had never been. Sight depends on *in*visibility or vanished images in addition to visual transformation, doubling, and refraction, a paradox that informs *2 Henry VI*'s depiction of Simpcox's false blindness and Margaret's loss of England's shore in her "dim and dusky spectacles." This cultural trope of visual-material vanishing, transformation, and doubling eventually manifested itself even in the physical structure of the early modern stage itself. In *Vision and Rhetoric in Shakespeare*, Alison Thorne describes the manipulation of visual perspective, originally championed by early modern artists such as Leon Battista Alberti, in English Renaissance theatre. Originally developed for the purpose of an ideal, unified perspective in visual art, perspectival manipulations grew to become intrigued by "illusionism in all its forms," particularly in the "illusionistic stage scenery" exemplified by the designs of Inigo Jones (37). Thorne argues that stage designers used artistic perspective for "optical tricks" that would give "the impression of deep space on a shallow stage" (37).

Even as "alehouse signs" such as the figure of Margaret locate and situate the play with visible symbols, in metatheatrical terms the entire procedure of watching the play unfold is called into question by the optical illusions of the stage and its scenery as well as the partial, manipulable nature of the audience's sight. Margaret's references to seeing, being seen, becoming a sign, and becoming an imprinted seal reveal the dangerously spectacular and permeable transaction between audience (or reader) and image. The eye was thought to be a vulnerable sense, a potential threshold for "vice" (McDermott 13), often "collapsing the boundaries between inner and outer worlds" (McDermott 8). Eyes could even become a medium for contagion, via images (Chalk 112). We may recall the impish Puck anointing the lovers' eyes in *Midsummer Night's Dream*, wreaking havoc and delusion. The visual relationship between theatrical imagery and viewers was, like Crooke's alterations, mutually transformative: early modern observers "could be physically changed by the object of their vision" (Lin 57), just as their own visual perspectives would shape what they would perceive. Early modern theatre mirrored audience affect and "impresses those features and images back onto spectators" in an interactive, refractive model (Hobgood 19). The phenomenology of the theatre allowed for a bodily amorphousness on the part of the audience, filtered through the uncertain eye. Paul Yachnin observes that the theatre was thought to be capable of mental and physical transformation in its play goers (76) – with potentially destructive consequences. As Michael O'Connell addresses, in early modern "antitheatrical arguments, the power of the stage entered through the eyes into the soul, with the potential for evil" (19). References to metaphors of visual refraction in *2 Henry VI* – the basilisk, the refraction of light on glass, the recoil of a gun – emphasize the altered, mediated nature of vision in a theatrical context where the observed and observer are potentially locked in a mutually destructive gaze. After the commons storm into court, Henry cries,

> Thou baleful messenger, out of my sight!
> Upon thy eyeballs murderous tyranny
> Sits in grim majesty, to fright the world.
> Look not upon me, for thine eyes are wounding.
> Yet do not go away. Come, basilisk,
> And kill the innocent gazer with thy sight.   (3.2.48–53)

A "basilisk," in the early modern imagination, was a serpentine monster that could kill one who gazed into its eyes. The eye itself, as shown in Henry's figuration of the eye as a tyrant and murderer, is diabolical and destructive in this trope, as well as operating, again, as a visual spectacle with multiple alterations and refractions. A basilisk gazes on the viewer who gazes at it, and it is this reflexivity (or refraction) that allows its violence. Sergei Lobanov-Rostovsky describes the basilisk symbol's role in early modern Petrarchan love poetry as one that "destroys the eye's claim to power" by reversing the male gaze: the basilisk trope represents the female beloved's eyes as active and violent (197). The very act of being an object of sight, then, is one that uneasily allows a violent reciprocity. When Margaret pleads Suffolk to curse his enemies, he exclaims, in a rather ineffectual *sententiae*: "Their sweetest shade a grove of cypress trees! / Their chiefest prospect murd'ring basilisks!" (3.2.323–4). Margaret's reply, "Enough, sweet Suffolk, thou torment'st thyself, / And these dread curses, like the sun 'gainst glass, / Or like an overcharged gun, recoil" (3.2.329–32), emphasizes the refractive nature of visual observation in this scene. Here, both vision itself and the ineffective rhetoric of Suffolk's curses – like the sun against glass – are basilisks, destroying speaker and observer.

This potential for mutual destruction through visual observation informs the precariousness of political performance in *2 Henry VI*.

Batch 125642   (North)

From 2 - 13 - 03 - 1 - 02

To 4 - 50 - 90 - 1 - 01

ISBN 978 - 1 - 4875 - 0069 - 6

READING BY DESIGN

Ord# 9024084   HFS NEW BOOKS RECEIVING

10/28/2025

Carton Qty	Move Qty	Move Ctns	Move Units	# of Ords	Pick Qty
20	1		1	1	1

In addition, play's references to books, texts, and print destabilize England's political hierarchies. While many antitheatrical writers believed that to read a play was less morally dangerous than to attend one (O'Connell 34), Shakespeare portrays stage and page as dually troubling to sociopolitical order in his portrayal of Margaret as imprint and sign, his theatricalization of Foxe, and Cade's revolutionary antipathy towards print. In the theatrics of her punishment, the Duchess Eleanor is "mail'd up in shame, with papers on my back" that have written verses as she proceeds through the common streets of London, suggesting a mutually between text and performance in both forming and, in this case, disintegrating, political status (2.4.31). Indeed, 2 *Henry VI* as a play seems to subvert attachments of image to power, portraying their mutual decomposition and inverting hierarchies of political theatrics. In this context, Margaret and Cade become the most visible emblems of political (dis)order. In contrast with the successful monarchs of Shakespeare's Henry IV and V, who successfully and consciously manage political theatre, Henry VI becomes fixated on imagery rather than on manipulating his own power over it: York laments that his "bookish" rule "hath pull'd fair England down" (1.2.259), and Margaret complains that "His study is his tilt-yard, and his loves / Are brazen images of canonized saints" (1.3.59–60). Here, books are as much associated with dangerous iconicity as plays. Ironically, it is his characterization as a reader that appears to blind Henry VI to political realities. The anti-bibliographical Cade, instead, as if filling a vacuum and inverting the figure of bookish Henry VI, becomes a wielder of horrific political theatrics as he mounts the heads of Say and his son-in-law, Sir James Cromer, on poles and has them "kiss" in "every corner" (4.7.136).[16] Margert E. Owens recounts this moment's "intense" attention to "theatrical spectacle" as it evokes the potent image of the Hydra, or many-headed monster, to symbolize a mass uprising (368; 371). The crude visual symbolism of duplicate heads in this scene replicates the history cycle's representation of competing political heads, a headlessness or the failure of authority, and an inverse duplication of the early modern state practice of decapitating political rebels. In a political and theatrical context where mastery over the image was a conduit for power, 2 *Henry VI* uses emblems, ciphers, and book materials to both vividly portray political disorder and to interrogate what is seen and, therefore, what can ever be impressed upon an audience of spectators.

Spectacle and Spectators

References to visual materials in *2 Henry VI* interrogate how the visual spectacle of performance could be seen and perceived. Neither the visual materials of stage/page nor the eye itself is capable of showing a total vision: this loss of sight, in Margaret's sea voyage, is also a loss of perception, as she loses "ken," or knowledge, of England. Even as a physician, Crooke himself situated his theory of visual perception in highly ambiguous terms. He sets forth several different possibilities for image impressions: "Sight must bee made either by an emission of spirites, or a reception of beames, or else by emission and reception both together" (569). He describes the anatomy of the eye as transparent, as it refracts the medium between the eye and object. This medium is coloured air (569). Crooke theorizes that the transparent eye receives light and colour from external forms without itself projecting light and colour; however, he immediately names several exceptions of dubious character: Tiberius Caesar; the physician Cardan; creatures who hunt at night; and John Baptista della Porta, who wrote of optical illusions and camera obscura in his *Natural Magic* (1558) (Crooke 569). Simpcox's falsely disabled reception of colours and Margaret's dusky eye combine to depict the troubled nature of visual perception in early modern culture through their transgressively ambiguous modes of delivery: in the false miracle of the sighted blind man and the dusky eye of an aggressively persuasive queen.

It is perhaps no accident that rhetorical figures of doubling and ambiguity are described as a "hall of mirrors" by Henry Louis Gates, Jr. The rhetoric of ambiguity and dissembling that represent the gender, class, and bodily subversions of Margaret, Cade, and Simpcox also figure their nature as images. These characters act as emblematic signs that disturbingly alter or refract the negotiated, uncertain relationship between the performing "cipher" in a theatrical spectacle and the visual perception of the audience. Shakespeare's portrayal of ambiguous visual delivery reflected a cultural understanding of visual materials as partial, precarious spectacles – one that would not last into the eighteenth century. Restoration critics of course famously attack Shakespeare's tendency to show his audience visual spectacles that transgressed the classical boundaries of decorum or propriety. This changing attitude towards theatrical decorum in visual delivery appears to reflect a more totalizing, direct relationship between sight and observation. A 1684 translation of Horace, for instance, situates decorum in terms of what should be appropriately displayed to a theatrical audience:

> Observe the just *decorum* of the Stage,
> And show those *Humors* still that *suit* the Age ...
> Things only *told,* tho of the same degree,
> Do raise our Passions less than what we *see:*
> For the *Spectator* takes in every part,
> The Ey's the faithfull'st Servant to the Heart:
> Yet do not every Part too freely shew,
> Some bear the telling, better than the view:
> Things *wild* or *cruel* do displease the Eyes,
> And yet when only *told,* the same surprise;
> *Medea* must not draw her murdering Knife,
> And on the *Stage* attempt her Childrens life.   (556)

Here, the eye and viewer are spectators rather than spectacles themselves. By the late seventeenth century, vision's relationship to perception and the "passions" is one of direct magnification, where the "spectator" (audience and eye) absorbs and observes the entire image. This description of a totalizing visual perception, so direct as to cause distress if the spectator views murder onstage, contrasts with Shakespeare's more ambiguous representation of the mediated, refractive, and altered gaze. As the following conclusion will examine, this empirical, direct conception of sight is being newly interrogated by new visual media, media that may be conceived of, like Shakespeare's visual ciphers, as species and spectacle.

Conclusion: Mediated Vision

Despite the disciplinary boundaries that exist between new media and bibliographical studies, the early modern book's problems of perception can help to illuminate how current visual media is discursively and socially constructed. Reading has been, as with the shift from manuscript to print, undergoing a paradigm shift in the early twenty-first century. E-books, digital texts, and hypertexts have shifted the visual interfaces and phenomenal context for the reading process, much as illustrated print called for an ambient, interactive form of reading for early modern viewers. In my previous chapters, I have explored the coterminous interrogation of visual perception and changing material aspects of visual print books in the early modern era. Here, I interrogate whether and how changing visual interfaces in new media may, as in the Renaissance, spur debate over visual perception. Will our new reading processes transform and destabilize epistemologies of sight, or will a continuing post-Cartesian relationship between observation and truth instead stabilize our interfaces with and experiences of new media? This question may ultimately be answerable only in time and after our reading methods have long shifted; but in this conclusion, I will seek to explore it.

The materials we use to communicate, whether books or screens, can transform phenomenological categories. In "A Telescope for the Mind?" Willard McCarthy revisits Margaret Masterman's 1962 article, "The Intellect's New Eye." McCarthy recalls the belief that computing media would create "a crisis of understanding from which a new, more adequate cosmology arises" (113). For example, Masterman advocated a role for the digital computer "not as a tool but as a telescope" (38). This digital telescope would expand our vision, both cognitively and culturally (38). This argument parallels a shift from seeing books as things or materials to books as phenomenal and ambient. Masterman's metaphorical relationship of computer to telescope also recalls the early modern figuration of the book as glass, prism, telescope, and mirror. Masterman anticipated changes in visual perception through digital technology: she links the computer to the technologies of the Renaissance, which brought about a similarly momentous shift in paradigms of sight, knowledge, and perception. Indeed, Jonathan Sawday claims that "some of the key linguistic terms we have begun to associate with computer culture (terms such as net, matrix, and web) have their founding moment in early modern writing" (27). As this book contends, metaphors for knowing (and unknowing) interweave with technical change to produce shifts in epistemic categories. While at times challenging Masterman's progressive narrative, McCarthy lauds her foresight in thinking through digital media's potential for "qualitative rather than quantitative change – different ideas rather than simply more evidence" (114). The mediating gaze of the computer as telescope, however, poses a less problematic relationship between medium and perception than do early modern English depictions of the book as mutable, illusory glass. This computer-telescope metaphor produces a relationship of knowledge's expansion and sight's extension, as opposed to the early modern book's metaphors of vision as a broken or dark glass. Masterman's analogy produces an understanding of visual media as an agent of phenomenological change, yet her concept of the computer as telescope obscures the complex intellectual history of sight as troubled episteme.

New media can invite us as users, readers, and designers to reconceive familiar empirical or straightforward notions of visual knowledge and visual materials. A broad application of phenomenological concerns to media, from book to blog, moves these media and their scholars from their current position as mere *technes* or "servant roles," to cite Alan Liu, and allows them to perform a vital role in our intellectual and cultural history (495). Discussions of visual rhetoric and visual media's affordances have inspired new classroom practices and new conceptions of knowledge production, but a neglect of visual media's function as an episteme limits these conversations to a situation of media as techne or telescopic aid to knowledge/vision. An attention to what Jenna Wortham calls "changes in perception," as well as changes to how we culturally *perceive* perception, will allow for new and productive questions to be asked of classroom technology and its potential applications.

For example, Johanna Drucker enjoins us to recognize the "gooeyness" of the online "GUI," or graphical user interface (213). Drucker argues against taking navigational icons, menus, and visual layouts of new media for granted. She instead advocates for reading GUIs as paratexts, a methodology that specifically parallels bibliographical scholarship on page paratexts (217). Such strategies counter what Chris Jenks calls a "doctrine of immaculate perception," where seeing equals knowing, a positivist method of observation from above (5). This doctrine is perhaps anti-rhetorical in its very nature: Catherine Hobbs tracks the growing eighteenth-century fear of rhetorical devices and symbolic language as "distortions of the objective representation of a visual reality" (41). By bringing together a pre-positivist methodology of producing and viewing the visual media of books with a post-positivist look at digital paratexts, we may begin to counter such cultural assumptions. This book's own investigation of the ways that book visuals specifically interacted with questions of politics and perception could also serve as a potential model for reading new media paratexts that would move us past a tool-based discourse, so that we may unravel the positivist model of sight as observation, or visual rhetoric as techne, alone.

From Disposable Materials to a Spectacle of Collection

A more comprehensive understanding of the philosophical concerns that lay behind the visual construction of different media platforms – whether paper, silicon, or glass – resists such a destructive streamlining of material history. Fortunately, as Ben McCorkle observes, the formal politics of different media have become more accessible now that we are in an era of flux: print "interfaces" that had become "invisible … conceptually understood as neutral containers for transmitting 'pure' language" (71) can now be perceived as "physical, performative object[s]" (74). Yet without conversations *between* media histories, the book and the digital page, the screen potentially becomes every bit as naturalized to users as the print page. This sense of familiarity and visual simplicity could lend new media the same false sense of material, epistemic, and ideological stability that has often plagued studies and sensations of the book. In our scholarship, we can resist this naturalization through actively analysing, constructing, and destabilizing visual formats in books and in new media. For example, Roger Chartier (among others) points to the e-text's mutability and collectivity due to its "palimpsestic and polyphonic" nature (145). Since I argue throughout my previous chapters for a more palimpsestic, polyphonic understanding of early books, I believe that it is necessary to situate *both* physical books and e-texts as palimpsests, or (re)collected, erasable, and reinscribable visual texts. After all, a fragmented, accumulative screen shot or social media blog may seem automatically unified to digital natives used to immediate visual scanning or scrolling. Social media spaces such as Twitter, Tumblr, Instagram, and especially Snapchat, which allows photographs to be hidden after a set period, approach digital space as palimpsest or partial, erasable collection of parts. The continued encouragement of a thoughtful reading and production of these visual materials could counter cultural assumptions of a simple observation or permanence of these new visual structures – the script is not forever but is a changeable and perishable jumble. Chartier points out what he argues to be a greater possibility of "textual intervention" in the e-text ("Languages, Books, and Reading" 144), as readers can go beyond inscribing text in physical blank pages to adding, removing, and (re)collecting different textual and visual material. We can particularly emphasize these possibilities to students accustomed to acting as consumers rather than producers within their everyday media use. Early modern reader and pedagogical practices such as commonplacing, miscellany binding, drawing within, blotting out, and physical collection situate the print text as potentially palimpsestic and "collective." Such practices speak to similar opportunities for visual (re)invention in digital and book media. Indeed, now that the print book is one option among many, its visual materials, such as its cover, its physical properties, and its illustrations, have become more important to how we teach, read, and collect books. Some publishers have even begun releasing physical books with illustrations and decorative covers alongside the ebook version of the same text, with the sense that physical books now (re)occupy a space of sensation and collection.

Navigators of both print and digital reading systems can sort through different books or works using "icons" as markers and inscribe or rearrange their spectacles of collecting in a personalized, inventive, and stylized (re)arrangement of print or online materials. Nicole Brown discusses the relationship between visible, physical materials and new media spaces in her discussion of literal and online graffiti as a form of "writing focused on (re)defining space in ways that its (re)construction and use are illuminated" (248). Graffiti, ancient and contemporary, has always demonstrated an attention to spatial location and a public, political rhetoric. Book collections, craft sites, and social media libraries similarly present the opportunity to attend to the rhetorical and political possibilities of space in the classroom and in our daily visual reading practices. An attention to the intersections between image, book, and screen gives us different ways to reconstruct *loci* as shared visual spaces for collection and invention.

As this study argues, the meanings of visual texts are constructed in the space between text and image, and through the arrangement of empty, negative spaces, in the reader's divided gaze. Scott McCloud in *Understanding Comics* and Meredith Badger in her early analysis of blogging practices argue that the reader invents meaning in the spaces between sequenced images, in the "gutter" of a visual page (McCloud 60; Badger, "Visual Blogs"). While McCloud's model has been pioneering and crucial to understanding images as meaningful objects of analysis, our scholarship's treatment of visuality's relationship to media needs further theory building if we are to analyse the arrangement, collection, and recollection of materials and images outside a narrative, sequential structure. The model of oscillation, which I follow and apply to tensions between part and whole in the early modern book, may ultimately be limited to the historical moment of early print. In the following section, I propose an alternative model of visual reading that can potentially account for both reader and object agency, as well as the paradoxical unity and fragmentation of spectacular materials, old and new.

Spectacles That Watch: Triangular Sight

The potential agency of visual construction, collection, and exchange does not lie with the reader alone, a dynamic perhaps ignored in discussions of new media spaces as potentially democratic and revolutionary in the classroom and public sphere. Johndan Johnson-Eilola contends that it is not just the reader or navigator that gazes on the visual interface of new media – these visible systems gaze back at us. As we read the online e-text, its "things are thinking with us, following us to detect trends in our interactions, our purchases, our interests, waiting to step forward to offer us something, such as ads targeted to our needs and wants" ("Polymorphous Perversity in Texts"). In other words, these online visual materials read *us*. For example, Samy Kamkar's "ever-cookie" application tracks user behaviour and navigation between browsers and browsing sessions, including our book preferences, purchases, and reviews (Johnson-Eilola). Such programs shift visual observation from human agent to material object, calling to mind, in a rather

Figure 6.1.

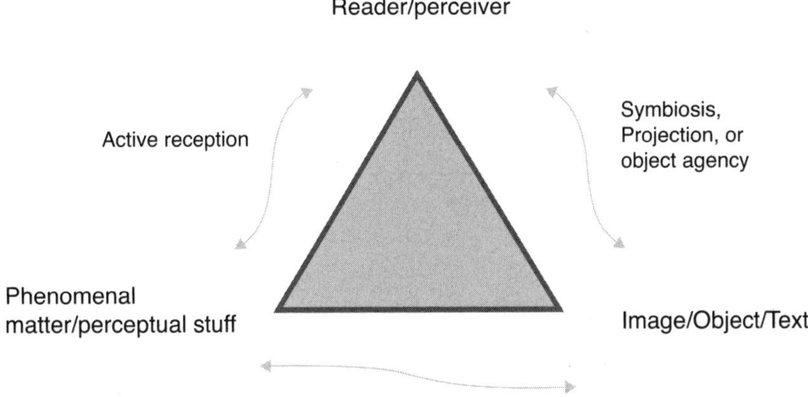

perverse sense, pre-Cartesian theories of entelechy or *species*. Like the model of entelechy, or materials enchanted with essential meaning, the materials of our contemporary reading systems are imparted with sentience and epistemic agency. Jane Bennett argues for a reinvigorated stance of what she calls vital materialism in *Vibrant Matter*. Bennett persuasively claims that an understanding of material agency will allow us to better understand complex ecologies. Bennett presents her vital materialism as a constructive theoretical alternative to the Frankfurt School's political materialism. Perhaps, however, the two models come together rather diabolically in the case of digital media's programmed, autonomous, and automatic observation and surveillance devices, as they form a complex, vital web of visual collection that also acts as a system of advertisement and exchange. To employ another relevant early modern theory of perception, these cookies and tracking devices operate as the visual *species* of our collective new-media spectacles, as they mediate, transmit, and potentially obstruct the image's relationship to the viewing eye. This troubled phenomenological relationship between image, reader, and visual matter can serve to complicate the practice of critical spatial theory, which often productively studies the politics, but not the perceptual problems, of space.[1] Indeed, I here posit a triangular structure of visual reading and perception that draws from classical and early modern theories of sight (Figure 6.1).

Figure 6.2.

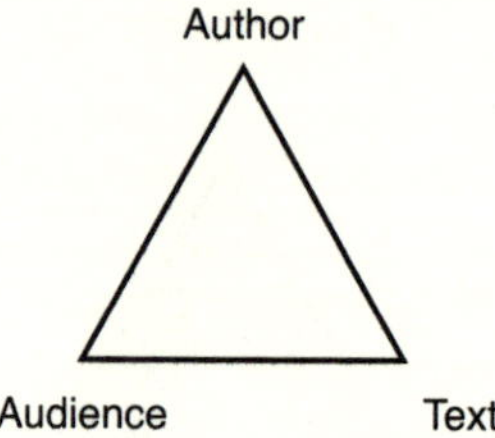

    This structure of triangular reading parallels, yet counters, the conventionally accepted model of the "rhetorical triangle" (Figure 6.2).

    In my model of triangular perception, each element does not merely "construct" the rhetorical situation or reading process. Rather, each element – reader or observer, phenomenal matter, and image/object/text – mediates, troubles, and even potentially *obstructs* the message, a relationship of both connection and fissure represented here by the squiggly and distorted rather than linear arrows. Since this structure is focused on the visual reading process, the author is omitted. Instead, the object's phenomenal matter, whether that may be best described as a network, replica, species, or imprint, operates as a point of mediation (or distortion) between image and viewer. This alternative model prohibits a clear, direct path of "immaculate perception." If we follow Platonic theories of vision, the reader or observer may even project their own phenomenal matter, to be combined with the perceptual "stuff" that the object or image emanates. Infinite obstacles and levels of mediation or, to paraphrase Helkiah Crooke, alteration can exist between viewer and image. Hence, the relationship between viewer and the perceptual "stuff" of the material or image may be, as in chapter 1's analysis of Hawes's and Caxton's rhetorical theories, best described as active reception, wherein readers might discover a pattern or detail from among the material constantly striking their eyes. With this phenomenal triangle in mind, the object itself could be empowered to shape what is viewed and encountered, particularly in a more receptive paradigm. A particular detail or image, for example, may draw the eye away from its unified message, fracturing or erasing the message itself. The relationship between viewer and the image or object could be one of projection, if the reader's agency dominates, or one of object agency, where the image itself overdetermines the pattern of visual observation. Alternatively, the image and reader could operate in a state of symbiosis, or mutuality. The nature of this relationship will necessarily be different and unique to each image, pattern, and text. Finally, phenomenal matter might alter, transform, reflect, or distort the object or image itself and will necessarily shape what the reader might envision. This new triangular model of visual reading transforms it from a simple merging of text/reader/author into (to paraphrase Richard Marback) a "wicked problem" of perception (399).[2] In this new triangle, the connections among vision, perception, and knowledge remain troublingly ambiguous: rather than a constructive triad, they instead present us with an unholy trinity.

Invention's New Libraries

If we assume sight to be a clear window into reality, it is difficult to design or envision alternative systems of visual rhetoric and visual reading: it is all too easy to overlook less visible, more marginalized possibilities with the assumption that they are unknowable and unforeseeable. Although this is a study that positions visual materials as central to an understanding of epistemic problems, it is also a study that argues for an uneasy relationship of vision to knowledge. As Spenser claims in his introduction to *The Faerie Queene*'s second book,

> Who euer heard of th'Indian *Peru*?
> Or who in venturous vessell measured
> The *Amazon* huge riuer now found trew?
> Or fruitfullest *Virginia* who did euer vew?
> Yet all these were, when no man did them know;
> Yet haue from wisest ages hidden beene:
> And later times things more vnknowne shall show [...]
> What if in euery other starre vnseene
> Of other worldes he happily should hear
> He wo[n]der would much more: yet such to some appeare   (185–6)

The interfaces we encounter shape what we can perceive but they should not limit us: we do not know what we do not know. But new ways of seeing our world – and new constructions of our political, material, and optical realities – might appear to some as shaded glimpses through a dark glass.

Notes

Introduction

1 See Ong's *Ramus, Method, and the Decay of Dialogue* (Chicago; U of Chicago P, 2005), and Elizabeth Eisenstein's *The Printing Press as an Agent of Change: Communications and Cultural Transformations in Early-Modern Europe* (Cambridge, Cambridge UP, 1980).

2 See, for example, his "Visible and Invisible Letters"; "The First Literary Hamlet and the Commonplacing of Professional Plays"; and "Hamlet and the Technologies of Writing in Renaissance England," *Shakespeare Quarterly* 55.4 (2004): 379–419. These recent publications radically illuminate the text-image multi-mediality of canonical early modern works.

3 See Smyth's "Burning to Read: Ben Jonson's Library Fire of 1623" 34–56, in this collection.

4 See "Looking into Aristotle's Eyes."

5 Although I dissent from Bolter's specific reading of the book as a linear, fixed structure, I borrow his term "remediation," which describes how new mediums maintain, transform, and adapt older mediums. For his discussion of the remediation of oral rhetoric to print, and from print to digital rhetoric, see *Writing Space* 23–6.

6 Also see Aristotle, *Generation of Animals* 5.1.779b20–35: 497. Aristotle here describes the eyes as "composed of water and not of air or of fire," although correct image reception is idiosyncratic and individuated: "some eyes contain too much fluid, some too little, to suit the right movement, others contain just the right amount" (497). In *De Sensu*, Aristotle again defends the watery nature of the eye against the Platonic theory of fire (47, 2.437a29–32) and calls the theory "that sight is effected by means of something which issues from the eye and that it travels as far as the stars

or, as some say, unites with something else after proceeding a certain distance," "wholly absurd" (51, 2.238a26–29).

7 "Each sense-organ is receptive of the object of perception without its matter" (*De Anima* 48, 3.2425b17–25). Also see Osborne, "Aristotle, De Anima 3.2" 402, and Hawhee 140.

8 *The Republic*, 107–20 (7.514–20).

9 For further discussions of epistemic certainty's relationship to rhetorical pedagogy in the academy, see Berlin, *Rhetoric and Reality*, and Ian Barnard, "The Ruse of Clarity" 434–51.

10 For further recent studies on the senses and sensation in the Renaissance, see for instance Drew Daniel, *The Melancholy Assemblage: Affect and Epistemology in the English Renaissance* (Fordham: Fordham UP, 2013); Holly Dugan, *The Ephemeral History of Perfume: Scent and Sense in Early Modern England* (Baltimore: Johns Hopkins UP, 2011); Keith M. Botelho, *Renaissance Earwitnesses: Rumor and Early Modern Masculinity* (New York: Palgrave, 2009); Gina Bloom, *Voice in Motion: Staging Gender, Shaping Sound in Early Modern England* (Philadelphia: U of Pennsylvania P, 2007); Elizabeth D. Harvey, *Sensible Flesh: On Touch in Early Modern Culture* (Philadelphia: U of Pennsylvania P, 2003); and Bruce R. Smith, *The Acoustic World of Early Modern England: Attending the O-Factor* (Chicago: University of Chicago Press, 1999).

11 See Richter, *Greek, Etruscan, and Roman Bronzes*.

12 See Rosenberg and Grafton, *Cartographies of Time* "Time in Print" 10–26.

13 See Klein, *Maps and the Writing of Space in Early Modern England* 42–76; and Cormack, *Charting an Empire* 48–90.

1 Through a Looking-Glass

1 This chapter primarily discusses the following two editions: William Caxton, *Hier begynneth the book callid the Myrrour and Dyscrypcyon of the Worlde with Many Mervaylles* … (Westminster, 1481), STC 24762, Early English Books Online; and Caxton, *Hier begynneth the book callid the Myrrour and Dyscrypcyon of the Worlde with Many Mervaylles* … (Westminster, 1490), STC 24763, Early English Books Online.

2 Hawhee and Holding situate rhetoric as material, emotive, and transformative in the works of Priestley and Austin, as they employ a language of chemistry to describe the relationship between language, rhetor, and audience. As I will discuss in greater length, Hawhee discusses rhetoric from a less material, more phenomenological approach in "Looking into Aristotle's Eyes: Toward a Theory of Rhetorical Vision."

Hawhee calls this phenomenal turn "rhetorical vision," rather than the more materially focused term of "visual rhetoric," 142.

3 Another, more contemporary parallel to the medieval imago mundi might be our own searchable, comprehensive *Wikipedia*, as Alex Mueller considers in "Wikipedia as Imago Mundi."

4 For an analysis of this dual role in Machiavelli's *Prince*, see Frank Tang's "Machiavelli's Image of the Ruler."

5 In *The Trojan Mirror*, Witalisz also notes the influence of the twelfth-century Latin version of the *Secretum Secretorum*, "believed to be Aristotle's council for Alexander the Great," on the genre's conventions, 97.

6 A later and important example of the genre's continued currency into the sixteenth century is the 1559 *Mirror for Magistrates*, a collection of poems developed as an expansion of Lydgate's *Fall of Princes*. For an extended analysis of the 1559 *Mirror* as a response to Tudor politics, see Scott Lucas, "'Let None Such Office Take, Save He That Can for Right His Prince Forsake.'"

7 Georgiana Donavin convincingly observes that the *Confessio Amantis*'s treatment of rhetoric draws from Aristotelian concepts of faculty psychology, particularly invention. As I will later discuss at length, portrayals of invention and imagination in Aristotelian and Platonic faculty psychology are important elements in the rhetoric of Caxton's *Mirrour* and Hawes's *Pastime*. See "Rhetorical Gower" 155.

8 As Anna Torti explains, the figure of Venus, the lady of the poem, and the temple itself all act as specula in this work. See "John Lydgate's Temple of Glas: 'Atwixen Two So Hang I in Balaunce,'" in *Intellectuals and Writers in Fourteenth-Century Europe*, ed. Piero Boitani and Anna Torti (Tübingen; Cambridge: Narr; Brewer, 1986) 231.

9 This language of goldsmithing and alchemy includes terms such as gathering together, melding, and multiplying, which Kuskin places in the context of market capitalism and social authority. In addition to these implications, I would add that this terminology indicates a phenomenal transformation of materials and objects to create new meaning, a metamorphosis that could include both the production and consumption, or reading, of Caxton's print works.

10 See Rita Copeland's "Lydgate, Hawes, and the Science of Rhetoric in the Late Middle Ages" 64–70.

11 Robert Gibbs notes that concave magnifying mirrors "despite their inconvenient habit of reversing the text, were used alongside lenses to enlarge small and faded handwriting" for reading in the medieval era (85n180). See also Edward Rosen, "The Invention of Eyeglasses," *Journal*

of the History of Medicine and Allied Sciences 11.1 (1956): 13–46. Lenses and concave mirrors shared properties and production methods: "the situation was the same for the fabrication of appropriate concave mirrors as it was for refractive lenses, since the necessary glass grinding and polishing technology was no different" (Falco http://fp.optics.arizona.edu/SSD/art-optics/historical.html). The ability of mirrors to magnify in the medieval era is not without controversy: see Sara J. Schechner, "Between Knowing and Doing" 145.

12 William Caxton, *The myrrour and dyscrypcyon of the worlde with many meruaylles … Enprynted by me Laurence Andrewe dwellynge in fletestrete, at the sygne of the golde[n] crosse by flete brydge* (London, 1527). STC 24764. Bodleian library, Shelfmark Lawn d. 72, bibliographic note in front matter.

13 See *OED*, "jumble," senses 1 and 3.

14 For an analysis of print's influence on the development of vernacular rhetoric for "practical, social, and commercial purposes," in the context of early modern English letter writing, see Newbold, "Traditional, Practical, Entertaining" 267–300.

15 In "Translating for Print," Knapp observes that several copies of this text show similar re-inscriptions of this proverb by readers (78).

16 Caxton, *Mirror* (2nd Ed. Westminster: printed by William Caxton, 1481). STC 15833, no. 48. John Rylands library incunable collection, Shelfmark RFE11.

17 As Knapp asserts, the gamble "known to be involved in printing illustrated books suggests that he would not have made this decision lightly … the introduction of illustrations into a printer's edition destroyed more than one printer's business" (76). The revolutionary nature of Caxton's illustrations, Knapp asserts, was that they "appealed to his audience" (76) and were employed in a situation in which Caxton may have considered the illustrations to be "essential for the understanding of the text" (75).

18 Corbett and Lightbown also trace this dialectical reading process between word and image through early modern illustrated title pages in *The Comely Frontispiece*. Of these illustrated devices, they claim that "in the sixteenth century it was even ruled that their explanation ought not to be wholly contained either in the image or the motto, but should emerge from the combination of the two" (10).

19 For this information on the medieval brain structure and its history as well as a wealth of visual illustrations of the medieval brain, see Clarke and Dewhurst, *An Illustrated History of Brain Function* 8–48. See also Minnis, "Medieval Imagination and Memory" 239, and A. Mark Smith, "History of Medieval Optics."

20 See Klarer, "*Ekphrasis*, or the Archaeology of Historical Theories of Representation" 36.

21 See also Carruthers, *The Book of Memory* 57. Some medieval thinkers, such as Thomas Aquinas, who divided the receptive from the composing imagination, theorized a five-part structure for the brain instead. This alternative organization, however, did not substantially change the primary focus on memory, imagination, and reason or judgment (Carruthers 62).

22 For instance, see Clarke and Dewhurst, 11, Figure 6, which shows lines that cross the animal brain with the optic nerve, as a visual chiasmus, in a fifteenth-century diagram; 32, Figure 39, which depicts channels that extend from the eyes and symbolize the "optic nerves," from a 1310 drawing; 38, Figure 48, a popular 1503 portrayal by Gregor Reisch in his encyclopedia *Margarita Philosophica*, which extends lines from the eye, nose, ear, and lips up to the brain to indicate sense data.

23 Kemp's *Cognitive Psychology in the Middle Ages* 45–60, contains a useful review of the Aristotelian and medieval brain structure. Imagination's important function in the productive impression and creation of visual sense data is further manifested by the medieval belief that a fetus could receive and retain an impression of an image (generally gruesome) that its mother viewed: see Macdonald, *History of the Concept of Mind* 261.

24 On the role of imagination in sleepwalking, sleep disturbances, and nightmares in medieval culture, see MacLehose, "Sleepwalking, Violence, and Desire in the Middle Ages."

25 See Collete, *Species, Phantasms, and Images* 9. Magnus further distinguishes phantasia and the imagination: "imagination is always connected with actual experience, *phantasy* with the play of the mind based on the images experience generates." Daniel Heller-Roazen cites medieval Jewish philosopher Isaac Israeli's "singular" claim that fantasia transmits "corporeal" things to the spiritual sense, or the imagination; here, phantasia acts as a cognitive mediator in a more metaphysical sense. See his "Common Sense: Greek, Arabic, Latin" 38.

26 Carruthers cites Galen, "Ibn Sina, Ibn Rushd, Albertus Magnus, Thomas Aquinas," and "Walter Burley" as proponents of this theory; the cognitive faculty of the "vis formalis," or "power of making forms," cooperated with phantasia to perform this purpose. See her "Mechanisms for the Transmission of Culture" 4–5.

27 In "Books and Bodies," Walter analyses how medieval English vernacular books employed a rhetoric of sensation, or the "boistous," through appealing to readers' sight, hearing, taste, smell, and touch.

28 In *The Acoustic World of Early Modern England*, Smith also employs these examples to further his analysis of physical memory in acoustics but does not emphasize their connection to the graphical elements of the book.

29 Later on, Descartes would specifically locate impressions as residing in a section of the brain as he connects sensation and cognition: he proposes that "ideas of objects are formed in the place assigned to the imagination and to common sense, how these ideas are retained in the memory, and how they cause the movement of all bodily parts." Descartes believed that "animal spirits," or a fluid in the brain, flow into the optic "nerves in a pattern that corresponds in some systemic way to the shapes impressed on the retina," then "stored for subsequent use by the memory" See Desmond Clarke, *Descartes's Theory of Mind* 54–5.

30 As Stark explains, "For most numinous philosophers, rhetorical style still carried the residue of the Word and the Name at the beginning of the world, which gave form to reality itself" (10).

31 Although it postdates the Tottel *Past-time*, philosopher-scientist Bernandino Telesio's *De Rerum Natura Iuxta Propria Principia* (*On the Nature of Things according to their Own Principles*) (1563) likewise connects fire with perception: "traditional psychological functions" were ascribed "to a material spirit, an imperceptibly thin and fiery body, which was located in the nervous system (Spruit 209).

32 See Ong, *Rhetoric, Romance, and Technology* 124–6, and Cummings, *Grammar and Grace* 10. Cummings's and Ong's discussion of punishment focuses on the later grammar-school era of rhetorical pedagogy; however, corporal punishment was also a traditional practice in scholastic education (although, as of the first publications of Caxton's *Mirrour* and Hawes's *Pastime*, not yet imprecated with the overtones of post-Reformation ideological warfare).

33 Copeland also interprets this scene as an elevation of rhetoric (68).

34 See Smyth's *"Profit and Delight"* 1–32, for a survey of common terms for rhetorical miscellanies.

35 *OED*, "magnify," sense 1a and Thomas Blount, *Glossographia or a Dictionary* (1656) "magnify (magnifacio): to make great account of, to honor much" (LEME: Lexicons of Early Modern English, leme.library.utoronto.ca/). Future citations from this database will be abbreviated to "LEME."

36 *OED*, "depute," sense 1a. See also Thomas Elyot, *The Dictionary of Sir Thomas Elyot*: "Addico, xi, dicere, to saye, to iudge, to appoynte, or depute," "Destino, aui, are, to pourpose, to appoynte, to depute, to prepare, to chese, to tye to a thinge, to sette a pryce" and Thomas Cooper, *Thesaurus Linguae Romanae et Britannicae* (1584): "Assigno, assignas,

assignâre. Liu. To giue: to distribute: to assigne: to appoint: to depute or ordeyne" (LEME).

37 *OED*, "speculate," sense 2a.

38 See *Pastime* sig. A3v.

39 In his classic article, Howell traces the early modern use of the terms *res* and *verba*. *Verba* was translated to "words" or, by extension, style/rhetoric, while *res* could imply either subject-matter/content (if derived from Quintilian) or literal, material "things" (if derived from Cicero). This *res*/*verba* binary began to be used pejoratively, against words for words' sake, in the seventeenth-century writings of Francis Bacon, Thomas Hobbes, and other plain-style partisans. See *"Res Et Verba."*

40 As the Groom of the Chamber in the court of Henry VII, this process of mirroring and dissembling in the political sphere may have been all too familiar to Hawes.

41 Francis Bacon would later write of "'coloring' an argument" as he tells us to fill our minds with images. See Hobbs, "Learning from the Past" 34; see also Francis Bacon, *The Philosophical Works of Francis Bacon* 77.

42 See *OED*, fumé, def. a. and *MED physiol.* def. 3.

43 See *OED*, "covert," senses 1 and 2, *MED* ppl. & adj. sense 1.

44 See John Foxe, Acts and Monuments 1596: "Bishops and priests ought not to come vnder the couert [1583 court] and controlment of temporall power" (1.195/1), cited in *OED* "covert," sense 6b.

45 See *OED*, "covert," sense 3 and Anonymous, *Verba Obsoleta et Alia* (ca 1558–93):

> Couptum: "Covert woody or Brushy grounde fit to defend deere in A Forrest or Parke" (LEME).

46 Where Blake emphasizes a continuity between the French manuscript's illustrations and the first print edition's woodcuts (33), Knapp notes several alterations between the two (76–81). Further, Blake argues that the illustrators of Caxton's *Mirrour* may have simply made their own adaptations and replications of the manuscript imagery without necessarily reading either text, perhaps even drawing their images from a cultural history of the genre (26–7). Alternatively, Knapp proposes a more author-based and systematic development of the woodcuts under Caxton's purview (64–9). While such discussions are speculative, the transformations of the woodcuts between each edition suggest both a larger process of cultural and technological transformation in visual print culture and a systemic, intellectual effort to suit image to text for each new audience.

47 Turner's *English Renaissance Stage* details the connection between mathematical discoveries, performance, and poetry in the sixteenth

and seventeenth centuries. In "Imaginary Conquests," Mullaney places the early modern map-mirror connection within the context of colonial encounter. Mirrors, maps, and compasses, Mullaney argues, were just as much of a source of fascination, awe, and value for early modern Europeans as they were for Native Americans.

48 As Mucklebauer discusses in "Imitation and Invention in Antiquity," these practices drew from a "classical framework" where "novelty emerges and invention occurs not by resisting the reproductive movement of imitation but by multiplying it, proliferating the number and type of models to be imitated" (75). Edward P.J. Corbett describes the dialectical practice of "Analysis," the study of rhetorical models, and "Genesis," the imitative and inventive (re)production of new models: see "The Theory and Practice of Imitation in Classical Rhetoric" 245.

49 *King James Version*, Genesis 28:16–17.

50 Lindgren, "Land Surveyors, Instruments, and Practitioners in the Renaissance" 492.

51 The measuring device of Jacob's staff may draw from Jacob's ladder in its name, but its etymology is unknown. A "Jacob's staff" could mean a pilgrim's staff, as well: The *OED* tracks its usage "from St. James (*Jacobus*), whose symbols in religious art are a pilgrim's staff and a scallop shell. In the other senses the name" Jacob's staff "is apparently more or less fanciful."

52 *King James Version*, Genesis 30:35.

53 *King James Version*, Genesis 11:7.

54 See Harman: "Assemblages are ad hoc groupings of diverse elements, of vibrant materials of all sorts. Assemblages are living, throbbing confederations that are able to function despite the persistent presence of energies that confound them from within" (23–4), and Latour 63–86 ("Objects too have Agency").

2 Memory Machines or Ephemera?

1 Both Marshall McLuhan and Walter Ong famously – and not without controversy – draw a link between the emergence of print and the displacement of oral memory onto the visual arrangement of the page. See especially Ong's *Ramus, Method, and the Decay of Dialogue*. Also see Ong, *Orality and Literacy* (New York: Routledge, 2012), and McLuhan, *The Gutenberg Galaxy* and *Understanding Media: The Extensions of Man* (Boston: MIT Press, 1994). While Mary Carruthers's scholarship on the memory canon interrogates this assumption of a mutually destructive

relationship between memory and print, Ong and McLuhan's narrative of displacement continues to dominate discussions of the memory canon. Of course, such criticisms of media's potential to destroy memory, and, by extension, true knowledge, can be traced from Plato's *Phaedrus*, which famously attacks writing itself for this reason.

2 See *Moonwalking with Einstein* (New York: Penguin, 2012) 89–107.

3 In "Clever Dogs and Nimble Spaniels," Höltgen also discusses the mnemonic imagery of collection and recollection in early modern print illustrations, particularly in images of hunting dogs and arrows drawn out of a quiver: "With Aristotle and Cicero, the topoi, loci, or places are *sedes argumentorum*, seats or 'resting places' for arguments. In the humanitistic treatises on logic and rhetoric these metaphors are elaborated and the places are often visualized as three-dimensional repositories, containers, or hiding places from which the arguments have to be drawn like arrows from a quiver" (20).

4 See Helfer's *Spenser's Ruins and the Art of Recollection* and "The Death of the 'New Poete.'"

5 Helfer sets this Ciceronian model of ongoing recollection against Virgil's: "while Virgil looks to himself to create a monument to repair the ruins of the past," in *De Oratore*: "Cicero looks to dialogue for Rome's continual edification and renovation" (725, "The Death of the 'New Poete'").

6 In "Memory Works in *The Faerie Queene*," Owens connects this invention/ memory dialectic to the construction of historical knowledge (28).

7 See Ivic's "Spenser and Interpellative Memory" in *Ars Reminiscindi*: "In its placement of Eumnestes's library atop the castle and in its representation of Eumnestes himself, this episode's materializing of memory also shares with the *ars memoriae* a deep fear of memory's vulnerability – that is, of forgetting" (290).

8 See also Carruthers 35–6.

9 See also John Baret, *An Alveary or Triple Dictionary, in English, Latin, and French* (1574), 711: "A coffer or other like place wherein iewels, or other secrete things are kepte, as euidences. Scri nium" (LEME).

10 As Landreth observes in "At Home with Mammon," the library books are not "present merely as the momentary vessels of some extra-material and immortal text; they are unique and vulnerable artifacts" (254).

11 Ann Moss's *Printed Commonplace Books and the Structuring of Renaissance Thought* – as well as Peter Beal's "Notions in Garrison: The Seventeenth-Century Commonplace Book," Renaissance English Text Society, 1987 – demonstrates the importance of commonplace books to English Renaissance thought at length.

12 See "Hamlet the Intellectual" in *The Public Intellectual*, ed. Helen Small; Miriam Jacobson, *Barbarous Antiquity: Reorienting the Past in the Poetry of Early Modern England* (Philadelphia: University of Pennsylvania Press, 2014); [and *OED*, etymology and definitions A1a, B1a, "antic"].

13 See *OED*, senses I.2, I.5, II.8, Thomas Elyot, *The Dictionary of Sir Thomas Elyot* (1538): "Commentarium, uel commentarius, a brigement or other boke, conteynynge thynges briefely writen. Also it signifieth a comment. Also a boke of remembrance or a Register or exposition" (LEME), and John Baret, *An Alveary or Triple Dictionary, in English, Latin, and French* (1574): "Raisonnette. A reckening booke: a register: a booke of accompt" (LEME).

14 The reference to a "Regester" could refer as well to a historical "remembrance" affected by print, that is, the Register of Writs, or Register of the Chancery, published in the Henrician reign by William Rastell in 1531, and re-published by Richard Tottel in 1553 with a table of contents. This register was essentially a "domesday book" of law for the sixteenth and seventeenth centuries; it included and assembled various common laws and writs into one book.

15 The varied and complex meanings of "devise" in part derive from its French and Italian etymology, in addition to its early modern English usage. To "devise" in Old French carried the alternate meanings of to divide and to invent, and later became a synonym for speech or discourse (*OED*); the *OED* also cites its definition in John Florio's 1611 Italian-English dictionary as "to deuise, to invent; also, to deuide or part a sunder; to discource, to talke or confer together; to blazon armes; also, to surmise, to thinke, to seeme vnto" (see "devise," etymology). See also *MED* 3(a) "A plan or design; a literary composition or device"; (b) "a disguise; a fashion in dress"; (c) "a device, scheme, stratagem, intrigue"; 4(a) "An artistic design, a work of art; an ornament"; (b) "a heraldic design, device"; 5 "A boundary, division"; Laurence Nowell, *Vocabularium Saxonicum* (ca 1567): "Cræftan. To devise or invente" (LEME), and Thomas Thomas, *Dictionarium Linguae Latinae et Anglicanae* (1587): "Imāgĭnor, āris, p.b. depon. Plin. Iun. To imagine, devise, or conceaue" (LEME).

16 Knight further notes several formal parallels, including blackletter type and the organization of glosses, between the *Calender* and early modern almanacs, particularly the *Kalender of Shepheardes*. He argues for a much wider and more variegated audience of readers for the *Calender* than is generally assumed by contemporary critics. See *Bound to Read* 127–33.

17 It should perhaps be noted that Quintilian approached this system with a substantial level of scepticism in his *Institutio Oratoria*. Quintilian's sceptical treatment of Metrodorus effectively divided memory as a

metaphysic and memory as a *techne*: "This makes me wonder all the more, how Metrodorus should have found three hundred and sixty different localities in the twelve signs of the Zodiac through which the sun passes. It was doubtless due to the vanity and boastfulness of a man who was inclined to vaunt his memory as being the result of art rather than of natural gifts" (225).

18 See Archer's "The Nostalgia of John Stow" for a larger discussion of nostalgic responses to the pre-Reform past and their relationship to the changing socio-religious rituals and institutions of early modern London (17–34). Archer observes a purposeful "ambiguity of the Elizabethan settlement on the question of images" (32).

19 See "The Politics of Time in Edmund Spenser's English Calendar."

20 Hackett (111) and Hadfield (50) remark on the mixture of images of fertility and virginity that they read as an attempt to dissuade Elizabeth from her marriage.

21 Wall, however, remarks on the division between Colin's erotic failure and Spenser's poetic success in this eclogue: "[W]hile Colin's poetic song to 'Eliza' (Queen Elizabeth) in the 'April' eclogue successfully fuses political praise, religious ardor, and poetic vision, he is finally unable to transform his erotic passions into a moral and nationally useful vocation. Incapable of creating a durable literary monument out of the trials of human experience, Colin throws into relief the greater achievements of the mysterious *Calender* writer, who does offer a model for integrating poetry into a Protestant and nationalist project" ("Authorship and the Material Conditions of Writing" 79).

22 Sannazaro's type is italic for the body of his poems; his annotations are in roman type, indicating a vernacular sensibility for the poems and a more scholastic, intellectual tradition in the notes.

23 Shaw and Bain sum up the many competing associations of blackletter type in an international context: "From the outset, the opposition between blackletter and roman has been colored by momentous polarities: medievalism vs. modernity, Protestantism vs. Catholicism, Lutheran Pietism vs. Italian Humanism, German Romanticisim vs. the French Enlightenment, the authority of the state vs. personal liberty and popular sovereignty, nationalism vs. cosmopolitanism, mysticism vs. rationality" (12). Blackletter was eventually associated with the German nationalism of Nazism, demonstrating that type can still carry loaded political meaning (13–14).

24 Nashe satirizes the euphuistic, Latinate style of Gabriel Harvey and his contemporaries: "[T]hey make such a miracle of musterd together in one

galimafrie or short Oration, most of the ridiculous senseles sentences, sinical launting phrases, and termagant inkhorne tearmes" (sig. G2r).

25 This annotator may have been Gabriel Harvey, Edmund Spenser, or someone else. My instinct is to read "E.K." as Spenser himself; however, my goal is not to submit one of the perpetual attempts to solve the unsolved mystery of E.K. but to analyse how these annotations may have been approached by early modern readers as visual markers.

26 Castiglione famously remarks that the ideal courtier is "to practice in all things a certain sprezzatura [nonchalance], so as to conceal all art and make whatever is done appear to be without effort and almost without any thought about it" (32).

27 The importance of the almanac genre itself in our understanding of early modern reading practices should not be ignored: as Alison Chapman underscores, "[A]strological almanacs enjoyed a remarkable rise in sales over the course of the sixteenth and seventeenth centuries and were arguably the most popular books of the early modern period" ("Marking Time" 1210). My recent search for almanacs that include tables or spaces for annotation on *Early English Books Online* (Web, 3 January 2015) indicates that many of these blanks were published anonymously, with the name of the printer alone marking authorship. As Adam Max Cohen observes, print editions of Spenser's *Calender*, too, were left anonymous, a choice that Cohen believes could indicate any number of factors, including the aristocratic tradition of avoiding print publicity, this text's political controversies, or a generalized antipathy to print, allegorized by the figure of Error in the Faerie Queene, whose "vomit full of books and papers was" (I.i.20) (Cohen 75). In the *Calender*, E.K.'s glosses may satirize popular print and its readers, although the epilogue seems to uphold print's potential for literary immortality.

28 Rhetorical commonplaces were a type of verbal and textual *loci* (place), literally "common places," or phrases and devices that could be memorized and communicated depending on the situation at hand.

29 See Anderson 87, and Fowler 3–5 and 99–100.

30 This 1569 English translation of Cicero's *Dream of Scipio* precedes Spenser's *Shepheardes Calender* by ten years. In this translation, Africanus continues: "For comonnly men do recken a yere only by the course and race of the sunne, that is to wit, of one Planet. But when all the signes & starres of firmamente are come againe to the same poinct, from whence they once set out, & begin again to renewe their former discription of the whole Heavuen, after long space & tract of time: then may that bee trulye named the *Turning yere*, wherein how many messages are contayned, I dare scarcely tell" (sig. Fiiir).

31 Smyth, in "Almanacs, Annotators, and Life-Writing in Early Modern England," cites the popular 1672 compilation *Poor Robin*, as well as early sixteenth-century mock almanacs by Thomas Middleton and William Rowley, as examples of this form (206n32). See also Meredith Molly Hand's discussion of Middleton's mock almanacs in "'More Lies Than True Tales': Scepticism in Middleton's Mock-Almanacs," *The Oxford Handbook of Thomas Middleton*, ed. Gary Taylor and Trish Thomas Henley (Oxford: Oxford UP, 2012).

32 As a non-aristocratic member of the Elizabethan court, Spenser perhaps here turns the satire on himself. As long contended by scholars such as S.K. Heninger, Louise Schleiner, Celeste Turner Wright, Agnes D. Kuersteiner, and more recently, James Kearney, D. Allen Caroll, and Penny McCarthy, the mysterious annotator E.K. may have been Gabriel Harvey, Edmund Spenser, Edmund Kent, or someone else. My instinct is to read "E.K." as Spenser himself; however, my goal is not to submit one of the perennial attempts to solve the unsolved mystery of E.K.

33 Another possibility for the nature of the annotations might be the potential collaboration of Gabriel Harvey, who could not "abide" "a bit of blank page" and in whose library "annotations abounded" (Kalas, *Frame, Glass, Verse* 68).

34 See also Thomas Thomas, *Dictionarium Linguae Latinae et Anglicanae* (1587) "Percommŏdus, a, um. * Verie meet, or seemly: very good, easie, and handsome" (LEME).

35 See *OED*, sense 1c, "The apparent path of a planet or star in the sky. Also: a point or position of the sun on the ecliptic"; sense 4, "*Obs.* A stone or other monument set up as a memorial"; sense 12, "*Obs.* a. A sign, badge, brand, etc., assumed by or imposed on a person. In *pl.*: †insignia (*obs.*)"; senses 13a and 13b; sense 14a, "A device, stamp, brand, label, inscription, etc., on an article, animal, etc., identifying it or its holder, or indicating ownership, origin, quality, etc.; †the stamp or impress of a coin (*obs.*)"; sense 19a, "A visible trace or impression on a surface (esp. skin), produced by nature, an accident, etc., as a stain, blemish, scar, fleck, stroke, dot"; sense 37, "Attention or notice; remark; esp. in worthy of mark. Now chiefly *arch*" and *MED*, "marken" v1 3a and 6.

36 See *OED*, "mark," sense†10, "A vestige, a trace. *Obs*" and *MED*, "marke" 7(a) "The trace left by the current of a river; an imprint made by teeth; *pl.* the tracks of an animal; (b) a depression in a horse's incisor as an indicator of the animal's age; (c) a scar; *med.* a pathological scar resulting from ulcers, pustules, etc.; *coll.* marks of the wounds in Christ's hands at Crucifixion; *fig.* the stain left by Original Sin; (d) a reminder; the result or consequence of a person's action."

3 Devising the Page

1 Parker Duchemin, in "Drayton's 'Poly-olbion' and the Alexandrine Couplet," *Studies in Philology* 77.2 (1980), notes that "Drayton had spent thirty-three years (at a conservative estimate) in his preoccupation with *Poly-olbion*, intermittently writing, brooding, struggling for patrons, and writing again" (146). Despite these efforts, the book was a commercial failure (145).
2 See Kerrigan's *Archipelagic English*, Walsham's *Reformation of the Landscape*, and Vine's *In Defiance of Time*.
3 See Dasgupta, "Drayton's 'Silent Spring'"; McCrae, "Tree-felling in Early Modern England"; and Trevisan's "'The Murmuring Woods Even Shuddred as With Feare.'"
4 McLuhan argues that the printed map "was key to the new vision of peripheries of power and wealth … the map brings forward at once a principle theme of King Lear, namely the isolation of the visual sense as a kind of blindness" (14).
5 This conveyance via images has close ties to the poetic, rhetorical figure of metaphor, whose etymology derives from the "ancient Greek μεταφορά < μετα- meta- prefix + φορά carrying (< the *o* -grade of the stem of φέρειν to bear, carry: see bear v.[1]), after μεταφέρειν to transfer" (*OED*, "metaphor"), and, in Puttenham's *Art of English Poesie*, was defined as "the figure of *transport*" (sig. Xr).
6 We could even assume that Michael Drayton had some encounter with the parallels between invention and imagination during his early modern education: "looking from the early sixteenth century schoolbooks, which continued to be used throughout the century, to the poetics and poems of the early 1580s and 90s, one is immediately struck that image and imagination become important and frequently used words" (Mack, *Elizabethan Rhetoric* 69).
7 Plett specifically draws this connection from Erasmus's *Copia* (1512), a highly influential rhetorical text of the Renaissance. See his *Enargeia in Classical Antiquity and the Early Modern Age* 24–8.
8 William Camden's earlier *Britannia* (first edition 1586) has been firmly established as a project of national unity and defined the genre of chorography, a genre that studied the material features of the landscape alongside antiquarian histories and engraved maps. I argue that *Poly-olbion*'s own portrayal of the British landscape is far more eclectic in form and content.
9 Rogationtide "beating of the bounds" also perhaps served to link ecological boundaries with a memory of violence in early modern English culture: Walsham recounts that these yearly perambulations included

"playfully whipping young boys or ducking them in streams and rivers to impress the limits of the parish upon their memory" (259), as the boundaries of their regions were (literally) beaten into their heads.

10 Trevisan counters Dasgupta and McCrae's concern with ecological history as she argues that Drayton uses deforestation to present a narrative of historical decline (263). She claims that Drayton is just as, or even more, concerned with the mutability of time as with the destruction of ecological space. However, as Walsham and Sanford establish, the material spaces of maps were also mnemonic spaces; temporal or historical uncertainties are mapped onto the visual landscapes of *Poly-olbion*'s maps.

11 As McCrae argues, the need for a greater preservation of trees in seventeenth-century discourse was primarily driven by concerns over naval capacity: oaks were a primary source for shipbuilding (414).

12 For a more lengthy account of James's view of sea rights, and Selden's possible reproduction of this state document's map, see Fulton, *The Sovereignty of the Sea.*

13 As Curran remarks of Drayton's text, oral culture "instead of being a liability is actually an aid to textual continuity. Books, Dee tells us, are quite vulnerable to the ravages of time" (503). Curran argues that Drayton associates himself with the vatic/prophetic tradition of the Celtic bards. This tradition allows Drayton to link a particularly oral, mythological memory to the prophesy and projection of a British state: Albion thus has a "once and future" status in Drayton's poetry.

14 Smyth notes in "'Reade in one age and understood i'th'next,'" that "print ballads frequently included familiar material: older woodcuts were often reused, presumably to keep down production costs, resulting, sometimes, in wildly incongruous couplings of word and image" (69). P.J. Voss also remarks on the common practice of recycling woodcuts both within and without print texts, citing the *Nuremberg Chronicle*'s "600 blocks" "printed in over 1800 instances" and William Copland's *The hystory of the two brethren Valentyne and Orson*, which reprinted around ten woodcuts 100 times, "used previously by Copland in Virgilius, again demonstrating woodcut recycling and repetition" (739 n.26). See "Books for Sale."

15 It was a common (though discredited) part of British mythology to place the first settlement of Britain with Brutus, a Trojan descendent of Aeneas.

16 See also John Palsgrave, *Lesclarcissement de la Langue Francoyse* (1530) "monster: a wonder" (LEME), and Thomas Thomas, *Dictionarium Linguae Latinae et Anglicanae* (1587): "Ostentum, ti, n.g. Euery thing that commeth against nature, or otherwise then nature giveth: a monster, a wonder: a strange thing or sight hapning seldome, and betokening some thing to come" (LEME).

17 Plato is far from the only classical philosopher to discuss to the concept of transanimation. His predecessor, Pythagoras, is believed to be a main influence on Plato in this issue. John Selden glosses this section with a reference to Plato's texts, *Phaedo* and *Phaedrus*, as well as Pythagoras's belief in transanimation: "*Lipsius* doubts whether *Pythagoras* receiued it from the *Druids*, or they from him, because in his trauels he conuerst as well with *Gaulish* as *Indian* Philosophers" (sig. Cv). Shakespeare's *Twelfth Night* also makes mention of the Pythagorean idea of transanimation. The Clown asks, "What is the opinion of Pythagoras concerning wild-fowl?" to which Malvolio answers, "That the soul of our grandam might happily inhabit a bird" (4.2.50–2). For a brief summary of Plato's references to transanimation and his potential Pythagorean influence, see Long's "Plato's Doctrine of Metempsychosis and Its Source" 154–5.

18 Yates argues that Bruno's *De Gli Eroici Furori* significantly influenced the symbols and conceits of English Petrarchan poetry after its publication. Further, she traces the winged heart symbol in Herman Hugo's Jesuit emblem book *Pia Desideria* (1624) that "shows the soul being released from a cage of sense by divine love" (108). This winged heart forms the title page of this book, demonstrating a continuity of this visual symbol from the late sixteenth to early seventeenth centuries.

19 In his "Blood in the Gutters" chapter of *Understanding Comics*, McCloud unpacks the use of "gutters," or the empty spaces between and below images in comics, to assert the reader's agency in creating meaning between panels. Although more material differences than similarities exist between contemporary comics and early modern illustrated books, this concept may be applied to Henry's engraving, which specifically plays with the white space and borders of the page to compel the reader's attention to the pike's movement within, and beyond, the page.

4 Image and Illusion in Francis Quarles's Emblems and Pamphlets

1 "Between 1639 and 1696 there were nine editions; the same number appeared between 1701 and 1777; and there were at least three times as many between 1800 and 1900" (Horden 32). Karl Josef Höltgen also notes that "Quarles's book is quite unique among English emblem books, religious or secular. Most of them did not have more than one edition. The only other work reprinted frequently is the *School of the Heart* (1647) by Christopher Harvey, erroneously attributed to Quarles and often published together with his *Emblemes*" (*Aspects of the Emblem* 32).

2 Stephen Orgel notes that in the early history of print illustrations, "woodblock books, such as the *Biblia Pauperum*, employed pictures to epitomize, recall and even control the interpretation of scriptural histories" (60). For a more detailed look at *The Mirror of Human Salvation*'s typology and theology, see Vrudny's *Friars, Scribes, and Corpses*. Vrudny extends Carruthers's scholarship on memory to the *Speculum Humanae*, as it channels readers' mnemonic, mimetic, and rhetorical responses through its text and images: "the *Speculum* serves well the mnemonic functions of picturing, experiencing, and internalizing the salvation won by Christ, but wrought by Mary" (viii).

3 "The tetragrammaton was ... a device for replacing the human representation of the first person of the trinity by a symbolic lettered presence, the four Hebrew letters or consonants of the God of Israel," in Protestant print texts (Aston 24).

4 See also Christopher Hill 190–1.

5 *MED* def. d., *OED*, senses A1, first documented use 1325, B1, first use 1581, and B2, first use 1584, Elisha Coles, *An English Dictionary* (1676) "Telescope, g. a large prospective glass" (LEME).

6 Englishman Thomas Harriot's, Galileo's, and Johannes and David Fabricius's discovery and exploration of sunspots in the early seventeenth century predate Quarles's publication of the *Emblemes*, although some of this scientific work was unpublished in England. A 1623 print version of John Webster's *Duchess of Malfi* contains a reference to Galileo's glass: "We need to goe borrow that fantasique glass / invented by Galileo the Florentine, / To view in an other spacious world i'th' Moone, / And looke to finde a constant woman there" (sig. E2v, Cardinal). This passage suggests an association between telescopes, optics, and Galileo's discoveries prior to Quarles's emblems.

7 *OED*, def. 1 and 2a, Thomas Blount, *Glossographia or a Dictionary* (1656) "Prism (Gr. πρίσμα) the powder or dust of those things that are cut with a Saw; Also a Geometrical figure so called" (LEME).

8 Stuart Clark cites Giambattista Della Porta's *Magiae Naturalis* (edition 1589) with its chapter "On Strange Glasses," as an influential text on optical and glass technologies in early modern culture (98). This work was translated to English in 1659.

9 See Samuel Clarke, *Medulla Theologiae*, and Thomas Wright, *The Passions of the Minde*, cited in Leah Knight, *Reading Green in Early Modern England* 32.

10 See *OED*, senses 1–3, John Baret, *An Alveary or Triple Dictionary, in English, Latin, and French* (1574) "to dishonour: to dishonest: to distaine ones ho nestie: to defile: to defame" (LEME), Timothy Bright, *Charactery: An Art*

of Short, Swift, and Secret Writing by Character (1588) "Distaine: Colour, or filth" (LEME), and Randle Cotgrave, *A Dictionary of the French and English Tongues* (1611) "Descoulorer. To discoulour, or distaine; to make pale, wanne, lew; to take away the hue of" (LEME).

11 My keyword search for "Anaxagoras" on the database *Early English Books Online* resulted in 108 "hits" in 66 records between the years 1620 and 1640 alone, although a few of these referenced the mythological king of Argos. References to Anaxagoras were not quite as plentiful as mid-seventeenth-century citations of Democritus, who likewise discussed visual phenomenology (in addition to rhetoric): my search produced 441 references to him in 138 records between 1620 and 1640.

12 Heywood mentions Anaxagoras in several texts, including his *Gynaikeion* (1624), *The hierarchie of the blessed angells* (1635), and *Pleasant dialogues and dramma's* (1637). Peacham, who created his own emblematic texts, references him in his miscellany, *The valley of varietie* (1638) (sig. G1v) and his polemical pamphlet, *The duty of all true subiects* (1639) (sig. D3r).

13 Including Burton's *Anatomy of Melancholy* (1621) in his "Digression of Air" (sig. X3v), Ingpen's *The secrets of numbers* (1624), and Ingpen's *A discourse concerning a new world* (1640).

14 Such as Du Moulin's *Coales from the altar* (1623) (sig. ¶3v), du Perron's *The reply of the most illustrious Cardinall of Perron* (1630) (sig. Ll2–Ll3), Fotherby, the Bishop of Salisbury's *Atheomastix clearing foure truthes* (1622) (see his Prologue, Book 1 chapter 5, and Book 2, chapters 1 and 4), and Granger's aptly named *Looking Glass for Christians* (1620) (sig. B4v).

15 See Horden's *Francis Quarles* for Quarles's family connections to Puritan leaders and education at the reform-minded Christ's college at Cambridge (5). His later article, "The Publication of the Early Editions," tracks Quarles's economic necessity to obtain royalties from the publication of his emblem books, as evident in his (and later, his widow's) numerous court suits against his printers.

16 The full list of pamphlets and texts in this book are as follows: *The Sheppeard's Oracle* (Quarles), *Coopers Hill: A Poem, Cupid and Psiche: A Spirit Poem, Argulus and Parthonia* (Quarles), *Poetical Varrieties* (Tho: Jordan), *Lingua or the Combats of th Toung: A Comedy, Sririly and Napes or the Fatall Union: a Comedy, A Ring and Not Ring: A Comedy by Beaumont & Fletcher, The Antiquary: A Comedy*, and *The Royall Slave: A Tragi-Comedy*. Shelfmark is Wood 330 (1).

17 For further information and resources on the seventeenth-century Royalist miscellany, see Smyth, *"Profit and Delight."*

18 As Catherine Belsey argues, Zeuxis's curtain, a trompe l'oeil or aesthetic technique that gives the optical illusion of realism, is a figure of desire as

it represents absence (257). See "Love as Trompe-l'oeil:." Her discussion of trompe l'oeil draws from Lacan's essay, "Of the Gaze," which posits that we enjoy this playful illusion because we are attracted to what is hidden and absent: see *The Four Fundamental Concepts of Psychoanalysis* 112.

19 The final pages of Adis's *Spie Sent Out of the Tower-Chamber*, however, are far more prosaic: Adis advertises his cleaning services, "commodious for people of all ranks and qualities … in these hard times" (sig. Ciiir). For more information on Adis's life and work, see Durso's *No Armor for the Back* 143–9.

20 Although it does not appear in this particular book, several publications of the *Shepheards Oracle*, including the 1646 edition held at Harvard's library, include an elaborate engraving by William Marshall that depicts reformers hacking away at the "tree of religion," with Charles I coming to the rescue, sword in hand.

21 These selections are by no means the only examples of the phrase "Up Go We" in mid- to late-seventeenth-century English broadside ballads. My search of the University of California Santa Barbara's broadside ballad archive uncovered forty-three ballads with the tune and phrase, including both political appropriations, such as "A Health to the Royal Family: A Tory's Delight" (1683), "A New Ballad from Whigg-Land" (1682), and "The Jesuits Exaltation" (1689) particularly surrounding the 1688 Glorious Revolution and deposing of James II. The tune also had its non-political uses, especially in comic marriage, love, and lust broadside ballads such as "The Good Fellows Consideration or the Bad Husbands Amendment" (1672–96?), "The Wanton Maidens Choice" (1671–1702?), and "The Crafty Maids Invention … How to Chuse Good Husbands" (1689). The political inversion of the Royalist and Whig ballads appears to mirror the gender inversions of the marriage and lust ballads.

5 Dead Lambs, False Miracles, and "Taintured Nests"

1 The combined work of John Colet and William Lily was authorized as a standard grammar text under King Edward in 1548 as *A Shorte Introduction of Grammar* and *Brevissima Institutio* (Cummings 207). This English grammar of 1548 was a symbol of the "vernacular authority" of the state as it sought to unify linguistic diversity (211).

2 In "Numeracy in Early Modern England," Keith describes the early modern era as marking a decisive shift in the practice of mathematics in everyday life: "For those concerned with the history of numbers and numerical skills, the period 1500–1700 in England is one of dramatic

transformation. It saw the replacement for most purposes of roman numerals by Arabic ones and the consequent supersession of the counting board or abacus by arithmetical calculation on paper. It witnessed the proliferation of textbooks on commercial arithmetic and double-entry bookkeeping; the introduction of decimals, logarithms and algebra; and the adoption of most of the arithmetical symbols with which we are now familiar" (103).

3 See *OED* sense 6. The *OED* sense 4a (the cipher as hieroglyph) and 4b (as "astrological sign or figure"), so that the term again connects numeracy, eschatology, and visuality. Its first example for sense 4b comes from Spenser's *Faerie Queen*, Book 3 Canto 2: "That bodie, wheresoever that it light, / May learned be by cyphers, or by Magicke might" (sig. Dd4r). This passage marks a conversation between a lovesick Britomart, who glimpses an image of the beautiful knight Artegall in a magic mirror devised by Merlin, and her nurse, Glauce. Glauce distinguishes the myth of Narcissus, or the act of falling in love with a mirror image, from a physical body that casts its "shadow" in Britomart's magic mirror. Cyphers, or visual signs, offer partial clues to distinguishing true from false sight in this scene. Again, numbers and even prosaic exchange intersect with the problematics of vision in early modern culture.

4 See LEME, Thomas Thomas, *Dictionarium Linguae Latinae et Anglicanae* (1587), "Nŏta, tæ, f.g. A note, a marke, a signe, a token, a spotte: a defamation, infamie, rebuke, a slaunderous name or report: a reprehension or correction of any writing: a cipher, note, or abbreuiation of that is read or written," and John Rider, *Bibliotheca Scholastica* (1589), "To Cypher, or vse cyphers, or abbreviations, in writing. 2 Scribire aliquid notis. A cypher, or abbreviation of that which is read, or written. 2 Nota, f. A cipher, vsed in numbring."

5 For a more in-depth look at the practice of commonplacing, especially in a print context, see Moss's *Printed Commonplace Books and the Structuring of Renaissance Thought*, and "Locating Knowledge," in *Cognition and the Book*, ed. Karl A.E. Enenkel and Wolfgang Neuber (Leiden and Boston: Brill, 2005) 35–50.

6 See *OED*, and Thomas Elyot, *The Dictionary of Sir Thomas Elyot* (1538): "Character, a token, a note made with a pen, a fygure, a style or fourme of speakynge" (LEME); Richard Huloet, *Abecedarium Anglico Latinum* (1552) "Token or note made wyth a penne. Character. Ris" (LEME).

7 See also *MED*, def. 2b "rasen": "to tear out (sth.), pluck out; root out (trees, etc.)," and Thomas Elyot, *The Dictionary of Sir Thomas Elyot* (1538) "Cancello, aui, are, to rase or put out, to cut or teare any thyng that is written" (LEME).

8 *OED, obs* sense 1.

9 Txapartegi dissents from this phenomenological and subjective reading of Plato's colour theories, offering instead a naturalistic model, in "Plato's Color Naturalism."

10 *OED*, "seal," sense 1a and 1b.

11 *OED*, "spectacle," *obs*. Sense 5a.

12 Crombie cites French surgeon Guy de Chauliac's La Grande Chirurgie (1363) as the earliest known medical work to mention eyeglasses or spectacles (204n53). Earlier, medieval English philosopher-scientists Roger Bacon and Robert Grosseteste, whose work dealt with philosophies of sight at length, "discussed the magnification and diminution of images by lenses," drawing from the work of Arabic scientist Alhazen (211).

13 While the *Microkosmographia* postdates *2 Henry VI*, its status as a compilation of existing medical knowledge may indicate a similar understanding of the eye and retina in Shakespeare's text; further, the printer William Jaggard published both Crooke's *Microkosmographia* and Shakespeare's *Comedies, Histories, and Tragedies* (1623), and may have even been treated by Crooke for his blindness (Willoughby 103).

14 *OED*, "alteration," sense 2b.

15 See *OED* sense 1b.

16 This scene closely follows Hall's historiographical account in his 1548 *Union of the two noble and illustre famelies of Lancastre and Yorke*: "And this cruell tyraunt not content with the murder of the lorde Say, wente to Myle ende, and there apprehended syr Iames Cromer, then shreve of Kent, and sonne in law to the sayd lord Say, & hym without confession or excuse heard, caused there likewyse to be hedded, and his head to be fixed on a poole, and with these two heddes, this blody butcher entered into the citie agayn, and in despyte caused them in euery strete, kysse to gether, to the great detestacion of all the beholders" (Fol. Clix).

Conclusion: Mediated Vision

1 Critical spatial theory draws from Henri Lefebvre and Michel de Certeau's theories of alternative narratives and constructions of material, visual spaces in everyday life. Barnett, while sympathetic to the goals of critical spatial theory, expresses scepticism regarding the unity of these alternative narratives: "all representations, even those of everyday spatial practices, are partial and those prone to multiple fissures and interruptions that serve to frustrate the ability of language to bring the everyday into presence as a concept" ("Psychogeographies of Writing").

2 Turning his pedagogical focus to the construction and design of visual compositions rather than their analysis, Marback theorizes design itself as a "wicked problem" in its response to "ambiguous" rhetorical situations that pose tensions between multiple audiences and infinite productive possibilities (399). His claim is influenced by Diana George, who popularized a movement away from critique of images and towards their design in the classroom as a way to understand "that images are not a reflection of a fixed reality, that, instead, our ways of understanding the world around us are somehow commingled with how we represent the world visually" (2multimed3). In a sense, design is a "wicked problem" because the process of visual perception has been a wicked problem since Plato's dialogues.

Bibliography

Aasand, Hardin L. "'Her Burning Face, Declines Apace': Ben Jonson and the Specter of Elizabeth." *Resurrecting Elizabeth I in Seventeenth-Century England.* Ed. Elizabeth Hageman and Katherine Conway. Madison, NJ: Fairleigh Dickinson UP, 2007. 95–110.

Acheson, Katherine. *Visual Rhetoric and Early Modern English Literature.* Burlington: Ashgate, 2013.

Adams, Frank. *Writing tables vvith a kalender for xxiiii. yeeres, with sundry necessarye rules.* 2nd ed. London, 1594. Printed by [R. Watkins and J. Roberts for] Frauncis Adams, stationer or bookbinder, dwelling in Distaffe lane, neare olde fishstreete, at the signe of the Aqua vite still, and are there to be sold. *Early English Books Online.* 2 January 2015.

Adis, Henry. *A Spie, Sent Out of the Tower-Chamber in the Fleet. Diogenes-like Argus is Sent to Spie, the Sequell Tells You Both By Whom and Why ...* London: 1648. Early *English Books Online.* Web. 15 March 2014.

Anderson, Benedict. *Imagined Communities: Reflections on the Origin and Spread of Capitalism.* New York and London: Verso, 2006.

Anderson, Judith. *Reading the Allegorical Intertext: Chaucer, Spenser, Shakespeare, Milton.* New York: Fordham UP, 2008.

Anon. *A blancke & perpetuall almanack, seruing as a memoriall, not only for al marchautes and occupiers, to note what debtes they haue to paie or receiue, in any moneth or daie of the yeare: but also for any other that will make & keepe notes ...* London, 1566. *Early English Books Online.* Web. 1 May 2012.

Anon. *The Passage of our most drad Soueraigne Lady Quene Elyzabeth through the citie of London to westminster the daye before her coronacion Anno 1558.* 2nd Ed. London (Printer Richard Tottel), 1558. *Early English Books Online.* Web. 27 November 2013.

Archer, Ian. "John Stow's *Survey of London*: The Nostalgia of John Stow." *The Theatrical City: Culture, Theatre, and Politics in London, 1576–1649*. Ed. David L. Smith, Richard Strier, and David Bevington. Cambridge: Cambridge UP, 1995. 17–34.

Aristotle, *De Anima*. Trans. W.W. Hamlyn. Oxford: Clarendon Press, 1993.

– *De Sensu*, Ed. G.R.T. Ross. New York: Arno Press, 1973.

– *Generation of Animals*. Cambridge: Harvard UP, 1958.

Armstrong, E. *A Ciceronian Sunburn: A Tudor Dialogue on Humanistic Rhetoric and Civic Poetics*. Columbia: University of South Carolina P, 2006.

Aston, Margaret. "Conversion: Properties of the Page in Reformation England." *Printed Images in Early Modern England*. Ed. Michael Hunter. Farnham: Ashgate, 2010.

The Atomists: Leucippus and Democritus (Fragments). Trans. and Commentary C.C.W. Taylor. Toronto: U of Toronto P, 1999.

Bacon, Francis. *Essayes Religious Meditations. Places of Perswasion and Disswasion. Seene and Allowed*. 2nd ed. London (Printed by John Windet): 1597. *Early English Books Online*. 13 October 2014.

– *New Atlantis: a work unfinished*. London: 1658. *Early English Books Online*. 23 July 2013.

– *The Oxford Francis Bacon: Novum Organum and Associated Texts*. Ed. Graham Rees and Maria Wakely. Oxford: Clarendon P, 2004.

– *The Philosophical Works of Francis Bacon*. Ed. Robert Leslie Ellis, James Spedding, and J.M. Robertson. Freeport, NY: Books for Libraries P, 1970.

Bacon, Roger. *Opus Maius. A Source Book in Medieval Science*. Trans. Robert B. Burke. Ed. Edward Grant. Cambridge, MA: Harvard UP, 1974.

Badger, Meredith. "Visual Blogs." *Into the Blogosphere: Rhetoric, Community, and Culture of Weblogs* (2004). Web. 8 September 2013.

Barber, Peter. "Mapmaking in England, ca. 1470–1650." *The History of Cartography, Volume III: Cartography in the European Renaissance*. Ed. David Woodward. Chicago: U of Chicago P, 2007. 1589–1669.

Barlow, Richard G. "Infinite Worlds: Robert Burton's Cosmic Voyage." *Journal of the History of Ideas* 34.2 (1973): 291–302.

Barnard, Ian. "The Ruse of Clarity." *College Composition and Communication* 61.3 (2010): 434–51.

Barnett, Scot. "Psychogeographies of Writing: Ma(r)king Space at the Limits of Representation." *Kairos: A Journal of Rhetoric, Technology, and Pedagogy* 16.3 (2012). n/p.

Baron, Naomi S. "Redefining Reading." *PMLA* 128.1 (2013): 193–200.

Bath, Michael, and Betty Willsher. "Emblems from Quarles on Scottish Gravestones." *Glasgow Emblem Studies: Emblems and Art History* 1 (1996): 169–201.

Belsey, Catherine. "Love as Trompe-l'oeil: Taxonomies of Desire in *Venus and Adonis*." *Shakespeare Quarterly* 46.3 (1995): 257–76.

Bennett, Jane. *Vibrant Matter: A Political Ecology of Things*. Duke: Duke UP, 2009.

Bensimon, Marc. "The Significance of Eye Imagery in the Renaissance from Bosch to Montaigne." *Yale French Studies* 47 (1972): 266–90.

Berlin, James. *Rhetoric and Reality: Writing Instruction in American Colleges, 1900–1985*. Carbondale: Southern Illinois UP, 1987.

Best, Stephen, and Sharon Marcus. "Surface Reading: An Introduction." *Representations* 108.1 (2009): 1–21.

Blake, N.F. *William Caxton and English Literary Culture*. London: Hambledon Press, 1991.

Bland, Mark. "The Appearance of the Text in Early Modern England." *Text* 11 (1998): 91–154.

Bolter, Jay. *Writing Space: Computers, Hypertext, and the Remediation of Print*. Mahwah, NJ: Lawrence Erlbaum Associates, 2001.

Brinsley, John. *A Consolation for Our Grammar Schooles* … London (Printed by Richard Field for Thomas Man), 1622. *Early English Books Online*. Web. 15 July 2018.

Brinsley, John. *Ludus Literarius: or, the Grammar Schoole Shewing How to Proceede from the First Entrance Into Learning, to the Highest Perfection Required in the Grammar Schooles, with Ease, Certainty and Delight to Both Masters and Schollars* … 2nd ed. London (Printed by Humphrey Lownes), 1612. *Early English Books Online*. Web. 21 May 2014.

Brown, Bill. "Introduction: Textual Materialism." *PMLA* 125.1 (2010): 24–8.

– "Thing Theory." *Critical Inquiry* 28.1 (2001): 1–22.

Brown, Nicole R. "Metaphors of Mobility: Emerging Spaces for Rhetorical Reflection and Communication." *Going Wireless: A Critical Exploration of Wireless and Mobile Technologies for Composition Teachers and Researchers*. Ed. Amy C. Kimme Hea. Cresskill, NJ: Hampton Press 2009. 239–54.

Burton, Robert. *The Anatomy of Melancholy*. 2nd ed. Oxford: 1621. *Early English Books Online*. Web. 15 December 2013.

Bynum, T.W. "A New Look at Aristotle's Theory of Perception." *History of Philosophy Quarterly* 4.2. (1987): 163–78.

Cahill, Patricia. "Take Five: Renaissance Literature and the Study of the Senses." *Literature Compass* 6.5 (2009): 1014–30.

Calhoun, Joshua. "The World Made Flax: Cheap Bibles, Textual Corruption, and the Politics of Paper." *PMLA* 126.2 (2011): 327–44.

Carlton, Charles. *This Seat of Mars: War and the British Isles, 1485–1746*. New Haven and London: Yale UP, 2011.

Carr, Nicholas. *The Shallows: What the Internet Is Doing to our Brains*. New York: W.W. Norton and Company, 2011.

Carroll, D. Allen. "The Meaning of 'EK.'" *Spenser Studies* 20 (2005): 169–81.

Carruthers, Mary. *The Book of Memory: A Study of Memory in Medieval Culture*. Cambridge: Cambridge UP, 2008.

– "Mechanisms for the Transmission of Culture: The Role of 'Place' in the Arts of Memory." *Translatio or the Transmission of Culture in the Middle Ages and the Renaissance: Modes and Messages*. Ed. Laura H. Hollengreen. Turnhout, Belgium: Brepols, 2008.

Castiglione, Baldesar. *The Book of the Courtier*. Ed. Daniel Javitch. New York: Norton, 2002.

Castoriadis, Cornelius. *The Imaginary Institution of Society*. Trans. Kathleen Blamey. Cambridge: MIT Press, 1998.

Caxton, William. *The Myrrour and Dyscrypcyon of the Worlde with Many Mervaylles*. Westminster, 1481. *Early English Books Online*. Web. 21 May 2013.

– 1490. *Early English Books Online*. Web. 21 May 2013.

– 2nd ed. London (Printed by Laurence Andrewes), 1627. *Early English Books Online*. Web. 21 May 2013.

Chalk, Darryl. "Make Me Not Sighted Like the Basilisk: Vision and Contagion in *The Winter's Tale*." *Embodied Cognition and Shakespeare's Theatre: The Early Modern Body-Mind*. Ed. Laurie Johnson, John Sutton, and Evelyn Tribble. Abingdon, UK: Routledge, 2014. 111–32.

Chapman, Alison A. "Marking Time: Astrology, Almanacs, and English Protestantism." *Renaissance Quarterly* 60.4 (2007): 1257–90.

– "The Politics of Time in Edmund Spenser's English Calendar." *SEL* 42.1 (2002): 1–24.

Chartier, Roger. "Jack Cade, the Skin of a Dead Lamb, and the Hatred for Writing." *Shakespeare Studies* 34 (2006): 77–89.

– "Languages, Books, and Reading from the Printed Word to the Digital Text." *Critical Inquiry* 31.1 (2004): 133–52.

Chess, Simone. "Performing Blindness: Representing Disability in Early Modern Popular Performance and Print." *Recovering Disability in Early Modern England*. Ed. Allison P. Hobgood and David Houston Wood. Columbus: Ohio State UP, 2013. 105–22.

Christiansen, Nancy L. "Rhetoric as Character-Fashioning: The Implications of Delivery's 'Places' in the British Renaissance *Paideia*." *Rhetorica: A Journal of the History of Rhetoric* 15.3 (1997): 297–334.

Cicero, Marcus Tullius. *Marcus Tullius Ciceroes thre bokes of duties to Marcus his sonne, turned out of latine into english, by Nicholas Grimalde*. 2nd ed. London

(Printed by Richard Tottell), 1556. *Early English Books Online*. Web. 15 January 2014.

– *The booke of Marcus Tullius Cicero entituled Paradoxa Stoicorum Contayninge a precise discourse of diuers poinctes and conclusions of vertue and phylosophie according the traditions and opinions of those philosophers, whiche were called Stoikes. Wherunto is also annexed a philosophicall treatyse of the same authoure called Scipio hys dreame*. Trans. Anon. 2nd ed. London, 1569. *Early English Books Online*. Web. 27 November 2013.

Clark, Stuart. *Vanities of the Eye: Vision in Early Modern European Culture*. Oxford: Oxford UP, 2007.

Clarke, Desmond. *Descartes's Theory of Mind*. Oxford: Oxford UP, 2003.

Clarke, Edwin, and Kenneth Dewhurst. *An Illustrated History of Brain Function: Imaging the Brain from Antiquity to the Present*. San Francisco: Norman Publishing, 1996.

Clarke, Samuel. *Medulla Theologiae, or, The Marrow of Divinity Contained in Sundry Questions and Cases of Conscience, Both Speculative and Practical*. London, 1659.

Coley, David K. "'Withyn a Temple Ymad of Glas': Glazing, Glossing, and Patronage in Chaucer's *House of Fame*." *The Chaucer Review* 45.1 (2010): 59–84.

Cohen, Adam Max. *Technology and the Early Modern Self*. New York: Palgrave Macmillan, 2009.

Colie, Rosalie. *Paradoxica Epidemica*. Princeton: Princeton UP, 1966.

Collete, Carolyn P. *Species, Phantasms, and Images: Vision and Medieval Psychology in the Canterbury Tales*. Ann Arbor: U of Michigan P, 2001.

Collins, Jim. *Bring on the Books for Everybody: How Literary Culture Became Popular Culture*. Durham: Duke UP, 2010.

Comenius, Johann Amos. *The Gate of the Latin Tongue Unlocked*. 2nd ed. London, 1656. *Early English Books Online*. Web. 15 December 2013.

Copeland, Rita. "Lydgate, Hawes, and the Science of Rhetoric in the Late Middle Ages." *Modern Language Quarterly* (1992): 57–82.

Copland, Richard. *The shepardes kalender: Here beginneth the kalender of shepardes newly augmented and corrected*. 2nd ed. London, 1570. Imprinted at London: By Thomas Este for Iohn Wally. *Early English Books Online*. Web. 2 January 2015.

Corbett, Edward P.J. "The Theory and Practice of Imitation in Classical Rhetoric." *College Composition and Communication* 22.3 (1971): 243–50.

Corbett, Margery, and Ronald Lightbown. *The Comely Frontispiece: The Emblematic Title-Page in England, 1550–1660*. London: Routledge, 1979.

Cormack, Lesley B. *Charting an Empire: Geography at the English Universities 1580–1620*, Chicago: U of Chicago P, 1997.

"The Crafty Maids Invention." Printed by T.M. in White-Friers, 1689. *USCB Broadside Ballad Archive*. STC R174375. Web. 16 December 2013.

Craik, Katherine A. *Reading Sensations in Early Modern England*. Basingstoke, UK: Palgrave Macmillan, 2007.

– "'The Material Point of Poesy': Reading, Writing, and Sensation in Puttenham's *Arte of English Poesie*." *Environment and Embodiment in Early Modern England*. Ed. Mary Floyd Wilson and Garrett A. Sullivan. Basingstoke, UK: Palgrave Macmillan, 2007. 153–70.

Cressy, David. "Book Burning in Tudor and Stuart England." *The Sixteenth Century Journal* 36.2 (2005): 359–74.

Crombie, Alistair C. *Science, Optics, and Music in Medieval and Early Modern Thought*. London: Hambledon P, 1990.

Crooke, Helkiah. *Microkosmographia: a description of the body of man*. 2nd ed. London (Printed by William Jaggard), 1615. *Early English Books Online*. Web. 15 January 2014.

Cummings, Brian. *The Book of Common Prayer: The Texts of 1549, 1559, and 1642*. Oxford: Oxford UP, 2011.

Cummings, Brian. *The Literary Culture of the Reformation: Grammar and Grace*. Oxford: Oxford UP, 2002.

Curd, Patricia. *Anaxagoras of Clazomenae: Fragments and Testimonia*. Toronto: U of Toronto P, 2007.

Curran, John E. "The History Never Written: Bards, Druids, and the Problem of Antiquarianism in *Poly-Olbion*." *Renaissance Quarterly* 51.2 (1998): 498–525.

D'Addario, Christopher. "Echo Chambers and Paper Memorials: Mid and Late- Seventeenth-Century Book-bindings and the Practices of Early Modern Reading." *Textual Cultures: Texts, Contexts, Interpretation* 7.2 (2012): 73–97.

Dasgupta, Sukanya. "Drayton's 'Silent Spring': *Poly-olbion* and the Politics of Landscape." *The Cambridge Quarterly* 39.2 (2010): 152–71.

Davis, David. "Images on the Move: The Virgin, The Kalender of Shepherds, and the Transmission of Woodcuts in Tudor England." *Journal of the Early Book Society for the Study of Manuscripts and Printing History* 12 (2009): 99–132.

Dawson, Anthony B. *The Culture of Playgoing in England: A Collaborative Debate*. Cambridge: Cambridge UP, 2001.

De Certeau, Michel. *The Practice of Everyday Life*. Berkeley: U of California P, 1984.

De Grazia, Margreta. "Hamlet the Intellectual." *The Public Intellectual*. Ed. Helen Small. Oxford: Blackwell Publishing, 2002. 89–109.

Delagrange, Susan H. *Technologies of Wonder: Rhetorical Practice in a Digital World*. Logan: Utah State UP, 2011.

Derrida, Jaques. "Structure, Sign, and Play in the Discourse of the Human Sciences." *A Postmodern Reader*. Ed. Joseph P. Natoli and Linda Hutcheon. New York: SUNY P, 1993.

Dickson, Lisa. "The Prince of Rays: Spectacular Invisibility in Spenser's *The Faerie Queene*." *EMLS* 12.2: 31 paragraphs.

Dobranski, Stephen B. *Readers and Authorship in Early Modern England*. Cambridge: Cambridge UP, 2005.

Donavin, Georgiana. "Rhetorical Gower: Aristotelianism in the Confessio Amantis's Treatment of 'Rethorique.'" *John Gower: Manuscripts, Readers, Contexts*. Ed. Malte Urban. Turnhout, Belgium: Brepols 2009. 155–73.

Dowland, John. *Andreas Ornithoparcus his Micrologus, or Introduction: containing the art of singing Digested into foure bookes*. 2nd ed. London (Printed by William Jaggard), 1609. *Early English Books Online*. Web. 15 January 2014.

Downe, John. *A Treatise of the True Nature and Definition of Justifying Faith*. Oxford: 1635. *Early English Books Online*. Web. 15 December 2013.

Drayton, Michael. *Poly-olbion*. London: 1612. Print.

Drucker, Johanna. "Reading Interface." *PMLA* 128.1 (2013): 213–20.

Duffy, Eamon. "The Shock of Change: Continuity and Discontinuity in the Elizabethan Church of England." *Ecclesiastical Law Journal* 7.35 (2004): 429–46.

Du Moulin, Pierre. *Coales From the Altar; Or Foure Religious Treatises to Kindle Devotion in this Colde Age*. 2nd ed. London: 1623. *Early English Books Online*. Web. 15 December 2013.

Du Perron, Jacques Davy. *The reply of the most illustrious Cardinall of Perron, to the ansvveare of the most excellent King of Great Britaine the first tome. Translated into English*. 2nd ed. Paris, 1630. *Early English Books Online*. Web. 15 December 2013.

Dupré, Sven. "Visualization in Renaissance Optics: The Function of Geometrical Diagrams and Pictures in the Transmission of Practical Knowledge." *Transmitting Knowledge: Words, Images, and Instruments in Early Modern Europe*. Ed. Sachiko Kukusawa and Ian Maclean. Oxford: Oxford UP, 2006. 11–40.

Durso, Keith E. *No Armor for the Back: Baptist Prison Writings, 1600s–1700s*. Macon, GA: Mercer UP, 2007.

Eggert, Katherine. *Showing Like a Queen: Female Authority and Literary Experiment in Spenser, Shakespeare, and Milton*. Philadelphia: U of Pennsylvania P, 2000.

Elam, Keir. *The Semiotics of Theatre and Drama*. London and New York: Methuen & Co., 1980.

Engel, William E. *Chiastic Designs in English Literature: From Sidney to Shakespeare*. Farnham: Ashgate, 2009.

England and Wales. Sovereign (1603–1625: James I). *[A Note] of the Head-Lands of England*. London: 1605. STC 1320:06. *Early English Books Online*. Web. 18 July 2014.

Enders, Jody. "Delivering Delivery: Theatricality and the Emasculation of Eloquence." *Rhetorica: A Journal of the History of Rhetoric* 15.3 (1997): 253–78.

Everson, Stephen. *Aristotle on Perception*. Oxford: Clarendon Press, 1999.

Falco, Charles M. "Historical Questions." *The Hockney-Falco Thesis*. Art-Optics. Web. 10 July 2016. http://fp.optics.arizona.edu/SSD/art-optics/historical.html.

Ferrell, Lori Ann. "Page *Techne*: Interpreting Diagrams in Early Modern English 'How-to' Books." *Printed Images in Early Modern Britain*. Ed. Michael Hunter. Farnham, UK: Ashgate, 2010. 113–26.

Fish, Stanley. *Self-Consuming Artifacts: The Experience of Seventeenth-Century Literature*. Berkeley: U of California P, 1974.

– *Surprised by Sin*. London: St Martin's, 1967.

Fisher, Joshua B. "'He Is Turned a Ballad-Maker': Broadside Appropriations in Early Modern England." *EMLS* 9.2 (2003).

Fleming, Juliet. *Graffiti and the Writing Arts of Early Modern England*. Philadelphia: U of Pennsylvania P, 2001.

Foxe, John. *Actes and Monuments of Matters Most Speciall and Memorable, Happenying in the Church with an Universall History of the Same, Wherein is Set Forth At Large the Whole Race and Course of the Church ...* 2nd ed. London (Printed by John Daye), 1583. *Early English Books Online*. Web. 3 July 2016.

Fotherby, Martin. *Atheomastix clearing foure truthes, against atheists and infidels*. 2nd ed. London, 1622. *Early English Books Online*. Web. 15 December 2013.

Fowler, Alastair. *Spenser and the Numbers of Time*. New York: Barnes & Noble, Inc., 1964.

Fulton, Thomas Wemyss. *The Sovereignty of the Sea*. The Lawbook Exchange, 1911.

Galbraith, Steven K. "'English' Black-Letter Type and Spenser's *Shepheardes Calender*." *Spenser Studies* 23 (2008): 13–40.

Galloway, Andrew. "Reassessing Gower's Dream-Visions." *John Gower, Trilingual Poet: Language, Translation, and Tradition*. Ed. Elizabeth Dutton, John Hines, and R.F. Yeager. Woodbridge, England: Brewer, 2010. 288–303.

Ganson, Todd Stuart. "The Platonic Approach to Sense-Perception." *History of Philosophy Quarterly* 22.1 (2005): 1–15.

Gates, Jr, Henry Louis. *The Signifying Monkey: A Theory of African-American Literary Criticism*. Oxford: Oxford UP, 1988.

George, Diana. "From Analysis to Design: Visual Communication in the Teaching of Writing." *College Composition and Communication* 54.1 (2002): 11–40.

Gheyn, Jacob de. *The exercise of armes for caliures, muskettes, and pikes.* 2nd Ed.: Amsterdam and Hage, 1608. *Early English Books Online.* Web. 3 February 2014.

Gibbs, Robert. *Tomaso da Modena.* Cambridge: Cambridge UP, 1989.

Gilman, Ernest B. "Word and Image in Quarles' *Emblemes.*" *Critical Inquiry* 6.3 (1980): 385–410.

Goeglein, Tamara A. "Reading English Ramist Logic Books As Modern Emblem Books: The Case of Abraham Fraunce." *Spenser Studies* 20 (2005): 225–52.

Gordon, Andrew. "'If My Sign Could Speak': The Signboard and the Visual Culture of Early Modern London." *Early Theatre* 8.1 (2005): 35–51.

– *Writing Early Modern London: Memory, Text, and Community.* London: Palgrave Macmillan, 2013.

Granger, Thomas. *A Looking-Glass for Christians.* London, 1620. *Early English Books Online.* Web. 8 December 2014.

Grabes, Herbert. *The Mutable Glass: Mirror-imagery in Titles and Texts of the Middle Ages and the English Renaissance.* Cambridge: Cambridge UP, 1973.

Grogan, Jane. *Exemplary Spenser: Visual and Poetic Pedagogy in* The Faerie Queene. Burlington, VT: Ashgate, 2009.

Gulley, N. *Plato's Theory of Knowledge.* London: Methuen & Co., 1962.Gurney, Evan. "Spenser's 'May' Eclogue and Charitable Admonition," *Spenser Studies: A Renaissance Poetry Annual* (2012): 193–219.

Gurr, Andrew. *Playgoing in Shakespeare's London.* Cambridge: Cambridge UP, 2004.

– *The Shakespearean Stage 1574–1642.* Cambridge: Cambridge UP, 1992.

Gutjahr, Paul C. "The Letter(s) of the Law: Four Centuries of Typography in the King James Bible." *Illuminating Letters: Typography and Literary Interpretation.* Ed. Paul C. Gutjahr and Megan L. Benton. Amherst: U of Massachusetts P, 2001. 17–44.

Gutjahr, Paul C., and Megan L. Benton. "Reading the Invisible." *Illuminating Letters: Typography and Literary Interpretation.* Ed. Paul C. Gutjahr and Megan L. Benton. Amherst: U of Massachusetts P, 2001. 1–19.

Hackel, Heidi Brayman. *Reading Material in Early Modern England: Print, Gender, and Literacy.* Cambridge: Cambridge UP, 2005.

Hackett, Helen. *Virgin Mother, Maiden Queen: Elizabeth I and the Cult of the Virgin Mary.* New York: Palgrave Macmillan, 1996.

Hadfield, Andrew. *Edmund Spenser: A Life.* Oxford: Oxford UP, 2012.

– "Politics." *A Critical Companion to Spenser Studies.* New York: Palgrave Macmillan, 2006. 42–57.

Haight, Gordon S. "Francis Quarles in the Civil War." *Review of English Studies* 12.46 (1936): 147–64.

Hall, Edward. *The union of two noble and illustre families of Lancastre and Yorke …* 2nd ed. London, 1548. *Early English Books Online*. Web. 15 January 2014.

Hamilton, A.C. *The Spenser Encyclopedia*. Toronto: U of Toronto P, 1990.

Hampton-Reeves, Stuart. "Kent's Best Man: Radical Chorographic Consciousness and the Identity Politics of Local History in Shakespeare's *2 Henry VI*." *Journal for Early Modern Cultural Studies*. 14.1 (2014): 63–87.

Harman, Graham. *Guerrilla Metaphysics: Phenomenology and the Carpentry of Things*. Open Court: Chicago and La Salle, IL, 2005.

Harvey, Elizabeth. *Sensible Flesh: On Touch in Early Modern Culture*. Philadelphia: U of Pennsylvania P, 2003.

Hawes, Stephen. *The History of Graund Amoure and la Bel Pucell, Called the Pastime of Pleasure Conteynyng the Knowledge of the Seven Sciences, and the Course of Mans Lyfe in this World*. 2nd ed. London (Printed by Richard Tottel), 1555. *Early English Books Online*. Web. 21 May 2013.

Hawhee, Debra. "Looking into Aristotle's Eyes: Toward a Theory of Rhetorical Vision." *Advances in the History of Rhetoric* 14 (2011): 139–65.

Hawhee, Debra, and Cory Holding. "Case Studies in Material Rhetoric: Joseph Priestly and Gilbert Austin." *Rhetorica* 28.3 (2010): 261–89.

"A Health to the Royal Family: Or, the Tories Delight." Printed for J. Wright, J. Clark, W. Thackeray, and T. Passenger, 1683. *USCB Broadside Ballad Archive*. STC R188205. Web. 16 December 2013.

Heidegger, Martin. *What Is a Thing?* Chicago: Henry Regnery Company, 1967.

Helfer, Receba. "The Death of the 'New Poete': Virgilian Ruin and Ciceronian Recollection in Spenser's *The Shepheardes Calender*." *Renaissance Quarterly* 56.3 (2003): 723–56.

– *Spenser's Ruins and the Art of Recollection*. Toronto: U of Toronto P, 2012.

Heller-Roazen, Daniel. "Common Sense: Greek, Arabic, Latin." *Rethinking the Medieval Senses: Heritage/Fascinations/Frames*. Ed. Stephen G. Nichols, Andreas Kablitz, and Alison Calhoun, Baltimore: Johns Hopkins UP, 2008.

Heninger, S.K., Jr. "The Typographical Layout of Spenser's *Shepheardes Calender*." *Word and Visual Imagination: Studies in the Interaction of English Literature and the Visual Arts*. Ed. Karl Höltgen, Peter Daly, and Wolfgang Lottes. Erlangen: Universitätsbibliothek Erlangen-Nürnberg, 1988. 33–71.

Herbert, George. *The Temple: Sacred Poems and Private Ejaculations*. 2nd ed. Cambridge, 1633. Printed by Thomas Buck and Roger Daniel. *Early English Books Online*. Web. 29 March 2014.

Heywood, Thomas. *Gynaikeion: or, Nine bookes of various history*. 2nd ed. London, 1624. *Early English Books Online*. Web. 15 December 2013.

– *The hierarchie of the blessed angells Their names, orders and offices*. 2nd ed. London, 1635. *Early English Books Online*. Web. 15 December 2013.

– *Pleasant dialogues and dramma's, selected out of Lucian, Erasmus, Textor, Ovid, &c. With sundry emblems extracted from the most elegant Iacobus Catsius*. 2nd ed. London, 1637. *Early English Books Online*. Web. 15 December 2013.

Hill, Christopher. "Francis Quarles and Edward Benlowes." *The Collected Essays of Christopher Hill: Writing and Revolution in 17th Century England*. Amherst: U of Massachusetts P, 1985. 188–207.

Hill, Thomas. *An Almanack Published at Large, in Forme of a Booke of Memorie Necessary for all Such, as Haue Occasion Daylie to Note Sundry Affayres, Eyther for Receytes, Payments, or Such Lyke. Nevvly set forth, by T.H. Londoner*. London, 1571. *Early English Books Online*. Web. 1 May 2014.

Hillman, David. "Puttenham, Shaksepeare, and the Abuse of Rhetoric." *SEL* 36.1 (1995): 73–90.

Hinde, William. *A faithfull remonstrance of the holy life and happy death of John Bruen …* London, 1641. Printed by R.B. for Philemon Stephens and Christopher Meredith. *Early English Books Online*. Web. 31 March 2014.

Hobbs, Catherine L. "Learning from the Past: Verbal and Visual Literacy in Early Modern Rhetoric and Writing Pedagogy." *Language and Image in the Reading-Writing Classroom: Teaching Vision*. Mahwah, New Jersey: Lawrence Erlbaum Associates, 2002. 27–44.

Hobgood, Allison. *Passionate Playgoing in Early Modern England*. Cambridge: Cambridge UP, 2014.

Höltgen, Karl Josef. *Aspects of the Emblem: Studies in the English Emblem Tradition and the European Context*. Kassel: Edition Reichenberger, 1986.

– "Clever Dogs and Nimble Spaniels: On the Iconography of Logic, Invention, and Imagination." *Explorations in Renaissance Culture* 24 (1998): 1–36.

– "Francis Quarles's Emblemes and Hieroglyphikes: Some Historical and Critical Perspectives." *The Telling Image: Explorations in the Emblem*. Ed Ayers L. Bagley, Edward M. Griffin, and Austin J. McLean. New York: AMS Press, 1996. 1–28.

– "Literary Art and Scientific Method in Robert Burton's *Anatomy of Melancholy*." *Explorations in Renaissance Culture* 16 (1990): 1–36.

Höltgen, Karl Josef, and Horden, John, editors. Introduction. *Francis Quarles' Emblemes and Hieroglyphikes of the Life of Man*. Hildesheim: Georg Olms Verlag, 1993. 1–22.

Hopkins, Jasper. *Nicholas of Cusa: Metaphysical Speculations*. Minneapolis: Arthur J. Banning Press, 1998.

Horace. *The Odes, Satyrs, and Epistles of Horace Done into English*. 2nd ed. London, 1684. *Early English Books Online*. Web. 15 January 2014.

Horden, John. *Francis Quarles: A Bibliography of His Works to 1800*. Oxford: Oxford UP, 1953.

– "The Publication of the Early Editions of Francis Quarles's *Emblemes* (1635) and *Hieroglyphikes* (1638)." *The Library: The Transactions of the Bibliographical Society* 8.1 (2007): 25–32.

Hotson, Howard. *Commonplace Learning: Ramism and its German Ramifications, 1543–1630*. Oxford: Oxford UP, 2007.

Howell, A.C. "Res et Verba: Words and Things." *ELH* 13.2 (1946): 131–42.

Hugo, Herman. *Pia Desideria*. 1624.

Hunter, Dard. *Papermaking: The History and Technique of an Ancient Craft*. New York: Dover, 1943.

Hunter, Michael. *Printed Images in Early Modern Britain*. Farnham: Ashgate, 2010.

Hutcheon, Linda. *A Theory of Adaptation*. New York: Routledge, 2006.

Ingpen, William. *A discourse concerning a new world & another planet in 2 bookes*. 2nd ed. London, 1640. *Early English Books Online*. Web. 15 December 2013.

– *The secrets of numbers according to theologicall, arithmeticall, geometricall and harmonicall computation*. London, 1624. *Early English Books Online*. Web. 15 December 2013.

Ivic, Christopher. "Spenser and Interpellative Memory." *Ars Reminiscendi*. Ed. Donald Beecher and Grant Williams. Toronto: Centre for Reformation and Renaissance Studies, 2009. 289–312.

Iyengar, Sujata. *Shakespeare's Medical Language: A Dictionary*. London: Continuum, 2011.

Jacobson, Miriam. "The Elizabethan Cipher in Shakespeare's *Lucrece*." *Studies in Philology* 107.3 (2010): 336–59.

Jameson, Fredric. *The Political Unconscious: Narrative As a Socially Symbolic Act*. London: Routledge, 1981.

"The Jesuits Exaltation." Printed for J. Back, 1688. *USCB Broadside Ballad Archive*. STC R188321. Web. 16 December 2013.

Jenks, Chris. *Visual Culture*. London and New York: Routledge, 2003.

Johns, Adrian. *The Nature of the Book: Print and Knowledge in the Making*. Chicago: U of Chicago P, 1998.

Johnson-Eilola, Johndan. "Polymorphous Perversity in Texts." *Kairos: A Journal of Rhetoric, Technology, and Pedagogy* 16.3 (2012).

Jonson, Ben. *Every Man Out of His Humour*. Ed. Helen Ostovich. Manchester: Manchester UP, 2001.

Kalas, Rayna. *Frame, Glass, Verse: The Technology of Poetic Invention in the English Renaissance*. Ithaca, New York: Cornell UP, 2007.

– "The Technology of Reflection: Renaissance Mirrors of Steel and Glass." *Journal of Medieval and Early Modern Studies*. 32.3 (2002): 519–42.

Kallendorf, Craig. *The Virgilian Tradition: Book History and the History of Reading in Early Modern Europe*. Aldershot, England: Ashgate, 2007.

Kantorowicz, Ernst H. *The King's Two Bodies: A Study in Mediaeval Political Theology*. Princeton: Princeton UP, 1997.

Kastan, David Scott. *Shakespeare and the Book*. Cambridge: Cambridge UP, 2001.

Kearney, James. "Reformed Ventriloquism: The Shepheardes Calender and the Craft of Commentary." *Spenser Studies: A Renaissance Poetry Annual* 26.1 (2011): 111–51.

Keith, Thomas. "Numeracy in Early Modern England." *Transactions of the Royal Historical Society* 36 (1987): 103–32.

Kemp, Simon. *Cognitive Psychology in the Middle Ages*. Westport, CT: Greenwood Press, 1996.

Kerrigan, John. *Archipelagic English: Literature, History, and Politics 1603–1707*. Oxford: Oxford UP, 2008.

Kiefer, Frederick. *Shakespeare's Visual Theatre: Staging the Personified Characters*. Cambridge: Cambridge UP, 2003.

Klarer, Mario. "*Ekphrasis*, or the Archaeology of Historical Theories of Representation: Medieval Brain Anatomy in Wernher der Gartenaere's *Helmbrecht*." *Word and Image: A Journal of Verbal/Visual Enquiry* 15.1 (1999): 34–40.

Klein, Bernard. *Maps and the Writing of Space in Early Modern England*. Basingstoke, UK: Palgrave Macmillan, 2001.

Knapp, James A. *Illustrating the Past in Early Modern England: The Representation of History in Printed Books*. Aldershot, UK: Ashgate, 2003.

– "Translating for Print: Continuity and Change in Caxton's *Mirrour of the World*." *Disputatio* 3 (1998): 64–90.

Knight, Jeffrey Todd. *Bound to Read: Compilations, Collections, and the Making of Renaissance Literature*. Philadelphia: U of Pennsylvania P, 2013.

Knight, Leah. *Reading Green in Early Modern England*. Burlington, VT: Ashgate, 2014.

Knowles, Katherine. "'This Little Abstract': Inscribing History upon the Child in Shakespeare's *King John*." eSharp 10 (Orality and Literacy): 1–24.

Kuersteiner, Agnes D. "EK is Spenser." *PMLA* 50.1 (1935): 140–55.

Kuskin, William. *Symbolic Caxton: Literary Culture and Print Capitalism*. Notre Dame: Notre Dame UP, 2008.

Lacan, Jacques. "Of the Gaze." *The Four Fundamental Concepts of Psychoanalysis*. Ed. Jacques-Alain Miller. Trans. Alan Sheridan. New York: Norton, 1998.

Landreth, David. "At Home with Mammon: Matter, Money, and Memory in Book II of the *Faerie Queene*." *ELH* 73.1 (2006): 245–74.

Lanfiere, Thomas. "The Good Fellows Consideration or The Bad Husbands Amendment." Printed for P. Brooksby at the Golden Ball in West Smithfield,

1672–1696?. *USCB Broadside Ballad Archive*. STC R228237. Web. 16 December 2014.

Lanham, Richard. *The Economics of Attention: Style and Substance in the Age of Information*. Chicago: U of Chicago P, 2006.

Latour, Bruno. *Reassembling the Social: An Introduction to Actor-Network-Theory*. Oxford: Oxford UP, 2005.

Lemnius, Levinus. *The touchstone of complexions generallye appliable, expedient and profitable for all such, as be desirous & carefull of their bodylye health …* 2nd ed. London: 1576. *Early English Books Online*. Web. 31 December 2013.

Levi-Strauss, Claude. *The Savage Mind*. Chicago: U of Chicago P, 1962.

Lewalski, Barbara. *Protestant Poetics and the Seventeenth-Century Religious Lyric*. Princeton: Princeton UP, 1979.

Lin, Erika T. *Shakespeare and the Materiality of Performance*. New York: Palgrave, 2012.

Lindgren, Uta. "Land Surveyors, Instruments, and Practitioners in the Renaissance." *The History of Cartography, Volume III: Cartography in the European Renaissance*. Ed. David Woodward. Chicago: U of Chicago P, 2007. 477–508.

Liu, Alan. "Imagining the New Media Encounter." *A Companion to Digital Literary Studies*. Ed. Susan Schreibman and Ray Siemens. Oxford: Blackwell, 2008. 1–25.

– "Where Is Cultural Criticism in the Digital Humanities?" *Debates in the Digital Humanities*. Minneapolis: U of Minnesota P, 2012. 490–510.

Loades, D.M. "The Press under the Early Tudors: A Study in Censorship and Sedition." *Transactions of the Cambridge Bibliographical Society* 4.1 (1964): 29–50.

Lobanov-Rostovsky, Sergei. "Taming the Basilisk." *The Body in Parts: Fantasies of Corporeality in Early Modern Europe*. Ed. David Hillman and Carla Mazzio. New York: Routledge, 1997.

Long, Herbert S. "Plato's Doctrine of Metempsychosis and Its Source." *The Classical Weekly* 41.10 (1948): 149–55.

Luborsky, Ruth Samson. "The Illustrations to *The Shepheardes Calender*." *Spenser Studies* 2 (1981): 3–54.

– "The Illustrations to the Shepheardes Calender II." *Spenser Studies* 9 (1988): 249–53.

Lucas, Scott. "'Let None Such Office Take, Save He That Can for Right His Prince Forsake': *A Mirror for Magistrates*, Resistance Theory and the Elizabethan Monarchical Republic." *The Monarchical Republic of Early Modern England: Essays in Response to Patrick Collinson*. Ed. John F. McDiarmid. Aldershot, England: Ashgate, 2007. 91–108.

Macdonald, Paul S. *History of the Concept of Mind: Speculations about the Soul, Mind, and Spirit from Homer to Hume.* Farnham: Ashgate, 2003.

MacLehose, William. "Sleepwalking, Violence, and Desire in the Middle Ages." *Culture, Medicine, and Psychiatry* 36.4 (2013): 601–24.

Mack, Peter. *Elizabethan Rhetoric: Theory and Practice.* Cambridge: Cambridge UP, 2002.

– "Early Modern Ideas of Imagination: The Rhetorical Tradition." *Imagination in the Later Middle Ages and Early Modern Times.* Ed. Lodi Nauta and Detlev Pätzold. Leuvan, Dudley, MA: Peeters, 2004. 59–60.

Mak, Bonnie. *How the Page Matters.* Toronto: U of Toronto P, 2012

Marback, Richard. "Embracing Wicked Problems: The Turn to Design in Composition Studies." *College Composition and Communication* 61.2 (2009): 397–419.

Marlowe, Christopher. *Dr. Faustus and Other Plays.* Ed. David Bevington and Eric Rasmussen. Oxford: Oxford UP, 1998.

Martin, Catherine Gimelli. "'What If the Sun Be Centre to the World?': Milton's Epistemology, Cosmology, and Paradise of Fools Reconsidered." *Modern Philology* 99.2 (2001): 231–65.

Masterman, Margaret. "The Intellect's New Eye." *Freeing the Mind: Articles and Letters from the Times Literary Supplement* (1962): 38–44.

Mazzaro, Jerome. "Shakespeare's 'Books of Memory': 1 and 2 *Henry VI.*" *Comparative Drama* 35.3/4 (2001): 393–414.

Mazzio, Carla. *The Inarticulate Renaissance: Language Trouble in the Age of Eloquence.* Philadelphia: U of Pennsylvania P, 2009.

McCarthy, Penny. "EK Was Only the Postman (Identifying Spenser and EK)." *Notes and Queries* 47.1 (2000): 28–31.

McCarthy, Willard. "A Telescope for the Mind?" *Debates in the Digital Humanities.* Ed. Matthew K. Gold and Lauren F. Klein. Minneapolis: U of Minnesota P, 2012. 113–23.

McCloud, Scott. *Understanding Comics.* New York: HarperCollins, 1994.

McCorkle, Ben. *Rhetorical Delivery as Technological Discourse: A Cross-Historical Study.* Carbondale: Southern Illinois UP, 2012.

McCrae, Andrew. "Tree-felling in Early Modern England: Michael Drayton's Environmentalism." *The Review of English Studies* 63.260 (2012): 410–30.

McCullough, Peter. "Lancelot Andrewes' Transforming Passions." *Huntington Library Quarterly.* 74.1 (2008): 573–89.

McDermott, Jennifer Rae. "Perceiving Shakespeare: A Study of Sight, Sound, and Stage." *Early Modern Literary Studies* 19 (2009): 1–38.

McKenzie, D.F. "Typography and Meaning." *Making Meaning: 'Printers of the Mind' and Other Essays*. Ed. Peter D. McDonald and Michael F. Suarez, S.J. Amherst: U of Massachusetts P, 2002. 198–236.

McKerrow, R.B. *An Introduction to Bibliography*. Oxford: Oxford UP, 1927.

McLane, Paul E. *Spenser's Shepheardes Calendar: A Study in Elizabethan Allegory*. Notre Dame: University of Notre Dame Press, 1969.

McLuhan, Marshall. *The Gutenberg Galaxy*. Toronto: U of Toronto P, 2011.

Merleau-Ponty, Maurice. *The Phenomenology of Perception*. Trans. Colin Smith. London: Routledge, 1981.

Michell. *The sence of Iohn Warners speech in his personall capacity, spoken by the Lord Mayor of London in his politique capacity: or A declaration delivered from Iohn, and my Lord, utterd from them both, with one mouth, Apr. 25. 1648. Dedicated to the Right Honourable Oliver Crumvvell and the rest of the saints militant*. 2nd Ed. London, 1648. *Early English Books Online*. Web. 16 December 2013.

Middleton, Thomas, and Thomas Dekker. *The Roaring Girl*. Ed. Paul A. Mulholland. Manchester: Manchester UP, 1999.

Milner, Matthew. *The Senses and the English Reformation*. Burlington, VT: Ashage, 2011.

Milton, John. *Comus and Other Poems*. Ed. F.T. Prince. Oxford: Oxford UP, 1968.

– *Paradise Lost*. Ed. Stephen Orgel and Jonathan Goldberg. Oxford: Oxford UP, 2008.

Minnis, Alastair. "Medieval Imagination and Memory." *The Cambridge History of Literary Criticism*. Ed. Alastair Minnis and Ian Johnson. Cambridge: Cambridge UP, 2005. 239–74.

Mischo, John Brett. "The Rhetoric of Poverty and the Poverty of Rhetoric: Shakespeare's Jack Cade and the Early Modern Rhetoric Manual." *English Language Notes* 41.1 (2003): 32–44.

Moncrief, Kathryn, and Kathryn McPherson. *Performing Pedagogy in Early Modern England*. Burlington, VT: Ashgate, 2011.

Montagu, Richard. *A gagg for the new Gospell? No: a nevv gagg for an old goose VVho would needes vndertake to stop all Protestants mouths for euer*. 2nd Ed. London: 1624. *Early English Books Online*. Web. 16 December 2013.

Montrose, Louis. "The Elizabethan Subject and the Spenserian Text." *Literary Theory/Renaissance Texts*. Ed. Patricia Parker and David Quint. Baltimore: Johns Hopkins UP, 1986. 303–40.

Moore, Philip. *An almanack and prognostication for. xxxvij, yeres, verie profitable for all men, specially for phisicions, chyrurgians, men of lawe, marchauntes, mariners, husbande men, and handicraftes men: gathered out of Ciprianus Leouicius workes with the reuolutions in the ende, and all the moste necessarie*

rules that is nedefull to be put in any almanack. / Gathered by Philip Moore.
practicioner of phisicke and chyrurgerie. 2nd ed. London, 1570. Printed by Ihon
Kyngston, for Henry Saunderson. *Early English Books Online.* Web. 2 January
2015.

More, Thomas. *Utopia. Three Early Modern Utopias: Utopia, New Atlantis, and the
Isle of Pines.* Ed. and Intro. Susan Bruce. Oxford: Oxford UP, 1999.

Moshenska, Joseph. *Feeling Pleasures: The Sense of Touch in Renaissance England.*
Oxford: Oxford UP, 2014.

Moss, Ann. *Printed Commonplace Books and the Structuring of Renaissance
Thought.* Oxford: Clarendon P, 1996.

Mucklebauer, John. "Imitation and Invention in Antiquity: A Historical-
Theoretical Revision." *Rhetorica* 21.2 (2003): 61–88.

Mueller, Alex. "*Wikipedia* as Imago Mundi." *Studies in Medieval and Renaissance
Teaching* 17.2 (2010): 11–25.

Mullaney, Steven. "Imaginary Conquests: European Material Technologies
and the Colonial Mirror Stage." *Early Modern Visual Culture: Representation,
Race, and Empire in Renaissance England.* Ed. Peter Erickson and Clark Huls.
Philadelphia: U of Pennsylvania P, 2000. 15–43.

Nakamura, Lisa. "'Words with Friends': Socially Networked Reading on
Goodreads." *PMLA* 128.1 (2013): 238–43.

Nebeker, Eric. "The Broadside Ballad and Textual Publics." *SEL* 51.1 (2011): 1–19.

"A New Ballad From Whigg-Land." London: Printed for N. Whigg, 1682.
USCB Broadside Ballad Archive. STC R12357. Web. 16 December 2013.

Newbold, W. Webster. "Traditional, Practical, Entertaining: Two Early English
Letter Writing Manuals." *Rhetorica* 26.3 (2008): 267–300.

O'Connell, Michael. *The Idolatrous Eye: Iconoclasm and Theater in Early Modern
England.* Oxford: Oxford UP, 2000.

Ong, Walter J. *Ramus, Method, and the Decay of Dialogue: From the Art of
Discourse to the Art of Reason.* Cambridge: Harvard UP, 1983.

– *Rhetoric, Romance, and Technology: Studies in the Interaction of Expression and
Culture.* Ithaca: Cornell, UP, 1971.

Osborne, Catherine. "Aristotle, De Anima 3.2: How Do We Perceive That We
See and Hear?" *Classical Quarterly* 33.2: 401–11.

Owens, Judith. "Memory Works in *The Faerie Queene.*" *Spenser Studies* 22
(2007): 27–46.

Owens, Margaret E. "The Many-Headed Monster in *Henry VI, Part 2.*"
Criticism 38.3 (1996): 367–82.

Ovid. *Metamorphoses.* Oxford: Oxford World's Classics, 1986.

Paré, Ambroise. *The workes of that famous chirurgion Ambrose Parey.* 2nd ed.
London: 1634. *Early English Books Online.* Web. 31 December 2013.

Paster, Gail Kern, Katherine Rowe, and Mary Floyd-Wilson. *Reading the Early Modern Passions*. Philadelphia: U of Pennsylvania P, 2004.

Peacham, Henry. *The duty of all true subiects to their King as also to their native countrey, in time of extremity and danger*. 2nd ed. London, 1639. *Early English Books Online*. Web. 15 December 2013.

– *The gentlemans exercise. Or an exquisite practise, as well for drawing all manner of beasts in their true portraitures: as also the making of all kinds of colours, to be vsed in lymming, painting, tricking, and blason of coates, and armes, with diuers others most delightfull and pleasurable obseruations, for all yong gentlemen and others*. 2nd ed. London, 1612. *Early English Books Online*. Web. 16 December 2013.

– *The valley of varietie: or, Discourse fitting for the times containing very learned and rare passages out of antiquity, philosophy, and history*. 2nd ed. London, 1638. *Early English Books Online*. Web. 15 December 2013.

Pearlman, E. "The Duke and the Beggar in Shakespeare's *2 Henry VI*." *Criticism* 41 (1999): 309–21.

Plato. *Phaedrus*. Cambridge: Cambridge UP, 1952.

– *The Republic*. Ed. and trans. Chris Emlyn-Jones and William Preddy. Cambridge: Harvard UP, 2013.

– *Theaetetus*. Trans. Robin H. Waterfield. London: Penguin, 1987.

– *Theaetetus*. Ed. John Henry McDowell. Oxford: Clarendon P, 1996.

Plett, Heinrich F. *Enargeia in Classical Antiquity and the Early Modern Age: The Aesthetics of Evidence*. Leiden: Brill, 2012.

Pope, Alexander. *The Dunciad in Four Books*. Ed. Valerie Rumbold. New York: Routledge, 2014.

"Poperys Downfal, and the Protestants Uprising by the Crowning of King William and Queen Mary." Printed for G.C. on Ludgate Hill, 1689. *USCB Broadside Ballad Archive*. STC R187323. Web. 16 December 2013.

Price, Leah. "From *The History of a Book* to a 'History of the Book.'" *Representations* 108.1 (2009): 120–38.

Printed Images in Early Modern England. Ed. Michael Hunter. Farnham: Ashgate, 2010.

Puttenham, George. *The Arte of English Poesie*. 2nd ed. London, 1589. *Early English Books Online*. Web. 15 January 2014.

Quarles, Francis. *Argolus and Parthenia* and *The Shepheards Oracle: Delivered in an Eglogue* [cropped]. 1644. Shelfmark: Wood 330 (1).

– *Emblemes with Quarleis by E. Benlowes*. London: 1634/35.

– *Enchiridion, Containing Institutions Divine, Cotemplative, Practicall, Morall, Ethicall, Oeconomical, Politicall*. 1644.

– *The Whipper Whipt. In England & Scotland, or, The proceedings of the parliament of England*. 1644. Shelfmark: Pamph. D.63 (1).

Quintilian. *The Institutio Oratoria of Quintilian*. Ed. H.E. Butler. New York: G.P. Putnam's Sons, 1921–2.

Remmert, Volker R. "In the Sign of Galileo: Pictorial Representation in the 17th-century Copernican Debate." *Endeavor* 27.1 (2003): 26–31.

Rhodes, Neil, and Jonathan Sawday. "Introduction: Paperworlds: Imagining the Renaissance Computer." *The Renaissance Computer: Knowledge Technology in the First Age of Print*. Ed. Neil Rhodes and Jonathan Sawday. London: Routledge, 2000. n/p.

Richter, Gisela Marie Augusta. *Greek, Etruscan, and Roman Bronzes*. New York: Gilliss, 1915.

Rickert, Thomas. *Ambient Rhetoric: The Attunements of Rhetorical Being*. Pittsburgh: University of Pittsburgh P, 2013.

Roberts, Lorraine M. "Francis Quarles." *Dictionary of Literary Biography Volume 126: Seventeenth-Century Nondramatic Poets*. Ed. M. Thomas Hester. Detroit: Gale Research, 1993.

Rosenberg, Daniel, and Anthony Grafton, *Cartographies of Time: A History of the Timeline*. New York: Princeton Architectural Press, 2010.

Rossi, Paolo. *Logic and the Art of Memory: The Quest for a Universal Language*. Chicago: U of Chicago P, 2000.

Row-Heyveld, Lindsey. "'The lying'st knave in Christendom': The Development of Disability in the False Miracle of St. Alban's." *Disability Studies Quarterly* 29.4 (2009): (not paginated).

Russell, Daniel S. "Perceiving, Seeing, and Meaning: Emblems and Some Approaches to Reading Early Modern Culture." *Aspects of Renaissance and Baroque Symbol Theory, 1500–1700*. Ed. Peter M. Daly and John Manning. New York: AMS Press, 1999.

Sanford, Rhonda Lemke. *Maps and Memory in Early Modern England: A Sense of Place*. New York: Palgrave, 2002.

Sawday, Jonathan. "Towards the Renaissance Computer." *The Renaissance Computer: Knowledge and Technology in the First Age of Print*. Ed. Neil Rhodes and Jonathan Sawday. London: Routledge, 2000. n/p.

Schechner, Sara J. "Between Knowing and Doing: Mirrors and Their imperfections in the Renaissance." *Early Science and Medicine* 10.2 (2005): 137–62.

Schleiner, Louise. "Spenser's 'EK' as Edmund Kent (Kenned/of Kent): Kyth (Couth), Kissed, and Kunning-Conning." *English Literary Renaissance* 20.3 (1990): 374–407.

Schutz, Andrea. "Absent and Present Images: Mirrors and Mirroring in John Gower's *Confessio Amantis*." *Chaucer Review: A Journal of Medieval Studies and Literary Criticism* 34.1 (1999): 107–24.

Schwyzer, Philip. *Literature, Nationalism, and Memory in Early Modern England and Wales*. Cambridge: Cambridge UP, 2004.

Sclater, William. *A briefe exposition vvith notes, vpon the second epistle to the Thessalonians. By William Sclater Doctor of Divinitie, and minister of Pitmister in Summerset*. 2nd ed. London: 1635. *Early English Books Online*. Web. 15 December 2013.

Selden, John. *Mare clausum, seu, De dominio maris libri duo*. London: 1636. *Early English Books Online* Web. 18 July 2014.

Shakespeare, William. *2 Henry IV*. *The Riverside Shakespeare*. Ed. G. Blakemore Evans et al. Boston: Houghton Mifflin, 1997.

– *A Midsummer Night's Dream*. *The Riverside Shakespeare*. Boston: Houghton Mifflin, 1997.

– *Richard II*. *The Riverside Shakespeare*. Boston: Houghton Mifflin, 1997.

– *The Sonnets*. Ed. G. Blakemore Evans. Cambridge: Cambridge UP, 1996.

– *Twelfth Night*. *The Riverside Shakespeare*. Boston: Houghton Mifflin, 1997.

– *The Winter's Tale*. *The Riverside Shakespeare*. Boston: Houghton Mifflin, 1997.

Shaw, Paul, and Peter Bain. "Blackletter vs. Roman: Type as Ideological Surrogate." *Blackletter: Type and National Identity*. Ed. Peter Bain and Paul Shaw. Princeton: Princeton Architectural P, 1998. 10–15.

Sherman, William H. *Used Books: Marking Readers in Renaissance England*. Philadelphia: U of Pennsylvania P, 2008.

– "What Did Renaissance Readers Write in their Books?" *Books and Readers in Early Modern England: Material Studies*. Ed. Jennifer Andersen and Elizabeth Sauer. Philadelphia: U of Pennsylvania P, 2002. 119–37.

Shinn, Abigail. "'Extraordinary Discourses of Unnecessarie Matter': Spenser's *Shepheardes Calender* and the Almanac Tradition." *Literature and Popular Culture in Early Modern England*. Ed. Matthew Dimmock and Andrew Hadfield. Burlington, VT: Ashgate, 2009.

Sidney, Sir Philip. *An Apologie for Poetrie*. 2nd ed. London, 1595. *Early English Books Online*. Web. 29 September 2013.

– *An Apology for Poetry, Or, The Defence of Poesy*. Ed. Robert W. Maslen. Manchester: Manchester UP, 2002.

Smart, I.M. "Francis Quarles: Professed Royalist and 'Puritanical Poet.'" *The Durham University Journal* 70 (1978): 187–92.

Smith, A. Mark. "What Is the History of Medieval Optics Really About?" *Proceedings of the American Philosophical Society* 148.2 (2004): 180–94.

Smith, Bruce R. *The Acoustic World of Early Modern England: Attending the O-Factor*. Chicago: U of Chicago P, 1999.

Smith, Helen. "'Imprinted by Simeon Such a Signe': Reading Early Modern Imprints." *Renaissance Paratexts*. Ed. Helen Smith and Louise Wilson. Cambridge: Cambridge UP, 2011. 17–33.

Smith, Helen, and Louise Wilson. "Introduction." *Renaissance Paratexts*. Ed. Helen Smith and Louise Wilson. Cambridge: Cambridge UP, 2011. 1–14

Smith, Ian. *Race and Rhetoric in the Renaissance: Barbarian Errors*. New York: Palgrave Macmillan, 2009.

Smyth, Adam. "Almanacs, Annotators, and Life-Writing in Early Modern England." *ELR* 38.2 (2008): 200–44.

– "Burning to Read: Ben Jonson's Library Fire of 1623." *Book Destruction from the Medieval to the Contemporary*. Ed. Gill Partington and Adam Smyth. New York: Palgrave, 2014. 34–54.

– *"Profit and Delight": Printed Miscellanies in England, 1640–1682*. Detroit: Wayne State UP, 2004.

– "'Reade in one age and understood i'th'next': Recycling Satire in the Mid-Seventeenth Century." *Huntington Library Quarterly* 69.1 (2006): 67–82.

Speed, Steven. "Cartographic Arrest: Harvey, Raleigh, Drayton and the Mapping of Sense." *At the Borders of the Human: Beasts, Bodies, and Natural Philosophy in the Early Modern Period*. Ed. Erica Fudge, Ruth Gilbert, and Susan Wiseman. New York: Palgrave, 2002.

Spenser, Edmund. *The faerie queene Disposed into twelue books, fashioning XII. morall vertues*. 2nd ed. London, 1590. *Early English Books Online*. Web. 1 May 2012.

– *The Shepheardes Calender Conteining Twelue Aeglogues Proportionable to the Twelue Monethes*. 2nd ed. London, 1579. *Early English Books Online*. Web. 1 May 2014.

Spiller, Elizabeth A. "Reading Through Galileo's Telescope: Margeret Cavendish and the Experience of Reading." Renaissance Quarterly 53.1 (2000): 192–221.

Spruit, Leen. "Renaissance Views of Active Perception." *Theories of Perception in Medieval and Early Modern Philosophy*. Ed. Simo Knuuttila and Pekka Kärkkäinen. Dordrecht and London: Springer, 2008. 203–24.

Stallybrass, Peter. "Afterword." *Renaissance Paratexts*. Ed. Helen Smith and Louise Wilson. Cambridge: Cambridge UP, 2011. 204–19.

– "The First Literary Hamlet and the Commonplacing of Professional Plays." *Shakespeare Quarterly* 59.4 (2008): 371–420.

– With Roger Chartier, John Franklin Mowery, and Heather Wolfe. "Hamlet's Tables and Technologies of Writing in Renaissance England." *Shakespeare Quarterly* 55.4 (2004): 379–419.

– "Visible and Invisible Letters: Text versus Image in Renaissance England and Europe." *Visible Writings: Cultures, Forms, Readings*. Ed. Marija Dalbello and Mary Shaw, New Brunswick, NJ: Rutgers UP, 2011. 77–98.

Stallybrass, Peter, and Margreta de Grazia, "The Materiality of the Shakespearian Text." *Shakespeare Quarterly* 44.3 (1993): 255–83.

Stark, Ryan J. *Rhetoric, Science, and Magic in Seventeenth-Century England*. Washington, D.C.: The Catholic University of America P, 2009.

Stewart, Alan. "'Worme-Eaten, and Full of Canker Holes': Materializing Memory in *The Faerie Queene* and *Lingua*." *Spenser Studies* 17 (2003): 215–38.

Stoichita, Victor. *The Self-Aware Image: An Insight into Early Modern Meta-Painting*. Trans. Anne-Marie Glasheen. Cambridge: Cambridge UP, 1997.

Summit, Jennifer. *Memory's Library: Medieval Books in Early Modern England*. Chicago: U of Chicago P, 2008.

– "Monuments and Ruins: Spenser and the Problem of the English Library." *ELH* 70.1 (2003): 1–34.

Tang, Frank. "Machiavelli's Image of the Ruler: 'Il Principe' and the Tradition of the Mirror for Princes." *Machiavelli: Figure-Reputation*. Ed. Joep Leerssen and Menno Spiering. Amsterdam: Rodopi, 1996. 187–200.

Thorne, Alison. *Vision and Rhetoric in Shakespeare: Looking through Language*. New York: Palgrave Macmillan, 2000.

Trevisan, Sara. "'The Murmuring Woods Even Shuddred As with Feare': Deforestation in Michael Drayton's *Poly-olbion*." *Seventeenth Century* 26.2 (2011): 240–63.

Turner, Henry S. *The English Renaissance Stage: Geometry, Poetics, and the Practical Spatial Arts, 1580–1630*. Oxford: Oxford UP, 2006.

Tuggle, Brad. "Memory, Aesthetics, and Ethical Thinking in the House of Busirane." *Spenser Studies* 23 (2008): 119–51.

Txapartegi, Ekai. "Plato's Color Naturalism." *History of Philosophy Quarterly* 28.4 (2011): 319–37.

Typus mundi in quo eius calamitates et pericula nec non diuini, humanique amoris antipathia, emblematicè proponuntur à rr. C.S.I.A. 1627.

Vine, Angus Edmund. *In Defiance of Time: Antiquarian Writing in Early Modern England*. Oxford: Oxford UP, 2010.

Virgil. *Here fynyssheth the boke yf [sic] Eneydos, compyled by Vyrgyle, which hathe be translated oute of latyne in to frenshe, and oute of frenshe reduced in to Englysshe by me wyll[ia]m Caxton* … 2nd ed. Westminster (Printed by William Caxton), 1490. *Early English Books Online*. Web. 4 July 2014.

Vogt-Spira, Gregor. "Senses, Imagination, and Literature: Some Epistemological Considerations." *Rethinking the Medieval Senses: Heritages/Fascinations/Frames*. Baltimore: Johns Hopkins UP, 2008.

Voss, P.J. "Books for Sale: Advertising and Patronage in Late Elizabethan England." *Sixteenth Century Journal* 29:3 (1998): 733–56.

Vrudny, Kimberly J. *Friars, Scribes, and Corpses: A Marian Cofraternal Reading of the Mirror of Human Salvation (Speculum Humanae Salvationis)*. Paris: Peeters, 2010.

Wall, Wendy. "Authorship and the Material Conditions of Writing." *The Cambridge Companion to English Literature 1500–1600*. Ed. Arthur F. Kinney. Cambridge: Cambridge UP, 2000. 64–89.

– "Letters, Characters, Roots." *Shakespeare in Our Time: A Shakespeare Association of America Collection*. Ed. Dympna Callaghan and Suzanna Gossettt. London: Bloomsbury, 2016. 25–8.

– *Staging Domesticity: Household Work and English Identity in Early Modern Drama*. Cambridge: Cambridge UP, 2002.

Walsham, Alexandra. *The Reformation of the Landscape: Religion, Identity, and Memory in Early Modern Britain and Ireland*. Oxford: Oxford UP, 2011.

Walter, Katie. "Books and Bodies: Ethics, Exemplarity, and the 'Boistous' in Medieval English Writings." *New Medieval Literatures* 14.1 (2012): 95–125.

"The Wanton Maidens Choice." Printed for J. Deacon at the Angel in Guiltspur-Street, 1671–1702? *USCB Broadside Ballad Archive*. STC R186233. Web. 16 December 2013.

Weaver, William P. "*Triplex Est Copia*: Philip Melanchthon's Invention of the Rhetorical Figures." *Rhetorica* 29.4 (2011): 367–402.

Webster, John. *The Tragedy of the Dutchesse of Malfy* ... 2nd ed. London, 1623. Early English Books Online. Web. 15 December 2013.

"The Whig Rampant." Printed for P. Brooksby at the Golden Ball in West Smithfield, 1672–1696? *USCB Broadside Ballad Archive*. STC R2621. Web. 16 December 2013.

"The Whig's Exaltation: A Pleasant New Song of 1682." London: Printed by Nath. Thompson, 1682. *USCB Broadside Ballad Archive*. STC R206506. Web. 16 December 2013.

Whitburn, Merrill D. "The Value of Book Collecting in Research and Teaching." *College Composition and Communication*. 61.2 (2009): 420–37.

White, Jason C. "Militant Protestants: British Identity in the Jacobean Period, 1603–1625." *History* 94.314 (2009): 154–75.

Wilcher, Robert. "Francis Quarles and the Crisis of Royalism." *Critical Survey* 5.3 (1993): 252–62.

Wilks, Timothy. "The Pike Charged: Henry as Militant Prince." *Prince Henry Revived: Image and Exemplarity in Early Modern England*. Ed. Timothy Wilks. London: Southampton Solent University and Paul Holberton, 2007.

Williams, Grant. "Phantastes's Flies: The Trauma of Amnesic Forgetting in Spenser's Memory Palace." *Spenser Studies* 28 (2003): 231–52.

– "The Transmateriality of Memory in Early Modern Psychophysiological Discourse." *Ars Reminiscendi: Mind and Memory in Renaissance Culture*. Ed. Donald Beecher and Grant Williams. Toronto: Centre for Reformation and Renaissance Studies, 2009. 313–38.

Willoughby, Edwin Eliot. *A Printer of Shakespeare: The Books and Times of William Jaggard*. New York: Haskell House Publishers, 1934.

Witalisz, Władysław. *The Trojan Mirror: Middle English Narratives of Troy as Books of Princely Advice*. Frankfurt: Peter Lang, 2011.

Woodward, David. "Techniques of Map Engraving, Printing, and Coloring in the European Renaissance." *The History of Cartography, Volume III: Cartography in the European Renaissance*. Ed. David Woodward. Chicago: U of Chicago P, 2007. 591–610.

Wortham, Jenna. "Relationships with (and Around) Google Glass." *JennyDeluxe*. Tumblr, 2013. Web. 8 September 2013.

Wright, Celeste Turner. "Anthony Mundy, 'Edward' Spenser, and EK." *PMLA* 76.1 (1961): 34–9.

Wright, Thomas. *The Passions of the Minde*. London, 1601.

Wymer, Rowland. "*The Tempest* and the Origins of Britain." *Critical Survey* (1999): 3–14.

Yachnin, Paul. "Eye to Eye Opposed." *The Culture of Playgoing in England: A Collaborative Debate*. Cambridge: Cambridge UP, 2001.

Yates, Frances A. *The Art of Memory*. Chicago: U of Chicago P, 1966.

– "The Emblematic Conceit in Giordano Bruno's De Gli Eroici Furori and in the Elizabethan Sonnet Sequences." *Journal of the Warburg and Courtauld Institutes* 6 (1943): 101–21.

Yates, Nigel. *Liturgical Space: Christian Worship and Church Buildings in Western Europe, 1500–2000*. Aldershot, UK: Ashgate, 2008.

Zumthor, Paul. "Intertextualité et mouvance," *Littérature* 41 (1981): 8–16.

Zwicker, Steven N. "Habits of Reading and Early Modern Literary Culture." *The Cambridge History of Early Modern English Literature*. Ed. David Loewenstein and Janel Mueller. Cambridge: Cambridge UP, 2002. 170–200.

Index